OXFORD MONOGRAPHS IN INTERNATIONAL HUMANITARIAN AND CRIMINAL LAW

Series Editors

SUZANNAH LINTON
Member of the Expert Committee, International Academy of the Red Cross & Red Crescent at Suzhou University and Adjunct Professor at the School of International Law, China University of Political Science and Law (CUPL)

SALVATORE ZAPPALÀ
Professor of International Law at the University of Catania

Non-Binding Norms in International Humanitarian Law

OXFORD MONOGRAPHS IN INTERNATIONAL HUMANITARIAN AND CRIMINAL LAW

This series emerged through the vision of the late Antonio Cassese. Since then the series has published original and innovative works on challenging issues in international humanitarian law and international criminal justice, primarily by emerging authors. Given the ever-growing intersection of these areas with other fields of international law such as the *jus ad bellum*, and disciplines such as criminology, sociology, and history, the scope of the series also incorporates these perspectives. Fresh approaches and new ideas for improving conceptual and practical challenges are welcomed. The series editors encourage submissions from around the world, and will consider edited collections, although the primary focus is on authored works.

ALSO PUBLISHED IN THIS SERIES

Doing Justice to History
Confronting the Past in International Criminal Courts
Barrie Sander

The Humanitarian Civilian
How the Idea of Distinction Circulates Within and Beyond International Humanitarian Law
Rebecca Sutton

Rules of Engagement and the International Law of Military Operations
J.F.R. Boddens Hosang

To Serve the Enemy
Informers, Collaborators, and the Laws of Armed Conflict
Shane Darcy

Non-Binding Norms in International Humanitarian Law

Efficacy, Legitimacy, and Legality

EMILY CRAWFORD

OXFORD
UNIVERSITY PRESS

OXFORD
UNIVERSITY PRESS

Great Clarendon Street, Oxford, OX2 6DP,
United Kingdom

Oxford University Press is a department of the University of Oxford.
It furthers the University's objective of excellence in research, scholarship,
and education by publishing worldwide. Oxford is a registered trade mark of
Oxford University Press in the UK and in certain other countries

First Edition published in 2021

Impression: 1

Published in the United States of America by Oxford University Press
198 Madison Avenue, New York, NY 10016, United States of America

British Library Cataloguing in Publication Data

Data available

Library of Congress Control Number: 2021946947

ISBN 978–0–19–881985–1

DOI: 10.1093/oso/9780198819851.001.0001

Printed and bound by
CPI Group (UK) Ltd, Croydon, CR0 4YY

For my mother and father

Captain:
Truly to speak, and with no addition,
We go to gain a little patch of ground
That hath in it no profit but the name.
To pay five ducats, five, I would not farm it;
Nor will it yield to Norway or the Pole
A ranker rate, should it be sold in fee.

. . .

Hamlet:
Two thousand souls and twenty thousand ducats
Will not debate the question of this straw:
This is the imposthume of much wealth and peace,
That inward breaks, and shows no cause without
Why the man dies. I humbly thank you, sir.

— *Hamlet,* Act IV, Scene IV

Series Editors' Preface

The shift towards informal or non-binding instruments in international relations, called 'soft law' in some quarters, has been discussed for decades now. It has spawned some fine theoretical observations in conferences, journal articles, and book chapters. Dr Emily Crawford's study introduces a new dimension, and it is not just because she focuses exclusively on international humanitarian law and some of its influential non-binding documents such as the *San Remo Manual on Naval Warfare* and the *Tallinn Manual*. Indeed, as one would expect, Dr Crawford reflects deeply on both the benefits and the drawbacks of the shift, and the implications for legitimacy and legality. She goes over and above that to bridge the conventional divide between theory and practice. In doing so, she presents a fascinating and methodologically rigorous study.

To identify 'soft' international humanitarian law, she takes up Chinkin's approach and includes instruments or provisions that meet any of the following: (1) 'articulated in non-binding form according to traditional modes of lawmaking'; (2) emanating 'from bodies lacking international lawmaking authority'; (3) directed at or designed to include 'non-state actors whose practice cannot constitute customary international law'; (4) and/or predicated on 'voluntary adherence, or [relies] upon non-juridical means of enforcement'. Dr Crawford's meticulous research uncovers that States and international adjudicative bodies regularly engage with non-binding humanitarian norms—either during or after their creation—while at the same time reaffirming their non-binding nature. How are we to view this equivocal behaviour? Dr Crawford's inquiry approaches this from several angles. The reasoning that lies behind this shift away from formal legality is relevant to our understanding, and she argues that 'hopes of influence, adaptability, and responsiveness have driven organisations and groups of experts to create soft law instruments, with the aims of having such instruments be of use to States and non-State actors'. This of course then leads her to interrogate if it has worked, and in turn how one evaluates success. How should one identify whether States and non-State groups actually engage with these instruments in practice, and abide by their rules or recommendations? How does one measure *impact*; can it be done scientifically or must one rely on a subjective evaluation? Or, should we be looking for *effectiveness*? The turn towards more litigation in International Law has certainly made the matter of proof something of a quest for international lawyers, and especially those working in international humanitarian law where practice is most often operational activity on the battlefield which few beyond the participants observe. This challenge was observed in the seminal ICTY Appeals Chamber's Interlocutory decision in *Tadić* as long ago as 1995.

However, as the author rightly points out, she is not engaged in a study of customary international humanitarian law, but seeks to determine 'whether these non-binding rules and instruments are having (or beginning to have) their intended impact'. She, therefore, takes up Yuval Shany's pragmatic 'goal-based approach' which holds that 'an action is effective if it accomplishes its specific objective aim', which applied to this study means considering whether the goals set out in the non-binding norm or instrument are achieved. Dr Crawford also draws from the International Law Commission's Commentaries to the Draft Conclusions on Identification of Customary International Law that give additional clarification as to the scope of these forms of practice. She emerges with her own standard of assessment:

> 'to what degree have States (or the other addressees of the non-binding norm) acknowledged and adopted some or all of the recommendations or provisions in their own conduct?'.

This is of course not a high standard, but it is one that is pragmatic, fits the circumstances, and is rooted in conceptual clarity. It leads Dr Crawford to search for explicit, positive affirmation, acknowledgement, or acceptance of the non-binding norm or instrument (e.g. citation in a court case, incorporation in domestic legislation, or positive affirmation or acknowledgement of the norm in official State documents, such as statements by authorised representatives). In the absence of explicit evidence of acknowledgement of the instrument (in the form of direct citation), she treats the source with caution.

We welcome this strong forensic approach. It leads to the following assessments, which are also a significant contribution to scholarship. Nearly all the 'soft' instruments had an impact on State practice. 'Through either citations in court cases, recognition in military manuals, or employment of the instruments before UN bodies, States and non-State groups are engaging with the soft law instruments'. Furthermore, Dr Crawford finds 'clear evidence that the rules contained in these instruments are being implemented in practice', even if that practice is inconsistent and variable depending on the types of instruments. Importantly, she observes that the mode of creation is relevant. Among the instruments aimed at modifying or influencing State behaviour, 'those that have significant State engagement in their formation (such as the Montreux Document and, to a lesser extent, the Copenhagen Principles) seem overall to have been more enthusiastically received by States than those that are the product of expert groups (with the notable exception of the San Remo Naval Manual)'. It appears especially relevant if the expert groups are small and/or have had limited State involvement in their formation, or have involved the ICRC. That being said, the response is chillier where the instruments are perceived as attempting to introduce innovations or new obligations into the law. 'Where the instrument is perceived as pushing the limits of State obligation beyond pre-existing hard law, the efficacy of the instrument seems limited.'

And so to the *crux* of the matter: do the demonstrable benefits of this turn towards informality outweigh the not-inconsequential theoretical problems and practical challenges such as accountability, transparency, and bias? This carefully considered study suggests that the proliferation of non-binding instruments and those who create them can be seen as both problem and opportunity. Dr Crawford predicts that their use will increase in international humanitarian law, stressing that 'both the creators of the instruments and the addressees and recipients of the instruments treat these instruments with care and consideration.' Although formally non-binding, 'these instruments are, in effect, making claims to authority and, as such, need to possess a degree of legitimacy in order to assert a compliance pull.' She, therefore, suggests that 'ensuring that there is some accountability, transparency, and a lack of bias in the non-binding norms seems crucial to their legitimacy and legality – and, therefore, their effectiveness.'

Non-Binding Norms in International Humanitarian Law is an original and important monograph, one that contributes not just to theory but practice, and also demonstrates admirable methodology. We really are delighted and proud to be able to publish it under this series.

The Editors

Acknowledgements

This book would not exist were it not for the generous assistance of friends and colleagues who provided unfailing support, feedback, and guidance. First, I could not have completed this work without the help of my outstanding research assistants, Eugene Cheung and Dunja Tatic. I was also ably assisted by the interns at the Sydney Centre for International Law at the University of Sydney Law School, Charlotte Lewis, Brendan Ma, and James Tanna. Michelle Nichols provided exceptional copyediting and has my enduring thanks, as does Shirley Morren at the Institute for International Humanitarian Law, for her kind assistance. Special thanks must also go to Jack McNichol and Merel Alstein at Oxford University Press.

I am also eternally thankful to friends and colleagues who provided feedback on chapters, and who discussed and debated my topic with me and helped me better formulate my thinking. These include Professor Nils Melzer, Professor Ben Saul, Dr Michael Sevel, Professor David Kinley, Dr Rosemary Grey, Professor Matthew Conaglen, Ms Netta Goussac, Dr Matt Killingsworth, Professor Dale Stephens, Professor Hitoshi Nasu, Associate Professor Jacqui Mowbray, Professor Sarah Williams, Professor Andrew Byrnes, Mr Steven Hill, Professor Tim McCormack, Professor Michael Schmitt, Dr Kubo Mačák, Professor Eric Talbot Jensen, and Dr Jeroen van den Boogaard.

Special thanks must go to Colonel Rob Holman and Professor Laurie Blank, for the wisdom and the wine; to Professor Bruce Oswald, the best cheerleader one could hope for; to Professor Rob McLaughlin, the academic I aspire to be; to Mr Robert McWhirter, for the education in clarity and the classics; to Dr Tanya Mitchell, for her generous collegiality and friendship; to Associate Professor Julien Pollack, for being an eternal source of uncomplicated joy; to Professor Shae McCrystal, for keeping me sane; and to Ms Irene Baghoomians, who is better than she could ever know.

Finally, thanks to my family, and, as ever, to James, for enduring The Hague in winter and Hobart in summer and still, somehow, sticking around. Grazie mille, amore mio, grazie mille.

The research in this book is current as of June 2021.

Contents

List of Abbreviations

ABASA	Alliance Burundo-Africaine pour le Salut
AMW	Air and Missile Warfare
ANADDE	Alliance Nationale pour le Droit et le Développement
API	Additional Protocol I
APII	Additional Protocol II
APM	Antipersonnel Mines
ASIL	American Society of International Law
AV-INTWARI	Alliance des Vaillants
BIMCO	Baltic and International Maritime Council
CCDCOE	Cooperative Cyber Defence Centre of Excellence
CERDS	Charter of the Economic Rights and Duties of States
CICR	Comité International de la Croix-Rouge
CIHL	Customary International Humanitarian Law
CNDD	Conseil National pour la Défense de la Démocratie
DCAF	Democratic Control of Armed Forces
DFT	Department for Transport
DoC	Deed of Commitment
DPH	Direct Participation in Hostilities
EOD	Explosive Ordnance Disposal
ERW	Explosive Remnants of War
FAO	Food and Agriculture Organization of the United Nations
FARC-EP	Revolutionary Armed Forces of Colombia—People's Army
FCO	Foreign and Commonwealth Office
FPI	Front Populaire Ivoirien
FRODEBU	Front pour la Démocratie au Burundi
FROLINA	Front pour la Libération Nationale
GRP-MILF	Government of the Philippines-Muslim Islamic Liberation Front
HDZ	Croatian Democratic Community
HPCR	Program on Humanitarian Policy and Conflict Research
ICAN	International Campaign to Abolish Nuclear Weapons
ICC	International Criminal Court
ICJ	International Court of Justice
ICoC	International Code of Conduct (for Private Security Providers)
ICoCA	International Code of Conduct Association
ICRC	International Committee of the Red Cross
ICRC CIHL Study	ICRC Study into Customary International Humanitarian Law
ICS	International Chamber of Shipping
ICTY	International Criminal Tribunal for the former Yugoslavia
IDP	internally displaced person

IEDs	Improvised Explosive Devices
IGNU	Interim Government of National Unity (Liberia)
IHL	international humanitarian law
IIHL	International Institute for Humanitarian Law
INKINZO	Parti Socialiste et Panafricaniste
IOSCO	International Organization of Securities Commissions
LOAC	Law of Armed Conflict
MDF	Montreux Document Forum
MFA	Mouvement des Forces d'Avenir
MILAMOS	Woomera Manual on the International Law of Military Space Operations and the Manual on International Law Applicable to Military Uses of Outer Space
MJP	Mouvement pour la Justice et la Paix
MLC	Mouvement de Libération du Congo
MoD	Ministry of Defence
MoU	memorandum of understanding
MPCI	Mouvement Patriotique de Côte d'Ivoire
MPIGO	Mouvement Populaire Ivoirien du Grand Ouest
NATO	North Atlantic Treaty Organization
NGO	non-governmental organisation
NIAC	Non-International Armed Conflict
NPFL	National Patriotic Front of Liberia
PALIPEHUTU	Parti pour la Libération du Peuple Hutu
PARENA	Parti pour le Redressement National
PDCI-RDA	Parti Démocratique de la Côte d'Ivoire-Rassemblement Démocratique Africain
PIT	Parti Indépendant des Travailleurs
PL	Parti Libéral
PMSC	Private Military and Security Company
PP	Parti du Peuple
PRIO	Peace Research Institute Oslo
PRP	Parti pour la Réconciliation du Peuple
PSD	Parti Social-Démocrate
PSSA	Private Security Services Provided Abroad
RADDES	Ralliement pour la Démocratie et le Développement Economique et Social
RAF	Royal Air Force (UK)
RCD/ML	Rassemblement Congolais pour la Démocratie/Mouvement de Libération
RCD/N	Rassemblement Congolais pour la Démocratie/National
RDR	Rassemblement des Républicains
RPB	Rassemblement du Peuple Burundais
SCEG	Security in Complex Environment Groups
SDA	Party of Democratic Action (Republic of Bosnia and Herzegovina)
SDS	Serbian Democratic Party

SIPRI	Stockholm International Peace Research Institute
SPLM/A	Sudan People's Liberation Movement/Army
UCDP	Uppsala Conflict Data Program
UDCY	Union Démocratique et Citoyenne
UDHR	Universal Declaration of Human Rights
UDPCI	Union pour la Démocratie et la Paix en Côte d'Ivoire
UKTI	UK Trade and Industry
ULIMO	United Movement of Liberia for Democracy
UN	United Nations
UNMAS	United Nations Mine Action Service
UNODC	United Nations Office on Drugs and Crime
UPRONA	Union pour le Progrès National
USAF	US Air Force
UXO	Unexploded Ordnance
WEOG	Western European and Others Group

Introduction

The law of armed conflict (also known as international humanitarian law or IHL)[1] is one of the most regulated fields of international law. Since the first treaty regarding conduct in armed conflict was adopted in 1864,[2] dozens of treaties have been adopted regulating the treatment of civilian populations,[3] prisoners of war,[4] specific means and methods of warfare,[5] and the protection of cultural property.[6] This proliferation of binding documents has been supplemented by comprehensive customary international law relating to armed conflicts.[7]

As political and social events, together with advances in technology, have changed the ways in which armed conflicts are conducted, so too has the law of armed conflict changed, with States adopting new treaties to better respond to new developments in practice.[8] However, a consistent criticism of the law of armed conflict has been its historical inability to effectively *predict* new developments and to proactively develop laws to deal with them.[9] There is some truth to this: IHL

[1] Also known, in the United States, as the law of war. The terms 'law of armed conflict' and 'international humanitarian law' (IHL) will be used interchangeably throughout this book (though there is debate as to whether the terms are genuinely synonymous in scope: see further Gary Solis, *The Law of Armed Conflict: International Humanitarian Law in War* (2nd edn, CUP 2016) 22–23).

[2] Convention for the Amelioration of the Condition of the Wounded in Armies in the Field (adopted 22 August 1864, entered into force 22 June 1865) 22 Stat 940; Treaty Series 377.

[3] Geneva Convention (IV) Relative to the Protection of Civilian Persons in Time of War of 12 August 1949 (adopted 12 August 1949, entered into force 21 October 1950) 75 UNTS 287.

[4] Geneva Convention (III) Relative to the Treatment of Prisoners of War of 12 August 1949 (adopted 12 August 1949, entered into force 21 October 1950) 75 UNTS 135 (Geneva Convention III).

[5] Convention on Prohibition or Restrictions on the Use of Certain Conventional Weapons which may be deemed to be Excessively Injurious or to Have Indiscriminate Effects (adopted 10 October 1983, entered into force 2 December 1983) 1342 UNTS 137 (Conventional Weapons Convention).

[6] Convention for the Protection of Cultural Property in the Event of Armed Conflict (adopted 14 May 1954, entered into force 7 August 1956) 249 UNTS 215.

[7] ICRC, *Customary IHL Database* <https://ihl-databases.icrc.org/customary-ihl/eng/docs/home> accessed 25 July 2021.

[8] For instance, the Convention on the Prohibition of Military or Any Other Hostile Use of Environmental Modification Techniques (adopted 10 December 1976, entered into force 5 October 1978) 1108 UNTS 151 (ENMOD) was adopted to respond to Cold War fears that technology for weather and other eco-modification could be weaponised. See further Emily Crawford, 'Accounting for the ENMOD Convention: Cold War Influences on the Origins and Development of the 1976 Convention on Environmental Modification Techniques' in Matthew Craven, Sundhya Pahuja, and Gerry Simpson (eds), *International Law and the Cold War* (CUP 2020).

[9] See, for example, Eric Talbot Jensen, 'The Future of the Law of Armed Conflict: Ostriches, Butterflies, and Nanobots' (2014) 35 Michigan Journal of International Law 253, 254; Glenn M Sulmasy, 'The Law of Armed Conflict in the Global War on Terror: International Lawyers Fighting the Last War' (2014) 19 Notre Dame Journal of Law, Ethics & Public Policy 309.

Non-Binding Norms in International Humanitarian Law. Emily Crawford, Oxford University Press. © Emily Crawford 2021.
DOI: 10.1093/oso/9780198819851.003.0001

treaties have, for the most part, been reactive, responding to the conduct of the most recent conflict, rather than predicting conduct yet to come.[10]

In recent years, there has been a trend towards reversing, or at least tempering, this reactive quality to IHL-making. States, civil society organisations, and experts, usually acting in small groups, have taken the initiative to draft and publish manuals of instruction on new and emergent means and methods of warfare that are either entirely unregulated or notably underregulated under the existing law. Rather than waiting for the international community to adopt new treaties, these small groups of interested stakeholders have instead, on their own initiative, engaged in norm development in the form of non-binding instruments.

These non-binding instruments have been designed as either 'best practice' guidelines or (re)statements of applicable law. They are not treaties and they are not intended to be binding. However, despite declarations regarding the non-binding nature of the instruments, they are, nonetheless, frequently positioned as authoritative statements of what the law *is*.[11] These instruments also share similar procedural methodologies. Standard practice has been to draw together a group of experts, usually from government agencies, the armed forces, academia, and legal practice. Over the course of a few years, these experts examine the questions and issues raised by their topic, ultimately drafting and adopting an instrument that, in many respects, resembles a treaty.

Non-binding instruments are not new to IHL; they have been part of IHL-making for decades, with States (and non-State actors) often adopting non-binding instruments, in the form of codes of conduct, manuals of instruction, or other draft or non-binding instruments.[12] For example, in 1880, the Institute of International Law[13] published its *Manual on the Laws of War on Land*.[14] The Oxford Manual, as it came to be known, was not intended to be adopted as 'an international treaty, which might perhaps be premature or at least very difficult to obtain',[15] but was nonetheless produced by the Institute in the belief that it was 'fulfilling a duty in offering to the governments a "Manual" suitable as the basis for national legislation in each State, and in accord with both the progress of juridical science and the needs of civilized armies'.[16]

[10] As noted by Marco Sassòli, Antoine A Bouvier, and Anne Quintin, the international law of armed conflict is often 'one war behind reality': Marco Sassòli, Antoine A Bouvier, and Anne Quintin, *How Does Law Protect in War? Cases, Documents and Teaching Materials on Contemporary Practice in International Humanitarian Law* (3rd edn, ICRC 2011) 52, 60.

[11] This is explored in more detail in Chapters 4 and 5.

[12] See further Chapter 3, which will explore the history of non-binding norms in IHL.

[13] Founded in 1873 and comprising renowned and respected international lawyers. See further Institut de Droit International (Institute of International Law), 'History' <http://www.idi-iil.org/en/histoire/> accessed 25 July 2021.

[14] *The Laws of War on Land* (Oxford Manual) (in French), adopted by the Institute of International Law at Oxford, 9 September 1880 http://www.idi-iil.org/app/uploads/2017/06/1880_oxf_02_fr.pdf accessed 25 July 2021.

[15] ibid Preamble.

[16] ibid Preamble.

Non-binding provisions have even been included in 'hard law' IHL treaties. For instance, Common Article 3 in the 1949 Geneva Conventions includes a provision that encourages parties to a non-international armed conflict to 'further endeavour to bring into force, by means of special agreements, all or part of the other provisions of the present Convention'.[17] Another statement of recommended practice can be found in Article 6(5) of Additional Protocol II,[18] encouraging the extension of amnesty to non-State participants in non-international armed conflicts.[19]

There is now a considerable number of non-binding instruments that are part of the landscape of the law of armed conflict. In many respects, these instruments are beneficial for those who engage with IHL—they are measured, thoughtful, well-researched statements of the law as it applies to new and complex situations. By drawing on the expertise of a small group of experts, these instruments can be debated and drafted in a timely manner—arguably more quickly than if the issues were left to the international community of 196 States to resolve. Additionally, because these instruments are not subject to debate at an international conference of States, the provisions are not subject to the usual revisions, reservations, and dilutions that come with attempts to reach consensus among numerous States. Non-binding instruments have the potential to be dynamic, prompt, and responsive measures to address pressing issues in armed conflicts.

However, the proliferation of these non-binding instruments raises some substantive and procedural issues. Concerns about legitimacy are obvious—as noted above, these documents are often debated and drafted by relatively small numbers of experts, sometimes as few as 30. Keeping the group of experts to a small number can make the drafting process more manageable but, equally, it can mean that it includes only a limited number of perspectives—especially if the experts are drawn from only a few specific legal systems and represent only select geographical, social-cultural, or political backgrounds. In practice, experts involved in one instrument's creation have often been involved in the drafting of other instruments; while drawing on the wealth of expertise offered by these individuals is obviously helpful, it might mean that only certain doctrinal or theoretical positions are reinforced and perpetuated. Finally, while attempts are clearly made to ensure that the final instrument reflects *lex lata*, in some instances the instrument is closer to *lex ferenda*.

Connected to concerns about the legitimacy of these instruments are issues regarding their legality. Are the instruments treated as legal documents in any way and, if so, what implications arise? Do they have any authority to claim themselves as being instructive, or to hope to influence behaviour? Do they deserve any

[17] Geneva Convention III (n 4) Art 3 (Common Article 3).

[18] Protocol Additional to the Geneva Conventions of 12 August 1949, and relating to the Protection of Victims of Non-International Armed Conflicts (Protocol II) (adopted 8 June 1977, entered into force 7 December 1978) 1125 UNTS 609 (Additional Protocol II or APII).

[19] ibid Art 6(5).

deference or respect as (semi-)authoritative statements, despite their non-binding status?

Finally, it is useful to examine whether these instruments are effective. How have they been received by States and other participants in armed conflicts? Do they shape or influence practice in conflicts? If these instruments *are* effective, and *are* followed in practice, the questions regarding their legitimacy and legality become even more pressing.

It is these questions that will be explored in this book. Chapter 1 will examine the concept of non-binding norms (also known as 'soft law'), proposing a working definition for this book and drawing on the literature on non-binding law in other fields of international law, such as international environmental law, international economic law, and international human rights law. This chapter will also briefly survey how non-binding norms and soft law have been received by States and by international judicial organs, such as the International Court of Justice (ICJ), to see what kind of consideration such instruments are afforded by international actors. Finally, the chapter will explore and assess the arguments for and against the very concept of soft law. This analysis will set the framework for the remaining chapters, which will focus on non-binding norms in IHL.

Chapters 2, 3, and 4 will begin the process of examining non-binding instruments in IHL. Chapter 2 will undertake a historical examination of the adoption of non-binding instruments. This chapter will provide historical context for the book, establishing that, while the proliferation of non-binding instruments in recent years is remarkable, it is not entirely unprecedented. Chapter 3 will then examine the inclusion of non-binding provisions in binding treaties—specifically, the 'special agreements' provision of Common Article 3 and the amnesty provision in Additional Protocol II.

Chapters 4 and 5 set out the remainder of the non-binding instruments under examination. Chapter 4 looks at the *San Remo Manual on International Law Applicable to Armed Conflicts at Sea*;[20] the *San Remo Manual on the Law of Non-International Armed Conflict*;[21] the *Montreux Document on Pertinent International Legal Obligations and Good Practices for States related to Operations of Private Military and Security Companies during Armed Conflict*;[22] the *Manual on International Law Applicable to Air and Missile Warfare*;[23] the *Copenhagen Process*

[20] Louise Doswald-Beck (ed), *San Remo Manual on International Law Applicable to Armed Conflicts at Sea* (CUP 1995) (San Remo Naval Manual).

[21] Michael Schmitt, Charles Garraway, and Yoram Dinstein (eds), *The Manual on the Law of Non-International Armed Conflict* (International Institute of Humanitarian Law 2006) (San Remo NIAC (Non-International Armed Conflict) Manual).

[22] *Montreux Document on Pertinent International Legal Obligations and Good Practices for States related to Operations of Private Military and Security Companies during Armed Conflict* (Swiss Federal Department of Foreign Affairs 2009) (Montreux Document).

[23] Program on Humanitarian Policy and Conflict Research at Harvard University, *Manual on International Law Applicable to Air and Missile Warfare* (CUP 2013) (AMW (Air and Missile Warfare) Manual).

Principles and Guidelines on the Handling of Detainees in International Military Operations;[24] the *Tallinn Manual on the International Law Applicable to Cyber Warfare*;[25] and *the Tallinn Manual 2.0 on the International Law Applicable to Cyber Operations*.[26] These documents can be broadly categorised as non-binding instruments that have resulted from a State-driven or expert group-driven process. The instruments aim to be statements of the applicable law (as well as, in some cases, additional statements of recommended practice) and are designed for use by States (and, to a lesser degree, non-State armed groups).

Chapter 5 examines the non-binding instruments that are not easily categorised as manuals of instruction for States; these are documents that have emanated from civil society organisations as research projects, or documents that are designed specifically for use by non-State actors. They include the International Committee of the Red Cross (ICRC) Study into Customary International Humanitarian Law;[27] the Interpretive Guidance on the Notion of Direct Participation in Hostilities under International Humanitarian Law;[28] the International Code of Conduct for Private Security Service Providers;[29] and the four Deeds of Commitment produced by the non-governmental organisation Geneva Call.[30]

These are not the only non-binding instruments relating to armed conflict or situations of armed violence.[31] However, these instruments have arguably been the most prominent, the most analysed, and, often, the most contentious. Chapters 4 and 5 will explore how and why these instruments came about, what their intended

[24] The Copenhagen Process on the Handling of Detainees in International Military Operations, *Copenhagen Process Principles and Guidelines* <https://um.dk/en/~/media/UM/English-site/Documents/Politics-and-diplomacy/Copenhangen%20Process%20Principles%20and%20Guidelines.pdf> accessed 25 July 2021 (Copenhagen Principles).

[25] Michael Schmitt (ed), *Tallinn Manual on the International Law Applicable to Cyber Warfare* (CUP 2013) (Tallinn Manual 1.0).

[26] Michael Schmitt (ed), *Tallinn Manual 2.0 on the International Law Applicable to Cyber Operations* (CUP 2017) (Tallinn Manual 2.0).

[27] ICRC, *Customary IHL Database* (n 7).

[28] Nils Melzer (ed), *Interpretive Guidance on the Notion of Direct Participation in Hostilities under International Humanitarian Law* (ICRC 2009) (Interpretive Guidance).

[29] *International Code of Conduct for Private Security Service Providers* (ICoC) <https://icoca.ch/the-code/>.

[30] Geneva Call, Deed of Commitment for Adherence to a Total Ban on Anti-Personnel Mines and for Cooperation in Mine Action (2000) <http://www.genevacall.org/wp-content/uploads/2019/07/DoC-Banning-anti-personnel-mines.pdf> accessed 25 July 2021; Geneva Call, Deed of Commitment for the Protection of Children from the Effects of Armed Conflict (2010) <http://www.genevacall.org/wp-content/uploads/2019/11/Official-DoC-Protecting-children-in-armed-conflict.pdf> accessed 25 July 2021; Geneva Call, Deed of Commitment for the Prohibition of Sexual Violence in Situations of Armed Conflict and towards the Elimination of Gender Discrimination (2012) <http://www.genevacall.org/wp-content/uploads/2019/07/DoC-Prohibiting-sexual-violence-and-gender-discrimination.pdf> accessed 25 July 2021; Geneva Call, Deed of Commitment for the Protection of Health Care in Armed Conflict (2018) <http://www.genevacall.org/wp-content/uploads/2019/07/Deed-of-Commitment-for-the-protection-of-health-care-in-armed-conflict-final-version-4.pdf> accessed 25 July 2021.

[31] See, for example, Terry Gill and others (eds), *Leuven Manual on the International Law Applicable to Peace Operations* (CUP 2017); Alan Cole and others (eds), *San Remo Handbook on Rules of Engagement* (Institute of International Humanitarian Law 2009).

scope and application are, which actors were involved in their creation, and whether they can be viewed as statements of the extant law or as progressive developments of the law.

Chapter 6 will begin the process of analysing *why* there has been a turn to non-binding norms in IHL. The statements of purpose behind the adoption of the various manuals, codes of conduct, and other non-binding norms will be examined to ascertain whether any common reasoning underpins the adoption of such instruments and documents. The discussion will be framed by an analysis of theories of soft law compliance, looking at why other branches of international law—such as economic and environmental law—have embraced non-binding norms, and whether there are any parallels for IHL.

Chapters 7 and 8 will examine three major theoretical and practical issues that arise in relation to non-binding instruments: questions of efficacy, legitimacy, and legality. Chapter 7 will examine whether these non-binding norms and instruments have been applied in practice, using two broad approaches to assessing efficacy: have the instruments been followed or adopted in their entirety, or have they instead been generally influential, but only in a limited way (that is, have only some of the recommendations been followed)? In doing so, this chapter will explore whether these instruments have been given effect through domestic legislative implementation or through incorporation into military manuals or official State policy, and/or whether they have been affirmed or used by State and international courts and tribunals.

Chapter 8 will examine the notions of legitimacy and legality in international law and will apply those theories to the IHL soft law instruments. The chapter will explore the idea of legitimacy, drawing on the extensive literature on legitimacy and international law that has emerged over the last 25 years, as well as the literature that has emerged on legitimacy and soft law more generally. Chapter 8 will examine and analyse some of the issues that are unique to IHL soft law instruments, looking at who initiated the process that led to the adoption of the instrument, what were the objectives behind the adoption, who was involved in the adoption of the instrument, and how the instrument has been received and perceived by its intended audience. In doing so, it will look at questions of whether the 'source' of the instrument influences its reception. For example, is an instrument issued by the ICRC considered more 'legitimate' than one from a non-affiliated group of experts? Does the involvement of certain experts make the instrument more (or less) acceptable to its target audience? To that end, Chapter 8 will explore public debate and expert commentary on the adoption and reception of certain IHL soft law instruments to see how they have been received, including any critiques of the instruments.

Chapter 8 will also examine the legality of soft law instruments in IHL and address several issues that are raised regarding the turn to soft law in IHL. Specifically, what is the interplay between non-binding documents and sources of international law? Given the proliferation of stakeholders directly or indirectly influencing the making of IHL, to what extent does the distinction between hard law and soft law continue to make sense? How far can soft law instruments be considered as State practice, or as showing State *opinio juris*?

Finally, Chapter 9 will attempt to account for what implications the turn to soft law has for IHL. Does it preclude or pre-empt the adoption of binding treaties? Can soft law instruments act as useful supplements for existing hard law norms, or are they used by States to avoid having to adopt hard law norms? (And, if so, does this matter?) Are non-binding instruments an incentive for States to no longer consider adopting treaties, and what are the implications of this?

With this outline in mind, the first substantive chapter examines the concept of non-binding norms, also known as soft law, and explores theories of and about soft law.

1

What is 'Soft' Law? An Analysis of the Concept of Non-Binding Instruments and Provisions in International Law

Introduction

Non-binding instruments are not unique to international humanitarian law (IHL); non-binding instruments and non-binding provisions have long been part of international law, in forms such as resolutions of the League of Nations or the General Assembly of the United Nations (UN),[1] draft articles or reports of the International Law Commission, or recommendations of UN organs. However, non-binding instruments have proliferated in the past few decades, as manifold new entities, organisations, and individuals begin to assert their influence on the international normative order[2] and to push at the boundaries of conventional sources of international law. These non-binding instruments cover a wide variety of topics, including international environmental law,[3] international economic law,[4]

[1] Not all General Assembly resolutions are non-binding, but most, as a rule, are recommendatory only. For an assessment of the legal weight of General Assembly resolutions, see Jorge Castañeda, *Legal Effects of United Nations Resolutions* (Alba Amoia tr, Columbia University Press 1969).

[2] As Ilhami Alkan Olsson notes, in addition to States, the international legal plane now hosts 'international organisations, formal and informal technical bodies, Treaty Bodies within the UN system, international conferences on various subject-matters as well as a wide range of non-state actors, including multinational enterprises (MNEs) [and] non-governmental organisations (NGOs)'—all of which have, to some degree or another, played the role of 'norm entrepreneur': Ilhami Alkan Olsson, 'Four Competing Approaches to International Soft Law' (2013) 58 Scandinavian Studies in Law 177, 179. The term 'norm entrepreneur' was coined by Cass R Sunstein to address the growing trend of actors, both within and outside existing political and legal systems, who seek to influence and change existing socio-legal systems: Cass R Sunstein, 'Social Norms and Social Roles' (1996) 96 Columbia Law Review 903. As Sunstein notes, '[p]rivate groups can test or even change norms. Indeed, the testing of current norms, meanings, and roles is a crucial function of groups that are intermediate between citizens and the state. Religious groups are in this sense norm entrepreneurs; the same is true for environmental and civil rights organizations': ibid 947.

[3] Such as the Declaration of the United Nations Conference on the Human Environment (Stockholm, 16 June 1972), *Report of the United Nations Conference on the Human Environment, Stockholm, 5–16 June 1972*, UN Doc A/CONF.48/14/Rev.1 (1973) <http://www.un-documents.net/aconf48-14r1.pdf> accessed 26 July 2021 (Stockholm Declaration) and the Rio Declaration on Environment and Development (Rio de Janeiro, 14 June 1992), *Report of the United Nations Conference on Environment and Development*, UN Doc A/CONF.151/26 (vol I) (12 August 1992) (Rio Declaration).

[4] Such as the Final Act, Conference on Security and Co-operation in Europe (Helsinki, 1 August 1975) <http://www.osce.org/files/f/documents/5/c/39501.pdf> 26 July 2021 (Helsinki Final Act).

Non-Binding Norms in International Humanitarian Law. Emily Crawford, Oxford University Press. © Emily Crawford 2021.
DOI: 10.1093/oso/9780198819851.003.0002

and international human rights law.[5] However, as noted in the introduction to this book, it has been in IHL that there has been a notable rise in the numbers of non-binding instruments in recent years, with nearly a dozen such instruments drafted and adopted.

Before examining these non-binding IHL instruments and provisions in more detail, it is helpful to examine the concept of non-binding instruments and provisions more generally. The notion of non-binding instruments in international law—also termed 'soft law'—is contentious.[6] There are differences of opinion on the benefits and drawbacks of creating and engaging with such instruments and provisions, and a spectrum of debate as to *how* to define the notion of soft law. With this framework in mind, this chapter will examine the different types of soft law instruments as identified in the literature, which can be broadly divided into two categories: non-binding norms in binding instruments and non-binding instruments. The chapter will also examine and analyse the arguments that have emerged in the literature, either in support of or in opposition to soft law instruments and provisions. Finally, the chapter will briefly survey how soft law has been received by States and by international judicial organs, such as the International Court of Justice (ICJ), to see what kind of consideration such instruments are afforded by these international actors. General analysis of the concept of soft law will set the framework for the remaining chapters of the text, which will focus on soft law in IHL, how such instruments have been drafted, how they have been received in practice, and how and whether such instruments are beneficial or detrimental to the overall aims of IHL.

Defining Non-Binding Instruments (or Soft Law)

As noted in the introduction, non-binding instruments have proliferated in the law of armed conflict in the last 20 years. To analyse the impact (if any) of these instruments, it is necessary to define what is meant by a 'non-binding instrument' or 'non-binding norm'. First, the entire concept of soft law is itself contested, with varied definitions and interpretations of scope.[7] Defining what a 'soft law' norm is depends, to some extent, on how one defines 'hard law'. However, the literature that examines the soft law–hard law spectrum often pays only the briefest attention to

[5] Such as the Universal Declaration of Human Rights, UN Doc A/RES/217(III) (10 December 1948) (UDHR).

[6] The terms 'soft law' and 'non-binding norm' will be used interchangeably in this book.

[7] For an assessment of the differing approaches to and definitions of soft law, see further RR Baxter, 'International Law in "Her Infinite Variety"' (1980) 29 International and Comparative Law Quarterly 549; Jaye Ellis, 'Shades of Grey: Soft Law and the Validity of Public International Law' (2012) 25 Leiden Journal of International Law 313, 315–23; Andrew Guzman and Timothy Meyer, 'Soft Law' in Eugene Kontorovich and Francesco Parisi (eds), *Economic Analysis of International Law* (Elgar 2015) 123–27.

defining soft law or hard law, and, in some instances, it does not attempt to define either.[8]

Additionally, the very idea that there is an easy and clear division between binding and non-binding rules is contestable. There is, arguably, a spectrum of normative force that exists in any set of rules or provisions in international law. As RR Baxter notes:

> [p]rovisions of treaties may create little or no obligations, although inserted in a form of instrument which presumptively creates rights and duties, while, on the other hand, instruments of lesser dignity may influence or control the conduct of States and individuals to a certain degree, even though their norms are not technically binding.[9]

Finally, there are authors who dispute the very existence of a category of 'soft law', something that will be discussed later in this chapter.

The first question to ask is what makes a provision (or an instrument) binding or non-binding under international law? In the literature on soft law, certain commonalities emerge, the first of which is recognition that there is no uniform or accepted definition of the term.[10] The second commonality in the literature is broad

[8] See, for example, Jon Birger Skjærseth, Olav Schram Stokke, and Jørgen Wettestad, 'Soft Law, Hard Law, and Effective Implementation of International Environmental Norms' (2006) 6 Global Environmental Politics 104, in which the authors only briefly touch on a definition of soft and hard law. '"Soft law" refers to international norms that are deliberately non-binding in character but still have legal relevance, located "in the twilight between law and politics". Important examples are resolutions by international organizations and international plans of action or codes of conduct. The essence of "hard law" is legally binding obligations': ibid 104. See also Julien Chaisse, 'Demystifying Public Security Exception and Limitations on Capital Movement: Hard Law, Soft Law and Sovereign Investments in the EU Internal Market' (2015–16) 37 University of Pennsylvania Journal of International Law 583. Chaisse does not define either hard law or soft law in his paper.

[9] Baxter (n 7) 565.

[10] See, for example, Francesco Francioni, 'International "Soft Law": A Contemporary Assessment' in Vaughan Lowe and Malgosia Fitzmaurice (eds), *Fifty Years of the International Court of Justice: Essays in Honour of Sir Robert Jennings* (CUP 1996) 167; Guzman and Meyer, 'Soft Law' (n 7) 123; Ulrika Mörth, 'Introduction' in Ulrika Mörth (ed), *Soft Law in Governance and Regulation: An Interdisciplinary Analysis* (Elgar 2004) 5. Common also to the literature on soft law is to credit Lord McNair with the genesis of the term. See, for example, AJP Tammes, 'Soft Law' in TMC Asser Institute and Board of the Netherlands International Law Review (eds), *Essays on International and Comparative Law in Honour of Judge Erades* (TMC Asser 1983) 187; Georges Abi-Saab, 'Cours général de droit international public' (1987) 207 Recueil des Cours 1, 132; Dinah Shelton, 'International Law and Relative Normativity' in Malcolm Evans (ed), *International Law* (OUP 2010) 164–65. However, McNair does not use the term 'soft law' in *The Law of Treaties: British Practice and Opinions* (OUP 1938) and none of the above literature specifically indicates where and when, if ever, McNair uses this term. It seems instead that the theory that McNair coined the term 'soft law' comes from René-Jean Dupuy, who calls soft law 'a term honoured by the authorship of Lord McNair': René-Jean Dupuy, 'Declaratory Law and Programmatory Law: From Revolutionary Custom to "Soft Law"' in Robert Akkerman, Peter van Krieken, and Charles Pannenborg (eds), *Declarations on Principles: A Quest for Universal Peace* (Martinus Nijhoff 1977) 252. However, as Robert Jennings would later clarify, McNair was 'devoted to identifying and distinguishing what he called "hard law", and from the beginning taught us to learn rigorously to distinguish between a proposition *de lege lata* and a proposition *de lege ferenda*': Robert Jennings, 'An International Lawyer Takes Stock' (1990) 39 International and Comparative Law Quarterly 513, 516. It seems more likely that McNair never used the term 'soft law', at least in his writings, but instead, as Jennings points out, used

acknowledgement that, as a minimum, what most—if not all—non-binding provisions or instruments share is their inability (intentional or otherwise) to create legal obligations for their addressees. For example, Oscar Schachter notes, 'it would probably be generally agreed that a nonbinding agreement, however seriously taken by the parties, does not engage their legal responsibility';[11] Francesco Francioni defines soft law as 'those international norms, principles, and procedures ... outside the system of formal sources of Article 38, paragraph 1 of the ICJ Statute ... [that lack] the requisite normative content to create enforceable rights and obligations';[12] and AJP Tammes categorises soft law as a term 'intended to indicate phenomena that have the characteristics of "law" in their directive effect to influence the will ... of those to whom the "soft law" is addressed ... [but] something is missing in the legal or binding nature'[13] of the soft law in question. Similar terminology is used by Francis Snyder, who defines soft law as 'rules of conduct which, in principle, have no legally binding force but which nevertheless may have practical effects'[14] and KC Wellens and GM Borchardt define it as:

> rules of conduct that find themselves on the legally non-binding level (in the sense of enforceable and sanctionable through international responsibility) but which ... are directed at ... and do have as effect (through international law), that the conduct of States, international organizations and individuals is influenced by these rules, however without containing international legal rights and obligations.[15]

Soft law can therefore be defined as any directive or instruction, in whatever form, that creates no binding obligations for its addressees. Put another way, where a 'treaty or international agreement ... requires an intention by the parties to create legal rights and obligations or to establish relations governed by international law',[16] no equivalent intention can be found with a soft law norm or non-binding instrument. Instead, such non-binding instruments exist outside the ambit of

the terms *de lege lata* and *de lege ferenda*. See also Jan Klabbers, *The Concept of Treaty in International Law* (Kluwer 1996) 160, who likewise doubts that McNair ever specifically used the term 'soft law'.

[11] Oscar Schachter, 'The Twilight Existence of Nonbinding International Agreements' (1977) 71 American Journal of International Law 296, 300.

[12] Francioni (n 10) 168.

[13] Tammes (n 10) 187.

[14] Francis Snyder, 'Soft Law and Institutional Practice in the European Community' in Stephen Martin (ed), *The Construction of Europe: Essays in Honour of Emile Noël* (Kluwer 1994) 198. See also Francis Snyder, 'The Effectiveness of European Community Law: Institutions, Processes, Tools and Techniques' (1993) 56 Modern Law Review 19, 32.

[15] KC Wellens and GM Borchardt, 'Soft Law in European Community Law' (1989) 14 European Law Review 267, 274.

[16] Schachter (n 11) 296. See also Dan O'Connell, *International Law* (2nd edn, Stevens 1970) 195; McNair, *The Law of Treaties* (1938) (n 10) 6.

pacta sunt servanda.[17] In the most basic, broad, and general sense, soft law and non-binding norms can be considered as all those rules, instruments, and provisions that do not (or are not intended to) have binding force and/or enforceability.

However, even within this broad definition, there are still distinct subcategories of soft law covering a wide spectrum. On one end of this definitional spectrum is what Baxter calls 'legally fragile'[18] treaties: political treaties[19] that establish alliances or demarcate neutral areas.[20] For Baxter, these treaties, though still binding sources of law, are essentially equivalent to 'joint statements of policy which will remain alive only so long as the States concerned see it to be in their mutual interest to concert their policies. One simply cannot think of "violations" of such instruments'.[21] These treaties are somehow 'less binding' than a treaty that, for example, establishes a joint agreement for the building of a dam—the terms of which, if violated, would give rise to a right to bring the dispute for adjudication.[22]

Baxter maintains that this 'less binding' quality is attributable to several factors. First, such treaties tend to be structured to allow denunciation or repudiation of the treaty for essentially subjective, non-legal reasons, with little or no consequence. Parties to such a treaty may decide that the treaty regime is simply too inconvenient or inappropriate to observe, and therefore may choose to terminate their participation. These treaties essentially create '"obligations" of such a fragility that legal enforcement may be difficult or even impossible'.[23] As an example, Baxter cites the Nuclear Test Ban Treaty of 1963,[24] which in Article IV allows a State party to withdraw from the treaty 'if it decides that extraordinary events, related to the subject matter of this Treaty, have jeopardized the supreme interests of its country'.[25] By allowing withdrawal from a treaty due to a subjective interpretation of events, a treaty regime 'from which easy release is available ... may not be enforceable in the strict legal sense'.[26] Additionally, such 'fragile' agreements might not lend themselves easily to enforcement. For example, if a treaty establishing a military alliance between two States were broken by one State refusing to provide

17 See further Hans Wehberg, 'Pacta Sunt Servanda' (1959) 53 American Journal of International Law 775.

18 Baxter (n 7) 551.

19 McNair, *The Law of Treaties* (1938) (n 10); see also McNair, *The Law of Treaties* (OUP 1961) 501–02.

20 Baxter (n 7) 551.

21 ibid.

22 Which was the issue in *Gabčikovo-Nagymaros Project (Hungary v Slovakia) (Merits)* [1997] ICJ Rep 3.

23 Baxter (n 7) 551.

24 Treaty Banning Nuclear Weapons Tests in the Atmosphere, in Outer Space and under Water (adopted 5 August 1963, entered into force 10 October 1963) 480 UNTS 43 (Nuclear Test Ban Treaty). Prosper Weil also considers the Nuclear Test Ban Treaty as one of these fragile instruments that outline 'norms whose substance is so vague, so uncompelling, that A's obligation and B's right all but elude the mind': Prosper Weil, 'Towards Relative Normativity in International Law' (1983) 77 American Journal of International Law 413, 414.

25 Nuclear Test Ban Treaty (n 24) Art VI.

26 Baxter (n 7) 551.

military assistance,[27] enforcing compliance with such a treaty would be difficult, if not impossible: 'if a State refuses to come to the aid of another under the terms of an alliance, nothing can force it to. It was never expected that the treaty would be "enforced" '.[28]

Connected to this definition of soft law would be those rules contained in binding instruments that either lack sufficient precision as to the content of the obligation, or else establish an obligation that is essentially unenforceable (due to imprecision in scope and/or content) and/or is otherwise, at best, recommendatory in nature.[29] An example of such a soft law provision would be the second-last sentence in Common Article 3 of the Geneva Conventions, which states that the '[p]arties to the conflict should further endeavour to bring into force, by means of special agreements, all or part of the other provisions of the present Convention'.[30] Such a provision as this—a recommendatory suggestion at most—is functionally unenforceable; it would not be possible to compel parties to a conflict to do something that the binding instrument in question presents as something they *should* do (rather than something they *must* do). These provisions are, as the ICJ has noted,[31] hortatory in nature, and therefore 'have the common characteristic of not creating legal obligations which are susceptible of enforcement, in whatever sense the concept of "enforcement" is employed'.[32] Such provisions are, however, meant to be taken 'seriously'[33] by States and treated with 'some measure of respect'.[34] According to this approach to soft law, the 'law' element is paramount. These

[27] ibid.

[28] ibid. However, cf Gerald Fitzmaurice, in his *Report on the Law of Treaties*, who argues that more weight should be given to the element of intention to establish relationships under treaty law. '[I]t seems difficult to refuse the designation of treaty to an instrument—such as for instance a treaty of peace and amity, or of alliance—even if it only establishes a bare relationship, and leaves the consequences to rest on the basis of an implication as to the rights and obligations involved, without these being expressed in any definite articles': Gerald Fitzmaurice, *Report on the Law of Treaties* (1956) 2 Yearbook of the International Law Commission, 104, 117; UN Doc A/CN.4/101.

[29] See further Michel Virally, 'La distinction entre textes internationaux ayant une portee juridique dans les relations mutuelles entres leurs auteurs et texts qui en sont depourvus' (1983) 60 IDI Annuaire 166. However, cf Vaughan Lowe, who argues against considering such norms within the soft law category, arguing that it is 'unhelpful to regard such rules as "soft law". They are binding in their own terms; and even rules that appeared clear at the time that they were drafted may come over time to reveal a range of possible interpretations and become "vague". Better to confine the term "soft law" to norms that are not binding but which colour the application of norms that are legally binding': Vaughan Lowe, *International Law* (OUP 2007) 96.

[30] Geneva Convention (III) Relative to the Treatment of Prisoners of War of 12 August 1949 (adopted 12 August 1949, entered into force 21 October 1950) 75 UNTS 135 (Geneva Convention III) Art 3. Chapter 3 will look at this provision in more detail.

[31] *Appeal Relating to the Jurisdiction of the ICAO Council (India v Pakistan)* [1972] ICJ Rep 46, 107, fn 1 (Judge Dillard), where it was stated that treaties (such as multilateral treaties establishing functioning institutions) 'frequently contain articles that represent ideals and aspirations which, being hortatory, are not considered to be legally binding except by those who seek to apply them to the other fellow'.

[32] Baxter (n 7) 554.

[33] Joseph Gold, 'Strengthening the Soft International Law of Exchange Arrangements' (1983) 77 American Journal of International Law 443, 443.

[34] ibid 443.

recommendations or vaguely defined norms have been adopted by States with the intention and understanding that State behaviour *should* be in compliance, even if there is no consequence from non-observance.[35] By including a hortatory norm in a binding treaty, the recommendation is therefore rendered more persuasive and is elevated to a level beyond mere ethical or political considerations.

A broader approach to the concept of soft law would include *any* non-binding instrument, provision, or set of instructions designed to restate, affirm, develop, and/or clarify existing binding norms that regulate conduct in a particular area.[36] For advocates of this definition, non-binding instruments 'cannot be considered mere moral or political directives ... [even though] the legally binding character ... [of the instruments] has been deliberately and sometimes explicitly denied by their drafters'.[37] The quintessential example of such a non-binding instrument would be resolutions of the UN General Assembly, such as Resolution 2444 on human rights in armed conflicts.[38] The resolution affirms the applicability of certain fundamental principles in situations of armed conflict (such as the principle of distinction and the prohibition on launching attacks against the civilian population)[39] and goes on to invite 'the Secretary-General, in consultation with the Red Cross and other appropriate international organisations, to study ... steps which could be taken to secure the better application of existing humanitarian international conventions and rules in all armed conflicts'.[40] The resolution then suggests that improvements and amendments to the law should be investigated, with a possible outcome being the adoption of new binding law regulating conduct in armed conflicts.[41] Resolution 2444 is an exemplar of this category of soft law: as a General Assembly resolution, it is non-binding[42] and, while it restates the applicability of existing customary law

[35] For an assessment of this approach, see ibid 443–45; Jonathan Carlson, 'Hunger, Agricultural Trade Liberalisation, and Soft International Law: Addressing the Legal Dimensions of a Political Problem' (1984–85) 70 Iowa Law Review 1187, 1200–04. However, cf Schachter, who rightly notes that 'imprecision and generalities are not unknown in treaties of unquestioned legal force ... if one were to apply strict requirements of definiteness and specificity to all treaties, many of them would have all or most of their provisions considered as without legal effect': Schachter (n 11) 298.

[36] See Christine Chinkin, 'Normative Development in the International Legal System' in Dinah Shelton (ed), *Commitment and Compliance: The Role of Non-Binding Norms in the International Legal System* (OUP 2000) 30–31.

[37] Daniel Thürer, 'Soft Law' in Anne Peters and Rüdiger Wolfrum (eds), *Max Planck Encyclopedia of Public International Law* (OUP 2021).

[38] General Assembly Resolution 2444 (XXIII), Respect for Human Rights in Armed Conflicts, UN Doc A/RES/2444(XXIII) (19 December 1968).

[39] ibid para 1.

[40] ibid para 2(a).

[41] ibid para 2(b).

[42] UN Charter, Art 10: 'The General Assembly may discuss any questions or any matters within the scope of the present Charter or relating to the powers and functions of any organs provided for in the present Charter, and, except as provided in Article 12, may make recommendations to the Members of the United Nations or to the Security Council or to both on any such questions or matters.' Note, however, the discussion on the potentially binding effect that UN resolutions can have. See further the 'Commentary to Article 10' in Bruno Simma and others (eds), *The Charter of the United Nations: A Commentary* (vol 1, 3rd edn, OUP 2012) 478–88. Note also Judge Lauterpacht's separate opinion in *South West Africa Cases (Advisory Opinion Concerning the Voting Procedure on Questions Relating to*

norms that apply in situations of armed conflicts,[43] it goes on to encourage but not mandate a particular course of action—that of inviting the UN Secretary-General, the International Committee of the Red Cross (ICRC), and any other interested stakeholders (in the form of international institutions) to examine how improved application of the laws of armed conflict may be enacted.

Finally, another theory of soft law is forwarded by Kenneth Abbott and Duncan Snidal, who take a reasonably broad approach to defining soft law but add the qualifier that the distinction between hard law and soft law is not a rigid binary and that 'soft law comes in many varieties'.[44] In coming to their definition, Abbott and Snidal, in conjunction with Robert Keohane, Andrew Moravcsik, and Anne-Marie Slaughter,[45] draw heavily on HLA Hart's *The Concept of Law*,[46] which defines a legal system as the 'union of primary and secondary rules',[47] with primary rules being all those rules that lay down obligations, while secondary rules are those 'concerned with the primary rules themselves. They specify the ways in which the primary rules may be conclusively ascertained, introduced, eliminated, varied, and the fact of their violation conclusively determined'.[48] Abbott and Snidal formulate a theory of soft law that sees hard and soft law as existing on a spectrum, one that is informed by three component elements of obligation, precision, and delegation. They conceive of hard law as any 'legally binding obligations that are precise (or can be made precise through adjudication or the issuance of detailed regulations) and that delegate authority for interpreting and implementing the law'.[49] Once any kind of agreement or arrangement that purports to be legally binding is 'weakened along one or more of the dimensions of obligation, precision, and delegation',[50] the agreement can be considered as having entered the 'realm of "soft law"'.[51] This approach is mirrored in the work of Samantha Besson, who argues that 'international legal norms ... well may have different degrees of normativity: their normativity

Reports and Petitions) [1955] ICJ Rep 67, 115, where he noted that while some decisions of the General Assembly can have limited and sometimes even full legal effect, 'it may be said by way of generalisation that they are not legally binding upon the Members of the United Nations ... they are in the nature of recommendations ... they do not create a legal obligation to comply with them'.

[43] The principles of distinction, and the prohibition on launching attacks against the civilian population, have long been considered customary international law. See further ICRC, *Customary IHL Database*, Rules 1 and 7 <https://ihl-databases.icrc.org/customary-ihl/eng/docs/home> 26 July 2021.

[44] Kenneth Abbott and Duncan Snidal, 'Hard and Soft Law in International Governance' (2000) 54 International Organisation 421, 422.

[45] Kenneth Abbott and others, 'The Concept of Legalisation' (2000) 54 International Organisation 401.

[46] HLA Hart, *The Concept of Law* (2nd edn, Clarendon 1994).

[47] ibid 79.

[48] ibid 94. Put more bluntly, 'rules of the first type impose duties; rules of the second type confer powers, public or private': ibid 81.

[49] Abbott and Snidal (n 44) 421.

[50] ibid.

[51] ibid. For a more detailed analysis of Abbott and Snidal's obligation/precision/delegation theory of legalisation, see further Abbott and others (n 45).

can range from being low (or soft) as with legal norms in the making to being imperative as with norms of *jus cogens*'.[52]

Despite the varied definitions of soft law in the literature, it is possible to discern two broad categories. The first category encompasses non-binding rules or provisions contained in binding instruments, which Tadeusz Gruchalla-Wesierski would call 'legal soft law'[53] and which Jean d'Aspremont terms soft *negotium*.[54] According to this approach, the provision, norm, or rule in question can be found in a binding instrument, such as a treaty. However, the provisions are 'purely indicative or suggestive [and] therefore do not formulate any obligations'.[55] As noted above, examples of such soft law would be the provision in Common Article 3 to the Geneva Conventions, which states that '[p]arties to the conflict should further endeavour to bring into force, by means of special agreements, all or part of the other provisions of the present Convention'.[56] In the second category, what d'Aspremont terms 'soft *instrumentum*',[57] are those instruments that are non-binding in their entirety. These non-binding instruments are, as Andrew Guzman and Timothy Meyer have identified,[58] similar in nature to a treaty 'but [fall] short of the requirements to be one'.[59] In the IHL context, such soft law instruments include, as mentioned above, the 1880 Oxford Manual, as well as the more recent examples of the *San Remo Manual on Non-International Armed Conflict* and the *Tallinn Manual 2.0 on the International Law Application to Cyber Operations*.[60]

This raises an interesting question: does the inclusion of a soft provision in a binding treaty make it 'less' soft than an entirely non-binding instrument? For d'Aspremont, form matters: in contrast to soft *negotium*, soft *instrumentum* are still capable of producing legal effects. Soft *instrumentum* can 'play a role in the

[52] Samantha Besson, 'Theorising the Sources of International Law' in Samantha Besson and John Tasioulas (eds), *The Philosophy of International Law* (OUP 2010) 175.

[53] Tadeusz Gruchalla-Wesierski, 'A Framework for Understanding "Soft Law"' (1984) 30 McGill Law Journal 38, 40.

[54] Jean d'Aspremont, 'Softness in International Law: A Self-Serving Quest for New Legal Materials' (2008) 19 European Journal of International Law 1075, 1084.

[55] ibid.

[56] Geneva Convention III (n 30) Art 3. See further Chapter 3.

[57] Jean d'Aspremont, *Formalism and the Sources of International Law: A Theory of the Ascertainment of Legal Rules* (OUP 2011) 129. Gruchalla-Wesierski (n 53) would use the phrase 'non-legal soft law': ibid 40.

[58] Andrew Guzman and Timothy Meyer, 'International Soft Law' (2010) 2 Journal of Legal Analysis 171, 187.

[59] ibid 187.

[60] Discussed in more detail in Chapter 4. See also Christine Chinkin, 'The Challenge of Soft Law: Development and Change in International Law' (1989) 38 International and Comparative Law Quarterly 850, 851. Dinah Shelton would categorise soft law into groups of primary and secondary, with primary soft law being those 'normative texts not adopted in treaty form that are addressed to the international community as a whole or the entire membership of the adopting institution or organisation' and secondary soft law being recommendations of international supervisory organs, jurisprudence of international courts and commissions, and resolutions of international bodies applying primary norms: Dinah Shelton, 'Soft Law' in Armstrong D (ed), *Routledge Handbook of International Law* (Abingdon 2009) 70. While this is an interesting approach, it will not be used in this book.

internationalization of the subject matter, provide guidelines for the interpretation of other legal acts, or pave the way for further subsequent practice which may one day be taken into account for the emergence of customary international norm'[61]—something that provisions that can be characterised as having a soft *negotium* cannot achieve because 'they have no normative character, as they fail to provide any directive as to which behaviour the parties should adopt irrespective of their own will'.[62] However, others, such as Gerald Fitzmaurice, would dispute such a characterisation and would argue that the choice to include such soft provisions in a hard law instrument is determinative, and that the inclusion of soft provisions in binding treaties does not deprive such provisions of their binding character, even if they lack specificity.[63]

Ultimately, as Alan Boyle and Christine Chinkin note, it is not so much the label attached to the soft law instrument or agreement that matters as its substance and intent:[64] did the parties involved in the drafting and adoption of the provision or instrument intend for it to have 'normative significance'?[65] Is there 'at least an element of good faith commitment, evidencing in some cases a desire to influence state practice or expressing some measure of law-making intention and progressive development'?[66]

For the purposes of this book, soft law will be defined broadly, using some of the key elements outlined by Chinkin. Non-binding norms include any instrument or provision that meets any of four possible determinants: it has 'been articulated in non-binding form according to traditional modes of law-making';[67] it emanates 'from bodies lacking international law-making authority';[68] it is directed at or designed to include 'non-state actors whose practice cannot constitute customary international law';[69] and/or it is predicated on 'voluntary adherence, or [relies] upon non-juridical means of enforcement'.[70]

Criticisms of and Support for the Concept of Soft Law

In assessing the different approaches to and definitions of non-binding norms and soft law, it should be noted that while some scholars see manifold benefits in an embrace of soft law and non-binding instruments, others reject or are resistant to the

61 d'Aspremont, 'Softness in International Law' (n 54) 1082.
62 ibid 1085.
63 Fitzmaurice (n 28) 117.
64 Alan Boyle and Christine Chinkin, *The Making of International Law* (OUP 2007) 213.
65 ibid 214.
66 ibid.
67 Chinkin, 'Normative Development' (n 36) 30.
68 ibid.
69 ibid.
70 ibid.

concept of soft law. This rejection or resistance stems from a belief that the concept of soft law is fundamentally incoherent. For these scholars, such as Jan Klabbers,[71] Prosper Weil,[72] and d'Aspremont,[73] a particular rule or norm is either binding or it is not. If it is not binding, it cannot be law, soft or otherwise. The reasons behind the resistance to soft law are varied. As this book will attempt to assess both the benefits and the drawbacks of the turn to non-binding instruments in IHL, it is necessary to examine some of these arguments in detail.

Soft Law as an Unhelpful, Counter-Productive, and Self-Defeating Concept

At a practical level, non-binding instruments might be considered problematic or undesirable precisely because of their non-binding nature. Why would a State (or other international organisation or group) go to the trouble of negotiating and producing a guidance document (or code of conduct or recommendation as to practice), only to undermine its ability to guide practice or regulate behaviour? Why create something knowing full well that it can and will be ignored?[74]

There are also compelling doctrinal arguments against embracing soft law. For Weil, the term 'soft law' is confusing and unhelpful, as it blurs two distinct categories of rule: binding legal norms that are imprecise or vague, and those provisions that:

> are precise, yet remain at the pre- or subnormative stage. To discuss both of these categories in terms of 'soft law' or 'hard law' is to foster confusion ... it would seem better to reserve the term 'soft law' for rules that are imprecise and not really compelling, since sublegal obligations are neither 'soft law' nor 'hard law': they are simply not law at all.[75]

Weil would limit designation of soft law norms to Baxter's 'legally fragile'[76] treaties—vague or unspecific provisions in binding treaties. However, Weil does not reject soft law outright, instead arguing that while soft law instruments or provisions:

[71] Jan Klabbers, 'The Redundancy of Soft Law' (1996) 65 Nordic Journal of International Law 167.
[72] Weil (n 24).
[73] d'Aspremont, *Formalism and the Sources of International Law* (n 57).
[74] See Anthony D'Amato, 'Softness in International Law: A Self-Serving Quest for New Legal Materials: A Reply to Jean d'Aspremont' (2009) 20 European Journal of International Law 897. 'The essence of any soft law rule is that it is not enforceable. A soft law is like a head without a body. The head knows where it wants to go but it lacks the means to get there': ibid 899.
[75] Weil (n 24) 415, n 7.
[76] Baxter (n 7) 551.

> may well constitute an important *stage* in the process of elaborating international norms ... they do not constitute the formal *source* of new norms. That does not mean, of course, that the jurist should ignore them; but between showing due interest in them and integrating them into the normative system under the cover of a sliding scale of normativity, there is a gap that can be bridged only at the cost of denying the specific nature of the legal phenomenon.[77]

Other critics of soft law are less amenable to non-binding instruments, arguing that they only add unnecessary confusion and indeterminacy to the legal landscape. For Klabbers, soft law not only is a redundant concept, but also has deleterious effects on the legal system itself. In making his argument, Klabbers notes the work of David Hume, specifically *A Treatise of Human Nature*, where Hume argues that while:

> all kinds of vice and virtue run insensibly into each other ... 'tis certain, that rights, and obligations, and property, admit of no such insensible gradation, but that a man either has a full and perfect property, or none at all; and is either entirely oblig'd to perform any action, or lies under no manner of obligation.... Half rights and obligations ... are perfect absurdities ....[78]

Drawing on Hume's reasoning, Klabbers critiques the possibility that one can have gradations of legal obligation; law is either binding or it is not—the very nature of law is that it can be 'more or less specific, more or less exact, more or less determinate, more or less wide in scope, more or less pressing, more or less serious, more or less far-reaching; the only thing it cannot be is more or less binding'.[79]

Klabbers rejects the argument sometimes put forward by proponents of soft law, that it provides a useful mechanism for addressing the areas of indeterminacy that sometimes exist in hard law (such as vaguely or generally worded provisions in treaties). For Klabbers, having recourse to additional guidelines to try and understand the scope of language used in treaties seems counterproductive, for:

> if language is itself indeterminate, it is difficult to see why the language of soft law instruments would be an exception. Hence, one would need another soft law instrument to give meaning to the terms of the previous one, and so on and so forth in an infinite regression. Moreover, and more seriously, quite a few soft law instruments are themselves deliberately kept vague; chances are, that they do not explain anything, but only add to the indeterminacy.[80]

77 Weil (n 24) 417.
78 David Hume, *A Treatise of Human Nature* (Clarendon Press 1896) bk III, pt II, ch VI, 529, 531.
79 Klabbers, 'The Redundancy of Soft Law' (n 71) 181.
80 ibid 178.

The embrace of soft law would seem to present considerable hazards for law, for its determinacy, its primacy, and its coherence.[81] If law is meant to be a knowable, definable system for regulating conduct, then by embracing soft law:

> we may end up in precisely the type of trouble that resort to soft law was supposed to help us overcome. By creating uncertainty at the edges of legal thinking, the concept of soft law contributes to the crumbling of the entire legal system. Once political or moral concerns are allowed to creep back into the law, the law loses its relative autonomy from politics or morality and therewith becomes a fig leaf for power.[82]

This opinion is shared by László Blutman, who argues that the wide disparity in definitions of what can be considered soft law is evidence of 'deeper conceptual and doctrinal problems',[83] and the term soft law is 'meaningless ... we have a term that denotes something vague, by which every author means different things, or even worse, does not mean any defined phenomenon leaving the term in its undetailed generality in common legal discourse'.[84] For Blutman, allowing the term 'soft law' to disseminate and flourish in international legal scholarship undermines the 'very existence of international law and the system of international legal sources'.[85] Anthony Arend also rejects soft law for these reasons, arguing that:

> [i]f a rule meets the criteria for law, then it should be called 'law'. If, however, the rule is not binding—as soft law has been described to be—then it should not have law anywhere in its name .... Given, in particular, the disdain with which international law is held by some international relations scholars, the concept of soft law seems to serve no purpose except to confuse matters and dilute the distinctive nature of legal rules.[86]

For another notable critic of soft law, d'Aspremont, the acceptance of soft law is also deeply problematic, in that it may well undermine the international legal system. By deformalising the process of 'law-ascertainment'[87]—the formal process of 'rigorously distinguishing law from non-law'[88]—and embracing the notion of normativity existing on a continuum rather than a binary system, the acceptance

[81] As noted by Klabbers, 'the very raison d'être of law is [its simplicity] ... knowing only categories of legal or illegal, in force or not in force, binding or not binding': Jan Klabbers, 'The Undesirability of Soft Law' (1998) 67 Nordic Journal of International Law 381, 387.
[82] ibid 391.
[83] László Blutman, 'In the Trap of a Legal Metaphor: International Soft Law' (2010) 59 International and Comparative Law Quarterly 605, 611.
[84] ibid 610–11.
[85] ibid 611.
[86] Anthony Clark Arend, *Legal Rules and International Society* (OUP 1999) 25.
[87] d'Aspremont, *Formalism and the Sources of International Law* (n 57) 1.
[88] ibid.

of soft law as a viable part of the international legal system may ultimately lead to undesirable outcomes. As d'Aspremont notes:

> [t]he illusory state of international law that is conveyed through the use of non-formal law-ascertainment may obfuscate the need to lobby for the adoption of new rules. In fact, the use of non-formal law-ascertainment criteria may bring about a feeling that the adoption of legal or non-legal regulations is no longer necessary. It can simultaneously dim the awareness of the possibility of resorting to non-legal instruments—which may prove more effective—to achieve the same political end.[89]

Additional concerns regarding the impact of soft law have been identified by Hilary Charlesworth, who has noted that the embrace of soft law could have anti-democratic outcomes—especially at the domestic level: 'if law can be created softly and informally in the international sphere, it will bypass the usual national processes for acceptance'.[90] Soft law norms, created to influence the behaviour of States, and the result of work undertaken by groups of experts operating in their personal capacity, would seem to pose a threat to a system of international law that places the State and its consent to be bound as the primary engine of international law-making. And while, of course, States can choose to reject such non-binding norms, those norms might still impact on State behaviour and 'force the hand' of States making a principled stand to reject a set of non-binding norms.[91]

The embrace of soft law potentially presents serious drawbacks, which raises the question: if soft law is so problematic, why do States and non-state groups embrace the form, and why would scholars and practitioners want to encourage the adoption of mechanisms that have been argued as heralding their own professional demise?[92]

[89] ibid 135.

[90] Hilary Charlesworth, 'Law-Making and Sources' in James Crawford and Martti Koskenniemi (eds), *The Cambridge Companion to International Law* (CUP 2012) 199.

[91] Indeed, as Shelton has argued, one of the reasons for recourse to soft law has been precisely this. 'Another reason for recourse to soft law is growing concern about the "free rider", the holdout State that benefits from legal regulation accepted by others while enhancing its own State interests, especially economic, through continued utilisation of a restricted resource .... The traditional consent-based international legal regime lacks a legislature to override the will of dissenting States but efforts to affect their behaviour can be made through "soft law" .... [Soft law can] resolve a pressing global problem over the objections of one or few States identifies as among those responsible for the problem, while avoiding the doctrinal barrier of their lack of consent to be bound by the norm': Shelton, 'Soft Law' (n 60) 75–76. Whether this is a true and/or desirable situation will be explored in Chapter 8 on the legitimacy and legality of soft law norms.

[92] d'Aspremont has a theory on the last component of this question. In his paper 'Softness in International Law: A Self-Serving Quest for New Legal Materials' (n 54), he contends that the embrace of soft law by scholars is a 'self-serving' endeavour on the part of international law scholars: ibid 1075. He argues that international legal scholarship is flourishing and proliferating as never before, and thus the field of international law 'is currently teeming with people devoting their entire careers to it, while it remains uncertain whether this discipline can still accommodate all of them': ibid 1093. In essence, then, the embrace of soft law is merely 'an attempt to extend the material studied by scholars with a view

Numerous scholars have suggested theories as to why soft law norms and instruments have been welcomed by States and other international actors. The question of why soft law and non-binding instruments have been embraced in IHL specifically will be examined in more detail in Chapter 6. It is worth examining here some of the general arguments that have been put forward as to why soft law norms are adopted. Guzman and Meyer have identified several broad theories for why non-binding norms may be favoured over binding norms, developing a number of categories, including coordination, loss avoidance, and delegation.[93] These theories, either singly or collectively, have also been forwarded or developed by other advocates for soft law. They join other theories, such as qualification, consistency, and clarity, as additional reasons why soft law is embraced.[94] These theories will be examined in the next section.

The Benefits of Soft Law: Coordinating, Qualifying, and Influencing Behaviour

One of the obvious benefits of non-binding instruments is their non-binding character. As the norm or instrument in question imposes no consequence for non-observance, States can embrace such a norm or instrument with the knowledge that non-compliance will not amount to an international wrong.[95] As Michael Bothe notes:

> [n]on-legal relations often serve as a compromise between sovereignty and order. Since there may be a difference in degree as to the certainty of the expectation of compliance between a legal and a non-legal obligation, and since there is a good

to providing more room for international scholarship': ibid 1093. Anthony D'Amato would seem to concur, arguing that soft law seems to be the result of international law scholars and students, 'repelled by the sluggish pace of traditional international law in advancing human rights and protecting the global ecosystem', pushing international law beyond its traditional consent-based law-making boundaries, effectively divorcing international law from the conduct of States: D'Amato (n 74) 898.

[93] Guzman and Meyer, 'International Soft Law' (n 58).

[94] Indeed, Hartmut Hillgenberg lists (but does not analyse in detail) numerous reasons why States would choose 'non-treaty agreements ... [including] the general need for mutual confidence-building; the need to stimulate developments still in progress; the creation of a preliminary, flexible regime possibly providing for its development in stages; impetus for coordinated national legislation; concern that international relations will be overburdened by a "hard" treaty, with the risk of failure and a deterioration in relations; simpler procedures, thereby facilitating more rapid finalisation (eg consensus rather than a treaty conference); avoidance of cumbersome domestic approval procedures in case of amendments; greater confidentiality ... agreements can be made with parties which do not have the power to conclude treaties under international law ... [and] agreements can be made with parties that other parties to the agreement are not willing to recognise': Hartmut Hillgenberg, 'A Fresh Look at Soft Law' (1999) 10 European Journal of International Law 499, 501.

[95] Malgosia Fitzmaurice and Olufemi Elias, *Contemporary Issues in the Law of Treaties* (Eleven 2005) 34–35.

> chance that the condemnation will be less in the case of a violation of a non-legal obligation, states often choose this approach when they wish to create a modus vivendi, but feel the necessity of preserving some way out.... [This] is particularly apparent where a situation is still fluid.[96]

For a State dealing with uncertainty as to its own capability for compliance, not to mention the likelihood of compliance by other States, 'a non-legal commitment is, thus, often much easier for a state to accept than a legal one'.[97] States can agree on certain basic principles or ground rules without the formality inherent in treaty relations,[98] which may be appealing for States dealing with controversial or problematic subject matter. As Bothe explains, 'States are often willing to face the facts and live with a situation which they do not like, but they will not formally recognise it. Therefore, they may be prepared to accept a situation in a non-legal modus vivendi which they would be loath to recognise in a treaty'.[99] For example, the historic reluctance of States to embrace additional regulations dealing with insurgents and rebels in armed conflict is ample evidence that States were willing to accept *some* guidance on conduct in non-international armed conflicts but were unprepared to be bound to apply the Geneva Conventions in their entirety.[100]

The voluntary nature of soft law is only one of the advantages of the form. Soft law norms have the capacity to contribute to, influence, and guide State and non-State behaviour, especially in fields where achieving consensus on binding rules has been notably difficult.[101] The fact that there is little or no consequence from failure to adhere to non-binding requirements can make adopting such norms so appealing. Soft law mechanisms can offer a convenient mechanism for States to coordinate their behaviour in relation to an existing (and conceivably ongoing) problem, without resort to a binding instrument.[102] Soft law or non-binding instruments can therefore provide a mechanism to establish basic rules for resolving ongoing or recurring problems. As an example, Guzman and Meyer cite documents such as the Paris Memorandum of Understanding on Port State Control as examples of how soft law can create an enduring instrument where recurring issues can find resolution, in the absence of pre-existing or new binding norms to regulate such issues.[103] Soft law instruments can have flow-on effects of influencing and

[96] Michael Bothe, 'Legal and Non-Legal Norms—A Meaningful Distinction in International Relations?' (1980) 11 Netherlands Yearbook of International Law 65, 91.

[97] ibid.

[98] Anthony Aust, 'The Theory and Practice of Informal International Instruments' (1986) 35 International and Comparative Law Quarterly 787, 789–96.

[99] Bothe, 'Legal and Non-Legal Norms' (n 96) 92.

[100] For an analysis of the debate around the adoption of Common Article 3, see Chapter 3 of this book.

[101] W Michael Reisman, 'The Concept and Functions of Soft Law in International Politics' in Emmanuel Bello and Bola A Ajibola (eds), *Essays in Honour of Judge Taslim Olawale Elias* (Martinus Nijhoff 1992) 138–39.

[102] Guzman and Meyer, 'International Soft Law' (n 58) 188.

[103] ibid.

changing behaviour, potentially in a more effective and efficient way than would be possible through more conventional means of treaty amendment (or treaty development).[104] Such instruments might also eventually contribute to the creation of customary international law by shaping State behaviour and *opinio juris*.[105] That is to say, an ostensibly non-legal instrument might eventually have a legal impact. As Baxter notes, soft law norms can:

> [e]stablish new standards of relevance for the negotiations between the parties. Certain arguments will be ruled out ... [and] the norm will establish the legal framework within which the dispute about its application may be resolved. It will establish presumptions, indicate the prevailing trend of opinion, provide a guiding principle which may have a certain inherent appeal for the parties, and channel negotiation and settlement into legal and ordered paths.[106]

In the IHL context, an example would be the *Copenhagen Process Principles and Guidelines on the Handling of Detainees in International Military Operations* (Copenhagen Principles) on detention in non-international armed conflicts: conceivably, non-international armed conflicts will continue, and detention of participants in such conflicts will continue to occur. Rather than attempt to develop additional or new treaty law on the question, the soft law instrument of the Copenhagen Principles can be called upon to provide some instruction.[107] As Gruchalla-Wesierski notes, 'where there is no other norm, any standard has a certain attractiveness'.[108]

[104] Shelton, 'Soft Law' (n 60) 75–76, who argues for soft law's ability to compel behaviour in States that are reluctant to adopt binding rules but that might be less resistant to persuasive recommendations.

[105] See Eric Suy, 'Innovations in International Law-Making Processes' in Ronald St John McDonald, Douglas Johnston, and Gerald Morris (eds), *International Law and Policy of Human Welfare* (Sijthoff and Noordhoof 1978) 190, where he states that General Assembly resolutions that have been adopted through 'overwhelming (or even unanimous) approval' can be an indication of *opinio juris*. However, both Suy and Stephen Schwebel (in 'The Effect of Resolutions of the UN General Assembly on Customary International Law' (1979) 73 American Society of International Law Proceedings 301, 305) affirm the centrality of State practice in the development of customary international law. Schwebel urges caution in giving weight to, as Suy puts it, 'the mere repetition of principles in subsequent resolutions to which states give their approval': ibid 190. For Schwebel, state practice cannot simply consist of further declarations or resolutions of the General Assembly: 'the actual behaviour of states must manifest itself so clearly and consistently as to evidence a practice': ibid 304. This position is also taken by Shelton ('Soft Law' (n 60) 70–71) and by Chinkin ('The Challenge of Soft Law' (n 60) 856–57), who argues that while soft law can potentially contribute to the formation of customary law, it cannot be customary law.

[106] Baxter (n 7) 565. Gruchalla-Wesierski (n 53) makes a similar point: 'soft law, by its nature, is the articulation of a norm. Thus, depending on its precision, it also has a significant political effect in guiding state practice, clarifying nascent law and accelerating potential state practice creating law. This result is due to the qualifying legal effect of soft law': ibid 69. See also Rosalyn Higgins, *Problems and Process: International Law and How We Use It* (Clarendon 1994), who notes that '[l]egal consequences can also flow from acts which are not, in the formal sense, "binding"': ibid 25.

[107] The Copenhagen Principles are discussed in more detail in Chapter 4 of this book.

[108] Gruchalla-Wesierski (n 53) 68. Shelton concurs, arguing that 'when the subject matter may not be ripe for treaty action because of scientific uncertainty or lack of political consensus ... the choice may not be between a treaty and a soft law text, but between a soft law text and no action at all: Shelton, 'Soft Law' (n 60) 75. See also Chinkin, 'The Challenge of Soft Law' (n 60) 861.

The notion that soft law is a useful means to coordinate behaviour is connected to another purported benefit of soft law—that of qualifying and clarifying behaviour.[109] According to this line of argument, soft law provides necessary clarity for those existing binding rules that might be vague as to scope.[110] In the IHL context, Common Article 3 refers to 'armed conflicts not of an international character' but provides no additional guidance as to how to define the term. By having recourse to, for example, the *San Remo Manual on the Law of Non-International Armed Conflict*, one might be better able to define the concept of a non-international armed conflict.[111]

Adopting soft law mechanisms can also offer a procedural benefit, which Guzman and Meyer call the theory of bureaucratic transaction costs.[112] According to this theory, the costs of negotiating and adopting a soft law provision 'may in some instances be lower than the costs of creating hard law'.[113] Because soft law instruments do not require the same degree of executive and legislative oversight and involvement that adopting a treaty would require, the costs involved in the creation and adoption of a voluntary instrument would be less onerous. For example, government lawyers could be sent to a meeting of experts drafting a code of conduct, rather than having to dispatch a minister for foreign affairs and diplomatic staff (and their retinues) to a treaty conference. As Gruchalla-Wesierski notes, such soft law instruments:

> do not require approval of parliaments but can be created or terminated by executive branches of governments alone. They do not need to be approved by constituent parts of federal states. Thus, they are much easier to bring into force. In addition, non-legal agreements are more easily extinguished given that they avoid the difficulties presented by termination procedures for legal obligations.[114]

Soft law instruments can offer clear financial, legislative, and administrative advantages to States that wish to regulate a particular type of behaviour, but do not wish (or are not able) to commit extensive resources to achieving such an aim.

Soft law also offers procedural benefits in terms of their potential for speedy and efficient adoption.[115] A soft law instrument may well be drafted far more quickly than a multilateral treaty. As noted by Bothe:

[109] See Ulrich Fastenrath, 'Relative Normativity in International Law' (1993) 4 European Journal of International Law 305, in which he cites the UN General Assembly Resolutions on Aggression (3314) and Friendly Relations (2625) as evidence of the clarifying effects of soft law, arguing that without these resolutions, the definitions of the concept of the use of force and aggression would be far less clear: ibid 314–15.

[110] As Gruchalla-Wesierski (n 53) notes, 'soft law makes clear the meaning of an act which might otherwise be ambiguous': ibid 58.

[111] In Article 1 of the NIAC Manual, discussed in more detail in Chapter 4.

[112] Guzman and Meyer, 'International Soft Law' (n 58) 177.

[113] ibid. See also Chinkin, 'The Challenge of Soft Law' (n 60) 853.

[114] Gruchalla-Wesierski (n 53) 43.

[115] See Hugh Thirlway, *The Sources of International Law* (OUP 2012) 164.

> [t]he process of negotiation and entry into force of international treaties is rather a slow one. Seventeen years elapsed from the date of adoption of the Universal Declaration of Human Rights until the adoption of the texts of the two UN Human Rights Covenants by the General Assembly, and it took ten years more before the Covenants entered into force.[116]

This protracted period of negotiation and adoption is further extended when one considers how lengthy domestic decision-making and law-making processes can be: a State that signs a treaty may never take the steps required to ratify the treaty. Or, as in case of the US approach to the Rome Statute of the International Criminal Court (ICC),[117] a State may vote in a new administration that is fundamentally opposed to the terms of a treaty previously embraced by the outgoing administration.[118] A soft law instrument may provide an efficient alternative to treaty-making, where domestic decision-making processes hinder the ability to develop the law. Recourse to soft law may be particularly useful when dealing with new and emergent technological and economic innovations that require a rapid response and may not be amendable to the kinds of legislative delays inherent in international and domestic law making.[119]

Soft law instruments can also offer innovative ways to address problems that traditional international law-making cannot. They can be negotiated and adopted by non-State groups, which are traditionally unable to participate in international law-making processes. As Dinah Shelton notes, soft law is:

> useful in addressing new topics of regulation that require innovative means of rule making with respect to non-state actors, which generally are not parties to treaties or involved in the creation of customary international law ... soft law texts [also] allow non-state actors to sign the instrument and participate in compliance mechanisms, both of which are far more difficult to do with treaties.[120]

116 Bothe, 'Legal and Non-Legal Norms' (n 96) 92. See also Shelton, 'Soft Law' (n 60), noting that 'non-binding instruments are faster to adopt, easier to change, and more useful for technical matters that may need rapid or repeated revision': ibid 75.

117 Rome Statute of the International Criminal Court (adopted 17 July 1998, entered into force 1 July 2002) 2187 UNTS 90 (ICC Statute).

118 See generally Angela Betti, '"Slay This Monster": The United States and Opposition to the Rome Statute on the International Criminal Court' (2016) 17 Human Rights Review 417; Leigh Monroe, 'The United States and the Statute of Rome' (2001) 95 American Journal of International Law 124.

119 See Pierre-Marie Dupuy, 'Soft Law and the International Law of the Environment' (1991) 12 Michigan Journal of International Law 420, who notes that the 'rapid evolution of the world economy and increasing State interdependence combined with the development of new fields of activity created by the unceasing progress of science and technology ... requires timely creation of new branches of international law that are adaptable and applicable to each new level of achievement reached as a result of technological advancement': ibid 421.

120 Shelton, 'Soft Law' (n 60) 76.

Soft law offers the possibility of engaging more participants in the international law-making process, creating the potential for better implementation and accountability under persuasive, if non-binding, rules.[121]

Given the diversity of arguments as to how to define and categorise soft law, and whether soft law is a good or bad addition to the realm of international law, it is clearly not possible to come up with a unifying definition of soft law or, for that matter, to develop a holistic account of why soft law is beneficial or detrimental to the international legal order. However, this is not, in itself, problematic. Defining soft law and quantifying the reasons for and against the embrace of soft law and non-binding instruments is useful, but only to a degree: while such an analysis can assist in understanding how and why these instruments and norms have come to prominence, it does not account for whether they have had any practical effect. One can spend considerable time disputing the scope of definitions of soft law and arguing over the merits and drawbacks of the category, but such arguments frequently pay insufficient attention to the fact that, desirable or not, soft law exists, and to how it is treated by those affected by the rule and those that implement the rule—namely, States and international courts and tribunals.

The debates surrounding the merits and drawbacks regarding soft law instruments will be explored in more detail in later chapters, looking at the specific IHL instruments under examination in this book. However, at this point, it is useful to examine some of the more general practice regarding soft law norms: how have they been received, either by States or by international courts and tribunals?[122]

The Reception and Treatment of Soft Law Instruments and Norms in International Law

There is a long history of States choosing to adopt non-binding instruments, which have routinely been cited by States as evidence of everything from best practice to customary international law, and which have been used by States to guide both their own behaviour and that of fellow States. Examples of such instruments include the UN Declaration of Human Rights, the Charter of Economic Rights and Duties of States,[123] the Helsinki Final Act, and the Rio Declaration. In this section, these instruments will be briefly explored to examine how they have been received in practice. It is the intent of the section not to explore these instruments in detail, but rather to examine why and how they were adopted, why the choice was made to adopt such instruments in non-binding form, how (and whether) they

[121] This is especially relevant in the context of IHL and will be discussed in more detail in Chapter 5.

[122] Questions relating to the efficacy of soft law instruments in IHL will also be subject to study in Chapter 7 of this book.

[123] Charter of Economic Rights and Duties of States, UN Doc A/RES/29/3281 (12 December 1974) (CERDS).

were embraced (or rejected) by the international community, and how they were received by international courts and tribunals. The section will examine whether, despite the debates about the validity of non-binding norms and soft law, States have, as a practical matter, turned to such instruments to achieve certain aims in a way that is not possible through binding treaties.

These instruments have been chosen for a variety of reasons: they emanate from different institutions or entities,[124] relate to different areas,[125] involve several different and varied States, and have had varying degrees of impact on the behaviour of States. They provide a useful insight into soft law norms more generally and assist in answering some of the central questions of this book. Does the *source* of the soft law norm influence its reception and treatment? Does a soft law norm emanating from the United Nations carry more weight than one from a regional organisation or grouping of States? Does it matter who was involved in the instrument's creation? And to what degree do the subject matter and objectives of the soft law instrument impact on how it is perceived and received? The objective is to begin to uncover whether practice in other fields of international law can help us better understand why and how non-binding instruments and norms have come to be adopted in IHL.

Soft Law Norms in the UN General Assembly—the Universal Declaration of Human Rights and the Charter of the Economic Rights and Duties of States

Soft law norms have played a notable part in international law and inter-State relations, especially following the establishment of the United Nations. Arguably, the quintessential non-binding instrument is the UN General Assembly resolution—the mechanism whereby States can express, in a non-binding document, their objectives, understandings, and beliefs regarding a particular situation. It was in this form—a General Assembly resolution—that one of the most influential non-binding instruments was adopted: the Universal Declaration of Human Rights (UDHR or Declaration). The UDHR was adopted in 1948, the final product of a year's worth of debate and discussion in the UN Commission on Human Rights. The aim had originally been to adopt a binding 'bill of rights';[126] however, before

[124] The UDHR (n 5) and CERDS (n 123) emanated from the UN General Assembly; the Rio Declaration from the UN Conference on Environment and Development (n 3); and the Helsinki Final Act from the Conference on Security and Cooperation in Europe (n 4).

[125] International economic law, international human rights law, international environmental law, and international security. These areas have, historically, readily embraced soft law norms and will be the subject of further examination in Chapter 6 of this book.

[126] See comments by US President Harry Truman, who, during his closing speech at the San Francisco Conference, stated his hopes that, under the Charter, 'we have good reason to expect the framing of an international bill of rights, acceptable to all the nations involved. That bill of rights will be as much a part of international life as our own Bill of Rights is a part of our Constitution': Documents of the

discussion could begin on the substance of the instrument, opinion was divided on whether the bill of rights should be in the form of a declaration, or whether a binding convention or covenant was the preferred instrument.[127] Ultimately, the Commission agreed to first adopt a more generally worded Declaration,[128] with the aim to later adopt a convention.[129] The reasons given for choosing a declaration in the first instance (rather than proceeding immediately to a convention) included that a 'lack of time'[130] prevented the drafting of a complete and comprehensive binding instrument and, given the relative newness of the principles to be outlined in the document, it was preferable to adopt a non-binding instrument, one with 'moral importance',[131] that could serve as a 'guide and inspiration to individuals and groups through the world',[132] and a 'statement of ideals, a goal towards which mankind should strive'.[133]

Despite the non-binding nature of the UDHR, it has had a notable impact on State practice and on the practice of international organisations.[134] Unsurprisingly, given it was one of the first significant documents of the General Assembly, the United Nations embraced the Declaration immediately. Numerous General Assembly[135] and Security Council[136] resolutions adopted from the period of 1949 onwards cite the Declaration and call on States to respect and observe its provisions. The UDHR was also affirmed in several treaties in the decade after its

United Nations Conference on International Organisation (United Nations Information Organisation 1945) vol I, 717. Similar comments to this effect were espoused by several State delegates throughout the Conference. See further discussions in Commission I, Documents of the United Nations Conference on International Organisation, vol VI, 296, 423, 456, 705).

[127] For a brief survey of the differing opinions of delegates (both in the Commission and in the General Assembly) as to whether to adopt a non-binding declaration or a binding treaty, see further Louis Sohn, 'The Universal Declaration of Human Rights: A Common Standard of Achievement? The Status of the Universal Declaration in International Law' (1967) 8 International Commission of Jurists Review 17, 18–23. For a complete record of the documents, including from the drafting committee and the Commission of Human Rights, see <http://research.un.org/en/undhr> accessed 27 July 2021.

[128] UN Doc E/CN.4/21 (1 July 1947) 3, 6.

[129] ibid.

[130] Commission I, Documents of the United Nations Conference on International Organisation, vol VI, 456, 707.

[131] Netherlands delegate, UN Doc E/CN.4/82/Rev.1 (22 April 1948) 3.

[132] US delegate, UN Doc E/CN.4/82/Rev.1 (22 April 1948) 18–20.

[133] UK delegate, UN Doc E/CN.4/82/Add.9 (10 May 1948) 2.

[134] For a comprehensive overview of the impact of the UDHR on domestic legislation and administrative acts, as well as its use in national courts, see further Hurst Hannam, 'The Status of the Universal Declaration of Human Rights in National and International Law' (1995–96) 25 Georgia Journal of International and Comparative Law 287.

[135] Including Resolution 285 (25 April 1949); Resolution 265 (14 May 1949); Resolution 395 (2 December 1950); Resolution 511 (12 January 1952); Resolution 615 (5 December 1952); Resolution 719 (11 November 1953); Resolution 721 (8 December 1953); Resolution 1142B (25 October 1957); Resolution 1179 (26 November 1957); Resolution 1302 (10 December 1958); Resolution 1510 (12 December 1960); Resolution 1514 (14 December 1960); Resolution 1597 (13 April 1961); Resolution 1662 (28 November 1961); Resolutions 1779, 1780, 1781 (7 December 1962); Resolution 1904 (20 November 1963).

[136] Resolution 182 (1963); Resolution 232 (1966).

adoption, most notably in the 1950 European Convention on Human Rights,[137] as well as in conventions on refugees, stateless persons, forced labour, the nationality of married women, and slavery and the slave trade.[138] In terms of its impact on States, the Declaration has, to varying degrees, been embraced in national legislation[139] and domestic judicial decisions.[140]

Another significant General Assembly resolution, though one that has had notably less impact than the UDHR, is Resolution 3281—the Charter of the Economic Rights and Duties of States (CERDS). The result of work undertaken by the United Nations Conference on Trade and Development, Resolution 45 (III) of 1972[141]:

> stressed the urgency to establish generally accepted norms to govern international economic relations systematically and recognized that it is not feasible to establish a just order and a stable world as long as a charter to protect the rights of all countries, and in particular the developing States, is not formulated.[142]

CERDS came about as part of larger ongoing efforts by the United Nations to further clarify the contours of international economic law.[143] Adopted by 120 States, with six votes against and 10 abstentions,[144] CERDS was considered a 'controversial'[145] and 'radical'[146] addition to international law, due to, among other factors, its

[137] Convention for the Protection of Human Rights and Fundamental Freedoms as amended by Protocols Nos 11 and 14 (adopted 4 November 1950, entered into force 3 September 1953) ETS 5 (ECHR).

[138] See Egon Schwelb, 'The Influence of the Universal Declaration of Human Rights on International and National Law' (1959) 53 ASIL Proceedings 217, 219–20.

[139] See, for example, the Preamble to the Constitution of the Republic of Guinea (UN Doc S/4122); Article 34 of the Lithuanian Law on the Legal Status of Foreigners; the Preamble to Australia's *Native Title Act 1993* (Cth); Article 16(2) of the Constitution of Portugal; Article 20(1) of the Constitution of Romania; Article 20(1) of the Constitution of Sao Tome and Principe; and Article 10(2) of the Constitution of Spain.

[140] See, for example, cases in Australia (*Dowal v Murray* (1978) 143 CLR 410); Botswana (*Attorney-General v Unity Dow*, Ct Appeal No 4/91, slip op, 52 (1991)); India (*Kesavananda Bharati v State of Kerala* (1973 AIR (SC)) 1461, 1510; *Maneka Gandhi v Union of India* (1978 AIR (SC) 597); Italy (*Ministry of Home Affairs v Kemali*, Cass, Foro It LXXXVII (1962) Part 1, 190); Mauritius (*Roussety v Attorney General* [1967] Mauritius Reports 45, High Court, reprinted in 44 ILR 108, 130); New Zealand (*Van Gorkom v Attorney-General* [1977] 1 NZLR 535); Nigeria (*Nolokwu v Commissioner of Police*, High Court of Nigeria (Agbakoba J, reprinted in *Law of Habeas Corpus* 96 (Chief Gani Fawehinmi (ed), 1986); Sri Lanka (*WMK Silva v Piyasena Senaratne* (SC Appl No 7, 1989)); Tanzania (*Ephrahim v Pastory Kaizilege*, reprinted in 87 ILR 106, 110 (High Court 1990)); the United Kingdom (*R v Miah* [1974] 1 All ER 1110); and the United States (*Filártiga v Peña-Irala* 630 F 2d 876 (2d Cir 1980)).

[141] See Proceedings of the United Nations Conference on Trade and Development, Third Session, vol I, Report and Annexes, annex I.A, 58.

[142] ibid.

[143] Also adopted in 1974 were the UN Declaration on the Establishment of a New International Economic Order, UN Doc A/RES/3201 (SVI) (9 May 1974) and the UN Programme of Action on the Establishment of a New International Economic Order, UN Doc A/RES/3202 (S-VI) (16 May 1974).

[144] For the voting record, see <http://www.un.org/ga/search/view_doc.asp?symbol = A/PV.2315> accessed 27 July 2021.

[145] Kristen Boon, 'Charter of Economic Rights and Duties of States (1974)' in Anne Peters and Rüdiger Wolfrum (eds), *Max Planck Encyclopedia of Public International Law*.

[146] SK Chatterjee, 'The Charter of Economic Rights and Duties of States: An Evaluation after 15 Years' (1991) 40 International and Comparative Law Quarterly 669, 677.

seeming rejection of established international law principles on the expropriation and nationalisation[147] of foreign property by the State. Where 'conventional international legal principles on expropriation ... required a showing of public purpose and payment of just compensation ... CERDS state[s] that expropriation and compensation are largely at the expropriating State's discretion'.[148] This approach, which seemed to run contrary to established customary international law, was rejected by States such as the United States, Germany, and the United Kingdom.[149]

CERDS, though not wholeheartedly embraced by the international community in its entirety, has nonetheless had some impact on international economic law. While the provisions on expropriation and compensation[150] were not accepted by developed States, other provisions, such as those on trade liberalisation[151] and technology transfers,[152] have been integrated into international documents[153] and have proven influential, such as during the negotiations for the World Trade Organization.[154]

Soft Law Norms in International Conferences—the Rio Declaration and the Helsinki Final Act

Soft law norms have also been embraced by States outside the forum of the General Assembly. In the field of international environmental law, the Rio Declaration on Environment and Development, adopted in 1992, has been influential in shaping

[147] As outlined in Resolution 1803 (14 December 1962), which the arbitrator in *Texaco v Libya* claimed as reflecting 'the state of customary law existing in this field': *Texaco Overseas Petroleum Co v Libyan Arab Republic* (1978) 17 ILM 1, para 87.

[148] Boon (n 145).

[149] For commentary on State objections to CERDS, see Chatterjee (n 146) 672–74.

[150] CERDS, Art 2(c).

[151] CERDS, Art 14.

[152] CERDS, Art 13.

[153] UN General Assembly Resolution 41/128 on the Declaration of the Right to Development (4 December 1986).

[154] Boon (n 145); Chatterjee (n 146) 677–83. CERDS has since been eclipsed, with the UN Economic and Social Council stating in 2004 that further monitoring of CERDS was unnecessary, as it had been effectively replaced by the Monterrey Consensus (Monterrey Consensus of the International Conference on Financing for Development <https://www.un.org/en/development/desa/population/migration/generalassembly/docs/globalcompact/A_CONF.198_11.pdf> accessed 27 July 2021): Report of the Secretary-General, Implementation of the Charter of Economic Rights and Duties of States, UN Doc A/59/99–E/2004/83 (18 June 2004) <http://www.un.org/en/development/desa/policy/publications/ecosoc/e_2004_83.pdf> accessed 27 July 2021. Furthermore, CERDS is not mentioned in the Millennium Development Goals (United Nations Millennium Declaration, UN GA Res 55/2 (8 September 2000)) or the Doha Declaration on the TRIPS Agreement (Declaration on the TRIPS Agreement and Public Health; Doha WTO Ministerial 2001: TRIPS WT/MIN(01)/DEC/2 (20 November 2001)). Furthermore, the contentious debate surrounding expropriation and compensation has been essentially rendered moot through the proliferation of bilateral investment treaties, which 'typically contain investor-friendly provisions for host State regulation of foreign investment, nationalisation, and expropriation': Boon (n 145).

the course of 'national and international environmental law and policy'.[155] The Rio Declaration came about as part of the programme of work undertaken by the United Nations to develop the international law relating to the protection and regulation of the natural environment. One of the first major developments in this field was the convening of the Stockholm Conference in June 1972,[156] which brought together States to draft a declaration on the 'rights and obligations of citizens and Governments with regard to the preservation and improvement of the human environment'.[157] The result of that conference was the adoption of the Stockholm Declaration, which outlined in seven preambular paragraphs and 26 principles that 'the protection and improvement of the human environment is a major issue which affects the well-being of peoples and economic development through the world'.[158]

Twenty years later, a second international conference was convened to assess developments in the field.[159] That conference adopted the Rio Declaration, a 27-principle document affirming, among other rights and duties, the need for sustainable development. Particularly influential was Principle 15, that 'in order to protect the environment, the precautionary approach shall be widely applied by States according to their capabilities. Where there are threats of serious or irreversible damage, lack of full scientific certainty shall not be used as a reason for postponing cost-effective measures to prevent environmental degradation.'[160]

As with the UDHR, divisions with regards to the aims and objectives of the Rio Conference emerged in the preparatory process—namely, was it the aim of the Conference to adopt a binding instrument, or was it preferable to produce a non-binding statement of aims? While developed and industrialised States advocated for a binding instrument, developing States wanted to adopt a document outlining 'only political commitments'.[161] Ultimately, the compromise was the adoption of the non-binding Rio Declaration.

Despite its non-binding character, the Declaration has been notably influential, especially with regards to the precautionary principle. Even though the precautionary principle was part of several international and domestic legal instruments[162] and

[155] Dinah Shelton, 'Stockholm Declaration (1972) and Rio Declaration (1992)' in Anne Peters and Rüdiger Wolfrum (eds), *Max Planck Encyclopedia of Public International Law*.

[156] UN General Assembly Resolution 2398 (XXIII), Problems of the Human Environment, UN Doc A/RES/2398/(XXIII) (3 December 1968), which approved the conference.

[157] UN General Assembly Preparatory Committee for the United Nations Conference on the Human Environment: Report of the Preparatory Committee on its Fourth Session, para 16.

[158] Preamble, para 2.

[159] UN General Assembly Resolution 44/228, United Nations Conference on Environment and Development, UN Doc A/RES/44/228 (22 December 1989).

[160] Known as the precautionary principle.

[161] Shelton, 'Stockholm Declaration (1972) and Rio Declaration (1992)' (n 155).

[162] See generally Ole Pedersen, 'From Abundance to Indeterminacy: The Precautionary Principle and Its Two Camps of Custom' (2014) 3 Transnational Environmental Law 323, 326–27; Meinhard Schröder, 'Precautionary Approach/Principle' in Anne Peters and Rüdiger Wolfrum (eds), *Max Planck Encyclopedia of Public International Law*.

materials[163] prior to its inclusion as Principle 15, the most 'commonly cited'[164] iteration of the principle since the Rio Conference has been Principle 15 of the Rio Declaration. And it has been *this* iteration that has been influential in State practice. As noted in the Commentary to the Rio Declaration,[165] Principle 15:

> has undeniably gained considerable weight since its formulation at the Rio de Janeiro Conference. In effect, the precautionary principle has become prevalent in State practice: it has been incorporated in a large number of preambles and operative articles of international agreements and is regularly invoked by parties to international disputes. Overall, it enjoys a prominent place in international environmental law.[166]

There is considerable evidence of the influence and embrace of the precautionary principle (as enunciated in the Rio Declaration specifically), with some domestic courts,[167] as well as international courts,[168] specifically citing the Declaration and its formulation of the precautionary principle in their decisions.

Another influential instrument that emanated from a conference of States was the Helsinki Final Act, adopted by the Conference on Security and Cooperation in Europe in 1975. The Conference was convened between July 1973 and August 1975. It had its origins in advocacy by the Soviet Union and Warsaw Pact States for the introduction of some form of collective security arrangement for Europe. Disputes and divisions over the exact make-up of conference participants, as well as the objectives and aims of the Conference, brought delays, but concessions on both sides, including allowing the participation of the United States and Canada, led to the Conference proceeding in 1973. The Final Act contained provisions regarding State sovereignty; the use of force; non-intervention; respect for human

[163] See generally Joakim Zander, *The Application of the Precautionary Principle in Practice* (CUP 2010) ch 5.

[164] Pedersen (n 162) 326. See also Agne Sirinskiene, 'The Status of Precautionary Principle: Moving towards a Rule of Customary Law' (2009) 4 Jurisprudence 349, 351; Simon Marr, 'The Southern Blue Fin Tuna Cases: The Precautionary Approach and Conservation and Management of Fish Resources' (2000) 11 European Journal of International Law 815, 820.

[165] Jorge E Viñuales (ed), *The Rio Declaration on Environment and Development: A Commentary* (OUP 2015).

[166] ibid 412.

[167] See, for example, the Supreme Court of Pakistan in *Zia v WAPDA PLD,* 1994 SC 693 (cited in Rajendra Ramlogan, *Sustainable Development: Towards a Judicial Interpretation* (Martinus Nijhoff 2011) 87), where it was stated: 'The Rio Declaration is the product of hectic discussion among the leaders of the nations of the world and it was after negotiations between the developed and the developing countries that an almost consensus declaration had been sorted out. Environment is an international problem having no frontiers creating transboundary effects. In this field every nation has to cooperate and contribute and for this reason the Rio Declaration would serve as a great binding force and to create discipline among the nations while dealing with environmental problems.'

[168] Discussed in the next section on the reception of soft law norms in international courts and tribunals.

rights and fundamental freedoms, including freedom of religion; self-determination; disarmament; economic, scientific, and technological cooperation; respect for family rights, including family reunification and respect for cross-border marriages; and protections for journalists, artists, and minority cultural and religious groups.

It was never the intention of the Act to be adopted as a binding instrument. As noted by Michael Wood and Daniel Purisch, 'the Final Act's drafters took pains to ensure that it would not be construed as legally binding, both by presenting it as a Final Act, rather than as an agreement, and by avoiding imperative language in favour of expressions of intent'.[169] The non-binding quality of the Final Act is evident in its language: the Final Act specifically outlines that it 'is not eligible for registration under Article 102 of the Charter of the United Nations'[170]—that is, it is not a treaty capable of registration with the United Nations. However, since its adoption, the Helsinki Final Act has influenced and shaped State practice, specifically the provisions in the Final Act that 'acknowledged that respect for human rights was a condition for peace and that the security of individuals was complementary to the security of States'.[171] As noted by US Ambassador Leonard Garment in 1976, '[t]he existence of a formal, written document, to which the Eastern regimes gave their public consent and their formal stamp of legitimacy, has made a difference. The words matter and are beginning to move human minds'.[172]

Commentators and scholars have since gone so far as to call the Helsinki Final Act the 'beginning of the end of the Cold War',[173] arguing that the 'human rights norms established by the Helsinki Final Act gradually transformed state–society relations across Eastern Europe and the Soviet Union … these norms contributed significantly to the demise of Communist Rule'.[174] The inclusion of human rights norms in an international document, even if non-binding, proved a persuasive force for change. As Wood and Purisch note, the Helsinki Final Act was legally important, in that 'to the extent that the areas covered by the Final Act had previously been within the sole domestic jurisdiction of the participating States, the conclusion of the Final Act made them a proper subject of discussion in the international area'.[175]

[169] Michael Wood and Daniel Purisch, 'Helsinki Final Act (1975)' in Anne Peters and Rüdiger Wolfrum (eds), *Max Planck Encyclopedia of Public International Law*. See also Pieter van Dijk, 'The Implementation of the Final Act of Helsinki: The Creation of New Structures or the Involvement of Existing Ones?' (1989) 10 Michigan Journal of International Law 110, 113–15.

[170] Helsinki Final Act (n 4) Basket IV.

[171] Christian Nünlist, 'Helsinki+40 in the Historical Context' (2014) 25 Security and Human Rights 198, 202–03.

[172] US Commission on Security and Cooperation in Europe, *The Belgrade Followup Meeting to the Conference on Security and Cooperation: A Report and Appraisal* (US Government Printing Office, 1978) App C, 70.

[173] Nünlist (n 171) 202.

[174] Daniel Thomas, *The Helsinki Effect: International Norms, Human Rights, and the Demise of Communism* (Princeton University Press 2001) 272.

[175] Wood and Purisch (n 169).

Soft Law Norms in International Courts and Tribunals

It is evident from this (admittedly brief) review of a few key non-binding instruments in international law that States can, and do, engage with such instruments. Moreover, there is compelling evidence to indicate that soft law norms have been treated with a measure of seriousness by States, as well as by international courts and tribunals, and, in several instances, have been examined and employed as a source of instruction for the parties involved in the dispute—if not as a source of obligation outright. This section will examine a few key cases to see how and why international courts and tribunals have engaged with the soft law norms already examined—the UDHR, the Charter of Economic Rights and Duties of States, the Rio Declaration, and the Helsinki Final Act—to see what kinds of judicial treatment these instruments have received.

The Universal Declaration of Human Rights and the Charter of Economic Rights and Duties of States

The non-binding instrument that has, of the four examined in this chapter, been given arguably the most judicial attention is the UDHR. However, in examining the impact of the Declaration in the context of international courts and tribunals, a note of caution is warranted. There is notable debate over *when* the Declaration could be considered as having attained customary status. At the point at which it attained customary status, the UDHR ceased to be a non-binding recommendation and become binding law, which means that any judicial reference to the Declaration has no value for the purposes of examining how a non-binding statement of principles impacts on State practice.

An additional complication arises in that some States[176] considered the UDHR, at the time of its drafting, to be not merely a statement outlining this new[177] field of international human rights law, but rather an interpretive instrument designed

[176] See, for example, comments made by the Mexican government during the UDHR's drafting, where it expressed the view that 'the usefulness and importance of the Declaration are not lessened by the fact that it includes no provisions for legal sanctions. The Declaration has a real and effective value in itself; first, because it states precisely the human rights and fundamental freedoms which States Members undertook in signing the Charter of the United Nations to promote and develop ... [I]n signing the Charter [States] undertook to fulfil in good faith the principles stated therein; and these principles include the promotion and respect of human rights': UN Doc E/CN.4/82/Add.1 (16 April 1948) 3.

[177] This was acknowledged by the French delegation, which noted that while the idea of human rights was not a new concept for domestic law, the idea that the human person could have rights at international law, as outlined in the Declaration, was entirely new, as 'the individual becomes a subject of international law in respect of his life and liberty; principles are affirmed, side by side with those already laid down by a majority of national laws, which no national or international authority had hitherto been able to proclaim, let alone enforce': Economic and Social Council, Official Records, Sixth Session, Supp 1, UN Doc E/600 (1948), 20.

to give tangible meaning to the binding obligations already outlined in the UN Charter with regards to human rights and fundamental freedoms.[178] According to this interpretation, the UDHR is 'a document interpreting the Charter, and therefore vested with the same mandatory force as the Charter itself'.[179] It is possible, therefore, to consider the provisions of the Declaration not as purely hortatory statements, but as restatements of existing binding obligations. However, it must also be noted that there were, arguably, many more States in 1948 that considered the Declaration as not having legally binding effect.[180]

It is possible to make a cautious assessment of how the UDHR has been received in international courts and tribunals. A somewhat arbitrary limit will be placed on the number of cases examined, which will be limited to those cases within the first dozen years following the adoption of the Declaration. This is done as an essentially simple (and simplistic) way to limit the possibility that the Declaration was, at the time of judicial examination, already considered customary international law. In the years immediately following the adoption of the UDHR, the ICJ noted the significance of the Declaration on three separate occasions: in the *Asylum* case,[181] in the *Anglo-Iranian Oil Company* case,[182] and in the *Nottebohm* case.[183] The Declaration was, in each of those cases, discussed briefly, but was nevertheless considered an important statement of applicable law. For example, in *Anglo-Iranian Oil*, Judge Levi Carneiro affirmed the importance of Article 17 of the UDHR, which outlines the human right to property and the right not to be deprived of such property.[184] In the *Nottebohm* case, Judge ad hoc Guggenheim noted the importance of Article 15 of the Declaration relating to a right to nationality, claiming that if a State refused to recognise nationality (and the connected right of diplomatic protection) for a person with disputed nationality, then 'the protection of the individual which is so precarious under existing international law would be weakened even further',[185] and would be 'contrary to the basic principle embodied in Article 15(1) of the Universal Declaration adopted by the General Assembly of the United

[178] See, for example, comments by the representative of Lebanon, who asserted that the Human Rights Commission, in drafting the Declaration, was essentially completing 'the work initiated by the Charter, in giving content and meaning to the phrase "the dignity and worth of the human person"': Lebanon, UN Doc E/CN.4/SR50 (4 June 1948) 4.

[179] Sohn (n 127) 20.

[180] See, for example, comments by the delegations of the Netherlands (UN Doc E/CN.4/82/Rev.1 (22 April 1948) 3); the United States (UN Doc E/CN.4/82/Rev.1 (22 April 1948) 18–20); the United Kingdom (UN Doc E/CN.4/82/Add.9 (10 May 1948) 2); New Zealand (UN Doc E/CN.4/82/Add.12 (3 June 1948) 4).

[181] *Colombian-Peruvian Asylum Case (Judgment)* [1950] ICJ Rep 266, 339 (dissenting opinion of Judge Azevedo).

[182] *Anglo-Iranian Oil Case (Jurisdiction)* [1952] ICJ Rep 93, 168 (dissenting opinion of Judge Levi Carneiro).

[183] *Nottebohm Case (Second Phase)* [1955] ICJ Rep 1, 63 (dissenting opinion of Judge ad hoc Guggenheim).

[184] *Anglo-Iranian Oil Case* (n 182) 168.

[185] *Nottebohm* (n 183) 63.

Nations on December 8th, 1948, according to which everyone has the right to a nationality'.[186] In the decades following its adoption, the Declaration would be cited with approval in a number of additional cases in the ICJ, including the *South West Africa* cases,[187] the *Namibia Advisory Opinion*,[188] the *Tehran Hostages Case*,[189] and the *Aegean Sea Continental Shelf Case*.[190]

Far less impactful than the UDHR has been the Charter of Economic Rights and Duties of States. One of the few attempts to utilise CERDS in arbitration, in *Texaco Overseas Petroleum Co v Government of the Libyan Arab Republic*,[191] was unsuccessful, as the International Arbitral Tribunal did not accept Libya's assertion that CERDS entitled it to nationalise property without the payment of compensation. The Tribunal noted that there were several factors that must militate against considering CERDS as having any legal value, including that it was adopted by non-industrialised States and attempts to have CERDS recognised in the General Assembly as a codification and progressive development of international law were rejected. These considerations led the Tribunal to the conclusion that 'the absence of any connection between the procedure of compensation and international law and the subjection of this procedure solely to municipal law cannot be regarded by this Tribunal except as a *de lege ferenda* formulation, which even appears *contra legem* in the eyes of many developed countries'.[192]

The Rio Declaration and the Helsinki Final Act

Turning now to the other two non-binding instruments under examination in this section, the Rio Declaration and the Helsinki Final Act have both been utilised by international courts and tribunals. However, as with the UDHR, a note of caution must be sounded. In both the Rio Declaration and the Helsinki Final Act, key provisions reaffirmed emergent or essentially extant principles of international law. The Rio Declaration codified the emergent notion of the precautionary principle, while the Helsinki Declaration reaffirmed the principle of non-intervention and

[186] ibid 63.

[187] Where Judge Tanaka cited the UDHR as 'not binding in itself' but still indicative of the interpretation and application of the human rights clauses in the UN Charter: *South West Africa Cases (Second Phase)* [1966] ICJ Rep 5, 289–90, 293 (dissenting opinion of Judge Tanaka).

[188] *Legal Consequences for States for the Continued Presence of South Africa in Namibia (South West Africa) Notwithstanding Security Council Resolution 276 (1970) (Advisory Opinion)* [1971] ICJ 16, 57 para 76.

[189] *United States Diplomatic and Consular Staff in Tehran (United States of America v Iran)* [1980] ICJ Rep 3, para 91.

[190] *Aegean Sea Continental Shelf Case* [1978] ICJ 3, 641–42. The UDHR was also cited in the *Application for Review of Judgment No 333 of the United Nations Administrative Tribunal* [1987] ICJ 18, 173, Judgment of 27 May, and the *Applicability of Article VI, Section 22, of the Convention on the Privileges and Immunities of the United Nations* [1989] ICJ 177, 211.

[191] *Texaco Overseas Petroleum Co v Libyan Arab Republic* (1978) 17 ILM 1.

[192] ibid para 88.

the protection of human rights. Neither of these concepts was foreign to international law at the time of its inclusion in the relevant document. However, what Principle 15 of the Rio Declaration and what the Helsinki Final Act *did* achieve was to codify in succinct and persuasive terms particular principles that (in the case of the precautionary principle) might have been of indeterminate or variable meaning, or that (in the case of the Helsinki Final Act) might have been a part of international law that was not generally accepted in a particular geopolitical region. In this way, both these instruments have been influential in that they form a locus around which a particular principle has been able to coalesce and evolve, and they have been used in the practice of courts and tribunals.

In the case of the precautionary principle, as enunciated in the Rio Declaration, the International Tribunal for the Law of the Sea, in its 2011 *Advisory Opinion on the Area*,[193] confirmed that the inclusion of Principle 15 in the International Seabed Authority Nodules and Sulphides Regulations transformed the non-binding statement of Principle 15 into a binding obligation, and observed that 'the precautionary approach has been incorporated into a growing number of international treaties and other instruments, many of which reflect the formulation of Principle 15 of the Rio Declaration. In the view of the Chamber, this has initiated a trend towards making this approach part of customary international law'.[194] In the 2009 case on gold mining in Romania, the European Court of Human Rights also noted 'the importance of the precautionary principle (enshrined for the first time in the Rio Declaration), which was intended to apply in order to ensure a level of high protection of health, the safety of consumers and the environment in all Community activities'.[195]

There has been less judicial attention paid to the Helsinki Final Act; however, it was used, by the ICJ, in the *Nicaragua* decision, as evidence of US *opinio juris* regarding non-intervention. As noted by the Court:

> [a]lso significant is United States acceptance of the principle of the prohibition of the use of force which is contained in the declaration on principles governing the mutual relations of States participating in the Conference on Security and Co-operation in Europe (Helsinki, 1 August 1975), whereby the participating States undertake to 'refrain in their mutual relations, as well as in their international relations in general', … from the threat or use of force. Acceptance of a text in these terms confirms the existence of an *opinio juris* of the participating States prohibiting the use of force in international relations.[196]

[193] *Responsibilities and Obligations of States with Respect to Activities in the Area (Advisory Opinion)* [2011] ITLOS Rep 10.

[194] ibid para 127.

[195] *Tatar v Romania*, ECtHR Application No 67021/01, Judgment (27 January 2009, Final 6 July 2009) para 120 (unofficial translation from the French original).

[196] *Military and Paramilitary Activities in and against Nicaragua (Nicaragua v United States of America) (Jurisdiction and Admissibility)* [1984] ICJ Rep 392, para 189; see also paras 204, 264.

Concluding Comments: Is Soft Law a 'Source' of International Law?

Evidence in this chapter demonstrates that States, and international courts and tribunals, will engage with non-binding norms even while they reaffirm the non-binding nature of the norm or instrument. Obvious issues arise from such practice: if soft law norms are being treated as relevant for States and judicial bodies, questions regarding the legality of such instruments must follow, as should questions regarding their legitimacy. These questions will be discussed in more detail in Chapter 8, but the next chapter turns to examine the history of soft law norms in IHL.

2

The History of Non-Binding Instruments in the History of International Humanitarian Law

Introduction

While there has been a proliferation of non-binding instruments relating to armed conflicts produced in the past 20 years, these documents are by no means outliers in the law of armed conflict. Since the advent of the modern treaty law of international humanitarian law (IHL), non-binding instruments have been an influential part of the law of armed conflict and have, on occasion, been pivotal in leading to the adoption of binding instruments. These non-binding instruments have taken various forms, including documents intended to be applied only to domestic actors,[1] documents intended to be adopted as binding instruments (but that failed to be so adopted),[2] and documents intentionally created as non-binding instruments of instruction.[3]

This chapter will outline the history of non-binding instruments in the law of armed conflict—specifically, those created prior to the non-binding instruments that are the primary subject of examination in this book. The focus will be on whether and how such instruments came to influence and impact on the binding law of armed conflict, the reasons behind the creation of these instruments, and why the non-binding path was chosen (if it was chosen, or, if it was not, why not). In doing so, the chapter will explore how non-binding instruments have been used in IHL historically and will set the stage for the analysis in the following two chapters of current non-binding instruments and provisions in IHL.

[1] Such as Instructions for the Government of Armies of the United States in the Field, General Order No 100.

[2] Such as the Brussels Declaration.

[3] Such as the *Oxford Manual on the Laws of War on Land.*

Non-Binding Norms in International Humanitarian Law. Emily Crawford, Oxford University Press. © Emily Crawford 2021.
DOI: 10.1093/oso/9780198819851.003.0003

The History of Non-Binding Norms in International Humanitarian Law

The Lieber Code (1863)

One of the first, and most influential, non-binding instruments adopted in the law of armed conflict was General Order 100—the Instructions for the Government of the Armies of the United States in the Field, better known as the Lieber Code. The Code was the result of work undertaken by both US government lawyers and military officials during the American Civil War, as well as advocacy and scholarship by Francis Lieber. Lieber, a scholar at Columbia's newly established law school, had written on international law and the law of armed conflict for many years. He had also experienced armed conflict first-hand, having fought with the Prussian Army against Napoleon following Napoleon's return from exile on Elba. In addition to Lieber's intellectual engagement with the law of armed conflict, there were personal reasons for his interest in the developing conflict in the United States. Lieber's three sons were soldiers in the Civil War, with two fighting for the Union and one for the Confederacy. Consequently, Lieber had good reason for his interest in the conflict and ensuring that certain minimum rules were followed.[4]

Following the Battle of Bull Run in 1861, Lieber wrote a series of letters to the *New York Times*, urging the Union to permit prisoner-of-war exchanges with the Confederacy. He followed up this correspondence with a series of public lectures at Columbia University, where he outlined the history of the international laws of war and detailed the history of rules governing questions such as the treatment of prisoners of war, the need to distinguish between combatants and non-combatants, and impermissible means and methods of war, such as the use of poison. Lieber's lectures were printed in the *New York Times*, and in other newspapers throughout the country, between October 1861 and March 1862.[5] In response to these lectures, Major General Henry Halleck—himself a scholar of the international law of armed conflict, and newly promoted General in Chief of the Union Armies—approached Lieber for advice on how to resolve some of the problems of the conflict, such as whether those who had taken up arms for the Confederacy were to be treated as regular combatants or should instead be considered as 'marauders'[6] not entitled to any special legal protections.[7]

[4] See generally Frank Freidel, *Francis Lieber: Nineteenth Century Liberal* (Peter Smith 1968) 305–06; David Crowe, *War Crimes, Genocide, and Justice* (Springer 2014) 80–81.

[5] A comprehensive history of the Lieber Code, as well as the history of the laws of armed conflict in US politics and law, can be found in John Fabian Witt's *Lincoln's Code: The Laws of War in American History* (Free Press 2012); Chapters 6–8 deal specifically with Lieber's work prior to General Order 100, as well as his work with the US government officials on General Order 100.

[6] Halleck, quoted in Daniel Sutherland, *A Savage Conflict: The Decisive Role of Guerrillas in the American Civil War* (University of North Carolina Press 2009) 64.

[7] Crowe (n 4) 81.

By 1863, Lieber had produced, and a committee of generals had endorsed, a short manual of 157 articles that outlined the accepted rules applicable in situations of armed conflict, as governed by international law. The articles covered a wide array of situations, including protections for ambassadors, the appropriate treatment of spies, special markings for hospitals, procedures for armistice and surrenders, prohibitions on acts such as assassination and the use of poison, the prohibition on causing further injury to persons 'already wholly disabled',[8] and rules on the treatment of civilians and civilian property. Following its approval by the Union government, the instructions were issued as an executive order (rather than as a codified instrument, which would have required legislative approval and, consequently, debate in Congress and possible alteration or delay in their issuance).[9] The order was then disseminated among Union officers in the field and also transmitted to Confederate military officers and officials.

Whether the Lieber Code helped mitigate the brutality of the American Civil War is debatable. John Fabian Witt argues that the Code 'did not reduce the suffering in the conflict. To the contrary, ... [the Code] helped produce some of the war's most enduring humanitarian crises'.[10] Patryk Labuda notes that 'historians agree that the Lieber Code's impact during the Civil War was probably scant. Most commanders knew but ignored the Code'.[11] However, there is almost universal agreement in the literature that the impact of the Code lies in its adoption by other sovereign nations in the years following the end of the Civil War. This is significant: the Lieber Code was a code of instruction, binding only as a domestic executive order, and applicable only to the Union armies. It was not intended as an international instrument. Nevertheless, the Code would go on to have a significant impact on the development of the international law of armed conflict. Following the Code's adoption in the United States, Lieber transmitted the document to lawyers and politicians across Europe, with the conviction that it would be 'adopted as a basis for similar works by the English, French and Germans'[12] in their dealings in armed conflict. Lieber's belief was soon affirmed: the Code was considered 'so consistent with accepted practice'[13] that in the years following the end of the American

[8] Lieber Code, Art 71.

[9] Patryk Labuda, 'The Lieber Code' in Anne Peters and Rüdiger Wolfrum (eds), *Max Planck Encyclopedia of Public International Law*.

[10] Witt (n 5) 249.

[11] Labuda (n 9). See also Richard Hartigan, *Lieber's Code and the Law of War* (Gryphon 1983), who notes that '[a]lthough "General Orders, no. 100" enjoyed the status of an official order of the United States government, it did not receive immediate recognition from Union commanders. Confederate officials dismissed it as propagandistic ... and derided it and the Union army applied it loosely': ibid Hartigan 20–21. The Code was, however, cited in the US Supreme Court case *Ex parte Vallandigham* 68 US (1 Wall) 243 (1864).

[12] Francis Lieber, letter to General Halleck, 20 May 1863, reprinted in Thomas Sargeant Perry (ed), *The Life and Letters of Francis Lieber* (Osgood and Company 1882) 333–34.

[13] Lindsay Green, *The Contemporary Law of Armed Conflict* (3rd edn, Manchester University Press 2008) 37.

Civil War, several States adopted Lieber-style codes for their own armed forces, including Prussia,[14] the Netherlands,[15] France,[16] Russia,[17] Serbia,[18] Argentina,[19] the United Kingdom,[20] Portugal,[21] and Spain.[22]

The Lieber Code was 'instantly influential';[23] it was, as Geoffrey Best has put it, 'the quarry from which all the subsequent codes were cut'.[24] This was evident not just in its adoption in State military manuals, as illustrated above, but also in the influence the Code would have on international treaty law. The first attempt to incorporate Lieber's Code into the law of nations would come less than 10 years after the end of the American Civil War, with the 1874 Project of an International Declaration concerning the Laws and Customs of War[25]—which would come to be known as the Brussels Declaration. The Declaration, though not successfully adopted as a binding international instrument, would nevertheless prove notably influential in bringing about the advent of comprehensive binding rules of international law, such as the Hague Conventions of 1899 and 1907.

The Brussels Declaration (1874)

The widespread acceptance of the Lieber Code by European governments[26] prompted diplomats in the Russian Ministry of Foreign Affairs to suggest that a European conference be convened, with the aim to draft, negotiate, and adopt a uniform set of laws applicable in situations of armed conflict. To that end, Fyodor von Martens, a civil servant in the Ministry, put together a draft instrument for debate, drawing heavily on the Lieber Code.[27] The similarities between this draft instrument and the Lieber Code were obvious: Swiss jurist (and friend and correspondent of Lieber) Johann Casper Bluntschli commented that the von Martens draft was nearly identical to Book VIII of his own *Das moderne Kriegsrecht der civilisirten Staten*, which was itself 'little more than a translation'[28] of the Lieber

[14] In 1870.
[15] In 1871.
[16] In 1877.
[17] In 1877; revised in 1904.
[18] In 1878.
[19] In 1881.
[20] In 1883; revised in 1904.
[21] In 1890.
[22] In 1893. For comments on the above-noted military codes, see further Thomas Erskine Holland, *The Laws of War on Land: Written and Unwritten* (Clarendon 1908) 72–73.
[23] Witt (n 5) 343.
[24] Geoffrey Best, *Humanity in Warfare: The Modern History of the International Law of Armed Conflicts* (Weidenfeld and Nicolson 1980) 171.
[25] Indeed, the Russian delegate and President of the Brussels Conference, Baron Jomini, explicitly noted that the Conference had its origins in the Lieber Code: Hartigan (n 11) 22.
[26] In addition to the adoption of the 1864 Geneva Convention and the 1868 St Petersburg Declaration.
[27] As Witt notes, 'Lieber's handiwork in 1862–63 was indeed apparent in the Russian proposal': Witt (n 5) 344. See also Karma Nabulsi, *Traditions of War: Occupation, Resistance and the Law* (OUP 1999) 5.
[28] Witt (n 5) 343.

Code, with the addition of the 1864 Geneva Convention—'one could almost say that the one is a copy of the other'.[29] The draft Brussels Declaration was essentially a repetition of the Lieber Code, taking into account the new international treaty law relating to the treatment of the wounded and sick in armies in the field, as had been codified in the 1864 Geneva Convention.[30]

The draft was sent to the States invited to the Brussels Conference, due to be held in July 1874.[31] The Conference, comprising 15 European States,[32] intended to produce a binding international instrument.[33] However, the draft proved unacceptable to several delegates, especially those from the smaller European States. Some delegates felt that the Russian draft protected only the larger military powers of Europe by seeming to enshrine an almost unfettered right of invasion and occupation, thereby favouring large States that had the manpower, materiel, and resources to mount such an invasion or occupation. At the same time, the draft limited the lawful right of States to resist invasion, which disadvantaged the smaller European States that did not have ample supplies of men and materiel to resist invasion and were consequently well acquainted with decades, if not centuries, of invasion at the hands of their larger European counterparts. As the French Ambassador to the Court of St James remarked of the Russian draft, 'all measures seem calculated to guarantee conquering armies the advantages of their organisation and their invading marching masses, and, on the other hand, to diminish the means of

[29] 23 July 1874, Brussels, Legations Fond A 25, quoted in Nabulsi (n 27) 6–7.

[30] As Martens himself noted, '[s]o it is to the United States of North America and to President Lincoln that belongs the honor of having taken the initiative in defining with precision the customs and laws of war. This first official attempt to codify the customs of war and to collect in a code the rules binding upon military forces has notably contributed to impress the character of humanity upon the conduct of the northern states in the course of that war': cited in Elihu Root, 'Francis Lieber' (1913) 7 American Journal of International Law 453, 457.

[31] Draft Project of an International Declaration Concerning the Laws and Customs of War, reprinted in James Lorimer, *The Institutes of the Law of Nations: A Treatise on the Jural Relations of Separate Political Communities* (vol 2, Blackwood 1884) 337 ff.

[32] In attendance were Austria-Hungary, Belgium, Denmark, France, Germany, Great Britain, Greece, the Netherlands, Portugal, Russia, Spain, Sweden, Norway, Switzerland, and Turkey (the Ottoman Empire). The United States had been invited but declined the invitation. See Gustave Rolin-Jaequemyns, 'Chronique du Droit International—1871–1874' (1875) 7 Revue de droit international et de législation comparée (1st ser) 70, 88. There was debate as to whether to invite delegates from South American States; however, the Conference ultimately decided that 'the number of attending powers was already so great that agreement on controversial questions would be difficult enough without adding delegates from South American countries': Doris Graber, *The Development of the Law of Belligerent Occupation, 1863–1914: A Historical Survey* (Columbia University Press 1949) 22. See also Rolin-Jaequemyns (n 32) 70, 88; 'Actes de la Conference Reuni a Bruxelles, du 27 Juillet au 27 Aout 1874, pour Regler le Lois et Coutumes de la Guerre', Nouveau Recueil General de Traites, 2nd Series, 1879–80, IV, 15 (note, however, that Tracey Leigh Dowdeswell asserts that an invitation *was* extended to South American States, as well as Persia, which declined to attend: Tracey Leigh Dowdeswell, 'The Brussels Peace Conference of 1874 and the Modern Laws of Belligerent Qualification' (2017) 54 Osgoode Hall Law Journal 805, 825–26).

[33] See Dietrich Schindler and Jiri Toman (eds), *The Laws of Armed Conflicts: A Collection of Conventions, Resolutions, and Other Documents* (4th edn, Martinus Nijhoff 2004) 21.

defence of populations surprised by such an invasion. It is, in truth, a code of conquest, rather than one of defence.'[34]

With this issue unresolved, the delegates met in Brussels to debate and, it was hoped, adopt the declaration. The Conference debated rules covering issues such as occupied territory, the status of combatants, targeting rules, the protection of prisoners of war, and the treatment of the wounded and sick. As with the Russian draft declaration, the amended text that emerged from debates in Brussels replicated or otherwise strongly echoed provisions in the Lieber Code. In fact, one can see this repetition (in scope, if not expression) when comparing both the Russian draft declaration and the final Brussels document with the provisions of the Lieber Code regarding treatment and parole for prisoners of war;[35] the prohibition on the use of poison as a weapon of war;[36] the prohibition on orders of no quarter;[37] prohibitions on misuse of the flag of truce;[38] rules on armistice;[39] and protections for buildings of religion, the arts, and sciences.[40]

Hopes that the Brussels document would be adopted as a binding international instrument were frustrated, as the Conference quickly stalled when the question of belligerent status was debated.[41] As anticipated in reactions to the Russian draft declaration, States were unable to reach a compromise over whether irregular fighters—including partisan fighters, insurgents, and participants in resistance warfare in occupied territory, as well as civilians in non-occupied territory resisting an invading army (*levée en masse*)—would be granted lawful combatant belligerent status (and the rights associated with such status, including combatant immunity and prisoner-of-war rights on capture).[42] The smaller European States argued that it was vital for resistance fighters to be protected by the law,[43] while the larger European States considered that partisan fighters were nothing more

[34] La Rochefoucauld to the Minister of Foreign Affairs, 26 June 1874, Brussels, Légations Fond A 25, quoted in Nabulsi (n 27) 6–7.

[35] Brussels Declaration, Draft Arts 23–34 (echoing provisions and wording in the Lieber Code, Arts 49–59, 72–80).

[36] Brussels Declaration, Art 13(a) (echoing provisions and wording in the Lieber Code, Art 70).

[37] Brussels Declaration, Art 13(d) (echoing provisions and wording in the Lieber Code, Art 60).

[38] Brussels Declaration, Art 13(f) (echoing provisions and wording in the Lieber Code, Art 114).

[39] Brussels Declaration, Arts 47–52 (echoing provisions and wording in the Lieber Code, Arts 135–47).

[40] Brussels Declaration, Art 8 (echoing provisions and wording in the Lieber Code, Arts 34–36).

[41] See generally *Actes de la Conférence de Bruxelles de 1874: sur le projet d'une convention internationale concernant la guerre: protocoles des séances plénières, protocoles de la Commission déleguée par la Conférence, annexes* (Librairie des publications législatives 1874) 28, 32–34, 50.

[42] See further Emily Crawford, *Identifying the Enemy: Civilian Participation in Armed Conflict* (OUP 2015) ch 2.

[43] For example, the Swiss, Netherlands, and Belgian delegates were concerned that placing restrictions on the rights of peoples to defend their homelands would put the smaller nations at a distinct disadvantage. As Baron Lambermont of Belgium put it, 'if citizens were to be sacrificed for having attempted to defend their country at the peril of their lives, they need not find inscribed on the post at the foot of which they are about to be shot, the article of a treaty signed by their own Government, which had in advance condemned them to death': cited in Lorimer (n 31) 380.

than brigands and bandits.[44] While some progress was made on extending protections to participants in *levées en masse* in non-occupied territory,[45] consensus could not be reached. The Declaration as finally drafted proved unacceptable to the Conference as a whole, and the Conference closed without the adoption of the Declaration as a binding instrument.

The Brussels Declaration, intended to be the first comprehensive binding instrument on the law of armed conflict in international law, was relegated to a non-binding statement of principles, the result of a Conference that had been, in the words of one of its chief architects, 'a complete failure'.[46] However, despite such a seeming setback in the codification of the law of armed conflict, the Brussels Declaration, an unintentional soft law instrument, would go on to have an impact on future parties interested in developing the law of armed conflict. Its influence was 'particularly apparent in French, English, German, Italian, and Russian [military] manuals'[47] adopted in the aftermath of the Conference,[48] with Martens making the claim that, for those States not adopting the Declaration, the 'moral force of the project was so great'[49] that even non-adopters followed the rules set down in Brussels.[50] Less than a decade later, the Brussels Declaration would find new life in a different form—that of the *Oxford Manual on the Laws of War on Land* (known as the Oxford Manual), itself an influential non-binding document in the laws of armed conflict.

The Oxford Manual (1880)

The failure to adopt a binding instrument at Brussels would prove only a temporary setback, as the 'debates that crystallized at Brussels brought the great powers to the threshold of a new understanding of the nature of law and its role in international relations'.[51] Before the end of the decade, international law scholars

[44] As Jean De Breucker noted, the larger European powers were of the opinion that 'without rules war would spell ruin for the countries invaded, since a people who wanted to defend itself should have the pluck to organise in peace time': Jean De Breucker, 'La Déclaration de Bruxelles de 1874 concernant les lois et coutumes de la guerre' *Chronique de politique étrangère* (vol XXVII, Institut royal des relations internationals, 1974), cited in DB, 'The Brussels International Declaration of 1874 concerning the Laws and Customs of War' (1974) 14 International Review of the Red Cross 616.

[45] See further comments by the Russian delegate, General Leer, in which he outlined what he considered an appropriate compromise solution: *Actes de la Conférence de Bruxelles de 1874* (n 41) 50, comments beginning 'M. le général de Leer s'exprime, au sujet de cet article, dans les termes suivants'.

[46] VV Pustogarov, *Our Martens: F.F. Martens, International Lawyer and Architect of Peace* (intro WE Butler, Simmonds 2000) 113.

[47] Graber (n 32) 26.

[48] Frantz Despagnet, *Cours de Droit International Public* (Charles de Boeck ed, 4th edn, Librairie de la Société du Recueil Sirey; L Larose et L Tenin 1910) 805; Fyodor Fyodorovich Martens, *La paix et la guerre: la conférence de Bruxelles 1874. Droits et devoirs des belligérants (leur application pendant la guerre d'Orient 1874–1878) la conférence de La Haye 1899* (Arthur Rousseau 1901) 120, 244.

[49] Graber (n 32) 27.

[50] Martens (n 48) 119.

[51] Dowdeswell, 'The Brussels Peace Conference of 1874' (n 32) 841.

and practitioners, under the auspices of the Institute of International Law, recommitted themselves to the process of codifying the laws of war, in the form of the 1880 Oxford Manual. Specifically presented as a non-binding instrument,[52] the Manual was intended to be utilised as a template for States in their conduct of armed conflicts.[53]

The Oxford Manual drew explicitly on the work of the Brussels Conference. In the Preface to the Manual, the Institute acknowledged the Brussels Declaration as 'a solemn pronouncement of the good intentions of governments'[54] regarding the codification of the law of armed conflict and acknowledged the failure at Brussels to adopt the declaration as binding international law. However, the Institute stated its belief that the legal and policy issues that prevented the adoption of the declaration as a treaty in 1874 would not prevent the reception of the Oxford Manual as an acceptable restatement of the extant law of armed conflict because 'although the governments have not ratified the draft issues by the Conference at Brussels … since 1874 ideas, aided by reflection and experience, have had time to mature, and because it seems less difficult than it did then to trace rules which would be acceptable to all peoples'.[55] The Institute believed that the Manual would be welcomed by States because 'rash and extreme rules will not … be found therein. The Institute has not sought innovations in drawing up the Manual; it has contented itself with stating clearly and codifying the accepted ideas of our age so far as this has appeared allowable and practicable'.[56]

Many of the provisions seen in the Brussels Declaration (and the Lieber Code) are replicated in the Oxford Manual, such as provisions limiting the means and methods of warfare;[57] the treatment of spies;[58] protections for objects of religion, science, and art;[59] and provisions on the treatment of prisoners of war.[60] However, the Oxford Manual was not accepted by the community of nations. While the Manual was adopted by Argentina,[61] there is no extant evidence that it was adopted by any other State or adapted as part of any other State military manuals.[62] Germany was particularly scathing of the Manual, stating that any attempt to regulate armed

[52] From the Preface to the Manual: 'The Institute … does not propose an international treaty, which might perhaps be premature or at least very difficult to obtain.'

[53] From the Preface to the Manual: 'being bound by its by-laws to work, among other things, for the observation of the laws of war, [the Institute] believes it is fulfilling a duty in offering to the governments a Manual suitable as the basis for national legislation in each State, and in accord with both the progress of juridical science and the needs of civilized armies.'

[54] Oxford Manual, Preface.

[55] ibid. See also Institut de Droit International, 'Reglementation des Lois et Coutumes de la Guerre. Manuel des Lois de la Guerre', *Annuaire de l'Institut de Droit International* (1881–82) vol 5, 150, 157–58.

[56] Oxford Manual, Preface.

[57] Oxford Manual, Art 4 (echoing the wording of the Brussels Declaration, Art 12).

[58] Oxford Manual, Arts 23–26 (echoing the wording of the Brussels Declaration, Arts 19–22).

[59] Oxford Manual, Art 34 (echoing the wording of the Brussels Declaration, Art 17).

[60] Oxford Manual, Arts 61–78 (echoing the wording of the Brussels Declaration, Arts 23–34).

[61] According to Crowe (n 4) 85 and Nabulsi (n 27) 9.

[62] See Graber (n 32) 30.

conflict was 'obscene .... When peace gives place to war, then passion and violence enter upon the great stage of history ... the expression "civilized warfare", used by Bluntschli, seems hardly intelligible; for war destroys this equilibrium'.[63]

The Oxford Manual on Law of Naval Warfare (1913) and the Hague Draft Rules on Air Warfare (1923)

By the end of the 1800s, the international community had made significant progress in developing the law of armed conflict, culminating in the adoption of the 1899 Hague Regulations. However, as technological developments changed the means and methods of warfare, it became apparent that the law as codified needed to be supplemented. The law of naval warfare was the focus of the first major non-binding instrument to be adopted after the Hague Regulations. While naval warfare had been subject to attention at the Hague in 1899 and again in 1907,[64] this had only been in discrete areas of naval warfare, such as the status of enemy merchant ships, rules on automatic submarine contact mines, and the establishment of an international prize court. There was no single Convention that comprehensively outlined the rules on the conduct of naval warfare. In fact, delegates at the 1907 Conference expressed the 'wish that the elaboration of a regulation relating to the laws and customs of maritime war should be included in the program of the next Conference, and that in all cases the Powers shall apply as far as possible to sea war the principles of The Convention on the Laws and Customs of War on Land'.[65]

The first attempts towards clarifying the law of naval warfare came in 1909 with the London Naval Conference, where the leading international naval powers[66] adopted the London Declaration concerning the laws of naval warfare. While the final instrument was signed by all Conference delegates, it failed to be ratified by any of the States involved, following the rejection of the document by the UK's House of Lords.[67] The declaration became a non-binding instrument, but one that

[63] Cited in Nabulsi (n 27) 9. See also Crowe (n 4) 85–86.

[64] Convention (VI) Relative to the Status of Enemy Merchant Ships at the Outbreak of Hostilities; Convention (VII) Relative to the Conversion of Merchant Ships into Warships; Convention (VIII) Relative to the Laying of Automatic Submarine Contact Mines; Convention (IX) Respecting Bombardment by Naval Forces in Time of War; Convention (X) for the Adaptation to Naval War of the Principles of the Geneva Convention (XI) Relative to Certain Restrictions with Regard to the Exercise of the Right of Capture in Naval War; Convention (XII) Relatives to the Creation of an International Prize Court; Convention (XIII) Concerning the Rights and Duties of Neutral Powers in Naval War.

[65] 'le voeu que l'elaboration d'un reglement relatif aux lois et coutumes de la guerre maritime figure au programme de la prochaine Conference et que, dans tous les cas, les Puissances appliquent, autant que possible, a la guerre sur mer les principes de la Convention relative aux lois et coutumes de la guerre sur terre': Acte final de la Deuxième Conférence de la Paix. La Haye, 18 Octobre 1907 <https://ihl-databases.icrc.org/dih-traites/WebART/185-180001?OpenDocument> accessed 28 July 2021.

[66] Comprising the United States, Japan, Austria-Hungary, France, Germany, Italy, the Netherlands, Russia, Spain, and the United Kingdom.

[67] Commentary to the London Declaration <https://ihl-databases.icrc.org/ihl/INTRO/255?OpenDocument> accessed 28 July 2021.

was considered a declaration of the existing customary law on naval warfare.[68] The adoption of the London Declaration was soon followed by action on behalf of the Institute of International Law, which determined to examine the law of naval warfare in more detail. The objective was to produce a manual for naval warfare equivalent to the 1880 Oxford Manual.[69] The result was the 1913 Oxford Manual on Naval Warfare, a 116-article document covering the law relating to the designation and status of warships and personnel engaged in naval warfare; permissible means and methods of naval warfare; rules on blockade, seizure, and prize; rules on the treatment of enemy personnel captured at sea; and protections for hospital ships.[70] In its study of the practice of naval warfare, the Institute was able to draw on existing naval warfare manuals from the United States, Italy, Japan, Russia, and the Netherlands;[71] both the London Declaration and the Oxford Manual on Naval Warfare were considered to be accurately reflective of the customary law of naval warfare of the time.[72]

The outbreak of the First World War precluded an examination of the Oxford Manual of Naval Warfare by States at the planned Third Hague Peace Conference, which was due to be held in Munich in 1914.[73] However, as the conflict continued, the practice of States with regards to naval warfare 'showed that the Hague treaties and traditional customary law had begun to be overtaken by developments in methods and means of warfare'.[74] Attempts at banning the use of submarines failed[75] and the outbreak of the Second World War, together with the new advances in military maritime technology, did little to clarify the legal situation, with widespread practice of 'arbitrary sinkings ... including many hospital ships and Red Cross vessels carrying relief supplies'.[76]

Following the end of the Second World War, naval warfare, once the focus of considerable legal attention by the international community, was largely ignored in treaty development, with only the Geneva Convention II on the Wounded, Sick, and Shipwrecked adopted in 1949. The dearth of specific treaty law on naval

68 J Ashley Roach, 'The Law of Naval Warfare at the Turn of Two Centuries' (2000) 94 American Journal of International Law 64, 65.

69 Natalino Ronzitti (ed), *Commentary to 1913 Manual on Naval Warfare: A Collection of Agreements and Documents with Commentaries* (Martinus Nijhoff 1988) 329–30.

70 *Oxford Manual on the Laws of Naval War Governing the Relations between Belligerents* (adopted by the Institute of International Law in 1913) (Oxford Manual on Naval Warfare).

71 ibid 330.

72 Louise Doswald-Beck, 'San Remo Manual on International Law Applicable to Armed Conflicts at Sea' (1995) 35 International Review of the Red Cross 583, 584.

73 Andrew White, 'The Third Peace Conference at the Hague' (1914) 76 The Advocate of Peace 183, 183; Nobuo Hayashi, *The Role and Importance of the Hague Conferences: A Historical Perspective* (UNIDIR 2017) 3.

74 Doswald Beck, 'San Remo Manual' (n 72) 584.

75 Doswald-Beck (ibid) notes that following the First World War, 'efforts were made, in particular by Great Britain in the 1920s, to outlaw submarines altogether, but ... this proposal was not accepted' (584), leading instead to the adoption of a treaty in 1936 that specified that submarines must abide by the same rules as warships.

76 ibid.

warfare, accompanied by significant changes in the means and methods of naval warfare, the expansive development of the international law of the sea, and the progressive development of the law of land warfare throughout the twentieth century led scholars and practitioners in the 1990s to note the 'troubling degree of uncertainty as to the content of contemporary international law applicable to armed conflicts at sea'.[77] Until the production of the San Remo Manual relating to Naval Warfare, the Oxford Manual on Naval Warfare remained the most recent instrument on the topic.

It was new technology, and its influence on the conduct of armed conflict, that prompted legal consideration of another aspect of modern warfare: that of air warfare. The aerial domain soon demonstrated its value as a venue for warfare: hot air balloons were used during both the American Civil War[78] and the Franco-Prussian War.[79] The potential for aircraft to be used as a weapons delivery system was clear; regulating aerial warfare was therefore included on the agenda in 1899 at The Hague, resulting in the adoption of the declaration prohibiting the launching of projectiles and explosives from balloons or by other similar new methods.[80] It was accompanied by Article 25 of the Hague Regulations IV, which provided that 'the attack or bombardment by any means whatsoever of towns, villages, habitations or buildings which are not defended is forbidden'.[81]

However, as with naval warfare, technology in relation to aerial warfare soon outpaced the law. By the end of the First World War, heavier-than-air craft were a fixture of warfare, as was the practice of (often indiscriminate) aerial bombardment. Even though the provisions adopted in The Hague in 1899 and 1907 were acknowledged to be 'merely declaratory of existing laws and customs of war . . . [and] binding independently of the status of the conventions of which they were a part',[82]

[77] ibid 585. As Doswald-Beck also notes, 'the customary law that developed prior to the First World War had made an appropriate balance between military and humanitarian needs that suited naval practices and the sailing ships of the nineteenth century. As it is not possible to return to those times, the law needs to be adjusted': ibid (584).

[78] See generally Jason Emerson, 'Great Weapon or "Fanciful Contraption"? The Rise and Fall of the Union Balloon Corps' (2012) 51 Civil War Times 33; Herman Herst, 'The Civil War's Attempt at Aerial Warfare' (1995) 253 Stamps 8, 8.

[79] Maurice Crosland, 'Science and the Franco-Prussian War' (1976) 6 Social Studies of Science 185, 203–05. Wyman argues that lighter-than-air machines were used by the French as a weapon of war as early as 1794, but does not cite in which instance: Richard Wyman, 'The First Rules of Air Warfare' (1984) 35 Air University Review 94, 94–95. John M Bacon (in 'The Balloon in Warfare', *Macmillan's Magazine* (1 May 1904) 108) argues that the balloon was used in the French Revolutionary wars. However, JM Spaight, writing in 1914, argued that 'when the first Hague Conference sat in 1899, flying, as we know it today, was non-existent': JM Spaight, *Aircraft in War* (MacMillan 1914) 11. While this is undoubtedly true for powered aircraft such as airplanes, the use of air balloons was commonplace by the adoption of the Hague Regulations in 1899—hence Declaration 1 prohibiting the launching of projectiles and explosives from balloons or by other similar new methods.

[80] Reaffirmed at the Second Hague Peace Conference in Declaration (XIV) Prohibiting the Discharge of Projectiles and Explosives from Balloons (The Hague, 18 October 1907).

[81] Hague Convention IV (1907), Art 25.

[82] JW Garner, *The German War Code: A Comparison of the German Manual of the Laws of War with Those of the United States, Great Britain, and France and with the Hague Convention Respecting the Laws and Customs of War on Land* (University of Illinois 1918) 5.

it was a function of the Hague Regulations (because of the *si omnes* or general participation clause[83]) that they were binding only in relation to conflicts involving signatories. If a State was not party to the Regulations, the Conventions did not apply. Therefore, when the First World War broke out, most of the belligerents were not bound by its provisions, as Italy, Bulgaria, Montenegro, Serbia, and Turkey had not ratified the Convention.[84] Widespread and indiscriminate aerial bombardment was commonplace during the First World War.[85]

In the aftermath of the War, the United States, the United Kingdom, France, Italy, and Japan met at a conference, convened by the United States in Washington in 1922, to further examine the development of the law of aerial warfare. However, the Washington conference ended up adopting a treaty on submarine warfare, rather than aerial warfare;[86] when it became clear that the Conference would not address air warfare, it adopted a resolution to establish a Commission of Jurists to examine the issue.[87] The Commission comprised the five States present at the Washington Conference, as well as a delegation from the Netherlands.[88] By early 1923, the Commission produced a draft document of 62 articles relating to aerial warfare (with an additional 12 provisions relating to the use of radio in warfare). The aerial rules covered several distinct areas, including the treatment and status of belligerents, classification and markings of aircraft, bombardment, espionage, and neutral aircraft.

The rules were never adopted in legally binding form, and there seems to be little evidence to indicate why this is: no follow-up international conference was organised, and no State involved in the Commission agreed to sign the instrument.[89] Contemporary (and near-contemporary) accounts of the work of the Commission speculate that the draft rules were not progressed to a binding instrument because the provisions limiting aerial bombardment were considered too strict and would have limited the ability of States to prosecute an air war[90] and that it was 'simply

[83] Hague Convention IV (1907), Art 2.

[84] JW Garner, *International Law and the World War* (vol 1, Longmans Green 1920) 467.

[85] William Wherry, 'Aerial Warfare in International Law' (Contemporary Law Pamphlets 1939) 3. See also Garner, *International Law and the World War* (n 84) 459–65.

[86] Treaty relating to the Use of Submarines and Noxious Gases in Warfare (Washington, 6 February 1922) (the treaty never entered into force, following the failure of France to ratify).

[87] Resolution Adopted by the Conference on the Limitation of Armament (1922) Establishing a Commission of Jurists to Consider Amendment of the Laws of War, Conference on the Limitation of Armament, 1640. For the adoption of these resolutions, see 'Report of the American Delegation', 306 and Foreign Relations of the United States (1922) vol 1, 288–97.

[88] For a detailed history of the Conference, see further Heinz Marcus Hanke, 'The 1923 Hague Rules of Air Warfare: A Contribution to the Development of International Law Protecting Civilians from Air Attack' (1993) 292 International Review of the Red Cross 12.

[89] JW Garner, 'International Regulation of Air Warfare' (1932) 3 Air Law Review 309, 317; Hanke (n 88) 19.

[90] Garner attributed the failure to adopt the Draft Rules as a treaty (or to adopting the draft rules as domestic law) to a general lack of interest on behalf of the citizens of the involved States, as well as a resistance by States to limit their ability to wage war in the future. '[T]here appears to be less and less readiness to prohibit or restrict the use of an instrumentality of such demonstrated potency and future possibility and a corresponding disposition to overlook the frightful consequences to civilisation to

too early for a set of rules as progressive as the Hague Rules'[91] to be adopted at that time.

The Tehran Declaration on Human Rights in Armed Conflict (1968) and the Turku Declaration of Minimum Humanitarian Standards (1990)

In 1968, the international community came together in Tehran at the first International Conference on Human Rights, to 'review the progress made in the twenty years since the adoption of the Universal Declaration of Human Rights and to formulate a program for the future'.[92] The Conference had been convened by the United Nations, which, in the 20 years since the adoption of the Universal Declaration of Human Rights, had been grappling with a number of significant human rights concerns, including decolonisation, racial discrimination, the human rights implications of economic development, and the divides between the developed world and the developing world, and between the East and the West, as played out in the Cold War.[93] The Conference was intended as an opportunity to review the progress of human rights in the United Nations since its inception, and to set the agenda for human rights implementation, enforcement, and development for the future.

The question of the human rights implications in situations of armed conflict was not initially considered in the draft agenda for the Conference,[94] but it found expression in one of the final resolutions of the Conference: Resolution XXIII.[95] The Resolution drew an explicit connection between human rights and situations of armed conflict by stating that 'peace is the underlying condition for the full observance of human rights and war is their negation' and that 'even during the periods of armed conflict, humanitarian principles must prevail'.[96] The Resolution called on States to ratify extant IHL treaties, and for the Secretary-General to examine the possibility of further developing the law of armed conflict, noting that 'the widespread violence and brutality of our times', including violations of the law of armed conflict, 'erode human rights'.[97]

which its unrestricted use may lead': Garner, 'International Regulation of Air Warfare' (n 89) 317. See also JM Spaight, *Air Power and War Rights* (Longmans 1925) 212 ff.

[91] Hanke (n 88) 20.

[92] Proclamation of Teheran, Final Act of the International Conference on Human Rights, Teheran, 22 April to 13 May 1968, UN Doc A/CONF.32/41 (1968) 3.

[93] See generally Roland Burke, 'From Individual Rights to National Development: The First UN International Conference on Human Rights, Tehran, 1968' (2008) 19 Journal of World History 275, 277–82.

[94] UN Doc A/6670, Annex II (12 June 1967).

[95] Final Act of the International Conference on Human Rights, UN Doc A/CONF.32/41 (1968) 18.

[96] ibid.

[97] ibid.

In coming to this position, the Tehran Conference drew on advocacy that had been undertaken previously by the International Committee of the Red Cross (ICRC), which, in 1965 at the XXth International Conference of the Red Cross in Vienna, also affirmed the links between human rights and humanitarian law. In Declaration X, entitled 'The Red Cross as a Factor in World Peace', the Conference noted 'its profound anxiety with regard to the suffering endured by the populations of a number of countries where armed conflicts are being waged', and specifically made mention of international human rights, in connection to colonial powers' 'repeated use of force directed against the independence or the right to self-determination of all peoples'.[98] The connection between human rights and humanitarian law was made more explicit during the Tehran Conference, when the ICRC delegate to the Conference stated that:

> [the laws of war are] ... based on certain of the fundamental rights proclaimed in [the Universal Declaration of Human Rights]—respect for the human person, protection against torture and against cruel, inhuman or degrading punishments or treatment. Those rights find their legal expression in the contractual engagements which [governments undertake] ... [T]he Universal Declaration of Human Rights and the Geneva Conventions are both derived from one and the same ideal, which humanity pursues increasingly in spite of passions and political strife and which it must not despair of attaining—namely, that of freeing human beings and nations from the suffering of which they are often at once the authors and the victims.[99]

The Tehran Declaration was one of the first international instruments that explicitly affirmed the linkages between human rights law and humanitarian law and initiated a process whereby human rights and humanitarian law would be considered in treaty law and practice as interrelated. The position taken in the Tehran Declaration would be echoed in numerous resolutions of the UN General Assembly and Security Council in later years.[100]

Also drawing the connection between human rights and humanitarian law was the Turku Declaration of Minimum Humanitarian Standards, which emerged from debate in the years following the adoption of Additional Protocol II in 1977. During that period, scholars of IHL began to explore the gaps in IHL in relation to

[98] Resolution X, XXth International Conference of the Red Cross, reprinted in (1965) 56 International Review of the Red Cross 570, 574–75.

[99] Statement of ICRC delegate to the International Conference on Human Rights in Teheran, 1968. Indeed, the Preamble to Protocol II refers to human rights. Regarding the place of human rights in Protocol II, see further Georges Abi-Saab, 'Human Rights and Humanitarian Law in Internal Conflicts' in Daniel Warner (ed), *Human Rights and Humanitarian Law: The Quest for Universality* (Martinus Nijhoff 1997) 112–14.

[100] Discussed in more detail later in this chapter.

what were being termed 'grey-zone conflicts'[101]—armed conflicts that did not meet the minimum requirements of either Protocol II or Common Article 3, yet were more than just 'minor' incidents, such as rioting or other internal tensions.

Theodor Meron was the first scholar and practitioner to take up the cause of a new instrument. Within five years of the adoption of the Protocols, Meron noted the 'inadequate reach of humanitarian and human rights law and the need for a new instrument'[102] and proposed the adoption of a 'short, simple and modest instrument ... [stating the] irreducible and nonderogable core of human rights that must be applied at a minimum in situations of internal strife and violence (even of low intensity)'.[103] Such a declaration, 'which would not require formal accession or ratification by states',[104] would be an important first step towards ensuring that there would be no 'twilight zone'[105] in the law, where the applicability of rules could be disputed.[106] Meron's advocacy led to the convening of an expert meeting at the Institute for Human Rights at Åbo Akademi University in Turku/Åbo, Finland. At that meeting, 17 experts[107] drafted and adopted a Declaration of Minimum Humanitarian Standards, which came to be known as the Turku Declaration.[108]

The Declaration's stated position was that 'international law relating to human rights and humanitarian norms applicable in armed conflicts do not adequately protect human beings in situations of internal violence, disturbances, tensions and public emergency',[109] and that certain minimum rules of human rights and humanitarian law should apply in all situations, without derogation, 'to all persons, groups and authorities, irrespective of their legal status and without any adverse discrimination'.[110] Of the 18 rules in the Declaration, nearly half are derived from fundamental rules of IHL, such as a prohibition on attacks against non-combatants; proportionality in the use of force; a prohibition on the use of illegal means and methods of warfare; and special protection for the sick and wounded, and for medical and religious personnel. The remainder of the articles in the Declaration

[101] See Asbjørn Eide, Allan Rosas, and Theodor Meron, 'Combating Lawlessness in Gray Zone Conflicts through Minimum Humanitarian Standards' (1995) 89 American Journal of International Law 215; Theodor Meron, 'On the Inadequate Reach of Humanitarian and Human Rights Law and the Need for a New Instrument' (1983) 77 American Journal of International Law 589.

[102] Meron, 'On the Inadequate Reach' (n 101) 589.

[103] ibid 606.

[104] ibid.

[105] ibid 603.

[106] Meron wrote on the issue several times: Theodor Meron, 'Towards a Humanitarian Declaration on Internal Strife' (1984) 78 American Journal of International Law 859; Theodor Meron, 'Draft Model Declaration on Internal Strife' (1988) 262 International Review of the Red Cross 59; Theodor Meron, *Human Rights in Internal Strife: Their International Protection* (CUP 1987).

[107] Including Theodor Meron and Hans-Peter Gasser, as well as other noted IHL practitioners and academics, such as Françoise Hampson, Asbjørn Eide, Luigi Condorelli, Allan Rosas, and Theo van Boven.

[108] Declaration of Minimum Humanitarian Standards (2 December 1990) (Turku Declaration).

[109] Turku Declaration, Preamble.

[110] Turku Declaration, Art 2.

are drawn from international human rights law,[111] including recognition of persons before the law; respect for the person, honour, and convictions of any person; freedom of thought, conscience, and religion; the right to humane treatment; and a prohibition on acts that are illegal under general international law, such as murder, torture, rape, collective punishments, hostage-taking, looting, enforced disappearance, and deliberate deprivation of food and health care.[112]

The Turku Declaration was sent first to the UN Sub-Commission on the Protection and Promotion of Human Rights in 1991,[113] and then to the Commission on Human Rights,[114] with the hope that it would eventually be adopted as a UN Declaration. However, the Declaration was ultimately abandoned in favour of an entirely new instrument,[115] on fundamental standards of humanity. That instrument was considered by the United Nations in several forums,[116] but did not eventuate into a UN declaration.

The Impact of Non-Binding Instruments in the History of International Humanitarian Law

From the above analysis, it is clear that non-binding instruments have often been looked to as mechanisms for addressing perceived shortcomings in the existing law and, in some instances, for the progressive development of the law. The remaining

[111] Jean-Daniel Vigny and Cecilia Thompson, 'Fundamental Standards of Humanity: What Future?' (2002) 20 Netherlands Quarterly of Human Rights 185, 189.

[112] See ibid 188–89.

[113] Sub-Commission on Prevention of Discrimination and Protection of Minorities, 43rd session, UN Doc E/CN.4/Sub.2/1991/55 (December 1991).

[114] UNCHR, Res 1994/26, 50th session, 36th meeting (26 August 1994).

[115] UNCHR, Res 1995/29, 51st session, 52nd meeting (3 March 1995).

[116] For the procedural history of the Declaration after it reached the United Nations, see further UNCHR, Res 1996/26, 52nd session, 51st meeting (19 April 1996) para 1; UNCHR, Report of the International Workshop on Minimum Humanitarian Standards, Cape Town, 27–29 September 1996, annexed to The Secretary-General, Report of the Secretary-General on Minimum Standards of Humanity, delivered to the Sub-Commission on Prevention of Discrimination and Protection of Minorities and the Commission on Human Rights, UN Doc E/CN.4/1997/77/Add.1 (28 January 1997). See also UNCHR, Res 1997/21, 53rd session, 56th meeting (11 April 1997); UN Doc E/CN.4/1996/80 (28 November 1995); UN Doc E/CN.4/1996/80/Add.1 (4 January 1996); UN Doc E/CN.4/1996/80/Add.2 (28 February 1996); UN Doc E/CN.4/1996/80/Add.3 (11 March 1996); UN Doc E/CN.4/1997/77 (24 December 1996); UNCHR, Res 1995/29; UNCHR, Res 1996/26; UNCHR, Res 1997/21; UN Doc E/CN.4/1998/87 (5 January 1998); UN Doc E/CN.4/1998/87/Add.1 (12 January 1998); UN Doc E/CN.4/1999/92 (18 December 1998); UN Doc E/CN.4/2000/94 (27 December 1999); UN Doc E/CN.4/2001/91 (12 January 2001); UN Doc E/CN.4/2002/103 (20 December 2001); UN Doc E/CN.4/2004/90 (25 February 2004); UN Doc E/CN.4/2006/87 (3 March 2006); UN Doc A/HRC/8/14 (3 June 2008). See further documents in the Commission on Human Rights and its successor body, the Human Rights Council: Res 1998/29, 54th session, 51st meeting (17 April 1998); Res 1999/65, 55th session, 58th meeting (28 April 1999); Res 2000/69, 56th session, 66th meeting (26 April 2000); December 2001/112, 57th session, 77th meeting (25 April 2001); December 2002/112, 58th session, 56th meeting (25 April 2002); December 2004/118, 60th session, 57th meeting (12 August 2004). See further David Petrasek, 'Moving Forward on the Development of Minimum Humanitarian Standards' (1998) 92 American Journal of International Law 557, 558.

part of this chapter will examine whether these instruments were later adopted by States or had any impact on State practice, and whether the non-binding character of the instruments had any impact on their reception.

The Lieber Code, the Brussels Declaration, and the Oxford Manual

By 1880, the international community of the time had engaged, to varying degrees, with three different non-binding instruments attempting to set out rules of conduct in armed conflicts: a domestic executive order, an unintentionally non-binding international document, and an intentionally non-binding manual of instruction. The instruments were, to varying degrees, either hailed as definitive statements of the extant law of armed conflicts or condemned as unacceptable incursions into a State's sovereign right to wage. There is a clear continuity between the provisions of the Lieber Code, the Brussels Declaration, and the Oxford Manual, and all three instruments (even the Oxford Manual) that helped set the groundwork for the adoption of the first major comprehensive treaty on the conduct of armed conflicts under international law. Indeed, it was the Brussels Declaration that proved to be hugely influential in shaping the course of the law of armed conflict: scholars and practitioners are almost universal in acknowledging that without the Brussels Declaration, there would have been no Hague Regulations in 1899.[117]

Did the fact that the Lieber Code, the Brussels Declaration, and the Oxford Manual were non-binding have any influence on how they were received, or was their non-binding nature essentially incidental to their ultimate impact? As Yutaka Arai-Takahashi notes, much of 'the famous Lieber Code, which was designed as the military manual of the US army during the American Civil War, may be considered codification (rather than new development) of pre-existing customary rules'.[118] If so, the Lieber Code and the Brussels Declaration were merely restatements of the extant binding law, and their form as non-binding instruments was not relevant: the rules they set down were already binding, and their communication in written form did not alter their legal status. Equally, while the Brussels Declaration and the Lieber Code helped to bring about the Hague Regulations, it must also be acknowledged that binding treaty law, in the form of the 1864 Geneva

[117] Pustogarov (n 46) 113. See also Katja Göcke, 'The Brussels Declaration' in Anne Peters and Rüdiger Wolfrum (eds), *Max Planck Encyclopedia of Public International Law*: 'many of the provisions contained in these two Hague Conventions can be traced back to the rules and regulations laid down in the Oxford Manual and the Brussels Declaration'; Green (n 13) notes that 'what appears in The Hague Regulations is the wording of Brussels, with but minor verbal changes': ibid 131.

[118] Yutaka Arai-Takahashi, *The Law of Occupation: Continuity and Change of International Humanitarian Law, and Its Interaction with International Human Rights Law* (Brill 2009) 57.

Convention and the 1868 St Petersburg Declaration, was also critical in paving the way for the adoption of the Hague Regulations in 1899.

However, there are additional elements to consider. First, while the drafters of the Lieber Code, the Brussels Declaration, and the Oxford Manual emphasised that their work was merely a restatement of the existing law and not a progressive or radical development, the instruments were still met with varying degrees of resistance as to their accuracy and applicability. As an example, it is illustrative to look to the debate that took place during the Brussels Conference regarding the inclusion of resistance fighters and participants in *levées en masse* in the categories of lawful combatant.

The question of recognising *levée en masse* as a form of lawful participation in armed conflict was included in the draft Brussels document and was immediately subject to considerable debate during the Conference.[119] The initial Russian draft declaration included proposed sections on the 'Rights of Belligerents with reference to Private Individuals',[120] and the relevant provisions relating to *levée en masse* were first outlined in Articles 45 and 46.[121] Article 45 stated that 'the inhabitants of a district not already occupied by the enemy, who shall take up arms in the defence of their country, ought to be regarded as belligerents, and if captured should be considered as prisoners of war'.[122] This provision was essentially in keeping with the Lieber Code and the national military codes previously adopted and was uncontroversial.

The Draft Declaration went further, however, and outlined in Article 46 that 'individuals belonging to the population of a country, in which the enemy's power is already established, who shall rise in arms against them, may be handed over to justice, and are not regarded as prisoners of war'.[123] It was *this* designation of resistance fighters as criminals rather than lawful combatants that divided the Conference, prompting the Belgian delegate to ask to have recorded in the written account of the Conference that no conclusion could be reached on the question of whether *levée en masse* could exist in occupied territory, and that participants in a levee must still be governed by the unwritten law of nations.[124] Further

[119] *Actes de la Conférence de Bruxelles de 1874* (n 41) 28, 32–34, 50.

[120] Draft Project of an International Declaration Concerning the Laws and Customs of War, reprinted in Lorimer (n 31) 337 ff.

[121] The Draft Declaration used section numbers (§) to indicate each provision; for convenience, the term 'Article' will be used when referring to provisions in the Draft Declaration.

[122] Draft Declaration, Art 45, reprinted in Lorimer (n 31) 377.

[123] ibid 378.

[124] 'M. le baron Lambermont constate de son côté que, l'accord n'existant pas sur ce point, l'accord n'existant pas sur ce point, la question de savoir si et sous quelles conditions les populations pourront prendre les armes dans le territoire occupé doit rester entière. Le protocole pourra mentionner que la question n'est tranchée ni dans un sens ni dans un autre. Si une guerre éclate, personne ne sera lié par un texte; on suivra les règles habituelles du droit des gens; rien ne sera préjugé ni pour ni contre par la convention projetée': ibid 34.

modifications of Articles 45 and 46 met with resistance; ultimately, following additional redrafting,[125] the provision first outlined in Article 45 was moved and become Article 10, with the more restrictive provision on *levée en masse* ultimately winning out.

What is the relevance of this example for the larger analysis of the impact of a non-binding instrument on the development of the law of armed conflict? Simply put, had it not been for the disputes over combatants that ultimately led to the Brussels Declaration failing to be adopted, there would have been no Martens Clause in the Hague Regulations, and no inclusion of resistance and partisan fighters as combatants in the 1949 Geneva Conventions. If one views the Brussels Declaration (and the Lieber Code and the Oxford Manual) as not just an instrument but as an *entire process*, involving both the final document and the drafts and debates that led to that document, one can see that the dispute over combatant status, and the attempt to progressively develop and expand the law by the smaller European States, was pivotal in laying the initial groundwork of thinking that would eventually lead to two significant developments in the law of armed conflict: the adoption of the Martens Clause in the 1899 Hague Regulations and the inclusion of partisan and resistance fighters in the categories of lawful combatant in Geneva in 1949. It was the *entire process* surrounding these non-binding instruments that would prove influential, not just for codifying and crystallising existing customary law but also for focusing and driving the debates over the *lex ferenda* of the law of armed conflict—debates that would mature into binding international law, either as custom or treaty, in the decades to come.

Additionally, it must also be noted that the *source* of these non-binding instruments no doubt influenced the degree to which they were embraced. That the Lieber Code had the imprimatur of the US government and was written and approved by men who were both lawyers and soldiers was no doubt fundamental to its acceptance as a definitive statement of the law of armed conflict. Likewise, that the Brussels Declaration was the product of State lawyers, diplomats, and military men was also no doubt central to its acceptance as a statement of the extant law. That the Oxford Manual was not so wholeheartedly embraced may well have had something to do with its origins as well—its dismissal by military and political figures as a scholarly work that seemed not to reflect existing trends in practice might have been influenced by the fact that the Institute was an organisation of lawyers and jurists, rather than politicians and military personnel.

[125] See further the comments by the Russian delegate, General Leer, in which he outlined what he considered an appropriate compromise solution: *Actes de la Conférence de Bruxelles de 1874* (n 41) 50, comments beginning 'M. le général de Leer s'exprime, au sujet de cet article, dans les termes suivants'.

Impact of the 1909, 1913, and 1923 Rules on Naval and Air Warfare

Turning to the impact of the London Declaration and the Oxford Rules on Naval Warfare and the Hague Rules on Aerial Warfare, did these documents in any way impact either the law or the practice of warfare following their production? While the 1909 London Declaration was not adopted as a binding instrument, it was reportedly recognised by several belligerents during World War I[126] and was considered an accurate statement of the customary law of naval warfare for the time.[127] However, an equivalent positive assessment of the 1913 Oxford Manual on Naval Warfare cannot easily be made out, with Ronzitti noting that:

> if the document . . . had been intended as a compendium of the rules of naval warfare—whether customary norms or the treaty norms to be found in the various international instruments—it must be said that this objective was not achieved. Many existing rules were not recorded in the Manual, which does not, therefore, serve as the research and coordinating tool it sets out to be.[128]

The Oxford Manual on Naval Warfare seems not to have had the impact its drafters intended—at least not on contemporary practice, with none of the literature, either at the time or more recently, citing the Oxford Manual as having been used in State practice. However, the ICRC, in its 2017 Commentary on the Second Geneva Convention, does make the connection between the Oxford Manual on Naval Warfare and the Second Geneva Convention, stating that several of the provisions of the Manual 'are direct precursors of articles in the Convention'.[129]

In contrast, the Hague Rules on Air Warfare were received favourably at the time, with contemporary assessment considering it 'an authoritative attempt to clarify and formulate rules of law governing the use of aircraft in war'.[130] The Rules were adopted in practice by some States: the Royal Air Force was prepared to accept the Draft Rules as the basis of its own code of conduct for air warfare,[131] with the British government later declaring the applicability of the Rules in its conflict in Abyssinia

126 Roach (n 68) 66; Schindler and Toman (n 33) 1111.

127 Schindler and Toman (n 33) 1111; Elizabeth Chadwick, 'Merchant Ship Conversion in Warfare, the Falklands (Malvinas) Conflict and the Requisition of the QE2' (2010) 12 Journal of the History of International Law 71, 82.

128 Ronzitti (n 69) 340.

129 ICRC, *Commentary on the Second Geneva Convention: Convention (II) for the Amelioration of the Condition of the Wounded, Sick and Shipwrecked Members of Armed Forces at Sea* (2nd edn 2017) Introduction, para 89.

130 Lassa Oppenheim, *International Law: A Treatise*, vol 2: *War and Neutrality* (ed Hersch Lauterpacht, 7th edn, Longmans 1952) 519.

131 See the note of 14 October 1932 (PRO AIR 8/141): 'His Majesty's Government . . . [was] prepared to accept as a basis for further elaboration the rules for air bombardment contained in the Hague Draft of 1922–1923'.

in 1935.[132] At the outbreak of the Second World War, the Hague provisions on bombardment were also called upon by the United Kingdom in its Instructions Governing Naval and Air Bombardment, as issued to the Royal Air Force,[133] and by Germany in its own Instructions Governing Aerial Warfare.[134] Contemporary accounts of the practice of Italy and Japan also strongly indicate that the Hague Rules were being implemented into instructions to armed forces.[135] Additionally, the rules first proposed in 1923 would eventually find binding expression in 1977 in Additional Protocol I,[136] where extensive rules on the protection of the civilian population from indiscriminate attack,[137] prohibitions on terror bombing,[138] and the definition of a military objective[139] were codified, drawing heavily on equivalent provisions first outlined in the Hague Draft Rules on Air Warfare.

It is possible to theorise why these instruments were (or were not) accepted. The Oxford Manuals on land warfare and naval warfare both emanated from a non-State organisation, the Institute of International Law. That the documents were developed by a scholarly institution might have been part of the reason why States were reluctant to accept them, especially when one considers that the London Declaration—an instrument that emerged from a conference of State delegates—*was* adopted by some States during the First World War. Equally, the failure of the 1913 Oxford Manual to adequately catalogue the extant law on naval warfare might also have contributed to its failed impact. It is also conceivable that the Hague Draft Rules, which were drafted under the auspices of a State-sanctioned and selected Commission of Jurists, were more palatable to States precisely because they had State imprimatur.

Impact of the Tehran and Turku Declarations

Finally, in examining the reception of both the Tehran and Turku Declarations, there are commonalities in their impact (or lack of impact) when compared to the other soft law instruments examined in this chapter. The Tehran Declaration on

[132] Otto von Nostitz-Wallwitz, 'Das Kriegsrecht im Italienisch-Abessinischen Krieg' *ZaoRV* (1936) 720.

[133] PRO AIR 8/283.

[134] Bundesarchiv/Militararchiv, Frieburg/BR, RW 5/v 336. See further Hanke (n 88) 35.

[135] J Ray, 'Les bombardements aeriens: Quelque aspects de la position prise par le Japon', Revue generale de droit aerien, 1938, 418, cited in Hanke (n 88) 36. Indeed, in 1963, the Tokyo District Court, in *Shimoda v The State*, affirmed the customary status of the Rules, stating that 'students of international law regard them as authoritative on the law of air warfare [as] rules of customary law in view of the fact that these are also found in common in the rules of land and sea warfare': (1963) 32 ILR 626.

[136] Protocol Additional to the Geneva Conventions of 12 August 1949, and relating to the Protection of Victims of International Armed Conflicts (Protocol I) (adopted 8 June 1977, entered into force 7 December 1978) 1125 UNTS 3 (Protocol I or API).

[137] API, Art 51(4)–(5).

[138] API, Art 51(2).

[139] API, Art 52(2).

Human Rights in Armed Conflict would have a significant impact on the development of IHL in the decade following its adoption. Following on from the Tehran Conference, it became commonplace for the United Nations to issue resolutions calling on States to respect human rights in armed conflicts. The first of these was Resolution 2444 (XXIII) on Respect for Human Rights in Armed Conflict.[140] Resolution 2444, unanimously adopted, recognised 'the necessity of applying basic humanitarian principles in all armed conflicts'[141] and stated that certain principles should be observed 'by all governmental and other authorities responsible for action in armed conflicts'.[142] In 1969, the UN Secretary-General issued a report on 'Respect for Human Rights in Armed Conflicts';[143] additional resolutions in respect for human rights in armed conflict followed, including Resolutions 2597,[144] 2674,[145] 2676,[146] 2677,[147] 2852,[148] 2853,[149] 3032,[150] 3102,[151] 3500,[152] 31/19,[153] and 32/44.[154]

That human rights law has a place in situations of armed conflict is now largely uncontested. While the Tehran Declaration on Human Rights did not initiate this merger between international human rights law and IHL,[155] it *has* been hailed by a number of commentators as pivotal in solidifying the merger.[156] As noted by Louise Doswald-Beck and Sylvain Vité, the Tehran Declaration was '[t]he true turning point, when humanitarian law and human rights gradually began to draw closer',[157] and

[140] 23 UN GAOR, Supp (No 18), UN Doc A/7433 (18 December 1968).
[141] ibid.
[142] ibid.
[143] UN Secretary-General, Report on Respect for Human Rights in Armed Conflicts, UN Doc A/7720 (20 November 1969), 11, 59–63, Sections 183–201.
[144] 24 UN GAOR Supp (No 30), UN Doc A/7909 (16 December 1969).
[145] 25 UN GAOR Supp (No 28), UN Doc A/8178 (9 December 1970).
[146] 25 UN GAOR Supp (No 28), UN Doc A/8178 (9 December 1970).
[147] 25 UN GAOR Supp (No 28), UN Doc A/8028 (9 December 1970).
[148] 26 UN GAOR Supp (No 29), UN Doc A/8429 (20 December 1971).
[149] 26 UN GAOR Supp (No 29), UN Doc A/8589 (20 December 1971).
[150] 27 UN GAOR Supp (No 30), UN Doc A/8966 (18 December 1972).
[151] 28 UN GAOR Supp (No 30), UN Doc A/9030 (12 December 1973).
[152] 30 UN GAOR Supp (No 34), UN Doc A/10463 (15 December 1975).
[153] 31 UN GAOR Supp (No 39), UN Doc A/31/295 (24 November 1976).
[154] 32 UN GAOR Supp (No 45), UN Doc A/32/396 (8 December 1977).
[155] See Noëlle Quénivet, 'The History of the Relationship between International Humanitarian Law and Human Rights Law' in Roberta Arnold and Noëlle Quénivet (eds), *International Humanitarian Law and Human Rights Law: Towards a New Merger in International Law* (Martinus Nijhoff 2008). See also Robert Kolb, 'The Relationship between International Humanitarian Law and Human Rights Law: A Brief History of the 1948 Universal Declaration of Human Rights and the 1949 Geneva Conventions' (1998) 324 International Review of the Red Cross 400, 409–19.
[156] Robert Kolb, 'Human Rights Law and International Humanitarian Law between 1945 and the Aftermath of the Teheran Conference of 1968' in Robert Kolb and Gloria Gaggioli (eds), *Research Handbook on Human Rights and Humanitarian Law* (Elgar 2013) 45; Louise Doswald-Beck and Sylvain Vité, 'Origin and Nature of Human Rights Law and Humanitarian Law' (1993) 293 International Review of the Red Cross 94, 94.
[157] Doswald-Beck and Vité (n 156) 112. See also Kolb, 'The Relationship between International Humanitarian Law and Human Rights Law' (n 155) 419.

the Additional Protocols of 1977 were the logical end product of the work of the 1968 Conference.[158]

Far less impactful was the Turku Declaration. Despite influential advocates, a declaration on fundamental standards of humanity has not been adopted by the United Nations, with the declaration last appearing on the UN agenda in 2008.[159] In the absence of 'official sanction' from the United Nations, the Turku Declaration, 'an important and useful document in its own right ... does not carry the imprimatur of an official text, formally agreed to by states ... the unofficial character of the text weakens its significance as a document intended to further develop international law'.[160] The lack of success of the Turku Declaration contrasts with the significant impact of the Tehran Declaration and raises questions as to whether the origins of and advocates for non-binding instruments effect how such instruments are received—something discussed in more detail in Chapter 8.

Concluding Thoughts on the History of Non-Binding Instruments in International Humanitarian Law

Non-binding documents have long been a part of the law of armed conflict and have proven, in some limited instances, to be useful tools for participants in armed conflicts. The next chapter of this book turns to examine two of the more impactful non-binding instruments that still have purchase today: the special agreements provision in Common Article 3 and the amnesty recommendation of Additional Protocol II.

158 'The adoption in 1977 of the two Protocols additional to the 1949 Geneva Conventions was, in a certain sense, a reflection of what had happened in Tehran nine years earlier': Doswald-Beck and Vité (n 156) 113.

159 UN Doc A/HRC/8/14 (3 June 2008).

160 Petrasek (n 116) 558.

3
Non-Binding Provisions in Binding Instruments

Introduction

As noted in Chapter 2, there is a long history of production, adoption, and utilisation of non-binding instruments in international humanitarian law (IHL). Whether the instruments were intended as non-binding, or whether their non-binding character was accidental, States have engaged with non-binding IHL instruments alongside binding IHL treaties. Additionally, non-binding standards have been included in binding treaties, most notably in the instruments related to the regulation of conduct in non-international armed conflict. Both Common Article 3 and Additional Protocol II contain non-binding standards that strongly encourage a particular course of action for parties to those instruments. Common Article 3 includes a provision that the 'Parties to the conflict should further endeavour to bring into force, by means of special agreements, all or part of the other provisions of the present Convention'.[1] Additional Protocol II includes a provision encouraging the authorities in power following the cessation of hostilities 'to grant the broadest possible amnesty to persons who have participated in the armed conflict, or those deprived of their liberty for reasons related to the armed conflict, whether they are interned or detained'.[2] This chapter will examine the drafting history of these two standards to explore why they were included in the Conventions and in Protocol II, whether these standards have been implemented, and how and why non-binding standards have been received by States and non-State groups. Of particular interest for this study is whether the inclusion of these non-binding standards within an existing binding treaty made it more likely that the standard would be implemented, and what that says about the nature of non-binding instruments and standards more generally.

[1] Common Article 3.
[2] APII, Art 6(5).

Non-Binding Norms in International Humanitarian Law. Emily Crawford, Oxford University Press. © Emily Crawford 2021.
DOI: 10.1093/oso/9780198819851.003.0004

Common Article 3's Special Agreements Provision in Historical Context, Theory, and Practice

The drafting history of Common Article 3 has been well-documented,[3] but it is helpful to briefly mention a few points in relation to the origins of international regulation of non-international armed conflicts. For some years prior to the adoption of Common Article 3, the International Committee of the Red Cross (ICRC) had advocated for internal armed conflicts to be regulated with the same scope and depth as international armed conflicts under international law. However, when States met at Geneva in 1949, they rejected such an expansive approach, preferring instead to embrace the narrower, more general principles of Common Article 3. Nonetheless, hopes for an expansive law of internal armed conflict were not entirely lost, but channelled instead into the special agreements provision of Common Article 3. The special agreements provision is a direct result of attempts by the ICRC in the decades leading up to the 1949 Conventions to broaden the application of the law of armed conflict to all types of armed conflict.

The Historical Background to the Adoption of Common Article 3 and the Special Agreements Provision

At the earliest stages of the development of the treaty law of armed conflict, both States and the ICRC believed that the international law of armed conflict should *not* extend to regulating internal conflicts. In 1863, the ICRC, at its second meeting, stated that the soon-to-be adopted Geneva Convention should not extend to internal armed conflicts.[4] States were also unwilling to accept the applicability of international law to civil wars, unless such conflicts reached a certain high-level degree of intensity and scope, and were impacting on the rights and obligations of neutral States.[5]

[3] See generally Sandesh Sivakumaran, *The Law of Non-International Armed Conflict* (OUP 2012) 35–42; Laura Perna, *The Formation of the Treaty Law of Non-International Armed Conflicts* (Martinus Nijhoff 2006) 49–60; Lindsay Moir, *The Law of Internal Armed Conflicts* (CUP 2002) 23–29; Anthony Cullen, *The Concept of Non-International Armed Conflict in International Humanitarian Law* (CUP 2012) 27–51.

[4] '[T]he Committee agreed, first and foremost, that, in its opinion, no action should be contemplated during civil wars, and that the [national] Committees should concern themselves only with European wars': ICRC, Meeting of 17 February 1863, minutes reprinted and translated in (1963) 3 International Review of the Red Cross 63, 67. The head of the Committee, Gustave Moynier, reaffirmed this statement in his 1870 work *Étude sur la convention de Genève pour l'amélioration du sort des militaires blessés dans les armées en campagne (1864 et 1868)*, stating that, regarding civil wars, 'international laws are not applicable to them' ('Nous ne parlons pas, cela va sans dire, des guerres civiles; les lois internationals ne leur sont pas applicables'): ibid 304.

[5] In such situations, States could choose to recognise the situation as one of belligerency under international law, which included consideration of factors such as '[w]hether the insurrection has or has not assumed the dimensions of war, and whether the legitimate interests of the neutral State do, or do not, require that she should claim from both parties the performance towards her of the obligations incident

However, during the first decades of the twentieth century, the ICRC and the national Red Cross and Red Crescent societies were increasingly involving themselves in internal conflicts.[6] By the XVIth ICRC Conference in 1938, the ICRC, informed by the civil conflict that had beset Spain during the 1930s, began to systematically advocate for the extension of international law to non-international armed conflicts.[7] When the societies were able to reconvene after the end of the Second World War,[8] the agenda for debate was the possibility of revision of the Geneva Conventions of 1929—debate that would ultimately lead to the adoption of the 1949 Geneva Conventions. One of the topics for consideration was allowing the Conventions to apply in their entirety to any cases of 'armed conflict within the borders of a State'.[9] The ICRC optimistically stated of such an approach: 'it is anticipated that no State or insurgent body would venture to proclaim, in the face of world opinion, its intention of disregarding the laws of humanity, whose value and essential character are universally recognised'.[10]

The work of the Preliminary Conference was transmitted to the Conference of Government Experts, which convened in April 1947 to consider the draft conventions. When the issue of expanding the Conventions to regulate civil wars was considered, the 1947 Conference declined to embrace the expansive approach advocated by the Preliminary Conference, instead stating that 'in case of civil war ... the *principles* of the Convention shall be equally applied by the said Party, subject to the adverse Party also conforming thereto'.[11] Revisions to the draft

to the status of belligerent ... the length of time during which the contest has existed; the number, order, and discipline of the rebel forces; their subordination to a de facto existing Government, capable of maintaining international relations with foreign States; the acts of the Government against which the rebels are in arms, both with respect to the rebels themselves and to foreign States': Opinion of the Law Officers (JB Karslake, CJ Selwyn, and R Phillimore) (14 August 1867), reprinted in Arnold McNair, *International Law Opinions, Selected and Annotated*, vol 1: *Peace* (CUP 1956) 143, 144. See also Robert McLaughlin, *Recognition of Belligerency and the Law of Armed Conflict* (OUP 2020).

[6] Sivakumaran, *The Law of Non-International Armed Conflict* (n 3) 31–35.

[7] Report of the ICRC to the XVIth International Red Cross Conference, London, June 1938, ICRC, 'Le Role et l'action de la Croix-Rouge en Temps de Guerre Civile' (1938) 20 Revue internationale de la Croix-Rouge 97, 110. See also Resolution XIV, 'Role and Activity of the Red Cross in time of Civil War', XVIth International Red Cross Conference, London, 1938. The Seventeenth Conference, which was to be held in 1942, was delayed by the hostilities of the Second World War (noted in the 1947 letter from the ICRC President, Count Folke Bernadotte, to the Presidents of the Central Committees of the Red Cross and Red Crescent Societies, reprinted in the *Report of the Seventeenth International Red Cross Conference, Stockholm, August 1948* (ICRC 1948) 3).

[8] ICRC, Circular Letter No 371, September 10, 1945, noted in ICRC, *Report on the Work of the Preliminary Conference of the National Red Cross Societies for the Study of the Conventions and of Various Problems Relative to the Red Cross, Geneva, July 26–August 3, 1946* (ICRC 1947) 1.

[9] ICRC, *Report on the Work of the Preliminary Conference* (n 8) 15.

[10] ibid. It is noteworthy that between the ICRC and the national societies, it was the ICRC that had been the more restrained in its recommendations. The ICRC had originally suggested that the new Conventions merely 'invite' States to apply the Conventions in their entirety in situations of civil war (and on the basis of reciprocity). However, the national societies took the position that States should be compelled, rather than invited, to apply the Conventions (but still bound by the principle of reciprocity): ibid.

[11] ICRC, *Report on the Work of the Conference of Government Experts for the Study of the Conventions for the Protection of War Victims (Geneva, April 14–26, 1947)* (ICRC 1947) 8 (emphasis added).

Convention were made,[12] with the new revised text dispensing with the provision that equal application of the Convention was 'subject to the adverse Party also conforming thereto', but retaining the wording that in civil war it was the 'principles' of the Convention that were to apply, and not the 'provisions'.[13]

At the Diplomatic Conference in Geneva, the question of extending international regulation to non-international armed conflict was, unsurprisingly, contentious.[14] Delegates from China,[15] the United States,[16] the United Kingdom,[17] France,[18] Greece,[19] Canada,[20] and Burma[21] were among those who voiced their concerns that too broad an extension of international protections to situations of internal conflict would present 'a very serious danger to sovereignty',[22] and that wholesale importation of the rules of international armed conflict to non-international armed conflict would bring immense 'practical difficulty'[23] for those obligated to apply such provisions. Divided opinion as to what kinds of internal conflict should be regulated, and to what degree, led to the formation of a special committee tasked with revising the provision of non-international armed conflict.[24]

[12] ICRC, *Draft Revised or New Conventions for The Protection of War Victims, Established by the International Committee of the Red Cross with the Assistance of Government Experts, National Red Cross Societies and other Humanitarian Associations* (ICRC May 1948).

[13] ibid Draft Art 2. However, this approach was, it seems, not intentional, but rather the result of an error in translation, whereby the French version of the text, which affirmed the idea of applying the provisions of the Conventions ('les dispositions de la présente Convention': Comité International de la Croix-Rouge (CICR), *Projets de Conventions Revisées ou Nouvelles Protégeant les Victimes de la Guerre* (CICR, May 1948) 6); the error was acknowledged at the Seventeenth International Conference (*VXIIe Conference Internationale de la Croix-Rouge (Stockholm, Août 1948), Commission Juridique, Sténogramme des Séances* Janvier 1949, 46: 'Il y a une erreur de traduction'). Sivakumaran considers this change the result of a simple translation error: Sivakumaran, *The Law of Non-International Armed Conflict* (n 3) 38. He notes, however, that David Elder considered the change intentional ('a slight but eminently important change was made; the term "principles" was replaced with "provisions", which marked a return to the initial proposal of the Preliminary Conference of National Red Cross Societies': David Elder, 'The Historical Background of Common Article 3 of the Geneva Convention of 1949' (1979) 11 Case Western Reserve Journal of International Law 37, 43).

[14] For a more detailed examination of the discussion around regulation of non-international armed conflict during the 1949 Geneva Conference, see Sivakumaran, *The Law of Non-International Armed Conflict* (n 3) 40–42; Cullen, *The Concept of Non-International Armed Conflict* (n 3) 27–51; Perna (n 3) 49–60. The discussion on what would become Common Article 3 (but was initially Article 2, then Article 2A) can be found in the *Final Record of the Diplomatic Conference of Geneva of 1949* (Federal Political Department, Berne) vol IIB, 9–16, 36–37, 38–39, 40–50, 53–55, 78–79, 82–84, 93–95, 97–102, 106, 120–27, 129, 325–39, 388.

[15] Final Record IIB (n 14) 12.

[16] ibid.

[17] ibid 10.

[18] ibid.

[19] ibid 10–11.

[20] ibid 13.

[21] ibid 15.

[22] ibid 327.

[23] ibid 10 (comments by Britain).

[24] ibid 16. An early attempt to introduce a provision prohibiting prosecution of persons taking direct part in a non-international armed conflict failed to be accepted (ibid 44 (comments by Norway)) but would resurface in debates surrounding the negotiation of the Additional Protocols in the 1970s.

It was in this Committee that the concept of 'special agreements' first made an appearance:[25] in an attempt to come to an agreement regarding when the Conventions should come into effect in a non-international armed conflict, a working party of the Special Committee drafted provisions that would have the Conventions apply in their entirety when recognition of belligerency occurred, or where the adverse party in a non-international armed conflict demonstrated the characteristics of a State.[26] However, in situations where neither recognition of belligerency nor de facto Statehood could be found, 'the parties to the conflict should endeavour to bring into force, by means of special agreements, all or part of the provisions of the present Convention, or, in all circumstances, to act in accordance with the underlying humanitarian principles of the present Convention'.[27] The text as submitted was considered by the Special Committee as being too onerous, with the delegate from the ICRC noting that if such a provision had been in place in the law, it 'could never have been applied in any recent case of civil war'[28] and thus 'did not represent a progress with regard to the present situation'.[29] This opinion was shared by other members of the Special Committee,[30] and the working party was asked to redraft the provision.[31]

Several texts were drafted and submitted to the Special Committee,[32] which attempted to either limit the number of Convention provisions that would apply to non-international armed conflicts, or limit the kinds of non-international armed conflicts to which the Conventions in their entirety would apply. In nearly all permutations, however, the special agreements provision was retained.[33] Drafts

[25] The idea that States should be 'invited to declare their readiness to apply the principles of the Convention' was first raised during the Work of the Preliminary Conference: *Report on the Work of the Preliminary Conference* (n 8) 15. However, this suggestion did not take the form of a special agreements provision. That is to say, the proposal at the Preliminary Conference was that the Conventions should apply to civil wars based on reciprocity, rather than on any requirement of States and non-State armed groups to separately negotiate a special agreement.

[26] Final Record IIB (n 14) 46–47.

[27] ibid 47.

[28] ibid 48 (Claude Pilloud).

[29] ibid.

[30] Such as the USSR: ibid.

[31] For the various permutations of the non-international armed conflict provision as drafted by the Working Party, see ibid 124–27.

[32] ibid 83. The USSR proposed revisions that would have deleted the 'special agreements' paragraph, along with the paragraph relating to ICRC assistance. Its proposed provision would have seen all parties to the conflict obliged to apply 'all the provisions of the present Convention' that guaranteed certain minimum fundamental standards: ibid 98. This would have rendered the special agreements provision unnecessary. The provision was specifically rejected by the United Kingdom, which felt that the special agreements provision was a necessary element to retain because 'if civil war developed to considerable proportions, there would be an inclination of both sides to introduce, by special agreements, as many as possible of the provisions of the Convention. It would therefore seem appropriate not to delete the paragraph on special agreements': ibid.

[33] Save for one attempt by the Soviet delegate, who felt that having a special agreements provision, rather than an obligatory application of the Conventions, 'would inevitably entail the renunciation of many provisions drawn up by the Conference for the protection of war victims:' ibid 98. However, Soviet delegate Morosov was eventually convinced of the virtue of retaining the special agreements provision: ibid 99.

and amendments were then taken to plenary for a vote, with several delegations speaking at length in favour of or against the article.[34] Ultimately, after choosing not to define non-international armed conflict as a concept and taking the '"principles" rather than the "provisions" approach',[35] Common Article 3 was adopted.

Central to the adoption of the special agreements provision (and of Common Article 3 in its entirety)[36] was the inclusion of paragraph 4 of Common Article 3: that 'the application of the preceding provisions shall not affect the legal status of the Parties to the conflict'.[37] The inclusion of this paragraph was pivotal to assuaging concerns, such as those voiced by Burma during the 1949 Conference, that the application of Common Article 3 during a non-international armed conflict would result in giving 'legal status to insurgents who sought by undemocratic methods, to overthrow a legally constituted government by force of arms'.[38] By including this provision, States reaffirmed their commitment to humanitarian ideals, while still acknowledging that the application of Common Article 3 did not alter the legal status of non-State parties, as the formal recognition of belligerency once did.

Common Article 3 Special Agreements—Scope and Interpretation of the Provision

Common Article 3, as finally adopted in the 1949 Geneva Conventions, provides that '[t]he Parties to the conflict should further endeavour to bring into force, by means of special agreements, all or part of the other provisions of the present Convention'. This provision, seemingly straightforward, has been subject to several possible interpretations regarding its scope and possible implementation. The first of these—namely, the binding force of the special agreements provision—is relatively easy to settle. A literal interpretation of the provision would hold that it acts merely as recommendatory practice. Parties involved in a Common Article 3 non-international armed conflict may, if they wish, decide to conclude an agreement between themselves to bring all or part of the entirety of the Geneva Conventions into effect to govern their behaviour during the non-international armed conflict.

[34] ibid 325–39.

[35] Sivakumaran, *The Law of Non-International Armed Conflict* (n 3) 42.

[36] As noted in the 2017 ICRC Commentary: 'The drafting history of the provision is straightforward. It was first suggested at the Conference of Government Experts convened by the ICRC in 1947 and was reintroduced with very little change in all successive drafts. Without it, neither common Article 3, nor any other article in its place, could have been adopted.' ICRC, *Commentary on the Second Geneva Convention: Convention (II) for the Amelioration of the Condition of the Wounded, Sick and Shipwrecked Members of Armed Forces at Sea* (2nd edn, 2017) para 889. See also *Report on the Work of the Conference of Government Experts* (n 11) 9.

[37] Common Article 3, para 4.

[38] Final Record IIB (n 14) (comments by Burma) 15, 102.

However, some publicists, most notably Jean Pictet in the 1952 Commentary to Geneva Convention I,[39] believed that the special agreements provision went beyond a mere invitation and was closer to a binding obligation:

> The provision does not merely offer a convenient possibility, but makes an urgent request, points out a duty: 'The Parties to the conflict should further endeavour . . .'. Although the only provisions which the individual Parties are bound to apply unilaterally are those contained in Article 3, they are nevertheless under an obligation to try to bring about a fuller application of the Convention by means of a bilateral agreement.[40]

This interpretation is reaffirmed in the 2016 ICRC Commentary to Geneva Convention I, where it is argued that:

> more than merely pointing out the possibility for the Parties to conclude such agreements, the provision encourages the Parties to make serious effort to bring into force obligations to protect victims and to limit the suffering caused by the armed conflict. The pressing nature of this exhortation is confirmed by the French version of the article, which uses the word 's'efforceront'.[41]

Such an interpretation is appealing for those hoping to apply the Conventions as broadly and as comprehensively as possible. Indeed, there is some logic in arguing that, because the provision is included in a binding treaty, and because it uses the imperative 'should', then such a non-binding recommendatory course of action should be given more weight, and should have more normative force, than a mere entreaty in a non-binding instrument suggesting only best practice. However, given the express intentions of the States at Geneva to *not* have the Conventions in their entirety apply in situations of internal conflict,[42] and considering subsequent practice (examined in the next section of this chapter, and in more detail in Chapter 7 of this book), such an optimistic interpretation of the normative force of

[39] Geneva Convention (I) for the Amelioration of the Condition of the Wounded and Sick in Armed Forces in the Field (adopted 12 August 1949, entered into force 21 October 1950) 75 UNTS 31 (Geneva Convention I or GC I).

[40] Jean Pictet (ed), *Commentary on the Geneva Conventions of 12 August 1949*, vol 1: *Geneva Convention for the Amelioration of the Condition of the Wounded and Sick in Armed Forces in the Field* (ICRC 1952) 59.

[41] ICRC, *Commentary on the First Geneva Convention: Convention (I) for the Amelioration of the Condition of the Wounded and Sick in Armed Forces in the Field* (2nd edn, ICRC 2016) para 848 <https://ihl-databases.icrc.org/applic/ihl/ihl.nsf/Comment.xsp?action = openDocument&documentId = 59F6CDFA490736C1C1257F7D004BA0EC> accessed 30 July 2021. *S'Efforceront* literally translates as 'to try hard' to do something: *Pocket Oxford-Hachette French Dictionary: French-English* (4th edn, Oxford 2012). A survey of several French legal dictionaries indicates that the word does not have a unique legal definition or character distinct from its ordinary meaning.

[42] See above regarding the discussions at Geneva in 1949.

the special agreements provision seems unlikely. Rather, the literal interpretation of the terms 'should further endeavour' is most appropriate.

Other questions relevant to interpretation arise. First, does the special agreements provision relate only to agreements between a State and an armed opposition group, or can it exist between two or more opposition groups that are party to a non-international armed conflict? Whether a Common Article 3 special agreement could include a third party, such as the United Nations or the ICRC, is not clear on the text of the provision. The Pictet Commentary to the Conventions seems to suggest that special agreements would only exist between States and armed opposition groups,[43] with the Commentary discussing the special agreements provision as something involving a rebel party and a *de jure* government—that is, a State and an armed opposition group.[44] However, the special agreements provision, as well as Common Article 3 more generally, refers only to 'Parties to the conflict', giving no indication that one of those Parties must be the State. It therefore seems reasonable to argue that a special agreement negotiated between two (or more) armed opposition groups engaged in a Common Article 3 armed conflict would still be considered a Common Article 3 special agreement.[45] As to whether a third party (that is, one not involved in the conflict) could be party to a Common Article 3 special agreement, the situation is less clear. The wording of Common Article 3 does not indicate whether third parties such as the United Nations or the ICRC would be excluded from concluding such treaties. Some of the literature suggests that such agreements would be included in Common Article 3, provided they were bilateral or multilateral agreements to implement provisions of IHL.[46] Therefore:

> an agreement between one party to the conflict and a third party comes under the purview of Common Article 3 only if it concerns the rights and obligations of all

[43] '[Common Article 3] applies to non-international armed conflicts only, and is only applicable to them until such time as a special agreement between the Parties has brought into force between them all or part of the other provisions of the Convention': Pictet, *Commentary on the Geneva Conventions*, vol 1 (n 40) 48; see also 59–60.

[44] See the wording used by Pictet: ibid.

[45] Liesbeth Zegveld, *The Accountability of Armed Opposition Groups in International Law* (CUP 2002) 29, who argues that a special agreement could exist between non-State parties to an armed conflict. See, for example, the Acte d'Engagement, a multilateral agreement between armed groups fighting in the Democratic Republic of the Congo to ensure 'strict observation of the rules of international humanitarian and human rights law' (the original agreement is in French: 'Article III: Des Principes Humanitaires Et Du Respect Des Droits De L'homme: Observation stricte des règles du droit international humanitaire et des droite de l'Homme') <https://peacemaker.un.org/sites/peacemaker.un.org/files/CD_080123_Acte%20d%27Engagement%2C%20Nord%20Kivu%20%28French%29.pdf> accessed 30 July 2021.

[46] Zegveld (n 45) 29, who argues that a special agreement could also exist between a party to the conflict and an organisation such as the ICRC. The 2017 ICRC Commentary to the Conventions also suggests that agreements involving international organisations can be considered special agreements under Common Article 3. 'What counts is the expression of consent of the Parties to respect or implement humanitarian law or specific obligations': ICRC, *Commentary on the Second Geneva Convention* (n 36) paras 852, 855–56.

> the contracting parties in terms of [IHL]. This means that if an agreement contains only a unilateral (not bilateral) undertaking by one party to the conflict to respect IHL or specifies only the rights and obligations of the third party, it cannot be considered as covered by Common Article 3.[47]

Must a special agreement only bring the Conventions into play, or can there be agreements to bring in other IHL or even human rights law rules? A narrow reading of the provision would suggest that 'only an agreement that explicitly brings into force other provisions of one or more of the four Geneva Conventions'[48] can be a special agreement. However, most of the literature advocates a broader view—that so long as *some* provisions of the Geneva Conventions are brought into effect by the agreement, it remains a Common Article 3 special agreement, regardless of whether human rights law norms are also introduced. As the ICRC Commentary to the Conventions notes:

> [a]s the purpose of the provision is to encourage Parties to an armed conflict to agree to a more comprehensive set of norms that protect those who are not or no longer taking direct part in hostilities, however, special agreements providing for the implementation of customary international humanitarian law, or which encompass a broader set of norms than those set down in the Geneva Conventions, in particular those of Additional Protocol I, may be considered special agreements under common Article 3.[49]

The Clapham Commentary to the Conventions concurs, stating that '[i]n our view also those agreements that, though formally not stipulated by virtue of Common Article 3, aim at putting in place additional humanitarian rules between the parties to the conflict, should qualify as ad hoc agreements since they fulfil the same objective pursued by Common Article 3 paragraph 3'.[50]

[47] Andrew Clapham, Paola Gaeta, and Marco Sassòli (eds), *The 1949 Geneva Conventions: A Commentary* (OUP 2016) 510, para 3.

[48] ICRC, *Commentary on the Second Geneva Convention* (n 36) para 846.

[49] ibid.

[50] Clapham, Gaeta, and Sassòli (n 47) 511. However, the Clapham Commentary adds the proviso that 'ad hoc agreements within the meaning of Common Article 3 of those mutual engagements that, though pursuing other than humanitarian aims, for example a ceasefire or peace proper, also contain rules of a humanitarian nature' should not be considered Common Article 3 special agreements 'since their prevailing object and purpose are not humanitarian': ibid 511. cf the 2017 ICRC Commentary, which argues that peace agreements and ceasefires could constitute Common Article 3 special agreements. '[I]t should be recalled that "peace agreements" concluded with a view to bringing an end to hostilities may contain provisions drawn from other humanitarian law treaties, such as the granting of amnesty for fighters . . . the release of all captured persons, or a commitment to search for the missing. If they contain provisions drawn from humanitarian law, or if they implement humanitarian law obligations already incumbent on the Parties, such agreements, or the relevant provisions as the case may be, may constitute special agreements under common Article 3': ICRC, *Commentary on the Second Geneva Convention* (n 36) para 850.

There seems no set rule as to what a special agreement should contain; it may simply be an agreement to apply the Conventions in their entirety[51] or it may be more limited, agreeing to apply parts of the Conventions. Any special agreement must not derogate from the minimum applicable IHL rules already in effect that a Party to the conflict may be obligated to apply (for instance, any obligations under treaties protecting cultural property, or banning the use of certain kinds of weapons). Logically, also, any special agreement may not purport to derogate from the protections outlined in Common Article 3. This is made clear from a plain reading of Common Article 3, which provides that 'each Party to the conflict shall be bound to apply, as a minimum, the following provisions'[52] of Common Article 3. A Common Article 3 special agreement would need to reaffirm the applicability of Common Article 3, and then extend the applicable law, even if only by reference to one additional provision of the Geneva Conventions proper, 'because the rationale underlying the Article is to bring into force IHL rules that would not otherwise bind the parties'.[53] Practice in relation to special agreements (discussed in more detail below and in Chapter 7) demonstrates that such agreements have tended to refer either 'generally to the Geneva Conventions, to some specific provisions of one or more of the Geneva Conventions, or by reformulating all or part of one or more Conventions'.[54]

One last question remains: are peace agreements special agreements under Common Article 3? An expansive approach to Common Article 3 special agreements would support an affirmative conclusion—that any agreement between parties to a non-international armed conflict in relation to the conduct of the armed conflict (including the termination of the conflict) is a special agreement under the Conventions. A narrow approach would hold that a peace agreement is not a Common Article special agreement unless it specifically brings 'into force ... all or part of the other provisions of the present Convention'.[55] The Geneva Conventions contain provisions regarding obligations applicable after the cessation of active hostilities (such as provisions on prisoners of war and occupied territory); therefore, *any* agreement that includes such provisions would be a Common Article 3 special agreement, even if included in a peace agreement. However, any agreement to bring about a ceasefire or armistice that *does not* include any reference to Geneva Conventions provisions, or to more general provisions of the law applicable in times of armed conflict, would not be a Common Article 3 special agreement.

[51] Indeed, this is the preferred approach outlined in the Pictet Commentary, which argues that in situations where more extensive IHL protections are necessary, then 'surely the most practical way of doing it is not to negotiate special agreements in great detail, but simply to refer to the Convention as it stands, or at all events to certain of its provisions': Pictet, *Commentary on the Geneva Conventions* (n 40) 59.

[52] Common Article 3, first sentence.

[53] Clapham, Gaeta, and Sassòli (n 47) 512, para 9.

[54] ibid 512, para 10.

[55] Common Article 3.

For the purposes of this book, the latter approach will be taken and only agreements containing Geneva Conventions provisions (or more general treaty or customary IHL) will be considered special agreements. Unilateral declarations by parties to the armed conflict to apply the Geneva Conventions will *not* be considered special agreements; rather, the agreements must be a bilateral or multilateral agreement between one or more parties to the conflict. This would include, however, bilateral or multilateral agreements that involve organisations such as the ICRC or the United Nations, which, according to Andrew Clapham, Paola Gaeta, and Marco Sassòli, 'comes under the purview of Common Article 3 only if it concerns the rights and obligations of all the contracting parties in terms of [IHL]'.[56] Whether Common Article 3 special agreements have been implemented in practice will be discussed further in Chapter 7.

Additional Protocol II's Amnesty Provision in Historical Context, Theory, and Practice

In the years following the adoption of Common Article 3, the deficiencies of its limited provisions were made clear.[57] While the adoption of any international legal regulation for non-international armed conflicts was ground-breaking,[58] the *de minimus* provisions of the article proved insufficient to the task of appropriately regulating conduct in non-international armed conflicts, which were becoming more frequent events.[59] The ICRC was at the forefront of calls to adopt new rules, which would become the 1977 Additional Protocols.[60]

Contained in Additional Protocol II was a hortatory provision, Article 6(5), that encouraged the authorities in government at the cessation of hostilities to 'grant the broadest possible amnesty to persons who have participated in the armed conflict, or those deprived of their liberty for reasons related to the armed conflict,

[56] Clapham, Gaeta, and Sassòli (n 47) 510, para 3.

[57] See the ICRC, in the Report submitted to the XXIst International Conference of the Red Cross, Istanbul, in September 1969, entitled *Reaffirmation and Development of the Law and Customs Applicable in Armed Conflicts: Report Submitted by the International Committee of the Red Cross, May 1969*. 'It has become clear to the ICRC, from its experience, that the existing provisions fail to meet all the humanitarian requirements of such conflicts. Article 3 common to the four Geneva Conventions especially, valuable as it has already proved to the ICRC, has in practice revealed inadequacies': ibid 98.

[58] Anthony Cullen, 'Key Developments Affecting the Scope of Internal Armed Conflict in International Humanitarian Law' (2005) 183 Military Law Review 66, 79–84.

[59] See generally Boško Jakovljević and Jovica Patrnogić, 'The Urgent Need to Apply the Rules of Humanitarian Law to So-Called Internal Armed Conflicts' (1961) 1 International Review of the Red Cross 250, noting that the non-international armed conflicts that had taken place since the Conventions came into force in 1950 'have unfortunately exposed one of the fundamental weaknesses of the Geneva Conventions, which is the following: the Conventions do not accord effective protection to victims of such conflicts, not having been nor are they being applied on such occasions, since conflicts of this sort are not of an "international character"': ibid 252.

[60] ICRC, *Reaffirmation and Development of the Law and Customs Applicable in Armed Conflicts* (n 57) 98.

whether they are interned or detained'.[61] As with the above section on Common Article 3, it is useful to know a little of the historical background that led to the adoption of Additional Protocol II in 1977. Specifically, it is helpful to examine how the question of non-State armed fighters in non-international armed conflict was dealt with during the drafting of Additional Protocol II.

The Historical Background to the Adoption of Additional Protocol II and Article 6(5) Amnesties

During the early discussions on the proposed Additional Protocols, there had been thoughts regarding the extension of some form of combatant status (or, at the very least, prisoner-of-war treatment) to fighters in non-international armed conflicts.[62] The move to extending combatant status was part of early advocacy by some States and the ICRC to expand the law of armed conflict to cover more, if not all, situations of armed conflict, regardless of whether such conflicts were international or non-international. This advocacy was informed by the shortcomings of Common Article 3, which were made clear almost immediately after the adoption of the Geneva Conventions in 1949. As early as 1956, only six years after the Conventions came into force, the ICRC was already advocating for additional rules to guide behaviour in all armed conflicts, including armed conflicts 'not of an international character',[63] driven by the knowledge that, '[i]n view of the developments which have taken place in methods of making war, and the continual invention of new weapons, a conflict would today be a catastrophe out of all proportion to the ends it might be hoped to attain'.[64]

That non-international armed conflicts were more frequent, and were frequently more brutal and protracted, was of increasing concern to the ICRC during this time. The XXth International Conference of the Red Cross in Vienna in 1965 adopted two resolutions that acknowledged the paucity of the law relating to non-international armed conflicts.[65] By 1969, the ICRC had reached out to a group of

[61] APII, Art 6(5).

[62] See Article 25 of the ICRC Draft Additional Protocol II submitted to the 1972 Conference of Government Experts. 'Members of regular armed forces and members of those armed forces which have fulfilled the conditions stipulated in Article 4 A (2) of the Geneva Convention relative to the Treatment of Prisoners of War of August 12, 1949, shall receive, after having fallen into the power of the adversary, a treatment similar to that provided for prisoners of war in the said Convention': ICRC, *Conference of Government Experts on the Reaffirmation and Development of International Humanitarian Law Applicable in Armed Conflicts, Second Session, 3 May–3 June 1972, Report on the Work of the Conference* (1972) vol I, 78.

[63] 1956 Draft Rules for the Limitation of the Dangers Incurred by the Civilian Population in Time of War, Art 2(b).

[64] ibid 3 (introduction to the draft prepared for the XIXth International Red Cross Conference, New Delhi, 1957).

[65] Resolution XIX, 'Protection of Civilian Population against the Dangers of Indiscriminate Warfare' and Resolution XXXI, 'Protection of Victims of Non-International Conflicts'; ICRC, *International Red Cross Handbook* (12th edn, Geneva 1984) 626–27, 643–45.

experts requesting their expertise on how the law relating to non-international armed conflict might be developed, with the findings serving as a basis for discussion at the XXIst International Conference of the Red Cross in Istanbul.[66] That study drew explicit attention to the fact that:

> while international wars involving the application of these Conventions have been few since 1945, non-international wars have been frequent and deadly. In these the only rules applicable are the basic rules contained in Article 3, common to the four Geneva Conventions; these moreover mainly concern the treatment of persons in enemy hands, not the conduct of hostilities. However valuable this Article 3, which was a veritable victory in 1949, succeeding internal conflicts have demonstrated that it was inadequate to ensure the human person all the necessary protection.[67]

The ICRC originally proposed further developing the principles contained in Common Article 3 to ensure 'respect of the red cross sign, hospitals, medical personnel or members of National Red Cross Societies; the treatment of regular combatants; relief for military or civilian detainees; blockade; supervision; drawing up of a model agreement for the application of the other provisions of the Geneva Conventions'.[68] There was limited agreement among the experts regarding the introduction of entirely new rules for non-international armed conflict beyond the fundamental principles outlined in Common Article 3; consensus seemed to be that the objective should not be 'the formulation of entirely new rules but at defining norms implicitly contained in Article 3, and more especially the fundamental principle of humane treatment'.[69]

By 1970, the United Nations had joined the ICRC in noting that there was 'a need to extend the scope of certain parts of existing humanitarian law to cover internal armed conflicts';[70] reports from the Secretary-General highlighted that there was a:

> substantial measure of agreement concerning the need to reaffirm or to set forth, in respect of internal conflicts, the principles embodied in the Hague Regulations (which, according to the Nuremberg judgment, have become customary law)

[66] ICRC, *Reaffirmation and Development of the Law and Customs Applicable in Armed Conflicts* (n 57).

[67] ibid 8.

[68] ibid 104.

[69] ibid.

[70] *Respect for Human Rights in Armed Conflicts*, Report of the Secretary-General, UN Doc A/7720 (20 November 1969) para 134. See also *Respect for Human Rights in Armed Conflicts*, Report of the Secretary-General, UN Doc A/8052 (18 September 1970) paras 127–65.

> and in other instruments concerning needlessly cruel or destructive weapons or methods of warfare against combatants as well as against non-combatants.[71]

It was at this time that a number of States expressed their openness to the possibility of adopting a new instrument to regulate armed conflict,[72] with some going so far as to suggest that a single instrument 'containing a suitably up-dated version of the provisions of the various Conventions signed between 1899 and the present' could be adopted,[73] or, at the very least, that 'certain provisions embodied in the laws of warfare as well as in the Geneva Conventions were to be extended so as to ensure the protection of persons involved in conflicts not of an international character, regardless of whether or not these persons have taken an active part in the hostilities'.[74]

In fact, the question of extending combatant privileges and protections to participants in non-international armed conflicts (an idea raised and then rejected at Geneva in 1949) arose again during the XXIst International Conference of the Red Cross, with Resolution XVIII on the 'Status of Combatants in Non-International Armed Conflict' containing a provision stating that:

> combatants and members of resistance moments who participate in non-international armed conflicts and who conform to the provision of Article 4 of the Third Geneva Convention of 12 August 1949 should when captured be protected against any inhumanity and brutality and receive treatment similar to that which that Convention lays down for prisoners of war.[75]

The issue was revisited during the 1971 Conference of Government Experts,[76] convened by the ICRC to facilitate the process of drafting and negotiating a new

[71] *Respect for Human Rights in Armed Conflicts*, Report of the Secretary-General, UN Doc A/8052 (18 September 1970) para 152. See also *Respect for Human Rights in Armed Conflicts*, Report of the Secretary-General, UN Doc A/8313 and Add.3.

[72] See generally *Respect for Human Rights in Armed Conflicts*, Comments by Governments on the reports of the Secretary-General, UN Doc A/8313, and Add.1, Add.2, and Add.3. For example, Canada remarked that 'the drafting of one or more protocols or other instruments directly linked to the Geneva Conventions, which would bind all parties in a treaty relationship, would be a more effective manner in which to proceed': A/8313, 15.

[73] Comments by the Dominican Republic, UN Doc A/8313, 29. See also comments by Norway, 'Efforts should be made to ensure the automatic application of the Hague Regulations and the Geneva Conventions in internal conflicts': UN Doc A8313, 44.

[74] Comments by the Federal Republic of Germany, UN Doc A/8313, 34.

[75] Resolution XVIII, 'Status of Combatants in Non-International Armed Conflict', XXIst International Conference of the Red Cross, Istanbul 1969.

[76] ICRC, *Conference of Government Experts on the Reaffirmation and Development of International Humanitarian Law Applicable in Armed Conflicts, Geneva, 24 May–12 June 1971, Report on the Work of the Conference* (August 1971), part V: *Protection of Victims of Non-International Armed Conflicts*, 61–62. The idea was also raised during the 1969 Conference: see *Reaffirmation and Development of the Law and Customs Applicable in Armed Conflicts* (n 57) 104.

instrument.[77] At this Conference,[78] and at the 1972 Conference of Government Experts[79] that followed, arguments for eliminating the distinction between international and non-international armed conflict were raised,[80] as was the prospect of extending prisoner-of-war and/or combatant rights to fighters in non-international armed conflicts.[81] The discussions that took place at the 1971 and 1972 Conferences were studied by the ICRC and formed the basis of the 1973 Draft Additional Protocols. The Swiss Federal Council then called a Diplomatic Conference in Geneva in 1974 to debate the 1973 draft.[82]

Diplomatic Conferences ran from 1974 to 1977. Draft Additional Protocol II was debated and numerous opinions were expressed on what kind of scope the Protocol should have. As with the 1949 debate on Common Article 3, debate on Additional Protocol II was divided between those States that wanted a more expansive set of rules put in place for regulating non-international armed conflicts and those States that wished to limit the degree of international legal incursion into what was considered a purely domestic concern. While some States believed that there should be a uniform instrument that dealt with international and non-international armed conflict alike,[83] others felt that the distinction between types of armed conflict should be maintained,[84] with yet other delegates arguing that, mindful of the practical and political difficulties in eliminating the distinction between types of armed conflicts, the new instruments should harmonise the law so that as many protections as possible for victims of international armed conflicts

[77] The Conference of Government Experts built on the work of ICRC experts, who produced the *Preliminary Report on the Consultation of Experts concerning Non-International Conflict and Guerrilla Warfare* (Geneva, 1970 (D 1153b)).

[78] See *Conference of Government Experts 1971* (n 76).

[79] See ICRC, *Conference of Government Experts on the Reaffirmation and Development of International Humanitarian Law Applicable in Armed Conflicts, Geneva, 3 May–3 June 1972, Basic Texts, Documentary Material Submitted by the International Committee of the Red Cross* (January 1972); *Conference of Government Experts 1972* (n 62).

[80] See *Conference of Government Experts 1971* (n 76) 20, paras 21–22; 36, paras 133–34. A more detailed description and analysis of the two sessions of work of the Conference of Government Experts can be found in Sivakumaran, *The Law of Non-International Armed Conflict* (n 3) 46–49; Claude Pilloud and others (eds), *Commentary on the Additional Protocols of 8 June 1977 to the Geneva Conventions of 12 August 1949* (ICRC 1987) 1326–33.

[81] See Article 25 of the ICRC Draft Additional Protocol II (n 62).

[82] See Pilloud and others (n 80) 1333–36. For a general analysis of the work of the two Conferences of Government Experts. See further Frits Kalshoven, 'The Conference of Government Experts on the Reaffirmation and Development of International Humanitarian Law Applicable in Armed Conflicts, 24 May–12 June, 1971' (1971) 2 Netherlands Yearbook of International Law 68; Frits Kalshoven, 'The Conference of Government Experts on the Reaffirmation and Development of International Humanitarian Law Applicable in Armed Conflicts (Second Session), 3 May–2 June, 1972' (1972) 3 Netherlands Yearbook of International Law 18.

[83] *Official Records of the Diplomatic Conference on the Reaffirmation and Development of International Humanitarian Law Applicable in Armed Conflicts, Geneva (1974–1977)* (Federal Political Department 1978) vol V, 91, para 3 (Norway); 149, para 40 (Australia); 186, para 15 (Finland); 193, para 54 (Syria); vol VIII, 218, para 17 (New Zealand).

[84] *Official Records* (83) vol V, 130, para 19 (Portugal); vol VIII, 221, para 33 (Romania); 232, para 17 (Nigeria); vol XI 248, para 18 (Indonesia); 108, para 40 (Monaco).

be made available to victims of non-international armed conflicts.[85] As with 1949, 'the provisions versus principles debate again reared its head'.[86]

Debate regarding Protocol II was further complicated by the debate surrounding Protocol I and the elevation of wars of national liberation to the stratum of international armed conflicts. The history of decolonisation and wars of national liberation has been documented extensively elsewhere. For the purposes of this book, it is sufficient to note that developments in the United Nations led to the adoption of resolutions declaring that any war fought against a colonial administration in a non-self-governing territory in pursuance of the right of self-determination was to be considered akin to a conflict between two sovereign States (rather than as a non-international armed conflict, as had previously been the case). As noted in UN General Assembly Resolution 3103 (XXVIII) on the Basic Principles of the Legal Status of the Combatants Struggling Against Colonial and Alien Domination and Racist Regimes, in 1973:

> The armed conflicts involving the struggle of peoples against colonial and alien domination and racist regimes are to be regarded as international armed conflicts in the sense of the 1949 Geneva Conventions, and the legal status envisaged to apply to the combatants in the 1949 Geneva Conventions and other international instruments is to apply to the persons engaged in armed struggle against colonial and alien domination and racist regimes.[87]

When the time came to debate and discuss the Additional Protocols, it was clear that Additional Protocol I would elevate 'wars of national liberation' from a non-international armed conflict to the stratum of an international armed conflict.[88]

A side-effect of this elevation of national liberation wars to the stratum of international armed conflict was that some States believed that an additional protocol relating to non-international armed conflict was unnecessary. The position was exemplified by India, which:

[85] ibid vol V, 142, para 7 (Sweden); 92, para 8 (Egypt). See also similar comments by the delegation from the International Commission of Jurists: vol V, 202, para 47.

[86] Sivakumaran, *The Law of Non-International Armed Conflict* (n 3) 50.

[87] 28 UN GAOR Supp (No 30), UN Doc A/9030 (12 December 1973).

[88] Cullen, 'Key Developments' (n 58) 89. For more detailed analysis of decolonisation and wars of national liberation, see further Theodor Meron and Detlev Vagts, 'The Geneva Conventions of 1949 and Wars of National Liberation' in Richard Baxter and others (eds), *Humanizing the Laws of War: Selected Writings of Richard Baxter* (OUP 2013); Jessica Whyte, 'The "Dangerous Concept of the Just War": Decolonization, Wars of National Liberation, and the Additional Protocols to the Geneva Conventions' (2018) 9 Humanity 313; Stephen Schwebel, 'Wars of Liberation—as Fought in UN Organs' in John Norton Moore (ed), *Law and Civil War in the Modern World* (Johns Hopkins Press 1974); Dietrich Schindler, 'The Different Types of Armed Conflicts According to the Geneva Conventions and Protocols' (1979) 163 Recueil des Cours 117; Heather Wilson, *International Law and the Use of Force by National Liberation Movements* (Clarendon 1988); Georges Abi-Saab, 'Wars of National Liberation and the Development of Humanitarian Law' in Robert Akkerman, Peter van Krieken, and Charles Pannenborg (eds), *Declarations on Principles: A Quest for Universal Peace* (Sijthoff 1977).

> raised strong objections to the very idea of a second protocol on the ground that once the national liberation movements had been included in paragraph 2 of Part I of draft Protocol I, giving them the status of international conflicts, then Protocol II would not be necessary, since any other conflict taking place within the territory of a sovereign State would be an internal conflict, and any international instrument designed to regulate non-international conflicts might in actual application impede the settlement of the conflict and lead to external interference.[89]

These concerns, together with the worries of other States about the expansive nature of draft Protocol II, meant that the very existence of an Additional Protocol regulating non-international armed conflict was at stake. Faced with the prospect of there being no instrument adopted regarding non-international armed conflict, the Pakistani delegation stepped in and produced a revised draft Protocol, comprising 28 articles (down from the 47 articles in the original draft Protocol II and compared to the 102 articles in Protocol I). This draft was eventually adopted as Additional Protocol II.

Despite this 'simplification'[90] of Protocol II, the treaty nonetheless significantly developed the law of non-international conflict to include more detailed and expansive provisions on the protection of the civilian population[91]—among them, for the first time in the treaty law of non-international armed conflict, provisions prohibiting the targeting of certain installations.[92] Absent, however, from Additional Protocol II was any provision extending any form of combatant immunity to fighters in non-international armed conflict. Combatant immunity was retained solely for fighters in international armed conflicts,[93] denying fighters in non-international armed conflict both the right to legitimately participate in armed hostilities and the guarantee that they would not be punished for mere participation in hostilities (provided they did not perpetrate war crimes).[94] While there had been limited debate at the Diplomatic Conference in support of extension of some combatant rights to fighters in non-international armed conflict,[95] this idea was quickly rejected.[96]

[89] *Official Records* (n 83) vol V, 345, para 50. See also similar comments from Romania (*Official Records*, vol V, 103, para 15), the Philippines (*Official Records*, vol V, 351, para 76), and Iraq (*Official Records*, vol V, 381, para 9).

[90] Pilloud and others (n 80) 1335–36.

[91] Articles 4–12.

[92] Articles 14, 15.

[93] Michael Bothe and others (eds), *New Rules for Victims of Armed Conflicts: Commentary on the Two 1977 Protocols Additional to the Geneva Conventions of 1949* (2nd edn, Martinus Nijhoff 2013) 243–44.

[94] Antonio Cassese, *International Law* (2nd edn, OUP 2005) 408.

[95] *Official Records* (n 83) vol V, 91, para 6 (Norway); 187, paras 20–21 (Bangladesh); vol VIII, 359, para 15 (Sweden).

[96] For criticisms of the suggestion, see comments by Burundi, *Official Records* (n 83) vol VIII, 293, para 41.

The only part of the Additional Protocol that approximates the combatant's immunity from prosecution at the cessation of hostilities is Article 6(5), which was originally Article 10 in the 1973 Draft Protocol II. Article 6(5) had been considered by both the 1971 and 1972 Conferences of Government Experts as part of a larger discussion regarding penal prosecutions, the death penalty, and the treatment of persons whose liberty has been restricted (contained in what was then Draft Articles 25, 26, and 28).[97] The Conference was grappling with the broader question of how to reconcile the (theoretical) granting of combatant status to fighters in non-international armed conflict with domestic laws imposing the death penalty, especially for the 'crime of insurrection'.[98] In light of these discussions, the ICRC suggested that one possible way the impasse could be overcome would be if, rather than granting outright pre-emptive immunity to fighters in non-international armed conflicts, provision could be made whereby 'no one could incur the death penalty solely for having belonged to armed forces which have fought in accordance with the laws and customs of armed conflicts'.[99] The ICRC also suggested that 'the authorities in power should not punish the fighter solely for having belonged to armed forces, unless imperative security requirements make this necessary'.[100] Moreover, it was argued that 'at the end of hostilities, it is desirable that normal life should be resumed as soon as possible. Hence, it would be fitting to generalize the proclamation of general amnesty, in the interest of both the victims and the authorities who will have to restore order and reconcile all elements of a divided people'.[101] Such a provision would not prevent the punishment of persons who had committed war crimes or other serious violations of IHL, but would encourage States not to prosecute fighters for participating in the hostilities—especially if such participation had been in all other respects compliant with the existing rules of IHL.

The 1971 and 1972 Conferences both retained the option of amnesty in non-international armed conflicts; when the ICRC came to put together draft Additional Protocol II, the amnesty provision was included in draft Article 10(6).[102] The inclusion of the amnesty provision in the final version of Additional Protocol II, in what would eventually be Article 6, was essentially uncontroversial; this was because, as noted by several delegates, 'provisions of that nature were included in the legislation of all States',[103] and the amnesty

[97] See *Conference of Government Experts 1971* (n 76) vol V, 56–60; *Conference of Government Experts 1972* (n 62) vol I, paras 2.148–2.152, 2.155–2.156, 2.209–2.235.

[98] *Conference of Government Experts 1972* (n 62) vol I, para 2.216.

[99] *Conference of Government Experts 1971* (n 76) vol V, 57.

[100] ibid.

[101] ibid 59. See also *Conference of Government Experts 1972* (n 62) vol I, 85–87, paras 2.220, 2.228, 2.229–2.235.

[102] See Draft Additional Protocols (n 61) 141–43, with Commentary.

[103] Comments by delegate from Pakistan, *Official Records* (n 83) vol VII, 92. See also similar comments by delegate from Canada: ibid 94.

provision 'laid no obligations on States'[104] but was merely a 'recommendation to States.'[105]

Amnesties in Article 6(5) of Additional Protocol II—Scope and Interpretation of the Provision

Additional Protocol II, as finally adopted, provides in Article 6(5) on penal prosecutions that: '[a]t the end of hostilities, the authorities in power shall endeavour to grant the broadest possible amnesty to persons who have participated in the armed conflict, or those deprived of their liberty for reasons related to the armed conflict, whether they are interned or detained.'

As noted by the ICRC in the Commentary to the Protocols, 'the object of this sub-paragraph is to encourage gestures of reconciliation which can contribute to reestablishing normal relations in the life of a nation which has been divided.'[106] However, the ICRC Commentary makes it clear that the question of amnesty is a matter solely 'within the competence of the authorities'.[107] Therefore, no breach of international law occurs should State authorities choose not to grant amnesty at the cessation of hostilities. The Commentary also makes it clear that the amnesty provision exists without prejudice in relation to requests for free pardon. As noted in the Commentary:

> [amnesty] is an act by the legislative power which eliminates the consequences of certain punishable offences, stops prosecutions and quashes convictions. Legally, a distinction is made between amnesty and a free pardon. The latter is granted by the Head of State and puts an end to the execution of the penalty, though in other respects the effects of the conviction remain in being. This paragraph deals only with amnesty, though this does not mean that free pardon is deliberately excluded. The draft adopted in Committee provided, on the one hand, that anyone convicted should have the right to seek a free pardon or commutation of sentence, and on the other hand, that amnesty, pardon or reprieve of a death sentence may be granted in all cases. That paragraph was not adopted in the end, in order to keep the text simple. Some delegations considered that it was unnecessary to include it because national legislation in all countries provides for the possibility of a free pardon.[108]

One possible exception to this recommendation exists: that amnesties are 'not to be construed to enable war criminals, or those guilty of crimes against humanity,

[104] Comments by delegate from Italy: ibid 93.
[105] Comments by delegate from Syrian Arab Republic: ibid.
[106] Pilloud and others (n 80) 1402.
[107] ibid.
[108] ibid.

to evade punishment'.[109] As Sivakumaran points out, the amnesty provision of Article 6(5) was never intended by States to amount to a general amnesty for all persons: the drafting history and the wording of draft Article 10 clearly indicate that 'the provision was drawn up in respect of persons "merely" taking a part in the armed conflict',[110] in order to 'mitigate the effects of the lack of combatant immunity in non-international armed conflicts'.[111] Debate exists as to whether this interpretation is held out in practice, as there has been conflicting practice in this regard—something that will be explored later in this book.

As a final note on the interpretation of Article 6(5), would a strict reading of Article 6(5) preclude amnesty agreements that were signed *during* an armed conflict? Article 6(5) states that '[a]t the end of hostilities, the authorities in power shall endeavour to grant the broadest possible amnesty'—which would seem to suggest that this article is designed to cover only post-conflict amnesties, and not those amnesties adopted during the conflict. However, given that Article 6(5) contains no other obligations, and is recommendatory only, nothing important seems to turn on this.

Concluding Thoughts

Does including a non-binding norm in a binding instrument have any impact on its reception? Put another way, does putting a hortatory provision in a binding treaty make it more likely that the recommendation will be implemented? State practice with regards to both the special agreements provision in Common Article 3 and the amnesty provision in Additional Protocol II seems to suggest different conclusions. Following the adoption of Common Article 3, there were examples of special agreements being concluded where none had existed prior to its adoption. Therefore, a strong case can be made that the inclusion of the special agreements provision did have an impact on State practice, by providing an option to States that had not previously been considered. In contrast, Article 6(5) of Protocol II seems to have had comparatively limited impact on State practice—amnesty agreements adopted after the introduction of Additional Protocol II seldom, if ever, cite Article 6(5). Additionally, a comparison of the number of amnesty agreements adopted prior to and after the coming into force of Protocol II do not suggest that Protocol II resulted in increased numbers of amnesty agreements being adopted.[112]

[109] From ICRC, *Customary IHL Database*, Commentary to Rule 159 <https://ihl-databases.icrc.org/customary-ihl/eng/docs/home> accessed 30 July 2021.

[110] Sivakumaran, *The Law of Non-International Armed Conflict* (n 3) 507.

[111] ibid.

[112] The impact of Common Article 3 and Protocol II on state practice is examined in more detail in Chapter 7.

One possible reason for the difference in impact might be the novelty of each provision. Article 6(5) only reaffirmed a practice that had always been considered a sovereign prerogative. States had always granted amnesties for any number of reasons; therefore, the inclusion of Article 6(5) in Protocol II may have had minimal impact on State practice because it was something that States were already doing, without the need for international sanction. However, Common Article 3 special agreements *were* genuinely new. While States had always had the right to extend full belligerent rights (and thus the full application of the laws of armed conflict) to insurgent groups in non-international armed conflicts, there was reluctance to do so. Common Article 3 special agreements introduced, in effect, a highly circumscribed version of recognition of belligerency. States were encouraged to implement the Conventions in their entirety, but the provision clearly stated that such special agreements *in no way* altered the legal status of the non-State group involved in the agreement. States could have the benefit of applying the laws of war without having to acknowledge that the non-State group possessed any measure of international personality—a development in State practice that was (unlike amnesty) genuinely novel.

Exploring why (or why not) these non-binding provisions have been taken up in practice will be explored more in later chapters. For now, this book turns to look at the newer non-binding norms that have been adopted in the last few decades, starting with the 1994 San Remo Manual on International Law Applicable to Armed Conflicts at Sea.

4
Non-Binding Instruments in International Humanitarian Law

State-Directed Non-Binding Instruments, and Non-Binding Instruments Created by Expert Groups

Introduction

The last 30 years have seen notable developments in the law of armed conflict. During the period 1994 to 2020, numerous treaties were adopted, joined by a considerable number of non-binding instruments that were created to regulate conduct in armed conflict—including the *San Remo Manual on International Law Applicable to Armed Conflicts at Sea* (1994); the *San Remo Manual on the Law of Non-International Armed Conflict* (2006); the *Montreux Document on Pertinent International Legal Obligations and Good Practices for States related to Operations of Private Military and Security Companies during Armed Conflict* (2008) (Montreux Document); the *Manual on International Law Applicable to Air and Missile Warfare* (2009); the *Copenhagen Process Principles and Guidelines on the Handling of Detainees in International Military Operations* (2012) (Copenhagen Principles); the *Tallinn Manual on the International Law Applicable to Cyber Warfare* (2013) and the *Tallinn Manual 2.0 on the International Law Applicable to Cyber Operations* (2017); the *Leuven Manual on the International Law Applicable to Peace Operations* (2018; Leuven Manual); and the *Oslo Manual on Select Topics of the Law of Armed Conflict* (2020; Oslo Manual). Currently in advanced stages of drafting are the *Woomera Manual on the International Law of Military Space Operations and the Manual on International Law Applicable to Military Uses of Outer Space* (MILAMOS).[1] In addition, there are *sui generis* instruments, including the International Committee of the Red Cross (ICRC) Study into Customary International Humanitarian Law (2005); the International Code of Conduct for Private Security Service Providers (2010); the *ICRC Interpretive Guidance on the Notion of Direct Participation in Hostilities under International Humanitarian Law* (2009) (DPH Guidance); and the four Geneva Call Deeds of Commitment (2000, 2010, 2015, and 2018).

[1] The author participated in her personal capacity as an expert in the early stages of the MILAMOS project and in the entirety of the Woomera project.

Non-Binding Norms in International Humanitarian Law. Emily Crawford, Oxford University Press. © Emily Crawford 2021.
DOI: 10.1093/oso/9780198819851.003.0005

These non-binding instruments have emerged from various spheres: some, like the Copenhagen Principles, were the initiatives of States; some, like the DPH Guidance, were the work of the ICRC; and some were the work of non-governmental civil society organisations, such as Geneva Call's Deeds of Commitment. The subject matter, scope, and breadth of the instruments is also notably varied: the instruments cover diverse topics, such as naval warfare, the use of private military and security companies, cyber operations, and the protection of health care workers. While some instruments are concise, both in the number of 'rules' outlined[2] and in the scope and depth of those rules,[3] others are lengthy and complex.[4] Some propose only to state the law as it currently exists,[5] while others employ the terminology of 'best practice'.[6]

Common to these instruments is their commitment to their non-binding status. Some instruments state this outright: the Montreux Document states in its Preface that 'this document is not a legally binding instrument', as does the Air and Missile Warfare Manual (AMW) Manual.[7] The manuals and non-binding instruments also frequently claim to be restatements of the law. For example, the AMW Manual states in its Introduction that its objective is to 'present a methodical restatement of existing international law on air and missile warfare, based on the general practice of States accepted as law (*opinio juris*) and treaties in force',[8] but affirms only a few pages later that the Manual 'does not have binding force'.[9] The manuals therefore occupy something of an unusual position—they affirm their non-binding status, while, somewhat paradoxically, proclaiming their status as declarations of the existing law. While it is true that the Manuals *themselves* do not have binding force per se, their very existence as a centralised statement of the law is nevertheless highly persuasive.

Also common among the manuals and instruments are their objectives to influence behaviour. For example, the ICRC DPH Guidance states that it 'does not aim to change binding rules of customary or treaty IHL',[10] but puts forward its hope that 'the comprehensive legal analysis and the careful balance of humanitarian and military interests underlying the Interpretive Guidance will render the resulting recommendations persuasive for States, non-State actors, practitioners, and academics alike'.[11] Likewise, the AMW Manual states that 'hopefully it will serve as a

[2] The Copenhagen Principles contain 16 rules.

[3] See, for example, the San Remo NIAC Manual, which has fewer than 40 rules and commentary spread over 75 pages.

[4] The Tallinn Manual 2.0 comprises 154 rules with commentary spread over 563 pages.

[5] AMW Manual, Introduction, x.

[6] Such as the International Code of Conduct for Private Security Service Providers, in Articles 12 and 13 of the Articles of Association of the International Code of Conduct for Private Security Service Providers' Association.

[7] Montreux Document, Preface, 9. See also AMW Manual, xiii.

[8] AMW Manual, x.

[9] ibid xiii.

[10] ICRC DPH Guidance, 9.

[11] ICRC DPH Guidance, 10.

valuable resource for armed forces in the development of rules of engagement, the writing of domestic military manuals, the preparation of training courses, and—above all—the actual conduct of armed forces in combat operations'.[12]

This chapter focuses on the 'recent' non-binding instruments, starting with the 1994 San Remo Manual on Naval Warfare. The chapter will analyse: the intention behind the adoption of these instruments; their scope and breadth; the originating institution or organisation, and the participants involved;[13] and a brief discussion of how the instruments have been received. The analysis will serve to establish the groundwork for the chapters that follow, which will explore the larger theoretical questions of how non-binding instruments generally (and these particular non-binding instruments specifically) have been received, whether they have actually made an impact on their extant topic areas, whether the processes by which they have been drafted and adopted in practice (if they have been adopted in practice) raise any concerns or challenges for the international law-making process, and the centrality of the State to that process.

A Note on the Methodology for Chapters 4 and 5

A brief note on methodology is useful here. The manuals and instruments under examination in this book have been chosen because they are the instruments that have been most commented on in the literature and because they are the ones that are most apposite for parties engaged in armed conflict.[14] Information about these instruments and manuals, such as their drafting history and the participants, has been drawn from publicly available information, and the analysis of the instruments focuses on both their substantive content and the procedural histories behind their creation. For convenience, analysis of these non-binding instruments will be divided across two chapters. Chapter 4 will examine two specific types of non-binding instruments: those that have been the result of State-sponsored initiatives, such as the Montreux and Copenhagen documents, and those non-binding instruments that have been initiatives of expert groups, primarily driven by academics, operating in close collaboration with government and armed forces experts, such as the San Remo and Tallinn Manuals. In the next chapter,

12 AMW Manual, xiii.

13 The titles and affiliations listed for the participants and experts in the manuals and instruments under examination in this book are reflective of the time of their participation, rather than their time of writing.

14 There were additional reasons for excluding the Leuven and Oslo Manuals: the Leuven Manual relates to peacekeeping operations and is therefore not solely related to armed conflict. The Oslo Manual was only published in 2020 and so there has been insufficient time to assess its reception in practice; the Oslo Manual also covers several areas where expert manuals or guidance already exist—for example, cyber operations and direct participation in hostilities. Therefore, it was decided to focus instead on the other manuals and guidance on topic.

the '*sui generis*' instruments of the ICRC Study into Customary International Humanitarian Law, the International Code of Conduct for Private Security Service Providers, the DPH Guidance, and the four Geneva Call Deeds of Commitment will be explored. These instruments have largely come from civil society organisations (such as the DPH Guidance) or are otherwise addressed entirely to non-State actors (such as the International Code of Conduct and the Deeds of Commitment). This is a somewhat arbitrary division but is done for the purpose of readability and chapter length.

The *San Remo Manual on International Law Applicable to Armed Conflicts at Sea*

The origins of the *San Remo Manual on International Law Applicable to Armed Conflicts at Sea*[15] (San Remo Naval Manual) can be traced back to the resolution adopted at the XXVth International Conference of the Red Cross in 1986, where it was noted that 'international humanitarian law relating to land warfare to a large extent has been reaffirmed and developed and that some areas of international humanitarian law relating to sea warfare are in need of reaffirmation and clarification on the basis of existing fundamental principles of international humanitarian law'.[16] The following year, the International Institute of Humanitarian Law, in conjunction with the Universities of Pisa and Syracuse, convened a roundtable in San Remo to review the law and draft a plan of action.

That the law on naval warfare needed to be updated was evident. As noted by the editor of the San Remo Manual, Louise Doswald-Beck, 'the need for an updated articulation of the law stems from the fact that treaty law on the conduct of hostilities at sea not only is fragmentary but also mostly dates back to 1907'.[17] The extant law on naval warfare was primarily located in the 1907 Hague Conventions and was supplemented by two non-binding instruments;[18] the written law had not been updated to reflect major technological and scientific developments in the conduct of naval warfare. Additionally, the adoption of major treaties on the law of the sea also impacted how naval warfare was being conducted in the latter part of the twentieth

[15] Note that, as of this writing, the San Remo Manual is currently being updated. See further <https://www.maritime-executive.com/editorials/standard-for-international-law-of-naval-warfare-is-set-for-an-update /> accessed 31 July 2021.

[16] Resolution VII, 'Work on International Humanitarian Law in Armed Conflicts at Sea and on Land' (adopted at the final plenary meeting on 31 October 1986), XXVth International Conference of the Red Cross, Geneva, 23 to 31 October 1986, reprinted in (1986) 26 International Review of the Red Cross 340, 349.

[17] Louise Doswald-Beck, 'The San Remo Manual on International Law Applicable to Armed Conflicts at Sea' (1995) 89 American Journal of International Law 192, 193.

[18] The London Declaration concerning the Laws of Naval War of 1909, and the *Oxford Manual on the Laws of Naval War Governing the Relations between Belligerents* (adopted by the Institute of International Law in 1913), discussed in more detail in the previous chapter.

century.[19] The experts who convened in San Remo in June of 1987 acknowledged that, driven by these new developments, study into how the contemporary law of armed conflict applied to naval warfare was vital.[20]

With the support of the ICRC, additional roundtables were held annually in Madrid (1988), Bochum (1989), Toulon (1989), Bergen (1991), Ottawa (1992), Geneva (1993), and Livorno (1994). It was in Madrid that it was decided that a 'contemporary restatement of the law of armed conflict at sea'[21] in the form of a manual should be adopted; the subsequent meetings culminated in the adoption in 1994 of the San Remo Naval Manual.

Following the Madrid Plan of Action, the first roundtable focused on 'The Military Objective and the Principle of Distinction in the Law of Naval Warfare'.[22] The rapporteur for this topic was Commander William Fenrick, who wrote an extensive report on the extant law of naval warfare and its historical development, taking into account both treaty law and State practice, and providing some conclusions. The report was sent to all participants prior to the first roundtable in November 1989, with the aim to solicit and collate any comments regarding the rapporteur's report. These comments were then, in turn, disseminated among the participants. At the roundtable itself, individual topics and issues covered by the rapporteur were assigned to working sessions, where a discussion leader facilitated and structured the discussion on the issue in plenary. Following the plenary discussion, the discussion leader produced an initial draft of the conclusions of the working session. Towards the end of the roundtable, all discussion leaders, in conjunction with the rapporteur and the editor, met to draft the overall conclusions of that roundtable. The results of the final drafting group meeting were submitted to the roundtable at the final session, with any agreed upon alterations being made. The process was followed at all subsequent roundtables, though with different rapporteurs dealing with different subjects.[23]

[19] See generally Vaughan Lowe, 'The Impact of the Law of the Sea on Naval Warfare' (1987) 14 Syracuse Journal of International Law and Commerce 657.

[20] See generally Doswald-Beck, 'The San Remo Manual' (n 17) 193–94.

[21] Known as the Madrid Plan of Action, reprinted in Louise Doswald-Beck (ed), *San Remo Manual on International Law Applicable to Armed Conflicts at Sea* (CUP 1995) 63. See also the Introduction, 5.

[22] ibid Doswald-Beck (ed), 64. For a summary of the process of drafting and adopting the San Remo Manual, see further Wolff Heintschel von Heinegg, 'The San Remo Manual – History, Methodology and Future Application' in Dale Stephens and Matthew Stubbs (eds), *The Law of Naval Warfare* (LexisNexis Butterworths 2019).

[23] The rapporteur for the second roundtable was Mr Gert-Jan F Van Hegelsom (Directorate of Legal Affairs, Ministry of Defence, The Netherlands), whose topic was 'Methods and Means of Combat in Naval Warfare'; the rapporteurs for the third roundtable were Professor Wolff Heintschel von Heinegg (Ruhr University), whose topic was 'Visit, Search, Diversion, and Capture', and Mr Christopher Greenwood (University of Cambridge), whose topic was 'The Effect of the United Nations Charter on the Law of Naval Warfare'; the rapporteur for the fourth roundtable was Professor Horace Robertson Jr, Rear Admiral, US Navy (ret) (Duke University), whose topic was 'Regions of Operations of Naval Warfare—Different Maritime Areas'; and the rapporteur for the fifth roundtable was Ms Louise Doswald-Beck (ICRC), whose topic was the 'Protection of Victims of Armed Conflicts at Sea'. See generally Doswald-Beck (ed), *San Remo Manual* (n 21) 64–66.

After the fourth roundtable at Ottawa in 1992, a 'harmonisation committee' was convened, with the aim of 'harmonising the terminology used in the various documents adopted at the end of each Round Table, deciding on a logical order of paragraphs, and reviewing the commentary that was written by the Rapporteurs for the Explanation'.[24] The Committee met again following the fifth roundtable, to finalise the harmonised text of the Manual and the Explanation. The final roundtable, held in Livorno in 1994, reviewed and approved the final text, and accepted (but did not formally approve) the Explanation.[25]

The experts involved in the debating and drafting of the San Remo Naval Manual can be broadly categorised into two groups: the participants, who were involved in the drafting process as well as the roundtable discussions, and the associated experts and observers, who attended the meetings but were not involved in the drafting process. The 56 participants included the rapporteurs,[26] authors of special reports,[27] authors of background papers,[28] and the members of the harmonisation group and authors of the Explanation,[29] as well as other experts drawn from academia, the armed forces, civil society, and government. In all, 22 of the participants were from academia, 29 from government and the armed forces, and five from civil

[24] 'Introduction to the Explanation' in Doswald-Beck (ed), *San Remo Manual* (n 21).

[25] The Introduction to the Explanation notes that this failure to provide formal approval was merely a reflection that the Explanation was the work of the individual authors, and not the product of the roundtables per se: ibid.

[26] Ms Louise Doswald-Beck (ICRC), Commander William Fenrick (Office of the Judge Advocate General, Canada), Mr Christopher Greenwood (University of Cambridge), Professor Wolff Heintschel von Heinegg (Ruhr University), Professor Horace Robertson Jr, Rear Admiral, US Navy (ret) (Duke University), and Mr Gert-Jan F Van Hegelsom (Directorate of Legal Affairs, Ministry of Defence, The Netherlands). See Doswald-Beck (ed), *San Remo Manual* (n 21) 46.

[27] Professor Salah El-Din Amer (Cairo University), Vice Admiral James H Doyle Jr (US Navy (ret)), Captain J Ashley Roach (Office of the Legal Adviser, US Department of State), and Professor Dietrich Schindler (Zurich University).

[28] Lieutenant-Colonel Kim Carter (Office of the Judge Advocate General, Canada) and Professor Wolff Heintschel von Heinegg (Ruhr University). The reports of the rapporteurs, as well as the background papers and special reports, were published (in English) in Wolff Heintschel von Heinegg (ed), *The Military Objective and the Principle of Distinction in the Law of Naval Warfare. Report, Commentaries and Proceedings of the Round-Table of Experts on International Humanitarian Law Applicable to Armed Conflicts at Sea, Ruhr-Universität Bochum, 10–14 November 1989* (Berliner Wissenschafts-Verlag 1991); *Methods and Means of Combat in Naval Warfare. Report and Commentaries of the Round-Table of Experts on International Humanitarian Law Applicable to Armed Conflicts at Sea. Institut Méditerranéen d'Etudes Stratégiques, Université de Toulon et du Var, 19–23 October 1991* (Berliner Wissenschafts-Verlag 1991); *Visit, Search, Diversion and Capture. The Effects of the United Nations Charter on the Law of Naval Warfare. Reports and Commentaries of the Round-Table of Experts on International Humanitarian Law Applicable to Armed Conflicts at Sea. Norwegian Navy School of Tactics, Norwegian Red Cross, Bergen, 20–24 September 1991* (Berliner Wissenschafts-Verlag 1995); and *Regions of Operations of Naval Warfare. Reports and Commentaries of the Round-Table of Experts on International Humanitarian Law Applicable to Armed Conflicts at Sea. Canadian Ministry of Defence, Canadian Red Cross, Ottawa, 25–28 September 1992* (Berliner Wissenschafts-Verlag 1995).

[29] Professor Salah El-Din Amer (Cairo University), Ms Louise Doswald-Beck (ICRC), Vice Admiral James H Doyle Jr (US Navy (ret)), Commander William Fenrick (Office of the Judge Advocate General, Canada), Mr Christopher Greenwood (University of Cambridge), Professor Wolff Heintschel von Heinegg (Ruhr University), Professor Horace Robertson Jr, Rear Admiral, US Navy (ret) (Duke University), and Mr Gert-Jan F Van Hegelsom (Directorate of Legal Affairs, Ministry of Defence, The Netherlands).

society organisations such as the ICRC. The participants were joined by 94 'experts and observers', who attended meetings but did not draft any of the relevant documents (such as special reports or background papers). All participants, experts, and observers participated in the process in their personal capacity, and not as official representatives of their States or their institutions.[30] The majority of the participants and observers were drawn from the Western European and Others Group (WEOG) of States:[31] of the 94 experts and observers, 63 were drawn from the WEOG States, and 44 of the 56 participants hailed from WEOG States. The Asia-Pacific Group accounted for the next largest group of participants and experts—20 in total—with 10 from the Eastern European Group, nine from the Latin American and Caribbean Group, and four from the African Group.

While the number of participants, experts, and observers totalled 150, not all of them were involved in all stages of the San Remo process. The Madrid Plan of Action had intended for the work to be undertaken by about 20 experts, with due regard paid to 'geographical representation'.[32] Ultimately, each meeting was attended by about 40 persons, with around 25 experts personally attending all or most of the meetings. Therefore, of the 150 involved in the process, only a small percentage was part of the 'core' group of experts who oversaw the final instrument. The Manual attributed this 'difference in numbers'[33] to several factors:

> First, some specialist experts were invited to some of the meetings in order to contribute their expertise to a specific issue. Secondly, interested observers attended some of the meetings and sometimes participated in discussions. Thirdly, some persons attended by virtue of their function, for example the senior Judge Advocates of certain navies (although, as with all participants, they attended in their personal capacity), but the individuals changed from time to time. Finally, some individuals attended only the first one or two meetings or only the last one or two meetings, but nevertheless made useful contributions to the work.[34]

Beyond indicating the names of the rapporteurs and other core experts, such as the authors of special reports and background papers, and the harmonisation group, the introduction to the Manual gives no indication of which participants, experts, and observers were at which roundtables, which makes it difficult to get a sense of who was involved in which meetings, and to what degree. Moreover, no indication is given as to the methodology behind the selection of the participants, experts,

[30] Doswald-Beck (ed), *San Remo Manual* (n 21) 67.

[31] The WEOG States comprise the Western European States, as well as Australia and New Zealand, with the United States as observer: <http://www.un.org/depts/DGACM/RegionalGroups.shtml> accessed 31 July 2021.

[32] Doswald-Beck (ed), *San Remo Manual* (n 21) 67.

[33] ibid.

[34] ibid.

and observers. While it is clear in some instances why certain participants were specifically chosen (being members of State navies, for instance), it is less clear why other experts were chosen, and why there was a lack of geographic representation from certain regional areas.[35]

The Manual as adopted comprises 183 'rules',[36] accompanied by an 'Explanation'—essentially a commentary to the rules, written by the rapporteurs for the roundtables. It is divided into six parts. Part I comprises general provisions on the scope and application of the rules within the Manual,[37] the law on the use of force and self-defence, including the role of the Security Council,[38] areas of naval warfare,[39] and a section on definitions of terms used in the Manual.[40] Part II covers regions of operations, and the obligations and rights of belligerents and neutrals within those different regions, including internal and archipelagic waters, and the territorial sea,[41] international straits and archipelagic sea lanes,[42] the exclusive economic zone and continental shelf,[43] and the high seas and sea-bed beyond national jurisdiction.[44] Part III covers the basic rules of international humanitarian law (IHL) as applicable to naval warfare,[45] including the rules on targeting, such as precautions in attack,[46] when enemy vessels may be attacked, and which enemy vessels and aircraft are exempt from attack;[47] and rules on neutral merchant vessels and civil aircraft.[48] Part IV details the relevant rules on methods[49] and means[50] of warfare at sea, with Part V outlining the rules on measures short of attack, such as interception, visit, search, diversion, and capture.[51] Part VI completes the rules, with details on protected persons, transports, and medical aircraft.[52] The Manual does not address the rules of State responsibility for violations of the law, war crimes, or questions of implementation, enforcement, and accountability. It does not expressly cover non-international armed conflicts, but nor does it expressly exclude them.[53]

35 Whether this is a significant issue regarding the ultimate instrument is something that will be further discussed later in this chapter, as well as in more detail in Chapter 8 on legitimacy and legality.
36 The Manual does not, itself, refer to the adopted provisions as rules; they instead are paragraphs of larger sections on specific IHL rules, such as, for example, precautions in attack (Section II).
37 Rules 1–2.
38 Rules 3–9.
39 Rules 10–12.
40 Rule 13.
41 Rules 14–22.
42 Rules 23–33.
43 Rules 34–35.
44 Rules 36–37.
45 Rules 38–45.
46 Rule 46.
47 Rules 47–66.
48 Rules 67–77.
49 Rules 93–111.
50 Rules 78–92.
51 Rules 112–58.
52 Rules 159–83.
53 'Introduction to the Explanation' in Doswald-Beck (ed), *San Remo Manual* (n 21) 64.

The stated intent of the Manual is to provide guidance for practitioners in the field of naval warfare. As noted in the Explanation to the Manual:

> [t]he participants in Madrid hoped that the results of such an endeavour by a group of specialists in international law and naval experts from different countries would aid the dissemination and the comprehension of the contemporary law, and would encourage the drafting of national naval manuals with a certain uniformity ... the Manual is not meant to be a binding document but it is of course not excluded that some or all of it could serve as a basis for diplomatic conferences at a later stage.[54]

For the most part, the Manual positions itself as *lex lata*. Any innovation or progressive development in the law is largely attributable to having to examine practical developments in related fields of international law, such as the law on the use of force and the law of the sea. Neither the UN Charter nor the UN Convention on the Law of the Sea were in existence at the time of the adoption of the extant treaty law on naval warfare; the developments in these areas—namely, the prohibition on the use of force and the peacetime legal regimes relating to certain parts of the sea—therefore needed to be acknowledged where they impacted with the law on naval warfare.[55] Other developments, such as changes in the law and technology relating to aircraft, were also noted. Additionally, developments in the 'general' law of armed conflict—namely, the adoption of the Additional Protocol I (API) concept of military objective[56]—also influenced the Manual, in that the concept of a military objective as understood in Additional Protocol I did not exist in the traditional law of naval warfare, but was included in the Manual.[57] The Manual's drafters also chose to use the terminology of the Geneva Conventions, employing the word 'neutral' to designate States not party to the conflict, rather than using the Additional Protocols terminology of 'neutral or other State which is not party to the conflict', so as to avoid possible complications that might arise should participants in an armed conflict feel compelled to distinguish between 'neutrals' and 'States not party to the conflict', which could 'introduce extreme uncertainty with regard to the rules applicable to the shipping of States not party to the conflict and to the protection of the waters of such States'.[58]

One final innovation, and one that was apparently controversial during the San Remo process,[59] was the inclusion of paragraphs on the 'rules applicable to zones which belligerents might establish and which adversely affect the use by others of

[54] ibid 62.
[55] ibid 67–68.
[56] As outlined in Article 52(2) of API.
[57] 'Explanation' in Doswald-Beck (ed), *San Remo Manual* (n 21) 68.
[58] ibid 68.
[59] ibid.

certain areas of the sea'[60]—that is, so-called exclusion zones. The inclusion of these paragraphs generated 'a certain amount of controversy amongst the participants as to whether rules applicable to such zones should be included in the Manual, for it was feared that doing so could encourage the belief that they are clearly lawful'.[61] State practice in relation to exclusion zones prior to the adoption of the San Remo Manual was mixed, with some evidence of States engaging in establishing exclusion zones, and other practice that treated the establishment of exclusion zones (at least prior to San Remo) as clearly unlawful under international law.[62] In including exclusion zones, despite their uncertain status, the majority of San Remo participants:

> thought that it was more useful to be pragmatic in this regard as such zones have been established and would probably continue to be used. Therefore, they thought it wise to specify certain criteria and restrictions so as to prevent the abusive establishment of zones as well as behaviour within the zone that would contravene international humanitarian law.[63]

For the most part, nearly all the 'innovations' introduced into the Manual were broadly agreed on by participants, with the Explanation at pains to indicate where divisions of opinion during the process took place. For example, the Explanation in relation to 'Zones' makes it clear that some experts were of the opinion that zones were 'simply unlawful',[64] while most felt that zones were a practical reality that needed to be addressed by the Manual.[65]

Within 10 years of the adoption of the San Remo Manual, there was clear evidence that it was 'widely accepted as being declaratory of the present law of naval warfare'.[66] The Manual has been noted approvingly in the military manuals of several States, particularly 'specially affected States'[67] that routinely engage in naval military operations.[68] For example, in the Australian military manual on the law of

[60] ibid 69.

[61] ibid.

[62] On the practice regarding exclusion zones prior to and post the adoption of the San Remo Manual, see generally Wolff Heintschel von Heinegg, 'The Law of Armed Conflict at Sea' in Dieter Fleck (ed), *The Handbook of International Humanitarian Law* (OUP 2013) 522–24.

[63] 'Explanation' in Doswald-Beck (ed), *San Remo Manual* (n 21) 69. For a more detailed examination of these 'innovations', see further Doswald-Beck, 'The San Remo Manual' (n 17).

[64] 'Explanation' in Doswald-Beck (ed), *San Remo Manual* (n 21) 181.

[65] ibid.

[66] Wolff Heintschel von Heinegg, 'Maritime Warfare' in Andrew Clapham and Paola Gaeta (eds), *The Oxford Handbook of International Law in Armed Conflict* (OUP 2014) 146.

[67] *North Sea Continental Shelf Cases (Germany/Denmark; Germany/Netherlands) (Judgment)* [1969] ICJ Rep 3, 43, para 74.

[68] See, for example, Office of the Chief of Naval Operations, US Department of the Navy, *The Commander's Handbook on the Law of Naval Operations* (2007, Naval Warfare Publication No NWP 1-14M); UK Ministry of Defence, *The Manual of the Law of Armed Conflict* (Oxford 2004) ch 13; German Navy, *Kommandanten-Handbuch* (Commander's Handbook) (Bonn 2002), 19, 140; the Norwegian armed forces manual—*Manual i krigens folkerett* (2013) 99, 168, 198. The French military manual is slightly more circumspect, noting that 'Bien qu'elles soient incluses dans le recueil de « droit

armed conflict, in the section on naval warfare it is noted that '[an] international document of significance in the area of naval warfare is the San Remo Manual on International Law Applicable to Armed Conflicts at Sea. It contains an extensive coverage of maritime issues directly connected with naval warfare. Although not a legally binding document, it represents a restatement of the law in part, and certain provisions of the manual are widely recognised as representing principles of customary international law.'[69]

Other military manuals endorse the San Remo Manual in even more explicit terms: the Argentinean military manual lists the San Remo Naval Manual as a source of law,[70] with both the Canadian and UK military manuals basing eventual chapters on military naval operations on the San Remo Manual.[71]

Academic and practitioner assessment of the Manual is likewise generally positive: the ICRC, when undertaking its study into the customary status of IHL,[72] decided not to examine the law of naval warfare, as 'this area of law was recently the subject of a major restatement, namely the San Remo Manual on Naval Warfare'.[73] Israel, in response to the 2010 *Mavi Marmara* incident, also justified its conduct by invoking the San Remo Manual;[74] the inquiries made into the incident,

international régissant la conduite des hostilités » publié par le Comité International de la Croix-Rouge (CICR) en 1996, les dispositions du manuel de San Remo ne constituent pas encore à proprement parler des règles de droit positif: la note liminaire rédigée par le CICR précise d'ailleurs que si la plupart des dispositions figurant dans le manuel sont considérées comme énonçant le droit actuellement en vigueur, certaines peuvent apparaître comme de simples développements du droit. Il convient donc de rester prudent dans l'appréciation de la valeur de ce texte, et de comparer ses dispositions avec le droit antérieur.' ('Although included in the collection of "international law governing the conduct of hostilities" published by the International Committee of the Red Cross (ICRC) in 1996, the provisions of the San Remo Handbook are not yet properly speaking positive rule of law: the ICRC's introductory note states that while most of the provisions contained in the manual are regarded as stating the law currently in force, some may appear as mere developments in law. It is therefore necessary to remain cautious in assessing the value of this text, and compare its provisions with the law prior.') Ministère de la Défense, *Manuel De Droit Des Conflits Armés* (2012) 42.

69 Australian Defence Force, *ADDP 06.4—Law of Armed Conflict* (2006) para 1.46.

70 In the Annex 'Convenciones Internacionales ordenadas cronológicamente' in Ministerio de Defensa, *Manual de Derecho Internacional de los Conflictos Armados* (2010) 165.

71 'This chapter is derived from the San Remo Manual on International Law Applicable to Armed Conflicts at Sea ... [It] is the most up to date version of the law taking into account recent developments such as the 1982 UN Law of the Sea Convention (UNCLOS)': Office of the Judge Advocate General, National Defence, Canada, *Law of Armed Conflict at the Operational and Tactical Levels* (B-GJ-005-104/FP-021, 2003) ch 8, 801.1. See also Stephen Haines, who was one of the co-authors of the chapter on naval warfare for the UK military manual: Stephen Haines, 'War at Sea: Nineteenth-Century Laws for Twenty-First Century Wars?' (2016) 98 International Review of the Red Cross 419, 434. Other States also reference the San Remo Manual in their domestic military manuals: see, for example, Norwegian Manual (n 68) 218; New Zealand Defence Force/Te Ope Kaatua O Aotearoa, *Manual of Armed Forces Law*, vol 4: *Law of Armed Conflict* (DM 69, 2 ed, 2017) 1–31; Danish Ministry of Defence, Defence Command Denmark, *Military Manual on International Law Relevant to Danish Armed Forces in International Operations* (2016) 579.

72 Discussed in more detail in Chapter 5 of this book.

73 Jean-Marie Henckaerts and Louise Doswald-Beck (eds), *Customary International Humanitarian Law* (ICRC 2005) vol 1, xxxvi.

74 See comments made on the Australian Broadcasting Corporation current affairs programme *Lateline* on 31 May 2010 by Israeli government official Mark Regev, who, when asked whether the

by both Israel and a UN panel of inquiry, also repeatedly made reference to the Manual as being a relevant source of law.[75] More recently, the ICRC, in its updated Commentary to the Second Geneva Convention[76] regarding the wounded, sick, and shipwrecked members of armed forces at sea, noted that the San Remo Manual is, 'for the most part, still a valid restatement of customary and treaty international law applicable to armed conflicts at sea'.[77] As Stephen Haines points out, there is 'strong evidence that the [San Remo Manual] is widely regarded as a reliable statement of the [law of armed conflict] to be applied at sea'.[78]

The *San Remo Manual on the Law of Non-International Armed Conflict*

Just over 10 years after the publication of the San Remo Manual on Naval Warfare, the International Institute for Humanitarian Law (IIHL) at San Remo produced another instruction manual for armed conflict, this time in relation to non-international armed conflict (NIAC). The work was initiated by the Institute while under the directorship of Dieter Fleck, as part of a major research project on the humanitarian law applicable in non-international armed conflicts. The project aimed to examine the law of non-international armed conflicts, an area that, as noted by the President of the IIHL, 'is gaining increasing importance and attention due to the growing frequency and menace of internal wars'.[79]

actions of the Israeli navy were compliant with international law, stated that 'the San Remo memorandum states, specifically 67A, that if you have a boat that is charging a blockaded area you are allowed to intercept even prior to it reaching the blockaded area if you've warned them in advance, and that we did a number of times and they had a stated goal which they openly expressed, of breaking the blockade. That blockade is in place to protect our people .... If you look at international law, if someone is breaking your blockade, intends to do so, has been warned, you are allowed to intercept, and that's exactly what we were doing.' Transcript at <http://www.abc.net.au/lateline/israeli-government-defends-raids/849144> accessed 31 July 2021.

[75] *Report of the Secretary-General's Panel of Inquiry on the 31 May 2010 Flotilla Incident* (the Palmer Report) <https://www.un.org/unispal/document/auto-insert-205969/> accessed 31 July 2021; and the report of the Israeli Government-created Public Commission to Examine the Maritime Incident of 31 May 2010 (the Turkel Commission) <https://www.jewishvirtuallibrary.org/the-turkel-commission-report-january-2011>. The Palmer Report cites or references the San Remo Manual nearly 100 times; the Turkel Report cites it over 50 times in Part 1.

[76] ICRC, *Commentary on the Second Geneva Convention: Convention (II) for the Amelioration of the Condition of the Wounded, Sick and Shipwrecked Members of Armed Forces at Sea* (2nd edn, ICRC 2017) Introduction, para 115.

[77] Bruno Demeyere and others, 'The Updated ICRC Commentary on the Second Geneva Convention: Demystifying the Law of Armed Conflict at Sea' (2016) 98 International Review of the Red Cross 401, 407.

[78] Haines (n 71) 434. See also Wolff Heintschel von Heinegg, 'The Current State of the Law of Naval Warfare: A Fresh Look at the San Remo Manual' (2006) 82 International Law Studies 269.

[79] Introduction, *The Manual on the Law of Non-International Armed Conflict, with Commentary* (International Institute of Humanitarian Law 2006) ii (San Remo NIAC Manual).

The process of debating and drafting the San Remo NIAC Manual commenced in March 1999, involving participants from academic, government, and military fields, as well as from civil society, including the ICRC and the Office of the United Nations High Commissioner for Human Rights.[80] However, information regarding *how* the Manual was created is limited: there is little publicly available information regarding the process undertaken for the Manual, with only one public statement that the participants followed the pattern set by the San Remo Naval Manual.[81] Information regarding the participants involved in drafting the Manual is also limited, with the only record of participants coming from the findings of the first meeting, reported in the 2000 edition of the Israel Yearbook on Human Rights.[82] The Yearbook detailed the intentions of the drafters of the Manual and the ambit of discussions, as well as reprinting the discussion and research papers produced by a number of participants for the first meeting;[83] but, beyond those names, any other information about participants, their States, and their institutions of origin, or any other relevant details about the debates that took place between the beginning of the project in 1999 and the eventual release of the Manual in 2006, is not available. Indeed, even the website of the Institute itself does not contain any information on the Manual; the last reference to the Manual on the IIHL site was in 2020:

> [t]he Manual on the Law of Non-International Armed Conflict which was published in March 2006, reflects the developments registered by humanitarian rules at a time where conflicts too often differ from classical warfare between States bound by the Hague Conventions and the Geneva Protocols. It has been now discussing the publication of an updated version.[84]

[80] See generally Dieter Fleck, 'Humanitarian Protection in Non-International Armed Conflicts: The New Research Project of the International Institute of Humanitarian Law' (2000) 30 Israel Yearbook on Human Rights 1, 10.

[81] It should be noted that this is, in large part, supposition. See further ibid 6. The San Remo NIAC Manual was not published as a standalone work as was the San Remo Naval Manual; the only record of participants in the manual and some of the processes followed come from the findings of the first meeting of the San Remo NIAC Manual, which were reported in (2000) 30 Israel Yearbook on Human Rights 1.

[82] (2000) 30 Israel Yearbook on Human Rights 1.

[83] Including Dino Kritsiotis, 'International Humanitarian Law and the Disintegration of States' (2000) 30 Israel Yearbook on Human Rights 17; Michel Veuthey, 'Remedies to Promote the Respect of Fundamental Human Values in Non-International Armed Conflict' (2000) 30 Israel Yearbook on Human Rights 37; George Walker, 'Responses to Humanitarian Law Violations in Non-International Armed Conflicts: Historical Perspectives and Considerations on Conflicts of Jurisdiction' (2000) 30 Israel Yearbook on Human Rights 79; Claus Kreß, 'War Crimes Committed in Non-International Armed Conflict and the Emerging System of International Criminal Justice' (2000) 30 Israel Yearbook on Human Rights 103; Daniel Garcia-Peña Jaramillo, 'Humanitarian Protection in Non-International Armed Conflicts: A Case Study of Colombia' (2000) 30 Israel Yearbook on Human Rights 179; Michael Hoffman, 'The Application of International Humanitarian Law in Sri Lanka: A Compliance Based Case Study on the Rules of War' (2000) 30 Israel Yearbook on Human Rights 209.

[84] <http://web.archive.org/web/20200710065220/http://iihl.org/research-and-publications/> accessed 27 September 2021. Copies of the Manual must be specially requested from the Institute.

By 2006, the drafting committee of Professor Michael Schmitt,[85] Professor Charles Garraway,[86] and Professor Yoram Dinstein[87] had produced a manual containing nearly 50 rules, covering the general principles of IHL applicable in non-international armed conflict,[88] targeting,[89] permissible means and methods of combat,[90] rules relating to persons entitled to special protection,[91] and rules related to specific objects and places,[92] such as cultural property[93] and the natural environment.[94] The Manual was accompanied by a commentary to indicate why certain rules were phrased in certain ways, as well as to provide definitional guidance on terms such as 'fighters'.[95]

The San Remo NIAC Manual replicates, for the most part, the extant treaty law on non-international armed conflict. Additionally, it includes reference to certain provisions of the law of international armed conflicts that are generally considered to be also customary in non-international armed conflicts, such as the definition of a military objective[96] and the principles prohibiting infliction of unnecessary suffering or superfluous injury.[97] Likewise, most of the provisions that might be considered as a progressive development of the law can still be conceptualised as part of pre-existing obligations: thus, the section on 'humane treatment' includes a provision that lists 'ethnic cleansing' as inhumane treatment.[98] While the concept of ethnic cleansing was not a part of the treaty law of non-international armed conflict, and was too recent a concept (at that time)[99] to be considered customary international law, its inclusion is warranted as being a violation of the principle of distinction.[100]

The Manual also includes some elements not found in the treaty or customary law of non-international armed conflict. The most obvious of these is Section 1.1.2, which relates to 'fighters'. The term does not exist in treaty or custom, and the Manual makes it clear that its use is meant only within the scope of the Manual.[101]

85 From the George C Marshall European Center for Security Studies.
86 From the Royal Institute of International Affairs (Chatham House).
87 From Tel Aviv University.
88 San Remo NIAC Manual, Section 1.2.
89 San Remo NIAC Manual, Section 2.1.
90 San Remo NIAC Manual, Sections 2.2, 2.3.
91 San Remo NIAC Manual, Sections 3.1–3.12.
92 San Remo NIAC Manual, Chapter 4.
93 San Remo NIAC Manual, Section 4.2.2.
94 San Remo NIAC Manual, Section 4.2.4.
95 San Remo NIAC Manual, Section 1.1.2, paras 1–4.
96 San Remo NIAC Manual, Section 1.1.4, but see also ICRC, *Customary IHL Database*, Rule 8 <https://ihl-databases.icrc.org/customary-ihl/eng/docs/home> accessed 2 August 2021.
97 San Remo NIAC Manual, Section 1.2.1, and see also ibid *Customary IHL Database*, Rule 70.
98 San Remo NIAC Manual, Section 1.2.4.
99 See further the Interim Report of the Commission of Experts Established Pursuant to Security Council Resolution 780 (1992), UN Doc S/35374 (1993), para 55, where the experts noted that 'the expression "ethnic cleansing" is relatively new'. For a brief history of the term 'ethnic cleansing' in law and practice, see further William Schabas, *Genocide in International Law: The Crime of Crimes* (CUP 2000) 189–201.
100 San Remo NIAC Manual, Section 1.2.4(f), para 11.
101 San Remo NIAC Manual, Section 1.1.2, paras 1–4.

The term 'fighters' is used to denote 'members of the regular armed forces fighting on behalf of the government and members of armed groups fighting against the government'.[102] It is employed 'in lieu of "combatants" in order to avoid any meaning of the latter term in the context of the international law of armed conflict'.[103] The only other rules that might be considered unusual—at least in the context of a manual on the law of non-international armed conflicts—are the inclusion of Section 3.8 on internally displaced persons (IDPs) and Section 3.9 on refugees. Neither Additional Protocol II nor Common Article 3 refers to IDPs or refugees.

As with the San Remo Naval Manual before it, the San Remo NIAC Manual was intended primarily as a restatement of the law applicable in non-international armed conflict;[104] this was no doubt influenced by the fact that an early stated aim of the manual was to replace the 2001 San Remo Code of Code in Non-International Armed Conflict, which had been used by the Institute in its training programs. However, the project's 'architect', Dieter Fleck, clearly intended the Manual to have an impact beyond those persons who attended training programs at the Institute. In discussing to whom the Manual was to be addressed, Fleck wrote that he hoped the Manual could 'further develop existing rules in an area of great political concern',[105] and that it 'could considerably help to support compliance with applicable legal principles and rules of conduct for fighters with a view to protect victims of non-international armed conflict'.[106] To that end, the Manual would have 'two levels of application ... one is the use in the field where rules have to be fairly simple. The other is at higher military and academic level to clarify more sophisticated legal and policy questions'.[107] This approach was reportedly affirmed in plenary, where it was 'agreed that the principal addresses of the Manual will be middle ranking officers and the Commentary will be written for higher authorities and for education'.[108]

As with the San Remo Naval Manual, the San Remo NIAC Manual existed in a somewhat liminal state—a restatement of the applicable law, but not an inherently binding document; an instrument intended for specific military personnel, but adopted in the hope that its influence would be wider. However, compared to the San Remo Naval Manual, the San Remo NIAC Manual did not have anywhere near the same impact on State practice. The Manual is not mentioned in the military manuals of the United Kingdom, Canada, or the United States;[109] nor is it

[102] San Remo NIAC Manual, Section 1.1.2, para 1.
[103] San Remo NIAC Manual, Section 1.1.2, para 1.
[104] San Remo NIAC Manual, Preface, 1.
[105] Fleck (n 80) 6.
[106] ibid.
[107] ibid.
[108] ibid 9.
[109] See, for example, UK *Manual of the Law of Armed Conflict* (n 68) ch 15 on Internal Armed Conflict; National Defence, Canada, *Law of Armed Conflict at the Operational and Tactical Levels* (B-GJ-005-104/FP-021, 2003) ch 17; US Department of Defense, *Law of War Manual* (2015) ch XVII. The San Remo NIAC Manual is, however, mentioned in the Danish Manual (n 71) 120.

mentioned in any of the major monographs on non-international armed conflict that have been produced since the manual's adoption, even in those works produced by participants in the NIAC Manual.[110] It was, however, cited in the Tallinn Manual as being 'considered ... when assessing whether a particular Rule applies during non-international armed conflict'.[111]

The *Montreux Document on Pertinent International Legal Obligations and Good Practices for States related to Operations of Private Military and Security Companies during Armed Conflict*

The next significant contribution to non-binding instruments in IHL came with the adoption of the Montreux Document on Pertinent International Legal Obligations and Good Practices for States related to Operations of Private Military and Security Companies during Armed Conflict. The Document was the result of a process[112] started in late 2005 by the ICRC, working in conjunction with the Swiss Federal Department of Foreign Affairs.[113] The process originated in response to the increasing use of private military and security companies (PMSCs) in situations of internal conflict,[114] most notably during the ongoing hostilities in Iraq and Afghanistan,[115] and the concern that these PMSCs were somehow operating in an international 'legal vacuum',[116] bound by no law regulating their behaviour.

The Swiss Initiative convened for its first meeting in January 2006, attended by government experts from Austria, Canada, France, Germany, South Africa,

[110] The San Remo NIAC Manual is not mentioned in Sandesh Sivakumaran, *The Law of Non-International Armed Conflict* (OUP 2012), Anthony Cullen, *The Concept of Non-International Armed Conflict in International Humanitarian Law* (CUP 2012), or Yoram Dinstein, *Non-International Armed Conflicts in International Law* (2nd edn, CUP 2021), which is interesting given that Dinstein was a contributing author to the San Remo NIAC Manual.

[111] Tallinn Manual, 7–8.

[112] Known as the 'Swiss Initiative'. See further Marie-Louise Tougas, 'Some Comments and Observations on the Montreux Document' (2009) 12 Yearbook of International Humanitarian Law 312; James Cockayne, 'Regulating Private Military and Security Companies: The Context, Negotiation, Weaknesses and Promise of the Montreux Document' (2008) 13 Journal of Conflict & Security Law 401.

[113] For a detailed history of the entire process, see < https://www.montreuxdocument.org/about/history.html > accessed 27 September 2021.

[114] For example, private military companies were used in Angola and Sierra Leone during the 1990s. See generally Peter Singer, *Corporate Warriors: The Rise of the Private Military Industry* (Cornell University Press 2008) 101–19, for a discussion of Executive Outcomes, the private military firm that had been employed to fight in the civil wars in Angola and Sierra Leone.

[115] See ibid 243–60 on the use of PMSCs in Iraq.

[116] See, for example, Chatham House, 'Private Military Companies: A Legal Vacuum?' Summary of International Law Programme Discussion Group (16 March 2005) <https://www.chathamhouse.org/sites/default/files/public/Research/International%20Law/il160305.pdf>; Thomas Catan, 'Private Armies March into a Legal Vacuum' *Financial Times* (10 February 2005); Peter Singer, 'War, Profits, and the Vacuum of Law: Privatized Military Firms and International Law' (2003) 42 Columbia Journal of Transnational Law 521.

Switzerland, Ukraine, the United Kingdom, and the United States, as well as representatives from the ICRC. Also joining the participants for the first day of the workshop were representatives from the private military and security industry,[117] as well as two independent experts.[118] The workshop heard presentations on a variety of topics, including 'Relevant International Standards: Overview, Use of Force, Mercenaries', 'Private Military and Security Companies and Human Rights: A Rough Sketch of the Legal Framework', 'Private Military/Security Companies under IHL', 'The Perspective of Contracting and "Headquarters" States', and 'Regional Organisations: What Role for the EU?'.[119]

This workshop was followed by a second meeting of experts in November 2006, where, among other things, the topic of accountability for and nationality of PMSCs was analysed.[120] Participants at this meeting included representatives from Afghanistan, Angola, Australia, Austria, Canada, France, Germany, Iraq, Poland, Sierra Leone, South Africa, Sweden, Switzerland, Ukraine, the United Kingdom, the United States, and the ICRC. Joining these government experts was a small number of representatives from industry associations and PMSCs, academic experts, and representatives from non-governmental organisations (NGOs).[121] The November 2006 meeting adjourned with the aim of reconvening later to develop a list of pertinent international obligations binding on States and PMSCs regarding the use of such organisations in situations of armed conflict (specifically, under IHL and international human rights law). It was also agreed that a list of 'good practice' for the employment and utilisation of PMSCs should be developed.

Between the November 2006 meeting and the third expert meeting in April 2008, civil society organisations became more involved in the process, with the Swiss government, the ICRC and two NGOs, the International Peace Institute, and the Geneva Centre for the Democratic Control of Armed Forces convening four informal expert consultations. These meetings involved academics, non-governmental organisations and institutes, industry representatives, and non-participant governments, who gave feedback on recommendations on the work to date, with the aim of improving the Montreux draft text.[122] At the third meeting in

117 From companies themselves, as well as industry associations, from the United States and the United Kingdom.

118 Workshop of Governmental Experts and Industry Representatives on Private Military/Security Companies, 16–17 January 2006, Zurich, Switzerland, Summary of the Chair, 1 September 2006, Swiss Federal Department of Foreign Affairs FDFA, Directorate of International Law <https://www.montreuxdocument.org/about/history.html > accessed 27 September 2021.

119 For complete records of the papers and other documentation used and produced by the process, see <http://www.eda.admin.ch/eda/en/home/foreign-policy/international-law/international-humanitarian-law/private-military-security-companies/montreux-document.html> accessed 3 August 2021 and <https://www.montreuxdocument.org/about/history.html > accessed 27 September 2021.

120 Expert Meeting of Governmental and Other Experts on Private Military and Security Companies, 13–14 November 2006, Montreux, Switzerland, Chair's Summary, 22 July 2007, Swiss Federal Department of Foreign Affairs FDFA, Directorate of International Law <https://www.montreuxdocument.org/about/history.html > accessed 27 September 2021.

121 ibid.

122 ibid.

April 2008,[123] experts from 18 States—including Afghanistan, Angola, Australia, Austria, Canada, China, France, Germany, Iraq, Poland, Russia, Sierra Leone, South Africa, Sweden, Switzerland, Ukraine, the United Kingdom, and the United States—as well as representatives from human rights organisations and industry bodies, 'made significant progress in elaborating and fine-tuning a draft text re-affirming existing legal obligations of States as well as PMSCs and their personnel and recommending good state practices in their regard'.[124] At the fourth meeting, held in September 2008, Afghanistan, Angola, Australia, Austria, Canada, China, France, Germany, Iraq, Poland, Sierra Leone, South Africa, Sweden, Switzerland, Ukraine, the United Kingdom, and the United States adopted, by consensus, the Montreux Document on pertinent legal obligations for States regarding PMSCs.[125]

The final text drew upon (and drew inspiration from) numerous sources of international and domestic law: for the first part of the document, the main sources were the Geneva Conventions and Protocols, the ICRC Customary International Humanitarian Law Study, and two UN 'best practice' documents: the UN Basic Principles on the Use of Force and Firearms by Law Enforcement Officials and the UN Code of Conduct for Law Enforcement Officials.[126] Also informing the discussion were regional and industry codes and other soft law instruments, including the EU Arms Export Code,[127] the CoESS/UNI Europa Code of Conduct and Ethics for the Private Security Sector,[128] the Sarajevo Code of Conduct and Client Procurement Guidelines,[129] and the International Peace Operations Association Code of Conduct.[130] Domestic legislation from participant and specially affected[131] States was also examined.[132] The Montreux Document, unlike the

[123] Detailed in the Third Meeting of Governmental and Other Experts on Private Military and Security Companies, 14–16 April 2008, Montreux, Switzerland, Chair's Summary, Swiss Federal Department of Foreign Affairs FDFA, Directorate of International Law <https://www.montreuxdocument.org/about/history.html > accessed 27 September 2021.

[124] ibid 2.

[125] Russia, which had been part of the discussion at the Third Expert Meeting, declined to endorse the final document, stating that to do so would be contrary to Russian domestic law proscribing the provision of private military services. Moreover, the Russian delegate stated that any discussion about the place of PMSCs in the IHL regime should be discussed by all parties to the Geneva Conventions, and not just a small group of States. The Russian delegate also reportedly felt that it was unacceptable to outright declare that PMSC personnel were prima facie civilians (reported in Cockayne (n 112) 423).

[126] Workshop of Governmental Experts and Industry Representatives on Private Military/Security Companies 16–17 January 2006, Zurich, Switzerland, Summary of the Chair, 1 September 2006, Swiss Federal Department of Foreign Affairs FDFA, Directorate of International Law <https://www.montreuxdocument.org/about/history.html> accessed 27 September 2021 >.

[127] <http://seesac.org/f/img/File/Res/EU-Documents/EU-Code-of-Conduct-on-Arms-Exports-512.pdf>.

[128] <http://psm.du.edu/media/documents/industry_initiatives/coess_code_of_conduct.pdf>.

[129] <www.seesac.org/f/docs/Private-Security-Companies/The-Sarajevo-Client-Guidelines-for-the-Procurement-of-Private-_1.pdf>.

[130] <https://lapa.princeton.edu/conferences/military07/restricted/ipoa_conduct_military07.pdf>.

[131] Specially affected in that these States were the territorial States of existing PMSCs and/or had either used or been subject to the use of private military and security firms during situations of armed conflict within their territory.

[132] Including from Afghanistan, Angola, Australia, Canada, France, Iraq, Sierra Leone, South Africa, the United Kingdom, and the United States. See generally Cockayne (n 112). Cockayne served as the

San Remo Manuals, was adopted as an intergovernmental statement, negotiated in a manner similar to a conventional treaty. As such, non-governmental actors were eventually removed from the final stages of the Document's negotiation, with NGOs even reportedly physically barred from attending the final 'face to face discussions'.[133]

The final instrument is divided into two parts. Part 1 covers the pertinent international legal obligations relating to PMSCs. It contains 27 operative paragraphs, covering the international law, IHL, and international human rights law obligations owed by contracting States, territorial States, and 'Home'[134] States, when engaging with PMSCs.[135] The remainder of Part 1 covers the relevant law that applies to other States (for example, that '[a]ll other States have an obligation, within their power, to ensure respect for international humanitarian law. They have an obligation to refrain from encouraging or assisting in violations of international humanitarian law by any party to an armed conflict').[136] Five paragraphs are dedicated to the specific obligations and rights that exist for PMSCs and their personnel under international law,[137] with the final paragraph affirming that the law on superior responsibility may apply to the conduct of PMSCs and their personnel.[138] Part 2 of the Montreux Document is a listing of 73 'good practices'[139] regarding those entities that might employ PMSCs, such as States, international organisations, non-government organisations, and companies. Where Part 1 drew on the treaty law of armed conflict, Part 2 draws more on domestic legislation, national and regional codes of conduct, corporate codes of conduct, and statements of policy. It covers broad topics, such as compliance monitoring and accountability mechanisms for PMSCs,[140] and establishing an authorisation procedure for the use of PMSCs,[141] as well as other recommendations, such as ensuring that PMSCs can be identifiable and distinguishable from the civilian population.[142]

facilitator for the first of the four Expert Consultation that took place in 2007 and participated in all four Expert Workshops during 2007.

[133] ibid 422.

[134] The Document defines these categories of States thusly: '"Contracting States" are States that directly contract for the services of PMSCs, including, as appropriate, where such a PMSC subcontracts with another PMSC ... "Territorial States" are States on whose territory PMSCs operate ... "Home States" are States of nationality of a PMSC, i.e. where a PMSC is registered or incorporated; if the State where the PMSC is incorporated is not the one where it has its principal place of management, then the State where the PMSC has its principal place of management is the "Home State"': Montreux Document, Preface, 10.

[135] Montreux Document, paras 1–17.

[136] Montreux Document, para 18.

[137] Montreux Document, paras 22–26.

[138] Montreux Document, para 27.

[139] Montreux Document, Part 2.

[140] Montreux Document, paras 19–23 (for Contracting States); 46–52 (for Territorial States); 68–73 (for Home States).

[141] Montreux Document, paras 25–42 (for Territorial States); 54–67 (for Home States).

[142] Montreux Document, para 44.

The Preface to the Montreux Document makes it clear that it is 'not a legally binding instrument and does not affect existing obligations of States under customary international law or under international agreements to which they are parties'.[143] The Montreux Document should therefore not 'be interpreted as limiting, prejudicing or enhancing in any manner existing obligations under international law, or as creating or developing new obligations under international law'.[144]

Part 1 has been appraised as a 'narrow',[145] 'conservative statement of the *lex lata*'[146] of IHL and international human rights law in relation to States and PMSCs. It restates the applicability of IHL for *all* parties in armed conflicts and affirms that the obligation to respect IHL applies for States that host, employ, or otherwise engage with PMSCs. Indeed, the very definition of PMSCs in the Montreux Document is itself significant: by stating that '"PMSCs" are private business entities that provide military and/or security services, irrespective of how they describe themselves',[147] the Document makes it clear that assessment of a PMSC is objective and not to be shaped by any attempted obfuscation on the part of a PMSC or State that may attempt to deny that it has engaged (or is engaging) in military and security services.

The Document also makes it clear that States are under a specific duty to respect international law when employing or hosting PMSCs, and that Contracting States cannot 'contract out' of their international obligations. It also acknowledges the customary law of State responsibility, in which Contracting States will be deemed responsible for the acts of PMSCs if they have been incorporated by the State into its regular armed forces in accordance with its domestic legislation;[148] if they can be considered members of organised armed forces, groups, or units under a command responsible to the State;[149] if they have been empowered to exercise elements of governmental authority if they are acting in that capacity (that is, they are formally authorised by law or regulation to carry out functions normally conducted by organs of the State);[150] or if they are acting on the instructions of the State or under its direction or control.[151]

Despite the cautious approach evidenced in the Document, there were some areas of contention. Certain areas were unaddressed, such as the legality of using force in self-defence.[152] Additionally, the difficult question of whether PMSCs should be considered as civilians taking direct part in hostilities, or whether

143 Montreux Document, Preface, para 3.
144 Montreux Document, Preface, para 4.
145 Cockayne (n 112) 404.
146 ibid.
147 Montreux Document, Preface, para 9(a).
148 Montreux Document, para 7(a).
149 Montreux Document, para 7(b).
150 Montreux Document, para 7(c).
151 Montreux Document, para 7(d).
152 Tougas (n 112) 344–45.

they should enjoy combatant status and rights, is essentially avoided. While the Document *does* list examples of activities that would be considered military or security in nature,[153] it does not make any definitive statement of whether PMSCs have a fixed status under the law. Rather, the relevant paragraphs of the Montreux Document state that the status of PMSCs should be assessed on a case-by-case basis 'according to the nature and circumstances of the functions in which they are involved',[154] reaffirming that, if they are civilians, 'the personnel of PMSCs may not be the object of attack, unless and for such time as they directly participate in hostilities'.[155] But, if they 'are incorporated into the regular armed forces of a State or are members of organized armed forces, groups or units under a command responsible to the State',[156] then they are entitled to prisoner-of-war status under Geneva Convention III 'if they are persons accompanying the armed forces meeting the requirements of article 4A(4) of the Third Geneva Convention',[157] and are 'obliged, regardless of their status, to comply with applicable international humanitarian law'.[158] The Montreux Document takes a functional rather than status-based approach to PMSCs, but avoids making any statement as to, for instance, whether PMSCs are civilians and therefore should not be placed in a position where they could be considered as taking a direct part in hostilities.[159]

Also controversial during the drafting stage were the specific definitions of 'Contracting State' and 'Home State', and the associated provisions on those States' obligations—specifically, that obligations under international human rights law exist 'regardless of the extra-jurisdictional location of the activities of the private entity'.[160] This was considered problematic from the perspective of due diligence obligations for States, and whether States could be held responsible for the activities of PMSCs who commit extra-territorial violations of human rights law specifically (as opposed to violations of IHL).[161] Some States[162] were concerned about the 'prominence of human rights language in the draft text',[163] and sought to downplay or minimise the effects of such language, while other States and non-governmental organisations felt that the

[153] Such as 'armed guarding and protection of persons and objects, such as convoys, buildings and other places; maintenance and operation of weapons systems; prisoner detention; and advice to or training or local forces and security personnel': Montreux Document, Preface, para 9(a).
[154] Montreux Document, para 24.
[155] Montreux Document, para 25.
[156] Montreux Document, para 26.
[157] Montreux Document, para 26.
[158] Montreux Document, para 26.
[159] Tougas (n 112) 342–44.
[160] Cockayne (n 112) 405.
[161] ibid 421.
[162] The United States, the United Kingdom, Canada, and Australia.
[163] Cockayne (n 112) 421.

human rights language should be reaffirmed and made stronger, rather than diminished. Ultimately, the push to downplay the human rights language won out, with overt references to matters such as 'due diligence' being excised from the final draft.[164] In response, human rights organisations involved in the Initiative voiced concerns that the instrument was heading in a notably conservative direction, and that it was ' "trading away" the Document's human rights language in an effort to secure the support of the widest possible group of States—and in particular the United States—on IHL issues'.[165] Some non-State participants even went so far as to hypothesise that their involvement in the entire Initiative was nothing more than a negotiation tactic, a ploy designed to 'play off' against any position taken by the ICRC, that would serve to make the ICRC position seem more moderate.[166] When the penultimate draft of the Document was distributed, Amnesty International and the International Commission of Jurists were highly critical, stating that the Document 'fell short, in substantial respect'[167] of the Initiative's stated goal of clarifying the situation regarding States and PMSCs, and that, in falling below the standards already set by international law, the Document ran the risk of being 'discounted and other sources of law invoked, a consequence which no doubt would devalue the currency of the initiative'.[168] Less controversial was Part 2, largely due to its ambit as 'good practice' rather than a restatement of the relevant law; its much broader scope and largely hortatory language meant that it was ultimately largely acceptable to participants in the Initiative, needing little revision.[169]

Once the Document was finally adopted, State and industry reception was essentially positive. Within a year, 15 more States had joined the original 17 in endorsing the Document; by 2020, that number would rise to 56,[170] with three intergovernmental organisations[171] also endorsing the Document. Of the States that have endorsed the document, five are from Africa, four are from the Latin America and Caribbean region, 25 are from the WEOG regional group, eight are from the Asia-Pacific region, and 12 are from Eastern Europe.[172]

[164] ibid.
[165] ibid.
[166] ibid.
[167] ibid 423.
[168] ibid.
[169] Third Meeting of Governmental and Other Experts, Chairs Summary, 2008.
[170] <http://www.eda.admin.ch/eda/en/home/foreign-policy/international-law/international-humanitarian-law/private-military-security-companies/participating-states.html> accessed 3 August 2021.
[171] North Atlantic Treaty Organization (NATO), the European Union, and the Organization for Security and Co-operation in Europe <http://www.eda.admin.ch/eda/en/home/foreign-policy/international-law/international-humanitarian-law/private-military-security-companies/participating-states.html> accessed 3 August 2021.
[172] <https://www.montreuxdocument.org/about/participants.html> accessed 27 September 2021.

The *Manual on International Law Applicable to Air and Missile Warfare*

At the same time that the Montreux Document was being conceived and debated, another non-binding manual was also in its preparatory stages—the *Manual on International Law Applicable to Air and Missile Warfare* (AMW Manual).[173] The Manual had its genesis in a meeting[174] co-convened by the Program on Humanitarian Policy and Conflict Research (HPCR) at Harvard University and the Swiss Federal Department of Foreign Affairs in January 2003.[175] The experts at that meeting identified the need to address possible gaps in the law when dealing with new technologies, with the field of air and missile warfare noted as a 'high-priority area for the restatement of existing international law'.[176] As with the law on naval warfare, the treaty law on aerial warfare was sparse, with only one *sui generis* document on aerial warfare—the 1923 Hague Rules of Air Warfare—in existence.[177] The Hague Rules, though not themselves binding, were considered by the experts at the 2003 meeting to have 'had considerable impact on the development of the customary law of armed conflict';[178] however, it was also noted that 'over the course of the recent decades, the challenges of applying existing law to the use of aircraft and missiles in time of hostilities has amply demonstrated that there are bones of contention regarding the scope and content of the international legal rules pertaining to air and missile warfare'.[179] With this in mind, it was felt that a restatement of the existing law of air and missile warfare was a valuable endeavour.[180]

The HPCR was tasked with overseeing this new project and, to that end, undertook consultations with governments and with representatives of the ICRC. Following these consultations, the HPCR convened a Group of Experts, numbering over 35, drawn from academia, government, the armed forces, and civil society. From there, the AMW Manual progressed in much the same fashion as the San Remo Naval Manual.[181] At the first meeting of the Group of Experts, a plan of

[173] The Manual was drafted under the auspices of the HPCR at Harvard University. While the HPCR uses its own acronym when referring to the Manual (that is, the HPCR Manual), this monograph will use the term AMW Manual.

[174] The Informal High-Level Expert Meeting on Current Challenges to International Humanitarian Law (also known as the Alabama I meeting). See further HPCR, *Manual on International Law Applicable to Air and Missile Warfare* (CUP 2013) xi.

[175] The HPCR was established in August 2000 as a joint venture of the Harvard TH Chan School of Public Health, the Executive Office of the United Nations Secretary-General, and the Swiss Federal Department of Foreign Affairs <htttp://www.hpcrresearch.org/> accessed 3 August 2021.

[176] HPCR (n 174) xi.

[177] Though the Additional Protocols had some specific rules relating to aerial warfare—such as rules on parachutists in distress, and rules on bombardments—the only standalone document on aerial warfare was the 1923 Hague Rules. The Hague Rules are discussed in more detail in Chapter 2.

[178] HPCR (n 174) ix.

[179] ibid.

[180] ibid.

[181] Indeed, the HPCR makes this connection between the two Manuals explicit, noting that 'the present project uses the San Remo Manual as a model' (ibid x) but that, 'like the San Remo Manual, the HPCR Manual must not be confused with a draft treaty . . . the goal is rather to present a methodical

action was developed, and topics were selected and assigned to experts, who then produced research papers for the remainder of the group. The Group of Experts then met to discuss the research papers and formulate rules based on agreed areas.

Eight meetings of the Group of Experts were held over the period of five years,[182] with most of the members of the Group of Experts in attendance at most of the meetings.[183] Of the 37 experts who were involved in the project through some or all of the meetings, one participant was from Africa,[184] one from the Asia-Pacific region,[185] and the remainder from WEOG States, with the largest subset of WEOG participants hailing from the United States.[186] Additional to the meetings of the Group of Experts, the draft manual was also the subject of consultations with States; bilateral,[187] regional,[188] and international and intergovernmental[189] meetings were held in a variety of locations to receive feedback and commentary on the

restatement of existing international law on air and missile warfare, based on the general practice of States accepted as law (opinio juris) and treaties in force': ibid.

[182] Following the first meeting at Harvard University in January 2004, the second meeting was in Luzern in September 2004; the third in Heidelberg in January 2005; the fourth in Oslo in September 2005; the fifth in Brussels in March 2006; the sixth in Spiez in December 2006; the seventh in Frankfurt in April 2008; and the eighth in Bern in 2009. Each meeting lasted on average of four full working days. See further HPCR (n 174) 409.

[183] See the appendices of the AMW Manual for the listing of participants and the sessions for which they were in attendance.

[184] Brigadier General Titus Githiora, Legal Advisor for the Kenyan Ministry of Defence, participated in the 2004 sessions of the Group of Experts.

[185] Professor Zhu Wenqi, Renmin University of China, was a 'core' expert in the entire process.

[186] In all, 10 participants were from US (or US-affiliated) institutions: Mr Claude Bruderlein from the HPCR at Harvard University; Rear-Admiral (ret) Jane Dalton, US Navy, and Attorney-Advisor to the US Department of State; Professor Yoram Dinstein, from the HPCR at Harvard University (though Professor Dinstein also held the position of Professor Emeritus of International Law at Tel Aviv University); Major General Charles Dunlap Jr, Deputy Judge Advocate General, US Airforce; Colonel (ret) W Hays Parks, Former Special Assistant to the Judge Advocate General for the Army for Law of War Matters, Office of the General Counsel, US Department of Defense; Professor Michael Schmitt, Dean and Professor of Law at The George C Marshall European Center for Security Studies (a joint United States Department of Defense and Federal Ministry of Defence security and Defense Studies Institute in Germany); Mr Bruno Demeyere, from HPCR at Harvard University; Colonel Edward Monaghan, Legal Adviser, US Air Force; Commander Angela Miller, Legal Adviser, US Navy; and Lt Colonel Philip T Wold, Legal Adviser, US Air Force.

[187] Those meetings were between China (March 2008), France (June 2008), Russia (March 2009), and the United States (June 2007).

[188] Three regional meetings were held: in Australia in November 2007 (for the Asia-Pacific region, with representatives of Australia, Cambodia, China, Indonesia, Japan, the Republic of Korea, Malaysia, New Zealand, Pakistan, the Philippines, Singapore, and Thailand in attendance); in Namibia in March 2008 (for the African region, with Australia, Belgium, China, Côte d'Ivoire, Denmark, Finland, France, Germany Greece, Latvia, Libya, Namibia, the Netherlands, Nigeria, Norway, Pakistan, Poland, Romania, Rwanda, South Africa, Spain, Tanzania, Uganda, Zambia, and Zimbabwe in attendance); and in Canada in September 2008 (with Argentina, Brazil, Canada, the United States, and Israel in attendance).

[189] At the Third Informal High Level Expert Meeting on Current Challenges to IHL (Alabama III), held in Montreux in May 2006, the attendees were representatives from Belgium, Brazil, Canada, the Democratic Republic of Congo, China, Denmark, Egypt, France, India, Italy, Japan, Jordan, the Republic of Korea, Mexico, the Netherlands, Nigeria, Norway, Pakistan, Russia, Saudi Arabia, Spain, Sweden, Switzerland, the United Kingdom, the United States, the European Union, the ICRC, and the Office for the Coordination of Humanitarian Affairs and Office of Legal Affairs, United Nations.

draft as it progressed. Suggestions and recommendations from those States were taken back to the Group of Experts and incorporated in revisions. These meetings meant that 'most of the leading States in the sphere of air and missile warfare'[190] were consulted at some point during the process, though State participation in consultations was undertaken on the understanding that it was not to 'imply official endorsement of the specific formulation of any given Black-letter Rules of the HPCR Manual'.[191] All stages of the Manual were overseen by a drafting committee,[192] whose task it was to steer the Manual from its first draft, as presented at the 2006 Brussels meeting, to the final text of the Manual, as adopted by the Group of Experts in Bern in 2009.

The AMW Manual, as finally adopted, contains 175 'Black-letter Rules',[193] divided into 24 sections covering topics such as basic definitions[194] and the general framework of the Manual;[195] weapons;[196] attacks;[197] military objectives;[198] direct participation in hostilities;[199] precautions that must be taken in both attack[200] and defence;[201] the protection of specific types of aircraft,[202] including civilian,[203] medical, and religious transports;[204] specific protections for certain persons and objects, such as the natural environment,[205] cultural property, objects indispensable to the survival of the civilian population, and UN personnel;[206] rules on humanitarian aid[207] and the establishment of exclusion and no-fly zones;[208] rules on certain methods of warfare, such as ruses, perfidy, and espionage;[209] surrender;[210] parachutists bailing out of aircraft in distress;[211] contraband, interception, inspection, and capture of neutral and/or enemy aircraft;[212] aerial blockade;[213] multilateral

190 HPCR (n 174) xii.
191 ibid.
192 The Drafting Committee comprised Arne Willy Dahl, Bruno Demeyere, Yoram Dinstein, Wolff Heintschel von Heinegg, Jean-François Quéguiner, and Michael Schmitt; the Committee met six times throughout the process (twice in 2008 and four times in 2009), with the final editing of the Manual in the hands of Yoram Dinstein and Bruno Demeyere.
193 To use the terminology in the Manual.
194 AMW Manual, Rule 1.
195 AMW Manual, Rules 2–4.
196 AMW Manual, Rules 5–9.
197 AMW Manual, Rules 10–21.
198 AMW Manual, Rules 22–27.
199 AMW Manual, Rules 28–29.
200 AMW Manual, Rules 30–41.
201 AMW Manual, Rules 42–46.
202 AMW Manual, Rules 58–70.
203 AMW Manual, Rules 47–57.
204 AMW Manual, Rules 71–87.
205 AMW Manual, Rules 88–89.
206 AMW Manual, Rules 88–99.
207 AMW Manual, Rules 100–04.
208 AMW Manual, Rules 105–10.
209 AMW Manual, Rules 111–24.
210 AMW Manual, Rules 125–31.
211 AMW Manual, Rules 132–33.
212 AMW Manual, Rules 134–46.
213 AMW Manual, Rules 147–59.

operations;[214] and the law of neutrality.[215] The AMW Manual is also accompanied by a Commentary, 'intended to provide user-friendly explanations for both legal advisers, and those who plan, approve, or execute air or missile operations on both sides of the armed conflict'.[216] The Manual notes that the ultimate responsibility for the rules lies with the Group of Experts, and that ultimate responsibility for the Commentary rests with the HPCR.[217]

Excluded from the Manual are rules on *jus ad bellum*, individual penal accountability under international criminal law, implementation and enforcement of the law (including the law on belligerent reprisals), the law on outer space, and the international human rights law implications for IHL in air and missile warfare. The reason given for these exclusions was that the aim of the Manual was to produce a document that had operational use in the conduct of hostilities.[218] Therefore, additional rules on criminal sanctions, for example, would arguably not have immediate operational use in the field in the same way as rules on how to define a military objective.

Also excluded from the Manual's ambit is the law on non-international armed conflict. The introduction notes that this was done because 'it was impossible to ignore serious terminological difficulties implicit'[219] in situations of non-international armed conflict, as certain terms, such as 'belligerent' and 'combatant', 'are overtly inappropriate for usage in non-international armed conflicts'.[220] Rather than employ imprecise or ambiguous terminology that could be used interchangeably between situations of international armed conflict and non-international armed conflict, the Group of Experts decided instead to concentrate on international armed conflict, but include in the Commentary indications where the Black-letter Rule 'is totally irrelevant to non-international armed conflicts or is applicable to them in a different fashion'.[221]

The AMW Manual makes it clear that the final rules, as adopted, 'reflect the overall consensus of the Group of Experts'.[222] The Introduction to the Manual outlines the process by which this consensus was reached, and what role dissenting voices played in the drafting process:

[214] AMW Manual, Rules 160–64.
[215] AMW Manual, Rules 165–75.
[216] HPCR (n 174) xv.
[217] 'The Group of Experts as a whole frequently determined what the Commentary on specific Black-letter Rules ought to include. All participants also had an opportunity to see an earlier version of the Commentary and to critique it. Still, for obvious practical purposes, it was impossible to seek a line-by-line approval of a rather lengthy text by the entire Group of Experts. Hence, whereas the Black-letter Rules of the *HPCR Manual* reflect the views of the members of the Group of Experts, the Commentary must be seen as the sole responsibility of HPCR': ibid xv.
[218] ibid xvii.
[219] ibid.
[220] ibid.
[221] ibid.
[222] ibid xiii.

> Consensus for the purposes of the drafting of the Black-letter Rules of the *HPCR Manual* was understood to mean that no more than two participants in the Group of Experts had reservations about the language in which the Black-letter Rules are couched (caveats were then inserted in the Commentary). Whenever three or more participants in the Group of Experts objected to a given text, it was changed to meet such objections or bridge over conflicting views. In the rare instances in which compromise formulas proved beyond the reach of the Group of Experts, it was agreed to follow in the text the majority view but to give in the Commentary full exposure to the dissenting opinions.[223]

The Commentary and Black-letter Rules therefore operate in tandem to give a full accounting for how particular rules have been arrived at, and how they should be interpreted.

The AMW Manual is also clear in noting that it should be taken as *lex lata* only. This is evident from use of the terminology 'Black-letter Rules', but is also affirmed in the introduction: 'no attempt has been made to be innovative or to propose new norms (*lex ferenda*), however desirable this may appear to be: the sole aim of this project has been to systematically capture in the text existing rules of international law (*lex lata*)'.[224] However, the Manual also affirms that it 'does not have binding force',[225] but the drafters hope that it will 'serve as a valuable resource for armed forces in the development of rules of engagement, the writing of domestic military manuals, the preparation of training courses, and—above all—the actual conduct of armed forces in combat operations'.[226] Indeed, the intended audience for the Manual is clearly stated as being operations officers, armed services lawyers, and military commanders in the field,[227] with the hope that the Manual could be of utility to 'other segments of the armed forces in time of armed conflict, as well by those organisations and entities mandated to monitor and report on the implementation of international law by parties to the armed conflicts'.[228]

On release of the AMW Manual, opinion was divided on its merits between those who praised it as a 'towering achievement'[229] and a 'tremendous accomplishment',[230] and those who considered that a number of its provisions did not 'reflect current international law ... are highly problematic, and, if actually implemented,

[223] ibid xiv.
[224] ibid x–xi.
[225] ibid xiii.
[226] ibid.
[227] ibid xv.
[228] ibid xiii.
[229] Charles Dunlap, 'Law of War Manuals and Warfighting: A Perspective' (2012) 47 Texas International Law Journal 265, 265. Dunlap was one of the experts involved in the drafting of the AMW Manual.
[230] ibid 275.

could result in war crime responsibility'.[231] Critics pointed to the 'rigid state-oriented definitions of belligerent party and international armed conflict'[232] as 'needlessly limiting'[233] and not reflective of the complex historical instances and customary law relating to non-State participants in international armed conflicts. The provisions that provided for the loss of protection for civilian aircraft in certain circumstances were also strongly criticised as being among several 'restrictive, regressive, and reprehensible rules'.[234] Indeed, even those who had been supportive of the Manual admitted that it may be 'too conservative'.[235]

The *Copenhagen Principles and Guidelines on the Handling of Detainees in International Military Operations*

The *Copenhagen Principles and Guidelines on the Handling of Detainees in International Military Operations* (Copenhagen Principles) were the result of an initiative spearheaded by the Danish government in 2007. Denmark's interest in the issue can be linked to its involvement in military operations in Afghanistan and, in particular, its bilateral memorandum of understanding (MoU) with Afghanistan concerning the transfer of persons between the Danish contingent of the International Security Assistance Force and the Afghan authorities, 'one of the first of such memorandums to be signed'.[236] While Denmark was of the opinion that such agreements and MoUs would offer 'a satisfactory solution to the challenges pertaining to the handling of detainees',[237] not all States involved in the international military operations in Afghanistan were able to reach a similar agreement with Afghan authorities. This led to the problematic outcome that 'the framework for the handling of detainees [would] vary according to the arrangements of the apprehending State'.[238] A uniform approach to the procedural and substantive rules applicable to the handling of detainees in multinational and international military operations was a necessity.

Denmark continued to raise the issue in international forums: during its tenure as president of the UN Security Council in 2006, Denmark presented a paper to the Council for discussion regarding the role of UN forces exercising detention

231 Jordan J Paust, 'A Critical Appraisal of the Air and Missile Warfare Manual' (2012) 47 Texas International Law Journal 277, 277.
232 ibid 279.
233 ibid.
234 ibid 282.
235 Dunlap (n 229) 275.
236 Thomas Winkler, 'The Copenhagen Process on Detainees: A Necessity' (2010) 78 Nordic Journal of International Law 489, 496. Winkler was Ambassador and Under Secretary for Legal Affairs for the Ministry of Foreign Affairs of Denmark and one of the representatives for Denmark during the Copenhagen Process.
237 ibid.
238 ibid.

powers during UN peace operations.[239] By the end of the year, the Danish Ministry of Foreign Affairs had arranged and hosted a small roundtable meeting in Copenhagen involving legal and diplomatic experts, who discussed the 'political, legal, and practical problems relating to dealing with the taking and handling of detainees in military operations'.[240] Following on from that meeting, the Danish government hosted a conference in 2007, inviting a number of State representatives,[241] as well as representatives from the United Nations, the North Atlantic Treaty Organization (NATO), and the ICRC.[242] During the 2007 conference, three topics in particular arose for further discussion. The first of these was which of the two legal regimes—IHL or international human rights law—applied under which conditions in international military operations, and what legal implications both regimes brought for States. The second topic was the standards for the handling of detainees in military operations (in particular, the conditions relating to the transfer of detainees to host or other countries). The third was what the best solution would be for the handling of detainees, considering the need for operational clarity.[243] It was generally agreed among participants at the conference that these concerns needed to be addressed.[244]

The Danish government was of the opinion that there was sufficient support among interested States[245] to develop a set of 'best practice guidelines for use in military operations'[246] to address specific areas of concern for States engaged in detention in international military operations, including the legal basis/mandate for detention in international military operations, the legal standards and procedures associated with transfers of detainees, the interaction between IHL and human rights norms in situations of non-international armed conflict, and the definition

239 Letter dated 7 June 2006 from the Permanent Representative of Denmark to the United Nations addressed to the Secretary-General, UN Doc S/2006/367 (2006). See also Bruce Oswald, 'The Copenhagen Process: Some Reflecting Concerning Soft Law' in Stéphanie Lagoutte, Thomas Gammeltoft-Hansen, and John Cerone (eds), *Tracing the Roles of Soft Law in Human Rights* (OUP 2016) 110.

240 Oswald (n 239) 110.

241 Argentina, Australia, Belgium, Canada, Denmark, France, Germany, the Netherlands, New Zealand, Nigeria, Norway, Pakistan, South Africa, Sweden, the United Kingdom, and the United States. By the end of the Copenhagen Process in 2012, additional States participating would include China, Finland, India, Malaysia, Russia, Tanzania, Turkey, and Uganda. See further Ministry of Foreign Affairs of Denmark, Legal Department, 'The Copenhagen Process on the Handling of Detainees in International Military Operations' (2007) 46 Military Law and the Law of War Review 363; Bruce Oswald and Thomas Winkler, 'The Copenhagen Process: Principles and Guidelines on the Handling of Detainees in International Military Operations' (2014) 83 Nordic Journal of International Law 128, 136.

242 Other intergovernmental organisations that would be involved in the process included the African Union, the European Union, and the Intergovernmental Authority on Development. See further Jonathan Horowitz, 'Introductory Note to the Copenhagen Process Principles and Guidelines on the Handling of Detainees in International Military Operations' (2012) 51 International Legal Materials 1364, 1364. At all meetings, the international organisations attended as observers only, rather than as participants. See further Oswald and Winkler (n 241) 144.

243 Ministry of Foreign Affairs of Denmark, Legal Department (n 241) 364.

244 ibid.

245 Oswald (n 239) 110.

246 Ministry of Foreign Affairs of Denmark, Legal Department (n 241) 364.

of detention 'inter alia questions of effective control'.[247] It was agreed at the 2007 conference that 'the solution was not the elaboration of new rules on handling of detainees, but to make the existing legal framework comprehensive and feasible to apply in practice'.[248]

These issues were examined in more detail at a seminar hosted by Denmark in May 2008,[249] where the narrower focus on best practices relating to detention from national, regional, and international perspectives were discussed and analysed.[250] During that meeting, the differing legal and policy approaches of States when dealing with detention in military operations were made manifest, with some States clearly favouring an IHL framework while others took a complementary approach of IHL and international human rights. Uncertainties about which of the international human rights law obligations must be considered applicable were also made evident at this time, as were divisions regarding whether there was a legal obligation to monitor the treatment of detainees after they were transferred from one State to another and, if so, how long such an obligation lasted.[251]

Drawing on the 2007 and 2008 discussions, the Danish Ministry of Foreign Affairs called for a second conference, held in Copenhagen in June 2009, where 23 States[252] and several international and intergovernmental organisations[253] met to discuss the results of the 2007 and 2008 meetings. During that conference, it was agreed that Denmark should elaborate a draft Copenhagen Process Outcome Document, known as the Copenhagen Process Declaration, for further discussion.[254] The broad aim of the Declaration was to affirm that both IHL and international human rights law would be respected when handling detainees, based on the best practices of States and international organisations previously discussed during the conferences and seminar.

By late 2010, the Danish government had produced and circulated a draft Declaration containing a preamble, 12 'guiding principles', and an explanatory note, which contained a commentary on the preamble and the principles.[255] The

[247] ibid 365.

[248] ibid.

[249] States participating at the 2008 Seminar were Argentina, Australia, Canada, Denmark, Finland, France, Germany, India, Malaysia, the Netherlands, Nigeria, Norway, Pakistan, South Africa, Sweden, Tanzania, Turkey, Uganda, the United Kingdom, and the United States. The international and intergovernmental institutions in attendance included the African Union, the European Union, NATO, the United Nations, the ICRC, and the Intergovernmental Authority on Development.

[250] Summary of Comments by Thomas Winkler, 'The Handling of Detainees in Military Operations: An Update on the Copenhagen Process' <www.biicl.org/files/4547_copenhagen_process.pdf>. See also Oswald and Winkler (n 241) 136.

[251] Oswald and Winkler (n 241) 138.

[252] Argentina, Australia, Belgium, Canada, Denmark, Finland, France, Germany, India, Malaysia, the Netherlands, New Zealand, Nigeria, Norway, Pakistan, Russia, South Africa, Sweden, Tanzania, Turkey, Uganda, the United Kingdom, and the United States.

[253] The African Union, the European Union, NATO, the United Nations, and the ICRC.

[254] Thomas Winkler, 'The Copenhagen Process on Detainees: A Necessity' (2010) 78 Nordic Journal of International Law 489, 497.

[255] The Declaration was not made publicly available; however, the substance has been reported on by Oswald and Winkler (n 241) 139–42.

preamble and the 12 guiding principles contained in the Declaration proceeded on the basis that detention is a 'necessary and legitimate means of achieving the objectives of military operations'.[256] The Declaration affirmed the importance of the Geneva Conventions and Additional Protocols, and reiterated that States have a responsibility to comply with their international obligations under both IHL and international human rights law in particular. The principles themselves covered several issues, including the definition of detention, the treatment of detainees, and procedural protections such as rules for the review of detention, as well as for the transfer and monitoring of detainees.[257]

The Declaration was then circulated among States and international organisations several times. The comments received were incorporated into revised drafts and the redrafted document was returned for comment to participants.[258] The Declaration and its contents were also the subject of a number of consultations with civil society,[259] including roundtables at the International Institute of Humanitarian Law[260] and academic conferences.[261] In all, the Declaration was 'open' for comments for almost two years.

Following this consultation period, the Danish government presented the redrafted Declaration, now known as the *Copenhagen Process Rules and Guidelines on the Handling of Detainees in International Military Operations*, at the final conference of the Copenhagen Process in October 2012.[262] During that final conference, various issues were discussed, culminating in the release of the now renamed *Copenhagen Process Principles and Guidelines on the Handling of Detainees in International Military Operations*. The Principles were 'welcomed' by nearly all States involved in the Process,[263] with the chairperson of the 2012 conference noting that 'by welcoming the Principles and Guidelines participants agreed that

[256] The Copenhagen Process Declaration, Preamble 3, as reported by Oswald and Winkler (n 241) 139.

[257] As reported in Oswald and Winkler (n 241) 139–42.

[258] This process is described in Oswald (n 239) 110–12.

[259] As noted in Oswald and Winkler (n 241) 141, the 'final engagement' with civil society prior to the adoption of the Copenhagen Principles included a roundtable hosted by Denmark, involving Amnesty International, the Danish Society of the Red Cross, Human Rights First, and members of Danish academia.

[260] See Thomas Winkler, 'Transfer of Detainees'(International Institute of Humanitarian Law 33rd Roundtable on Current Issues of International Humanitarian Law, 'Global Violence: Consequences and Responses', San Remo, 9–11 September 2010) <www.iihl.org/full-list-congresses-international-conferences-round-tables-since-institutes-foundation/>.

[261] Reported in Oswald and Winkler (n 241) 140.

[262] See generally Ministry of Foreign Affairs of Denmark, 'Copenhagen Process on the Handling of Detainees in International Military Operations: Introductory Comments by the Chair, Principles and Guidelines with Chairman's Commentary, and Minutes of the Third Copenhagen Conference' (2012) 51 Military Law and the Law of War Review 182. The States at the 2012 conference included Argentina, Australia, Belgium, Canada, China, Denmark, Finland, France, Germany, India, Malaysia, New Zealand, the Netherlands, Nigeria, Norway, Pakistan, Russia, South Africa, Sweden, Tanzania, Turkey, Uganda, the United Kingdom, and the United States. Civil society and international organisations in attendance were the African Union, the European Union, NATO, the United Nations, and the ICRC.

[263] Only Russia declined to 'welcome' the Principles, as discussed further below.

the Principles and Guidelines accurately reflect the discussions held during the final conference, and that the Principles and Guidelines are an expression of a global approach to the issue of detention'.[264]

The Copenhagen Principles as finally adopted, consist of a preamble, the 16 principles and guidelines, and a commentary for each principle and guideline.[265] The Principles identify the participant States and observer organisations,[266] noting that the participants 'while not seeking to create new legal obligations or authorisations under international law ... [nonetheless] confirmed the desire to develop principles to guide the implementation of the existing obligations with respect to detention in international military operations'.[267] Starting from the agreed position that 'detention is a necessary, lawful and legitimate means of achieving the objectives of international military operations',[268] the Principles and Guidelines outline a number of basic substantive and procedural protections and instructions for detention operations in international military operations, including, inter alia, that detention must be carried out in accordance with applicable international law,[269] that detainees should be informed of the reasons for their detention,[270] that certain protections are to be afforded to detainees in relation to the material conditions of their detention,[271] that security detainees should be able to have the decision leading to their detention subject to periodical review by an impartial and objective authority,[272] and that a detainee will only be transferred to another State or authority 'in compliance with the transferring State's or international organisation's international law obligations'.[273]

The Copenhagen Principles did not ultimately come to a settled position on the relationship between IHL and international human rights law, but essentially 'sidestepped' the issue with the Principle 16 'savings clause',[274] which provides that '[n]othing in *The Copenhagen Process Principles and Guidelines* affects the applicability of international law to international military operations conducted by the States or international organisations; or the obligations of their personnel to respect such law; or the applicability of international or national law to non-State actors'.[275]

264 As reported in Oswald and Winkler (n 241) 146.

265 The 'Chairman's Commentary' is expressly affirmed as representing only the chairman's views 'of how the Principles and Guidelines should be interpreted or applied', and while 'no participant during the final conference stated that the commentaries might not be ... considered as part of the Principles and Guidelines, it is open for states to argue so in future. At the very least the commentaries should be viewed as a tool that can be used by states and international organisations to add more substance to the Principles and Guidelines when they apply them': ibid 151.

266 Copenhagen Principles and Guidelines, Preamble I.

267 Copenhagen Principles and Guidelines, Preamble II.

268 Copenhagen Principles and Guidelines, Preamble III.

269 Copenhagen Principles and Guidelines, Principle 4.

270 Copenhagen Principles and Guidelines, Principle 7.

271 Copenhagen Principles and Guidelines, Principles 9–11.

272 Copenhagen Principles and Guidelines, Principle 12.

273 Copenhagen Principles and Guidelines, Principle 15.

274 Copenhagen Principles and Guidelines, Commentary to Principle 16, 16.2.

275 Copenhagen Principles and Guidelines, Principle 16.

This sidestepping of the issue of the role of international human rights law and its interplay with IHL was met with some criticism during the Process. While Russia 'welcomed the conclusion' of the Process and 'took note of' the Guidelines,[276] the Russian delegation was of the opinion that 'the Copenhagen Process could contribute more to the safeguarding of the humane treatment of detainees by placing greater emphasis on their inherent rights which derive from international human rights law and international humanitarian law'.[277] This echoed the approach taken by Sweden, which went on record as stating that its 'interpretation of the reference to international law in Principle 16 is that this also includes human rights law and that Sweden would have preferred if this had been stated explicitly in Principle 16'.[278]

The Principles as adopted were also narrower in focus than had been wanted by some States, applying to international military operations but not to law enforcement operations and counter-piracy operations. As noted by Oswald and Winkler:

> [t]he use of the term 'international military operations' signifies that the Principles and Guidelines apply only to military operations that have a cross-border component and include situations where one state deploys forces in the territory of another state to assist the latter in an internal armed conflict or to maintain peace and security. The term 'military' signifies that the Principles and Guidelines are not intended to apply to civilian police operations or those operations that are considered law enforcement, such as counter-piracy.[279]

Additional areas not dealt with by the Principles include the 'triggering standards'[280] for security or criminal detention, the situation with regards to voluntary detainees, and a number of procedural rules regarding detention reviews, such as a right of representation, the exact nature of review tribunals, the role of detainees in ongoing reviews, and principles that might be relevant during detainee repatriation.

That the Guidelines were never intended to be binding, and should not be taken as such, is repeatedly reaffirmed in the Guidelines themselves.[281] Indeed, the change of the terminology from 'Rules and Guidelines' to 'Principles and Guidelines' during the 2012 conference is indicative of the degree to which some States were determined to 'avoid reference to the word "rules" to ensure that the outcome document was not seen as ... binding'.[282] Furthermore, the Commentary

[276] Ministry of Foreign Affairs of Denmark (n 262) 214.
[277] ibid.
[278] As reported in Oswald and Winkler (n 241) 146.
[279] As reported in ibid 150.
[280] ibid 165.
[281] See Commentary to the Copenhagen Principles, 16.2.
[282] As reported in Oswald and Winkler (n 241) 144.

to Principle 16 reaffirms that the Principles and Guidelines are not to be taken as restatements of customary international law or evidence of *opinio juris*,[283] or as creating any new obligations or commitments for detaining authorities.[284] That being said, those involved in the drafting of the Copenhagen Principles have stated the hope that the Principles could be 'used as a basis for the progressive development of law',[285] and that 'seen from the perspective of both the detaining soldier and the detainee the Copenhagen Process Principles and Guidelines will lead to improvements both in its own right but also in comparison to situations where no such non-binding principles and guidelines exist'.[286] Thomas Winkler and Bruce Oswald went so far as to assert that, notwithstanding the non-binding nature of the Principles, they nevertheless 'contribute to the development of international law in a number of ways',[287] including that the Principles reinforce the principle of legality, that there is recognition of a base level for defining detention, that there is a framework of legal protections for detainees regardless of the reasons for their detention, and that two forms of review of detention—security and criminal—add to the existing law on review.[288]

When the Principles were released, they were praised as a 'valuable'[289] document for States, noteworthy for the fact that they were 'endorsed by a sizable and diverse group of countries and international organisations'.[290] Other comments in support included praise for the Principles as having successfully brought the question of detainee handling and treatment to international attention, resulting in a set of principles that were a good foundation for future discussions,[291] noting that such an achievement is particularly impressive given the failure of the similar attempt by the ICRC in 2003.[292] Most academic appraisal of the Principles acknowledges

[283] Commentary to the Copenhagen Principles, 16.2.
[284] ibid.
[285] Oswald and Winkler (n 241) 150.
[286] ibid 156.
[287] ibid 165.
[288] Outlined in more detail in ibid.
[289] John Bellinger, 'Completion of Copenhagen Process Principles and Guidelines on Detainees in International Military Operations' (*Lawfare*, 3 December 2012) <http://www.lawfareblog.com/completion-copenhagen-process-principles-and-guidelines-detainees-international-military-operations> accessed 3 August 2021.
[290] ibid. See also Cedric De Koker, 'The Copenhagen Process on the Handling of Detainees in International Military Operations: Principles and Guidelines—A Critical Appraisal' in Joanna Shapland and others (eds), *Desistance, Social Order and Responses to Crime* (Maklu 2014), who also argues that 'perhaps the most impressive achievement of the Copenhagen Process ... is that it persuaded the Permanent Five (5) and several other major contributors to international military operations to sit at the same table, discuss the subject and agree upon a set of principles. The fact that ... these states acknowledged that there are holes in the legal protection and that there is a need to further clarify some aspects of the handling of detainees is very significant': ibid 178; Lawrence Hill-Cawthorne, 'The Copenhagen Principles of the Handling of Detainees: Implications for the Procedural Regulation of Internment' (2013) 18 Journal of Conflict & Security Law 481: 'it is also a positive development for such principles to be agreed upon multilaterally': Hill-Cawthorne 496.
[291] William Boothby, *Conflict Law* (Springer 2014) 311.
[292] De Koker (n 290) 178.

that it is a measured set of guidelines that hew closely to the procedural rules on civilian internment in international armed conflict,[293] and that 'in an area of law that is plagued with uncertainty, a collection of the accepted standards among a significant number of states is an invaluable resource'.[294] Indeed, some have gone so far as to proclaim the Principles as a progressive development of the law, providing for 'more extensive protection than the international humanitarian law treaties',[295] particularly in relation to, inter alia, Principle Seven, which requires that persons detained are to be informed promptly of the reasons for their detention, as well as Principle Ten, which states that detainees should be held in designated places of detention. These Principles 'go well beyond what is required in NIACs ... [a]s such, these principles definitely provide "added value" because they reflect what states believe to be the appropriate way of handling detainees'.[296]

However, the Principles were not without vocal critics. Amnesty International, among other civil society organisations, was particularly critical of both the Copenhagen Process and the eventual Principles and Guidelines. Of the Process, Amnesty condemned it as having taken place in 'quasi-secrecy',[297] accusing Denmark of having 'deliberately convened discussions outside of any established international organisation in order to retain the ability to exclude certain states and civil society'.[298] Amnesty further condemned the adopted Principles as 'allowing for a lowering of standards to a kind of muddled compromise that in some respects falls even below the "lowest common denominator" among participating states' and that, ultimately, the entire Copenhagen Process 'that purported to aim at "ensuring humane treatment of detainees" ... has actually [established] ... a framework

[293] Hill-Cawthorne (n 290) 492.

[294] ibid 496.

[295] De Koker (n 290) 179.

[296] ibid.

[297] Amnesty International, 'Copenhagen "Principles" on Military Detainees Undermine Human Rights' (22 October 2012) <http://www.amnesty.org/en/latest/news/2012/10/copenhagen-principles-military-detainees-undermine-human-rights/> accessed 3 August 2021.

[298] ibid. In response to this criticism, Winkler and Oswald acknowledged that while the process was indeed State-centric (with only a few select intergovernmental organisations (IGOs) and the ICRC invited to observe), this served a specific purpose—namely, to ensure that States could participate in a forum where they could willingly and openly discuss their concerns, practices, and solutions, and that by including human rights NGOS, this open environment could have been derailed entirely: Thomas Winkler and Bruce 'Ossie' Oswald, 'The Copenhagen Process Principles and Guidelines on the Handling of Detainees in International Military Operations' (2012) 16(39) American Society of International Law Insights <http://www.asil.org/insights/volume/16/issue/39/copenhagen-process-principles-and-guidelines-handling-detainees> accessed 3 August 2021. Indeed, as noted by John Bellinger, the US voiced this exact concern at the commencement of the Process. Initially sceptical that the Process 'would simply become a forum to criticize U.S. detention practices', the US was convinced otherwise by the Danish strategy—that 'by including so many countries and international organizations involved in armed conflicts and peacekeeping operations, the Danish government was able to demonstrate that detention operations pose legal challenges for all countries and that the rules for detention in NIACs are quite hazy. The U.S. Government has endorsed the Copenhagen principles and is reportedly satisfied with them': Bellinger (n 289).

that will at best be ineffective, and at worst could fundamentally damage human rights'.[299]

The *Tallinn Manual on the International Law Applicable to Cyber Warfare and the Tallinn Manual 2.0 on Cyber Operations*

Tallinn '1.0'

The Tallinn Manual on the International Law Applicable to Cyber Warfare was adopted in response to the increasing awareness among practitioners and experts that cyber means of warfare were presenting a growing threat to States' military operations. Cyber operations had been the focus of academic, practitioner, and military attention for some years,[300] with the attacks launched against Estonia in 2007,[301] Georgia in 2008,[302] and Iran in 2010[303] demonstrating that cyber-attacks could create significant disruption and damage to infrastructure. At the initiative of the NATO Cooperative Cyber Defence Centre of Excellence (NATO CCDCOE),[304] an international military organisation based in Tallinn, Estonia,

[299] Amnesty International, 'Copenhagen "Principles" on Military Detainees Undermine Human Rights', 22 October 2012 <http://www.amnesty.org/en/latest/news/2012/10/copenhagen-principles-military-detainees-undermine-human-rights/> accessed 3 August 2021. Winkler and Oswald responded to these criticisms by noting that '[w]hile the Principles and Guidelines are not exhaustive (i.e., they do not cover all aspects of detention) the broad language of its substantive provisions could address a number of concerns identified by Amnesty International. For example, both the mandatory registration of detainees and the holding of detainees in designated places should address concerns of enforced disappearances and secret detention facilities. Similarly, the broad language used to deal with security and criminal detention reviews should sufficiently diminish fears of indefinite detention without review': Winkler and Oswald (n 298).

[300] Michael Schmitt, 'Computer Network Attack and the Use of Force in International Law: Thoughts on a Normative Framework' (1999) 37 Columbia Journal of Transnational Law 885; US Joint Chiefs of Staff, 'Information Operations' (Joint Publication 3-13, 13 February 2006) II-4–II-5 <http://www.globalsecurity.org/intell/library/policy/dod/joint/jp3_13_2006.pdf> accessed 3 August 2021; Ruth Wedgwood, 'Proportionality, Cyberwar and the Law of War' (2000) 76 International Law Studies 219; James Terry, 'The Lawfulness of Attacking Computer Networks in Armed Conflict and in Self-Defence in Periods Short of Armed Conflict: What Are the Targeting Constraints?' (2001) 169 Military Law Review 70; JTG Kelsey, 'Hacking into International Law: The Principles of Distinction and Neutrality in the Age of Cyber Warfare' (2008) 106 Michigan Law Review 1427.

[301] See Stephen Korns and Joshua Kastenberg, 'Georgia's Cyber Left Hook' (2008–09) 38 Parameters 60.

[302] Ian Traynor, 'Russia Accused of Unleashing Cyberwar to Disable Estonia', *The Guardian* (17 May 2007) <http://www.theguardian.com/world/2007/may/17/topstories3.russia> accessed 3 August 2021.

[303] John Markoff, 'A Silent Attack, But Not a Subtle One', *The New York Times* (26 September 2010) <http://www.nytimes.com/2010/09/27/technology/27virus.html> accessed 3 August 2021.

[304] <https://ccdcoe.org/about-us/> accessed 3 August 2021. The Cooperative Cyber Defence Centre of Excellence (CCDCOE) is 'a multinational and interdisciplinary hub of cyber defence expertise ... [comprising] a diverse group of experts—researchers, analysts, trainers, educators—from 20 nations. As of 2017, Belgium, the Czech Republic, Estonia, France, Germany, Greece, Hungary, Italy, Latvia, Lithuania, the Netherlands, Poland, Slovakia, Spain, Turkey, the United Kingdom, and the United States are signed on as Sponsoring Nations of the NATO Cooperative Cyber Defence Centre of Excellence. Austria and Finland have become Contributing Participants and Sweden is well on its way

a small group of experts agreed that the development of a manual of instruction would, it was hoped, assist in 'bringing some degree of clarity to the complex legal issue surrounding cyber operations',[305] particularly in relation the law of the use of force and IHL.

Following the first small group meeting in September 2009, a larger international Group of Experts was convened, drawing on legal practitioners, academics, and technical experts, as well as observers from civil society.[306] This Group of Experts was tasked with drafting rules for eventual inclusion in the manual; members of the group would research and prepare proposed rules, also providing a draft commentary to accompany the rule. These draft rules were then compiled to form the first draft of the eventual Tallinn Manual.[307] The first draft was then divided among three teams of experts, led by group facilitators, tasked with refining the draft. Revised drafts were then sent to discussion in plenary meetings of the entire Groups of Experts and returned for further revision and resubmission. In all, eight three-day meetings were held in Tallinn between 2010 and 2012.

After plenary meetings concluded, an Editorial Committee drawn from the Group of Experts worked on the Manual, meeting 12 times in Berlin and Tallinn, ensuring that the rules and their commentaries were of a high standard of 'accuracy, thoroughness, and clarity'.[308] The result of this work was distributed to a number of peer reviewers, who were each given sections of the Manual to review and comment on; these comments were returned to the Editorial Committee, which revised the draft in response. In July 2012, the Group of Experts convened in Tallinn for its last meeting, where it considered the final draft of the Manual, made any final changes, and approved the rules and commentary.

The result of the process was the adoption of 95 rules on the *jus ad bellum* and *jus in bello* applicable in cyber warfare. The Tallinn Manual proceeded from the position that international law *does* apply to new technologies and that cyberspace is not an area beyond the reach of the law on the use of force and the law on the conduct of hostilities.[309] The Manual outlined a number of different rules of instruction on cyber warfare, applicable in both international and non-international armed conflicts, including the law on sovereignty, jurisdiction, and control of States in cyberspace;[310] State responsibility in cyberspace;[311] the prohibition

of doing the same. The Centre is staffed and financed by member nations and is not part of NATO's military command or force structure': ibid.

305 Tallinn Manual 1.0, 4.

306 Civil society observers participated in discussion, but did not 'vote' on the rules, which were the sole domain of the Group of Experts: Tallinn Manual 1.0, 6.

307 The entire drafting process is recounted in Tallinn Manual 1.0, 9–11.

308 Tallinn Manual 1.0, 10.

309 Tallinn Manual 1.0, 3.

310 Tallinn Manual 1.0, Rules 1–5.

311 Tallinn Manual 1.0, Rules 6–9.

on the use of force;[312] the law on self-defence,[313] including the rules on regional, international, and intergovernmental organisations;[314] the applicability of IHL,[315] including conflict characterisation,[316] the geographical scope of hostilities,[317] and the law on command responsibility;[318] the law on the conduct of hostilities, including rules regarding the characterisation of persons in situations of armed conflict;[319] the definition of cyber-attack;[320] the principle of distinction;[321] lawful and unlawful attacks against persons;[322] lawful and unlawful attacks against objects;[323] permissible and impermissible means and methods of attack;[324] permissible and impermissible types of attack;[325] precautions that must be taken in both attack and defence;[326] unlawful and lawful means and methods of warfare;[327] the law on blockades and zones;[328] special rules on protected persons and objects;[329] the relevance of the law on occupation;[330] and the law of neutrality.[331]

In all, around 40 persons were involved in the drafting of the Tallinn Manual. Twenty-three of those participants served as members of the Group of Experts, including the six members of the Editorial Committee,[332] the two Legal Group Facilitators,[333] and two Technical Experts,[334] with four persons serving as observers.[335] The remaining numbers included 13 peer reviewers and various administrative, technical, and research personnel. In terms of the geographical and

[312] Tallinn Manual 1.0, Rules 10–12.
[313] Tallinn Manual 1.0, Rules 13–17.
[314] Tallinn Manual 1.0, Rules 18–19.
[315] Tallinn Manual 1.0, Rule 20.
[316] Tallinn Manual 1.0, Rules 22–23.
[317] Tallinn Manual 1.0, Rule 21.
[318] Tallinn Manual 1.0, Rule 24.
[319] Tallinn Manual 1.0, Rules 25–29.
[320] Tallinn Manual 1.0, Rule 30.
[321] Tallinn Manual 1.0, Rule 31.
[322] Tallinn Manual 1.0, Rules 32–36.
[323] Tallinn Manual 1.0, Rules 37–40.
[324] Tallinn Manual 1.0, Rules 41–48.
[325] Tallinn Manual 1.0, Rules 49–51.
[326] Tallinn Manual 1.0, Rules 52–59.
[327] Tallinn Manual 1.0, Rules 60–66.
[328] Tallinn Manual 1.0, Rules 67–69.
[329] Tallinn Manual 1.0, Rules 70–86.
[330] Tallinn Manual 1.0, Rules 87–90.
[331] Tallinn Manual 1.0, Rules 91–95.
[332] Professor Michael Schmitt, US Naval War College (who also served as Director); Air Commodore (ret) William H Boothby, former Deputy Director of Legal Services, Royal Air Force; Bruno Demeyere, Catholic University of Leuven; Professor Wolff Heintschel von Heinegg, Europa-Universität Viadrina; Professor James Bret Michael, US Naval Postgraduate School; and Professor Thomas Wingfield, George C Marshall European Centre for Security Studies.
[333] Professor Eric Talbot Jensen, Brigham Young University Law School, and Professor Sean Watts, Creighton University Law School.
[334] Dr Kenneth Geers, NATO CCDCOE, and Dr Rain Ottis, NATO CCDCOE.
[335] Colonel Gary Brown, US Air Force, US Cyber Command; Dr Cordula Droege and Dr Jean-François Quéguiner, ICRC; and Ulf Häußler, Headquarters, Supreme Allied Commander Transformation, NATO.

institutional origins of the participants,[336] most experts were drawn from WEOG States,[337] with two from the Eastern European Group.[338] There were no representatives from African, South American, Asian, or Middle Eastern States. Most experts were from academia, with 21 drawn from universities, eight from civil society or international organisations,[339] and seven from the armed forces.[340] All experts participated in their personal capacity and there were no persons present as authorised State observers.

The project limited itself to considering 'cyber-to-cyber' operations. The Manual was not 'intended for use in considering the legal issues surrounding kinetic-to-cyber operations, such as an aerial attack employing bombs against a cyber-control centre', and did not 'address traditional electronic warfare attacks, like jamming'.[341] Also excluded from the ambit of Tallinn 1.0 were cyber activities that fell below the threshold for a use of force, cyber 'criminality' of a purely domestic nature (including individual criminal liability under domestic law), and cyber security issues that could not be strictly classified as falling within a use of force or IHL framework, such as cyber espionage and intellectual property theft.[342]

The rules were adopted by consensus and reflected the general opinion held by the Group of Experts that the Manual reflected the applicable '*lex lata*, that is, the law currently governing cyber conflict' and not '*lex ferenda*, best practice, or preferred policy'.[343] The Commentary to the rules was designed to reflect the discussions held during the Tallinn process and to indicate where competing views on certain issues were voiced, where consensus could (and could not) be achieved, and when particular rules were considered to be of customary status in international armed conflict, non-international armed conflict, or both. In doing so, both the Commentary and the Rules proper drew heavily on other non-binding instruments, including the AMW Manual, the San Remo NIAC Manual, and the ICRC Customary International Humanitarian Law Study. The Commentary outlined that:

> [t]he Manual draws heavily on the ICRC Customary IHL Study, as it is a valuable repository of evidence and analysis regarding customary law in both international and non-international armed conflict. The AMW Manual also proved

[336] Not including the administrative and research personnel, but including observers and peer reviewers.

[337] Thirty-one, including Australia, Belgium, Canada, Germany, the Netherlands, Sweden, Switzerland, the United Kingdom, and the United States.

[338] Estonia.

[339] Including the NATO CCDCOE, the ICRC, the Geneva Centre for Security Policy, and Chatham House.

[340] For the purposes of this analysis, the War College and the US Military Academy have been classified as academic.

[341] Tallinn Manual 1.0, 5.

[342] Tallinn Manual 1.0, 4.

[343] Tallinn Manual 1.0, 5.

> especially valuable because it addresses customary law in both international and non-international law. Finally, the International Group of Experts frequently considered the NIAC Manual when assessing whether a particular Rule applies during non-international armed conflict. With the exception of treaty law, all of the aforementioned sources were persuasive, but not dispositive, evidence of a norm's status as customary international law.[344]

The Manual also referred to only four military manuals—those of Canada, Germany, the United Kingdom, and the United States. This reliance on so few manuals of instruction to State armed forces was justified with the statement that '[t]he international legal community generally considers these four manuals to be especially useful during legal research and analysis with respect to conflict issues'.[345] However, it was also noted that while 'many sources are cited as support for the legal principles set forth in the *Tallinn Manual* … this does not necessarily mean that the International Group of Experts viewed them as legal sources'.[346]

The non-binding nature of the Tallinn Manual is asserted in the first paragraph of the Introduction[347] and reaffirmed in the section entitled 'Authority of the Manual' at the end of the Introduction.[348] However, the drafters also clearly affirm their hope that the Manual will, like its predecessors the San Remo and AMW Manuals, contribute to 'bringing some degree of clarity to the complex legal issue surrounding cyber operations',[349] though it makes no explicit statements as to its intended audience. As noted above, the Manual asserts that it is stating the *lex lata* and is not *lex ferenda*.[350]

Indeed, the Manual takes a conservative approach to applying the law of armed conflict to the realm of cyber hostilities, with essentially restrained approaches to, for instance, the level of intensity required for cyber operations to be considered a non-international armed conflict,[351] and how precisely to define direct participation in cyber hostilities.[352] The Manual does not define data destruction as an attack under IHL, taking the position that to be considered an such,[353] a cyberattack

344 Tallinn Manual 1.0, 7–8.

345 Tallinn Manual 1.0, 8—though no substantiating references are offered to support this claim. However, the Manual does go on to note that failure to reference other military manuals 'should not be interpreted as a comment on the quality of any other such manuals' and that the reliance on such manuals had much to do with the fact that the Group of Experts 'included members who participated in the drafting of each of the four manuals. These members were able to provide invaluable insight into the genesis, basis, and meaning of specific provisions. Finally, unlike many other military manuals, these four are all publicly available': Tallinn Manual 1.0, 8.

346 Tallinn Manual 1.0, 9.

347 Tallinn Manual 1.0, 1.

348 Tallinn Manual 1.0, 11.

349 Tallinn Manual 1.0, 4.

350 Tallinn Manual 1.0, 5.

351 Tallinn Manual 1.0, Rule 23.

352 Tallinn Manual 1.0. Rule 35.

353 Tallinn Manual 1.0, Rule 30.

must produce kinetic effects—such as injury or death to persons or damage or destruction to objects. An attack that produces purely digital damage—that is, the erasure of data—but creates no physical kinetic effects is not considered an attack for the purposes of the Manual.[354] This was one of the more contentious areas of discussion during the drafting, with extensive debate over, inter alia, whether destruction of data that resulted in loss of functionality could reach the threshold of 'attack'.[355]

On its release, the Tallinn Manual was commended by some as a 'very valuable contribution to the interpretation of international law with regard to the novel challenges posed by cyber warfare',[356] and was rapidly embraced as the 'authoritative statement of international legal norms in cyberspace'.[357] However, Tallinn 1.0 was not without detractors; in addition to concerns about the limited scope of the Manual, one recurrent complaint was how narrow, in terms of geographic representation,[358] the Group of Experts was, being drawn overwhelmingly from WEOG States with no representation from Asia, Africa, or South America. Critics decried the Manual as having a 'certain neo-imperialist aftertaste'.[359] That only a few military manuals were consulted was also singled out for criticism: 'there is a clear problem of representativeness here and this pattern follows the arrogant practice criticised by Onuma Yasuaki where the "rule of international law" has been derived from the practice of some leading Western countries'.[360] Also singled out for

[354] See Commentary to Rule 30.

[355] See Commentary to Rule 30.

[356] Kubo Mačák, 'Military Objectives 2.0: The Case for Interpreting Computer Data as Objects under International Humanitarian Law' (2015) 48 Israel Law Review 55, 80.

[357] Ian Yuying Liu, 'The Due Diligence Doctrine under Tallinn Manual 2.0' (2017) 33 Computer Law and Security Review 390, 390. See also David O'Brien, a senior researcher at Harvard's Berkman Klein Center for Internet & Society, who described Tallinn 1.0 as 'one of the most authoritative and comprehensive texts on the application of international law to cyberwar': cited in Graham Templeton, 'Cyber Attack Response for Idiots and Presidents: The Tallinn Manual Provides Guidance on How to React to Hacking. But Will the U.S. Follow It?' (*Inverse*, 15 February 2017) <http://www.inverse.com/article/27810-tallinn-manual-2-0-dnc-russia-us-hack-fbi-clinton-trump-obama> accessed 3 August 2021. Templeton goes on to assert that '[w]ithin policy circles, the tome is ubiquitous' (though he does not cite substantiating evidence).

[358] Klée Aiken and Jessica Woodall, 'Tallin 2.0: Cyberspace and the Law', *The Strategist* (Australian Strategic Policy Institute, 14 May 2015) <http://www.aspistrategist.org.au/tallinn-2-0-cyberspace-and-the-law/> accessed 3 August 2021. See also Colin Sweet, 'Review: The Tallinn Manual on the International Law Applicable to Cyber Warfare' (2014) 66 Europe-Asia Studies 669, 669; Kristen Eichensehr, 'Review: The Tallinn Manual on the International Law Applicable to Cyber Warfare' (2014) 108 American Journal of International Law 585, 585.

[359] Lauri Mälksoo, 'The Tallinn Manual as an International Event' (*Diplomaatia*, 8 August 2013) <https://icds.ee/en/the-tallinn-manual-as-an-international-event/> accessed 3 August 2021. See also Yaroslav Radziwill, *Cyber Attacks and the Exploitable Imperfections of International Law* (Brill 2015) 21.

[360] Mälksoo (n 359), citing Onuma Yasuaki, *A Transcivilizational Perspective on International Law* (Martinus Nijhoff 2010) 228 ff. Tim McCormack and Rain Liivoja also criticised this geographical narrowness: Tim McCormack and Rain Liivoja, 'Law in the Virtual Battlespace: The Tallinn Manual and the Jus in Bello' (2012) 15 Yearbook of International Humanitarian Law 45, 49. See also Ashley Deeks, 'Tallinn 2.0 and a Chinese View on the Tallinn Process' (*Lawfare*, 31 May 2015) <http://www.lawfareblog.com/tallinn-20-and-chinese-view-tallinn-process> accessed 3 August 2021; Anthea Roberts, *Is International Law International?* (OUP 2017) 313–15.

criticism was the lack of State involvement in the drafting, with States neither invited to observe the proceedings nor consulted at any stage during the drafting.[361] Both of these procedural complaints would be, to some degree, rectified when the Tallinn Manual 1.0 was revised and reissued as the Tallinn Manual 2.0 in 2016.

Tallinn 2.0 (2016)

Almost as soon as Tallinn 1.0 was published, moves were underway by the North Atlantic Treaty Organization Cooperative Cyber Defence Centre of Excellence (NATO CCDCOE) to begin revising and expanding it to 'include the public international law governing cyber operations during peacetime'.[362] The justification for revising the Manual so soon after its publication was explained as a recognition that while hostile cyber operations as explored in Tallinn 1.0 'will typically be more worrisome from a national security perspective than those that occur in peacetime, States have to deal with cyber issues that lie below the use of force threshold on a daily basis'.[363] To that end, a new International Group of Experts was convened, with the aim of producing an expanded Manual that would replace Tallinn 1.0.[364]

In drafting Tallinn 2.0, much the same process was followed as was involved in producing Tallinn 1.0. Members of the International Group of Experts, comprising legal practitioners, academics, and technical experts, met over the course of three years to draft, debate, and ultimately adopt a new Manual.[365] As with Tallinn 1.0, Tallinn 2.0 contains rules outlining the relevant law applicable to cyber operations, agreed upon by consensus, and accompanied by a Commentary that explains the scope and interpretation of the rule, as well as giving some insight into the drafting of the rule, where areas of contention arose, and where the Group of Experts could and could not come to agreement on either scope or interpretation.[366] The Manual notes where particular rules are considered to be customary international law, and when the rules apply to either (or both) international and non-international armed conflicts. In this respect, Tallinn 2.0 and the process by which it was drafted and adopted are substantially similar to Tallinn 1.0.

However, due to the expanded scope of the Manual, and considering some of the criticisms of Tallinn 1.0, some significant changes were made to the process. Due to the considerably higher numbers of expert participants in the process,[367] and given

[361] See Michael Adams, 'A Warning about Tallinn ... Whatever It Says' (*Lawfare*, 4 January 2017) <http://www.lawfareblog.com/warning-about-tallinn-20-%E2%80%A6-whatever-it-says> accessed 3 August 2021.

[362] Tallinn Manual 2.0, 1.

[363] Tallinn Manual 2.0, 1.

[364] Tallinn Manual 2.0, 1–2.

[365] Many of the Tallinn 1.0 experts contributed to Tallinn 2.0.

[366] Tallinn Manual 2.0, 4.

[367] Tallinn 1.0 had 19 members of the International Group of Experts, four observers, and 13 peer reviewers, totalling 36 persons. Tallinn 2.0 had 20 members of the International Group of Experts, one

the increase in topic areas, only a handful of experts or contributors were involved in preparing initial drafts and commentaries on proposed rules.[368] Those draft rules and commentaries were then reviewed and refined by editors and peer reviewers, with the revised drafts sent to the International Group of Experts for discussion during three week-long sessions held between 2015 and 2016. Following on from these sessions, the rules and commentaries went through additional peer review in the lead-up to the 2016 final plenary meeting, where all draft rules and commentaries were vetted and approved by the International Groups of Experts.[369]

Alongside these expert meetings, three workshops were held by the NATO CCDCOE: one at the University of Tartu in 2014 and two at Syracuse University in 2015, touching on Tallinn-relevant issues such as the law on State responsibility, cyber espionage, and international human rights law in cyber space. More significant than the workshops was a process that took place contemporaneously to the workshops and the Tallinn 2.0 drafting process: the so-called 'Hague Process'. This was an initiative of the Netherlands Ministry of Foreign Affairs and the NATO CCDCOE, with the stated aim of ensuring that the Tallinn 2.0 process was transparent and that the 'States have a voice in this effort to set forth the international law that governs their activities in cyberspace'.[370] The Hague Process involved representatives and delegations from over 50 States and intergovernmental and international organisations, who, operating under Chatham House Rules, unofficially commented on the working drafts of the Manual.[371] While the final Manual was considered the sole product of the Group of Experts, it was acknowledged by the

technical expert, nine contributors, 58 legal peer reviewers, and two technical peer reviewers, bringing the number of participants to 90, plus one non-voting observer.

[368] These were Professor Michael Schmitt (US Naval War College and University of Exeter); Liis Vihul (NATO CCDCOE); Colonel (ret US Air Force (USAF)) Gary D Brown (Marine Corps University); Professor Wolff Heintschel von Heinegg (Europa-Universität Viadrina); Dr Gleider Hernández (Durham University School of Law); Deborah Housen-Couriel (University of Haifa Faculty of Law); Professor Eric Talbot Jensen (Brigham Young University); Gabor Rona (Cardozo Law School); Phillip Spector (former Senior Adviser to the Legal Adviser, US Department of State); Professor Sean Watts (Creighton University School of Law); Air Commodore (ret) William H Boothby (former Deputy Director of Legal Services, Royal Air Force (RAF) UK); Professor Michel Bourbonnière (Royal Military College Canada); Dr Robert Heinsch (Leiden University); Professor Stephan Hobe (University of Cologne); Colonel Darren Huskisson (USAF); Professor Jann Kleffner (Swedish Defence University); Professor James Kraska (US Naval War College); and Dr Rob McLaughlin (Australian National University).

[369] This process is discussed in Tallinn Manual 2.0, 5–6.

[370] <https://ccdcoe.org/news/2016/over-50-states-consult-tallinn-manual-2-0/> accessed 27 September 2021.

[371] In 2015, 35 legal advisers from European, North and Latin American, African, Asian, and Asia-Pacific states, as well as delegates from NATO and the European Union, attended consultations: <https://www.ccdcoe.org/news/2015/35-states-attend-tallinn-manual-consultations/> accessed 27 September 2021. The NATO CCDCOE goes on to say that 50 States were eventually involved in the entire process but does not name those States: <https://ccdcoe.org/news/2016/over-50-states-consult-tallinn-manual-2-0/> accessed 27 September 2021. However, the Australian Strategic Policy Institute names the Asia Pacific States as including Australia, China, India, Japan, Pakistan, the Philippines, South Korea, Sri Lanka, and Thailand: Aiken and Woodall (n 358).

editors of Tallinn 2.0 that the '"Hague Process" proved invaluable'[372] to the final product, by helping experts engage more clearly with the aims and objectives of States in dealing with cyber operations.[373]

Other changes witnessed during the Tallinn 2.0 process included a more broadly representative membership of both the International Group of Experts and the peer reviewers. Where Tallinn 1.0 had been criticised for its 'transatlantic framing and lack of global representation',[374] Tallinn 2.0 included experts and peer reviewers from institutions and organisations outside the Western European (or related States, such as the United States, Canada, and Australia) bloc, including Israel, Japan, China, Chile, South Korea, Kazakhstan, and India.[375] The experts and peer reviewers involved in Tallinn 2.0 were also more representative in relation to the institutions from which they were drawn; while Tallinn 1.0 membership was overwhelmingly academic in character, Tallinn 2.0 members were drawn from the armed forces,[376] government,[377] civil society and international organisations,[378] and the private sector[379] more broadly.

Tallinn 2.0, as finally adopted, comprises 154 rules on sovereignty,[380] due diligence,[381] jurisdiction,[382] international responsibility,[383] cyber operations not regulated by public international law,[384] international human rights law and cyber space,[385] diplomatic and consular law,[386] the law of the

[372] Tallinn Manual 2.0, 6.

[373] The Hague Process itself ran concurrent to the ongoing UN-led Group of Government Experts on Developments in the Field of Information and Telecommunications in the Context of International Security, which was tasked with exploring issues related to cyber security and international law: <http://www.un.org/disarmament/topics/informationsecurity/> accessed XXX. While the first rounds of meetings were successful in producing consensus documents on various issues relating to cyberspace and international security, the fifth Group of Government Experts meeting was unable to reach consensus on a number of issues. See further 'Developments in the Field of Information and Telecommunications in the Context of International Security' (UN Fact Sheet, July 2015) <https://unoda-web.s3-accelerate.amazonaws.com/wp-content/uploads/2015/07/Information-Security-Fact-Sheet-July2015.pdf> accessed 3 August 2021; Michael Schmitt and Liis Vihul, 'International Cyber Law Politicized: The UN GGE's Failure to Advance Cyber Norms' (*Just Security*, 30 June 2017) <http://www.justsecurity.org/42768/international-cyber-law-politicized-gges-failure-advance-cyber-norms/> accessed 3 August 2021.

[374] Aiken and Woodall (n 358).

[375] Tallinn Manual 2.0, xii–xviii.

[376] Eighteen experts and peer reviewers were drawn from State armed forces.

[377] Five experts were drawn from government: Phillip Spector, former Senior Adviser to the Legal Adviser, US Department of State; Eileen Denza, former Legal Counsellor to the UK Foreign and Commonwealth Office; Dr Dieter Fleck, former Director of the International Agreements and Policy Department of the German Ministry of Defence; Dr Chanaka Wickremasinghe, UK Foreign and Commonwealth Office; and Dr Martin Zwanenburg, Ministry of Foreign Affairs of the Netherlands.

[378] Including the United Nations, the NATO CCDCOE, NATO, the International Civil Aviation Organization, and the International Law Commission.

[379] Three experts were from industry: Daniel Garrie, from Law and Forensics LLC; David Simon, from Sidley Austin LLP; and Jeffrey Carr, from Taia Global.

[380] Tallinn Manual 2.0, Rules 1–5.

[381] Tallinn Manual 2.0, Rules 6–7.

[382] Tallinn Manual 2.0, Rules 8–13.

[383] Tallinn Manual 2.0, Rules 14–31.

[384] Tallinn Manual 2.0, Rules 32–33.

[385] Tallinn Manual 2.0, Rules 34–38.

[386] Tallinn Manual 2.0, Rules 39–44.

sea,[387] air and space law,[388] international telecommunications law,[389] the peaceful settlement of disputes under international law,[390] the rule on non-intervention,[391] the law on the use of force and self-defence,[392] collective security,[393] and comprehensive rules on cyber warfare, including applicability,[394] geographical scope of application,[395] characterisation of conflicts,[396] individual and command responsibility,[397] the law on the conduct of hostilities,[398] rules on specially protected persons and objects,[399] the law of occupation,[400] and the law of neutrality.[401] Excluded from Tallinn 2.0 were any rules pertaining to trade law, intellectual property, international criminal law, private international law, and any rules on cyber operations that could be considered as solely within the domain of domestic law.[402]

Tallinn 2.0 was much more upfront regarding its aims and objectives; unlike Tallinn 1.0, which made no statement as to its intended audience, Tallinn 2.0 states that its 'primary audience consists of State legal advisers charged with providing international law advice to governmental decision makers, both civilian and military. However, it is hoped that Tallinn Manual 2.0 also will prove valuable in academic and other endeavours'.[403] Tallinn 2.0 also strongly emphasises its non-binding nature: three paragraphs of its 24-paragraph introduction are dedicated to affirming the Tallinn's non-binding nature, with the Introduction making it clear that the Manual 'is not an official document, nor does it reflect the position of any other organisation or State represented by observers or any of the States involved in the "Hague Process"'.[404] The Manual also emphasises its *lex lata* status: '*Tallinn Manual 2.0* is intended as an objective restatement of the *lex lata*. Therefore, the Experts involved ... assiduously avoided including statements reflecting *lex ferenda*'.[405]

Following its launch, Tallinn 2.0 was critiqued in relation to several areas. One particular area of concern was the wording of the 'due diligence' obligation in Rules 6 and 7, with some States and commentators resisting the wording of the Rule

387 Tallinn Manual 2.0, Rules 45–54.
388 Tallinn Manual 2.0, Rules 55–60.
389 Tallinn Manual 2.0, Rules 61–64.
390 Tallinn Manual 2.0, Rule 65.
391 Tallinn Manual 2.0, Rules 66–67.
392 Tallinn Manual 2.0, Rules 68–75.
393 Tallinn Manual 2.0, Rules 76–79.
394 Tallinn Manual 2.0, Rule 80.
395 Tallinn Manual 2.0, Rule 81.
396 Tallinn Manual 2.0, Rule 82–83.
397 Tallinn Manual 2.0, Rules 84–85.
398 Tallinn Manual 2.0, Rules 86–130.
399 Tallinn Manual 2.0, Rules 131–45.
400 Tallinn Manual 2.0, Rules 146–49.
401 Tallinn Manual 2.0, Rules 150–54.
402 Tallinn Manual 2.0, 3.
403 Tallinn Manual 2.0, 2.
404 Tallinn Manual 2.0, 2.
405 Tallinn Manual 2.0, 3.

that 'a State must exercise due diligence in not allowing its territory, or territory or cyber infrastructure under its governmental control, to be used for cyber operations that affect the rights of, and produce serious adverse consequences for, other States',[406] when the preferred terminology was 'should' (rather than 'must').[407] Other criticisms levelled at the Manual were its approach to international human rights law[408] and its potentially problematic conceptualisations of necessity[409] and sovereignty.[410]

Conclusion

The above analysis has shown that the process of drafting many of these instruments has been almost identical: groups of experts convene to debate and draft a final document over a period of several years; the final instrument is then published with proclamations of its non-binding nature but accompanied with statements professing hopes for its influence and impact. The next chapter turns to look at other non-binding instruments that share similar objectives, but that have eventuated through, in some instances, notably different processes.

406 Tallinn Manual 2.0, Rule 6.

407 The issue of due diligence and attribution was raised in the meetings of the UN Group of Government Experts. See Group of Governmental Experts on Developments in the Field of Information and Telecommunications in the Context of International Security, Note by the Secretary-General, UN Doc A/68/98 (24 June 2013) 8; Group of Governmental Experts on Developments in the Field of Information and Telecommunications in the Context of International Security, Note by the Secretary-General, UN Doc A/70/174 (22 July 2015) 17. See also Eric Talbot Jensen and Sean Watts, 'A Cyber Duty of Due Diligence: Gentle Civilizer or Crude Destabiliser?' (2017) 95 Texas Law Review 1555; Liu (n 357).

408 See Robert Barnsby and Shane Reeves, 'Give Them an Inch, They'll Take a Terabyte: How States May Interpret Tallinn Manual 2.0's International Human Rights Law Chapter' (2017) 95 Texas Law Review 1515; Dinah PoKempner, 'Squinting through the Pinhole: A Dim View of Human Rights from Tallinn 2.0' (2017) 95 Texas Law Review 1599.

409 Christian Schaller, 'Beyond Self-Defence and Countermeasures: A Critical Assessment of the Tallinn Manual's Conception of Necessity' (2017) 95 Texas Law Review 1619.

410 See Gary Corn and Robert Taylor, 'Sovereignty in the Age of Cyber' (2017) 111 American Journal of International Law (unbound) 207; cf Michael Schmitt and Liis Vihul, 'Sovereignty in Cyberspace: Lex Lata Vel Non?' (2017) 111 American Journal of International Law (unbound) 213: 'some States have hesitated to confirm the principle of sovereignty as one that prohibits certain types of cyber operations … hesitant States appear to see the greater latitude to pursue national security objectives in cyberspace that derives from the absence of a primary rule of sovereignty as outweighing the likely costs of hostile cyber operations that might violate their sovereignty': Schmitt and Vihul 214.

5

Non-Binding Instruments in International Humanitarian Law

Civil Society Contributions to the Development of Non-Binding Norms

Introduction

Chapter 4 examined the various manuals and guidelines that have proliferated in the last 30 years in the law of armed conflict, designed to guide State practice in relation to certain distinct situations of armed conflict. This chapter will examine similar instruments and documents that have been adopted to guide practice, but that are dissimilar to the instruments discussed in previous chapters—either because they are directed only at very specific non-State entities (such as Private Military and Security Companies (PMSCs), or armed non-State groups), or because they have originated from civil society organisations, such as the International Committee of the Red Cross (ICRC). These instruments include the ICRC Study into Customary International Humanitarian Law, the International Code of Conduct for Private Security Providers, the ICRC's Interpretive Guidance on Direct Participation in Hostilities (DPH), and Geneva Call's Deeds of Commitment.

The ICRC Study into Customary International Humanitarian Law

The ICRC study on customary international humanitarian law (IHL) originated from the January 1995 meeting of the Intergovernmental Group of Experts for the Protection of War Victims in Geneva.[1] At that meeting, the Group of Experts adopted Recommendation II, which proposed that:

> the ICRC be invited to prepare, with the assistance of experts on IHL representing various geographical regions and different legal systems, and in consultation with

[1] This meeting was convened as a follow-up to the International Conference for the Protection of War Victims, Geneva, 30 August–1 September 1993, Final Declaration, reprinted in (1993) 296 International Review of the Red Cross 381.

Non-Binding Norms in International Humanitarian Law. Emily Crawford, Oxford University Press. © Emily Crawford 2021.
DOI: 10.1093/oso/9780198819851.003.0006

> experts from governments and international organisations, a report on customary rules of IHL applicable in international and non-international armed conflicts, and to circulate the report to States and competent international bodies.[2]

By the end of the year, the XXVIth International Conference of the Red Cross and Red Crescent endorsed the recommendation, officially authorising the ICRC to begin preparing a report on the customary rules of IHL applicable in both international and non-international armed conflict.[3]

In order to produce this study, the ICRC began by consulting with a group of academic experts, comprising Professor Georges Abi-Saab, Professor Sala El-Din Amer, Professor Ove Bring, Professor Eric David, Professor John Dugard, Professor Florentino Feliciano, Professor Horst Fischer, Professor Françoise Hampson, Professor Theodor Meron, Professor Djamchid Momtaz, Professor Milan Šahović, and Professor Raúl Emilio Vinuesa.[4] This Steering Committee proceeded to devise a Plan of Action, which was adopted in June 1996, with research beginning in October 1996.[5] The Plan of Action outlined the six key areas on which the Study would focus: the principle of distinction, specifically protected persons and objects, specific methods of warfare, weapons, the treatment of civilians and persons *hors de combat*, and implementation of IHL.[6]

Once the Plan of Action was adopted, it was necessary to determine how the research would be undertaken. Working off the logical assumption that 'national sources are more easily accessible within a country',[7] national researchers in nearly 50 countries through Africa, Asia, Europe, the Americas, and Australasia were approached. International sources were the purview of six teams of rapporteurs and researchers, who each had ownership of one of the six key areas in the Plan of Action.[8] The ICRC also undertook research into its own archives in relation

[2] Meeting of the Intergovernmental Group of Experts for the Protection of War Victims, Geneva, 23–27 January 1995, Recommendation II, reprinted in (1996) 310 International Review of the Red Cross 84.

[3] 26th International Conference of the Red Cross and Red Crescent, Geneva, 3–7 December 1995, Resolution 1, International Humanitarian Law: From Law to Action; Report on the Follow-up to the International Conference for the Protection of War Victims, reprinted in (1996) 310 International Review of the Red Cross 58.

[4] ICRC, Study on Customary International Humanitarian Law, Report submitted pursuant to Resolution 1 of the 28th International Conference of the Red Cross and Red Crescent, 30th International Conference of the Red Cross and Red Crescent, Geneva, Switzerland, 26–30 November 2007, 30IC/07/8.3, Annex I.

[5] ibid 2.

[6] How and why certain topics were chosen or excluded will be discussed in more detail later.

[7] Jean-Marie Henckaerts and Louise Doswald-Beck, *Customary International Humanitarian Law* (ICRC 2005), vol 1 (ICRC CIHL Study) xlv.

[8] Rapporteur Georges Abi-Saab and Researcher Jean-Francois Quéguiner (distinction); Rapporteur Horst Fischer and Researchers Gregor Schotten and Heike Spieker (specifically protected persons and objects); Rapporteur Theodor Meron and Researcher Richard Desgagné (specific methods of warfare); Rapporteur Ove Bring and Researcher Gustaf Lind (weapons); Rapporteur Françoise Hampson and Researcher Camille Giffard (treatment of civilians and persons *hors de combat*); and Rapporteur Eric David and Researcher Richard Desgagné (implementation).

to 40 'recent armed conflicts'.[9] The result of the 'three-pronged approach—that is, research into national, international and ICRC sources—is that practice from all parts of the world is cited'.[10] Of the national State practice examined, the researchers included 'military manuals, national legislation, national case-law, instructions to armed and security forces, military communiques issued during war time, diplomatic protests, opinions of official legal advisers, comments by governments on draft treaties, executive decisions and regulations, pleadings before international tribunals, statements in international organisations and at international conferences and government positions taken with respect to resolutions of international organisations'.[11]

The international sources examined included any relevant practice within the institutional framework of numerous international organisations, including the United Nations, the Organisation for African Unity/African Union, the Council of Europe, the Gulf Cooperation Council, the European Union, the League of Arab States, the Organisation of American States, the Organisation of the Islamic Conference, and the Organisation for Security and Cooperation in Europe, as well as the practice of the Commonwealth of Independent States, the Inter-Parliamentary Union, and the Non-Aligned Movement. Additionally, the practice of the UN Security Council, General Assembly, and Commission on Human Rights was examined, as were ad hoc UN investigations, work undertaken by the International Law Commission (as well as comments in response to its work), UN General Assembly committee work, reports from the UN Secretary-General, reporting procedures under various international treaty regimes (such as the Committee against Torture), the *travaux préparatoires* of treaties, State submissions before international and regional courts, and international case law (to the extent that such case law provided evidence of the existence of custom).[12]

On completion of this initial process, the reported State practice was summarised and consolidated into the six key areas. The ICRC then invited the international research teams to produce executive summaries, delivering an initial assessment of the current state of customary IHL. These executive summaries were discussed by the Steering Committee at meetings in Geneva and updated in light of those discussions; they were sent to academic and government experts, who were invited to Geneva to further discuss and update the findings.[13] The work of the Steering Committee in response to these consultations and updates served as the basis for the final written report, which involved a re-examination of the collated practice in light of any developments in the law and included a review of the rules

[9] ICRC CIHL Study, Introduction, xlvii.
[10] ibid.
[11] ibid xlv–xlvi.
[12] ibid xlvi–xlvii.
[13] For full details of the participants, locations, and dates for these meetings, see the ICRC CIHL Study, Introduction, l–li.

as drafted and ordered. The Commentaries to the rules were written and sent to the ICRC Legal Division for comment; each of the six 'parts' of the study were also reviewed by additional experts.[14] Comments from the ICRC and the experts were incorporated into a second draft, which was re-evaluated by the Steering Committee, the academic and governmental experts, and the ICRC Legal Division. Final comments were incorporated into the text and the work finalised under the guidance of the authors, Louise Doswald-Beck (in her capacity as Deputy and then Head of the ICRC Legal Division) and Jean-Marie Henckaerts (ICRC).

The final Study comprised 161 rules. The rules, the accompanying Commentaries, and the summary of practice are contained in Volume I of the printed version of Study, with the reporting of practice contained in Volumes II and III.[15] The Study has since been digitised and is available online.[16] Though the Study was the work of ICRC experts and mandated by the Conference of the Red Cross and Red Crescent, it is not strictly considered an official ICRC statement on the status of customary IHL: as noted by the ICRC, the institution 'respected the academic freedom both of the report's authors and the experts consulted'.[17]

As noted earlier, the six key areas included were the principle of distinction, specifically protected persons and objects, specific methods of warfare, weapons, the treatment of civilians and persons *hors de combat*, and implementation of IHL. Early on, certain choices regarding methodology and scope were made, which impacted on what was included and why. First, it was decided that the Study would not be an article-by-article assessment of the customary status of every treaty in IHL, but rather would take a more 'macro' approach, analysing broad issues and concepts in IHL, such as distinction and targeting, rather than individual provisions of treaties.[18] Also excluded from the Study was any investigation of the customary status of the law of naval warfare. This was justified on the grounds that 'this area of law was recently the subject of a major restatement, namely the San Remo Manual on Naval Warfare'.[19] Furthermore, other parts of IHL—such as the Martens Clause, the identification of specially protected persons and objects, and civil defence—were also excluded from the scope of the study, as they 'could not be developed in sufficient detail for inclusion'[20] in the first edition, though 'they might be included in a future update'.[21] The authors also noted that while relevant international human rights law provisions were consulted in the course of the

[14] Maurice Mendelson (Introductory section); Knut Dörmann (Part I); Theodor Meron (Part II); Horst Fischer (Part III); Peter Herby and the Mines and Arms Division of the ICRC (Part IV); William Fenrick (Part V); and Antonio Cassese (Part VI).

[15] Nearly 7,000 pages of Rules, Commentary, and Practice make up the hard copy of the Study.

[16] ICRC, *Customary IHL Database* <https://ihl-databases.icrc.org/customary-ihl/eng/docs/home> accessed 5 August 2021.

[17] Kellenberger, Foreword, ICRC CIHL Study, xi.

[18] ICRC CIHL Study, Introduction, xxx.

[19] ibid.

[20] ibid.

[21] ibid.

Study, this was only done where such provisions were found to 'support, strengthen and clarify analogous principles of international humanitarian law';[22] the authors made it clear that there was no intent to assess the customary status of international human rights law.

The aim of the Study was to provide a central source of reference for customary IHL. The authors noted that:

> [t]he general opinion is that violations of international humanitarian law are not due to the inadequacy of its rules, but rather to a lack of willingness to respect them, to a lack of means to enforce them ... to uncertainty as to their application in some circumstances ... [and] to ignorance of the rules on the part of political leaders, commanders, combatants and the general public.[23]

To that end, producing a compendium on the customary status of certain fundamental rules of IHL, noting that such rules are binding on all participants in armed conflicts, would, in theory, go a considerable way to ensuring a diminution of non-application of IHL. As noted in the Study:

> [k]nowledge of the rules of customary international humanitarian law is therefore of use to the many actors involved in the application, dissemination and enforcement of international humanitarian law, such as governmental authorities, arms bearers, international organisations, components of the International Red Cross and Red Crescent Movement and non-governmental organisations. A study on customary international humanitarian law may also be helpful in reducing the uncertainties and the scope for argument inherent in the concept of customary international law.[24]

In addition to assisting stakeholders in implementing the law of armed conflict, the authors of the Study had aims for it to serve as instruction for States in the enforcement of IHL:

> [k]nowledge of the rules of customary international law may also be of service in a number of situations where reliance on customary international law is required. This is especially relevant for the work of courts and international organisations. Indeed, courts are frequently required to apply customary international law.... [I]n addition, in many countries, customary international law is a source of domestic law and can be invoked before and adjudicated by national courts.

22 ibid xxxi.
23 ibid xxvii.
24 ibid xxix.

> Customary international law is also relevant to the work of international organisations in that it generally represents the law binding upon all member States.[25]

Unlike the non-binding manuals discussed in Chapter 4, the ICRC Study makes no reference to its binding or non-binding status. Instead, in one of the forewords to the work, the Study is claimed to be:

> a still photograph of reality, taken with great concern for absolute honesty, that is, without trying to make the law say what one wishes it would say. I am convinced that this is what lends the study international credibility. But though it represents the truest possible reflection of reality, the study makes no claim to be the final word. It is not all-encompassing—choices had to be made—and no-one is infallible. In the introduction to *De jure belli ac pacis*, Grotius says this to his readers: 'I beg and adjure all those into whose hands this work shall come, that they assumed towards me the same liberty that I have assumed in passing upon the opinions and writings of others.' What better way to express the objectives of those who have carried out this study? May it be read, discussed and commented on. May it prompt renewed examination of international humanitarian law and the means of bringing about greater compliance and of developing the law. Perhaps it could even go beyond the subject of war and spur us to think about the value of the principles on which the law is based in order to build universal peace—the utopian imperative—in the century on which we have now embarked.[26]

Another foreword to the work also affirms that 'the ICRC believes that the study does indeed present an accurate assessment of the current state of customary international humanitarian law … the ICRC's sincere hope is that it will clarify the meaning and significance of a number of rules of international humanitarian law and that it will ensure greater protection for war victims'.[27]

Upon the publication of the Study in March 2005, the authors were almost universally commended for having undertaken such a mammoth task. Commentators praised the Study as a 'significant contribution',[28] a 'remarkable feat',[29] and a work of 'extraordinary breadth, depth and vision'[30] that provides an 'invaluable service'[31]

[25] ibid xxix–xxx.

[26] Yves Sandoz, Foreword, ICRC CIHL Study, xvii–xviii.

[27] Jacob Kellenberger, Foreword, ICRC CIHL Study, xi. Similar sentiments were included in the Foreword by Justice Abdul Koroma (xiii).

[28] Daniel Bethlehem, 'The Methodological Framework of the Study' in Elizabeth Wilmshurst and Susan Breau (eds), *Perspectives on the ICRC Study on Customary International Humanitarian Law* (CUP/Chatham House/BIICL 2007) 3.

[29] ibid.

[30] Robert Cryer, 'Of Custom, Treaties, Scholars and the Gavel: The Influence of the International Criminal Tribunals on the ICRC Customary Law Study' (2006) 11 Journal of Conflict & Security Law 239, 263.

[31] Michael Bothe, 'Customary International Humanitarian Law: Some Reflections on the ICRC Study' (2005) 8 Yearbook of International Humanitarian Law 143, 177.

for all persons involved with IHL and its implementation. The Study was soon in use by several actors in international law. It was cited in international[32] and domestic[33] court cases within a year of its publication, a trend that would continue in the years that followed.[34] The ICRC Study would also be cited with approval in non-binding manuals, such as the Tallinn Manual.[35] Since its publication, the Study has been consistently updated with new practice, with the new findings published on the ICRC website.[36]

However, numerous criticisms were levelled at the Study, mainly directed at its methodology. The United States,[37] among others,[38] voiced concerns that the State practice cited as evidence of custom was 'insufficiently dense to meet the "extensive and virtually uniform" standard generally required to demonstrate the existence of a customary rule';[39] in particular, criticism was levelled at the Study for its seeming over-reliance on certain *types* of evidence (such as military manuals and resolutions of international or intergovernmental organisations). Criticisms included that some cited pieces of evidence were not strictly examples of State practice,[40] or that some evidence might be more indicative of a State acting for reasons of comity rather than *opinio juris* (therefore undermining any probative customary value).[41]

[32] In the International Criminal Tribunal for the former Yugoslavia in *Prosecutor v Hadžihasanović (Decision on Joint Defence Interlocutory Appeal of Trial Chamber Decision on Rule 98bis Motions for Acquittal)* (Case No IT-01-47-AR73.3, 11 March 2005) paras 29–30, 38, 45–56; *Prosecutor v Stakić (Judgment)* (Case No IT-97-24-A, 22 March 2006) para 296.

[33] In the Israel Supreme Court in *Adalah v GOC Central Command* (HCJ 3799/02, 23 June 2005) paras 20, 21, 24.

[34] *Gherebi v Obama* 609 F Supp 2d 43, 109 (DDC 2009); Israel Supreme Court sitting as the High Court of Justice, *Public Committee against Torture in Israel and other v Government of Israel* (HCJ 769/02, 13 December 2006) paras 23, 29–30, 33–34, 40–42, 46; *Hamdan v Rumsfeld* 548 US 557, 632 (2006). The Study would also prove instructive for the work of the Ethiopia-Eritrea Claims Commission, the Special Court for Sierra Leone, and the International Commission of Inquiry on Darfur. See further Jean-Marie Henckaerts, 'Customary International Humanitarian Law: Taking Stock of the ICRC Study' (2010) 78 Nordic Journal of International Law 435, 437–441.

[35] Tallinn Manual 2.0, 405, fn 975.

[36] ICRC, *Customary IHL Database* (n 16).

[37] John Bellinger, Legal Advisor of the US Department of State, and William Haynes, General Counsel of the US Department of Defense, Letter to the President of the ICRC, excerpted in 'United States Responds to ICRC Study on Customary International Law' (2007) 101 American Journal of International Law 639, 640.

[38] See, for example, Claude Emanuelli, 'Comments on the ICRC Study on Customary International Humanitarian Law' (2006) 44 Canadian Yearbook of International Law 437; Bethlehem (n 28).

[39] Bellinger and Haynes, Letter to the President of the ICRC (n 37) 640.

[40] See, for example, Emanuelli (n 38) 444–46, specifically noting that the inclusion of ICRC practice is problematic: 'The ICRC is not a State . . . its practice should not have the same weight as that of States' ibid 446.

[41] 'We are troubled by the type of practice on which the Study has, in too many places, relied . . . [T]he Study places too much emphasis on written materials, such as military manuals and other guidelines published by States, as opposed to actual operational practice by States during armed conflict . . . . We are also troubled by the extent to which the Study relies on non-binding resolutions of the General Assembly, given that States may lend their support to a particular resolution, or determine not to break consensus in regard to such a resolution, for reasons having nothing to do with a belief that the propositions in it reflect customary international law': Bellinger and Haynes, Letter to the President of the ICRC (n 37) 640.

Concerns were also raised that the Study, coming as it does with the imprimatur of the ICRC, would be unquestioningly accepted by stakeholders, leading to the parts of the Study considered *lex ferenda* being considered as law, rather than as academic opinion. As argued by Daniel Bethlehem, the Study 'has the benefit of momentum that derives from the name, stature and authority of the ICRC',[42] with Iain Scobbie adding that the Study is 'anointed with the prestige and authority of the ICRC and it should be expected that it will assume the mantle of status and persuasion accorded to the ICRC Commentaries on the Geneva Conventions and Additional Protocols because of its provenance'.[43] Additional uneasiness about the Study's impact has been voiced along the lines that the ICRC essentially overstepped its mandate, engaging in law-creation or treating *lex ferenda* as *lex lata*, rather than merely restating the law:

> The findings themselves pose awkward questions about the ICRC's efforts to 'establish' customary IHL. Above all, the Study has served to narrow the gap between the highly regulated treaty regime applicable in IAC and the rudimentary provisions in NIAC by documenting a convergence in the respective customary rules. These rules are set out in the Study under the guise of settled customary law: the research is presented as an exercise in 'finding' the law in force and the outcome as a restatement of what already exists. The reality, however, may well be otherwise. As one scholar put it, did not the contributors to the Study in fact, consciously or unconsciously, craft new rules in the shadow of the law or at least extend the law to hitherto unregulated concerns?[44]

The scholar mentioned by MacLaren and Schwendimann is Daniel Thürer,[45] who referred to the ICRC as a 'codifying' body, and declared the ICRC's work as not 'merely "tidying up" areas of international law but … engaging in their progressive development'.[46] In doing this, Thürer argues, the ICRC has intruded on the traditionally exclusive prerogative of States as law creators.[47]

[42] Bethlehem (n 28) 14.

[43] Iain Scobbie, 'The Approach to Customary International Law in the Study' in Elizabeth Wilmshurst and Susan Breau (eds), *Perspectives on the ICRC Study on Customary International Humanitarian Law* (CUP/Chatham House/BIICL 2007) 16.

[44] Malcolm MacLaren and Felix Schwendimann, 'An Exercise in the Development of International Law: The New ICRC Study on Customary International Humanitarian Law' (2005) 6 German Law Journal 1217, 1236.

[45] Daniel Thürer, 'Comment—The Democratization of Contemporary International Law-Making Processes and the Differentiation of Their Application' in Rüdiger Wolfrum and Volker Röben (eds), *Developments of International Law in Treaty Making* (Springer 2005) 58–59.

[46] ibid 59.

[47] Questions regarding the legitimacy and legality of this supposed law-making are discussed in more detail in Chapter 8 of this book.

The International Code of Conduct for Private Security Providers

At the same time as States were debating the *Montreux Document on Pertinent International Legal Obligations and Good Practices for States related to Operations of Private Military and Security Companies during Armed Conflict* (Montreux Document) on PMSCs, the Swiss government[48] initiated a parallel project to adapt and adopt the Montreux rules to create a set of guidelines for PMSCs themselves. To that end, a series of preliminary workshops with the private security industry,[49] civil society and academia,[50] and States and international organisations[51] was convened, so that the facilitators of the project could understand and map the contours of how and why PMSCs are employed, and what the PMSCs themselves considered to be necessary in terms of developing rules and guidelines regarding their operations.[52] These preliminary workshops were followed in June 2009 with a 'multi-stakeholder' workshop held in Nyon, Switzerland, involving nearly 50 representatives from PMSCs, civil society, academia, and both State and non-State employers of PMSCs, including China, Russia, the United Kingdom, and the United States.[53] As a result of all of these workshops, broad consensus was reached that a draft international code of conduct for PMSCs should be adopted, drawing on IHL and international human rights law, and including oversight and accountability mechanisms.[54]

[48] In conjunction with the Geneva Academy of International Humanitarian Law and Human Rights, an educational institution established in 2007 by the Faculty of Law of the University of Geneva and the Graduate Institute of International and Development Studies, which 'provides post-graduate education, conducts academic legal research and policy studies, and organizes training courses and expert meetings' (<http://www.geneva-academy.ch/the-academy/about-us/mission> accessed 5 August 2021), and the Geneva Centre for the Democratic Control of Armed Forces (DCAF), a civil society institution which 'assists partner states in developing laws, institutions, policies and practices to improve the governance of their security sector through inclusive and participatory reforms based on international norms and good practices ... [and] advises governments and international organizations in designing and implementing their own programmes for supporting states in developing their security sector governance. DCAF creates innovative knowledge products, promotes norms and good practices, and provides legal and policy advice. DCAF supports capacity building of state, civil society and private sector stakeholders by providing access to independent expertise and information on Security Sector Governance and Reform (SSG/R)' (<http://www.dcaf.ch/about-us> accessed 5 August 2021).

[49] Held in March 2009.

[50] Held in April 2009.

[51] Held in May 2009.

[52] For a more detailed explanation of the workshops (and the Code more generally), see Corinna Seiberth, *Private Military and Security Companies in International Law* (Intersentia 2014) 161–91; Anne-Marie Buzatu, 'Towards an International Code of Conduct for Private Security Providers: A View from Inside a Multi-Stakeholder Process' (2015) Geneva Centre for the Democratic Control of Armed Forces, SSR Paper 12, 31–35.

[53] Buzatu (n 52) 34.

[54] As outlined in Wilton Park, 'Report on Wilton Park Conference 979, Private Military and Security Companies: Working towards an International Code of Conduct, Thursday 4–6 June 2009 in Nyon, Switzerland' <http://www.wiltonpark.org.uk/wp-content/uploads/wp979-report.pdf> accessed 5 August 2021.

Responsibility for drafting such a code fell to the facilitators—a group comprising members of the Swiss government, the Geneva Academy of International Humanitarian Law and Human Rights, and the Geneva Centre for the Democratic Control of Armed Forces. Together, this group met following the workshops to 'sift through and analyse the contents of those discussions, putting together draft texts that would then be circulated to the next round of multistakeholder meetings for further feedback, starting the process over again'.[55] Following on from the Nyon Conference, an additional eight workshops were held between September 2009 and September 2010. Two of these workshops were attended primarily by industry representatives, with the remaining six workshops involving all stakeholders. The result of the workshops was two draft versions of an International Code of Conduct for Private Security Providers (ICoC), the first produced in January 2010 and the second in August 2010. The text of the ICoC was then officially adopted on 9 November 2010, with 58 private security companies[56] signing up to the Code.[57]

The Code contains 70 provisions covering a number of areas, such as the law on the use of force;[58] the apprehension and detention of persons;[59] prohibitions on torture and other cruel, inhuman, or degrading treatment or punishment,[60] gender-based violence,[61] human trafficking,[62] slavery and forced labour,[63] including child labour,[64] and discrimination;[65] requirements for identification and registering of personnel of PMSCs (or private security companies (PSCs), as they are referred to in the Code);[66] and a comprehensive list of commitments on management and governance, including the selection and vetting of personnel;[67] training and management requirements in relation to personnel, weapons, and materiel;[68] and health and safety commitments for personnel and management.[69]

Under the Code, signatory companies:

[55] Buzatu (n 52) 36.

[56] The companies are listed in David Wallace, 'International Code of Conduct for Private Security Service Providers' (2011) 50 International Legal Materials 89, 103–04.

[57] <https://icoca.ch/wp-content/uploads/2020/12/Annual-Report-2020-web.pdf> accessed 27 September 2021. See further 'The International Code of Conduct for Private Security Service Providers' (August 2013) Geneva Academy of International Humanitarian Law and Human Rights Academy Briefing No 4 <http://www.geneva-academy.ch/joomlatools-files/docman-files/Publications/Academy%20Briefings/Icoc_web_final.pdf> accessed 5 August 2021.

[58] ICoC, Principles 29–32.

[59] ICoC, Principles 33–34.

[60] ICoC, Principles 35–37.

[61] ICoC, Principle 38.

[62] ICoC, Principle 39.

[63] ICoC, Principle 40.

[64] ICoC, Principle 41.

[65] ICoC, Principle 42.

[66] ICoC, Principle 43.

[67] ICoC, Commitments 45–51.

[68] ICoC, Commitments 55–62.

[69] ICoC, Commitments 63–68.

> endorse the principles of the Montreux Document ... [and] commit to the responsible provision of Security Services so as to support the rule of law, respect the human rights of all persons, and protect the interests of their clients ... [and] affirm that they have a responsibility to respect the human rights of, and fulfil humanitarian responsibilities towards, all those affected by their business activities, including Personnel, Clients, suppliers, shareholders, and the population of the area in which services are provided. The Signatory Companies also recognize the importance of respecting the various cultures encountered in their work, as well as the individuals they come into contact with as a result of those activities.[70]

While the Code contains comprehensive principles and commitments regarding the conduct and management of PMSCs, the Code affirms that it:

> does not limit or alter applicable international law or relevant national law. The Code itself creates no legal obligations and no legal liabilities on the Signatory Companies, beyond those which already exist under national or international law. Nothing in this Code shall be interpreted as limiting or prejudicing in any way existing or developing rules of international law.[71]

However, the Code makes it clear that, despite its non-binding nature, the ultimate intent is that the Code will 'set forth a commonly-agreed set of principles for PSCs and ... establish a foundation to translate those principles into related standards as well as governance and oversight mechanisms',[72] with the aim that such standard can be harmonised on both a domestic and an international level.[73]

Upon its adoption, the ICoC was generally well received: commentators called it a 'remarkable and unique effort'[74] and a 'welcome'[75] and 'promising step'[76] towards better regulation of PMSCs. That the principles apply 'directly to PMSCs ... thereby overcoming the structural weaknesses of international law'[77] was also singled out for praise. This 'direct address' to the industry seems to have worked; 708 companies had formally committed to the Code of Conduct by 2013, the same year that saw the successful creation of an ICoC oversight mechanism, the International

70 ICoC, Preamble, paras 3–4.

71 ICoC, para 14.

72 ICoC, Preamble, para 5.

73 ICoC, para 10.

74 Whitney Grespin, 'An Act of Faith: Building the International Code of Conduct for Private Security Providers' *Diplomatic Courier* (July/August 2012) 68.

75 David Wallace, 'International Code of Conduct for Private Security Service Providers' (2011) 50 International Legal Materials 89, 90.

76 Reema Shah, 'Beating Blackwater: Using Domestic Legislation to Enforce the International Code of Conduct for Private Military Companies' (2014) 123 Yale Law Journal 2559, 2563.

77 Nigel White, 'Regulatory Initiatives at the International Level' in Christine Bakker and Mirko Sossai (eds), *Multilevel Regulation of Military and Security Contractors: The Interplay between International, European and Domestic Norms* (Hart 2011) 16.

Code of Conduct Association (ICoCA).[78] Additionally, there was clear adoption of the ICoC in domestic and international practice, with States and organisations such as the United Nations,[79] the United Kingdom,[80] the United States,[81] Switzerland,[82] and Australia[83] all including the ICoC as part of security policy.

However, there has been almost uniform criticism of the implementation and enforcement mechanisms of the ICoC. In the immediate aftermath of the adoption of the ICoC, one line of criticism was its failure to include a 'strong regulatory mechanism to oversee the implementation of the Code',[84] leading to the possibility that the ICoC will be at best 'limited and at worst will be tokenistic',[85] while another criticism was that, in placing obligations to respect international law on PMSCs, States could be considered as effectively evading their own duties and responsibilities under IHL and international human rights law.[86]

[78] <http://www.icoca.ch/en>. See also <http://www.admin.ch/gov/en/start/dokumentation/medienmitteilungen.msg-id-47889.html> accessed 5 August 2021. The ICoCA had always been envisaged as being part of the process and, following the adoption of the ICoC, additional working groups, led by a Steering Committee, met between 2010 and 2013, finally adopting the Articles of Association of the ICoCA: <http://www.icoca.ch/en/articles_of_association> accessed 5 August 2021. For a more detailed analysis of the process that led to the creation of the ICoCA, see further Buzatu (n 52) 45–62.

[79] The UN Department of Safety and Security adopted guidelines in 2012 requiring that any PMSCs employed by the United Nations be members of the ICoCA, and that they meet ICoC guidelines on the use of force and weapons handling. See further United Nations Security Management System, *Security Policy Manual* (2017) 95 <https://www.un.org/sites/un2.un.org/files/undss-security_policy_manual_e-book.pdf> accessed 27 September 2021.

[80] Security in Complex Environment Groups (SCEG) is a public–private UK entity 'for security companies who are committed to the development and implementation of international standards for the private security sector . . . [which] engages across government on a sustained basis on a range of issues pertinent to the industry. The Foreign and Commonwealth Office (FCO) is the principal conduit for the partnership but SCEG is also actively engaged with the Department for Transport, (DfT) the Home Office, the Department for International Trade, UK Trade and Industry (UKTI) and the Ministry of Defence (MoD)': <http://www.sceguk.org.uk/about-sceg/> accessed 5 August 2021. All SCEG members are required to abide by the ICoC.

[81] See the US Department of State Fact Sheet on Business and Human Rights, which states that 'We participate in The International Code of Conduct for Private Security Service Providers (ICoCA), an oversight and governance mechanism for private security companies promoting respect for human rights and humanitarian law in complex environments. ICoCA includes a certification, monitoring, and complaint mechanism': <https://www.state.gov/business-and-human-rights/> accessed 27 September 2021.

[82] Swiss law requires any PMSC domiciled in Switzerland or operating from Swiss territory (and providing services outside of Switzerland and the European Union/European Free Trade Area States) to be a member of the ICoCA: Article 7, Federal Act on Private Security Services Provided Abroad (PSSA) of 27 September 2013 (Status as at 1 September 2015): <http://www.eda.admin.ch/dam/eda/en/documents/aussenpolitik/sicherheitspolitik/Bundesgesetz-ueber-die-im-Ausland-erbrachten-privaten-Sicherheitsdienstleistungen-BPS_EN.pdf> accessed 5 August 2021. See further <http://www.eda.admin.ch/eda/en/home/aussenpolitik/sicherheitspolitik/bundesgesetz-ueber-die-im-ausland-erbrachten-privaten-sicherheit.html> accessed 5 August 2021.

[83] Australia is a foundation member of the ICoCA: <http://dfat.gov.au/news/media/Pages/australia-taking-lead-role-in-international-efforts-to-raise-standards-and-accountability-for-private-security-contractors.aspx> accessed 5 August 2021.

[84] White, 'Regulatory Initiatives' (n 77) 16.

[85] ibid.

[86] See generally Sorcha MacLeod, 'Private Security Companies and Shared Responsibility: The Turn to Multistakeholder Standard-Setting and Monitoring through Self-Regulation-"Plus"' (2015) 62 Netherlands International Law Review 119.

Even after the creation of the ICoCA, the body created for the purposes of ensuring compliance with the ICoC, the structural inadequacies of the ICoCA were critiqued, with one commentator noting that '[t]he absence of a judicial body or forum where PMCs can be held accountable if they persist in violating norms makes adherence to the Code largely voluntary'[87] and thus, arguably, incapable of being 'meaningfully enforced',[88] which itself renders the ICoCA fundamentally 'inadequate'.[89]

The ICRC Interpretive Guidance on the Notion of Direct Participation in Hostilities under International Humanitarian Law

The ICRC Interpretive Guidance was a process initiated by the ICRC, in conjunction with the TMC Asser Institute. The impetus for initiating the project came about because of changes in the conduct of armed conflicts, specifically that there has been:

> [a] continued shift of the battlefield into civilian population centers [which] has led to an increased intermingling of civilians with armed actors and has facilitated their involvement in activities more closely related to military operations .... As a result, civilians are more likely to fall victim to erroneous or arbitrary targeting, while armed forces—unable to properly identify their adversary—run an increased risk of being attacked by persons they cannot distinguish from the civilian population.[90]

To that end, the ICRC sought to bring together experts in an informal expert process to clarify the extant law on three specific questions, namely: (1) who is a civilian for the purposes of the principle of distinction? (2) what conduct amounts to direct participation in hostilities? And (3) what modalities govern the loss of protection against direct attack?[91] Over the course of five years, five informal expert meetings were held in The Hague and Geneva, involving around 50 legal experts from the military, government, and academia, as well as experts from international

[87] Reema Shah (n 76) 2564.
[88] ibid.
[89] ibid.
[90] Nils Melzer, 'The ICRC's Clarification Process on the Notion of Direct Participation in Hostilities under International Humanitarian Law' (2009) 103 ASIL Proceedings 299, 299.
[91] ICRC, Interpretive Guidance on the Notion of Direct Participation in Hostilities under International Humanitarian Law, Adopted by the Assembly of the International Committee of the Red Cross on 26 February 2009, published in (2008) 90 International Review of the Red Cross 991, 994 (DPHIG).

and non-governmental organisations (NGOs). All experts attended in their personal capacity.[92]

The aim of the Expert Process was the production of a non-binding document that outlined an approach to defining the scope of the term 'direct participation in hostilities'.[93] The process involved the preparation of questionnaires, background documents, and reports, which informed the debate at the expert meetings.[94] The meetings were conducted under Chatham House Rules[95] and no official list of participants was published.[96] However, a number of experts made their participation known to the public via publication of articles on the process,[97] as well as through identification on the papers from the Expert Process.[98]

The result of this Expert Process was the publication of the ICRC Interpretive Guidance. The Interpretive Guidance, as finally adopted, comprised 10 Recommendations of how to approach the concept of direct participation, defined as:

> [a] specific act [which] must meet the following cumulative criteria: (1) the act must be likely to adversely affect the military operations of military capacity of a party to an armed conflict or alternatively to inflict death, injury, or destruction on persons or objects protected against direct attack (threshold of harm); (2) there must be a direct causal link between the act and the harm likely to result from that act, or from a coordinated military operation of which that act

[92] ICRC, 'Overview of the ICRC's Expert Process (2003–2008)' 3 <www.icrc.org/eng/assets/files/other/overview-of-the-icrcs-expert-process-icrc.pdf>.

[93] DPHIG 991. For full papers for the Expert Process, see <www.icrc.org/eng/resources/documents/article/other/direct-participation-article-020709.htm>.

[94] William Fenrick, 'The ICRC Guidance on Direct Participation in Hostilities' (2009) 12 Yearbook of International Humanitarian Law 287, 288.

[95] ICRC, Fifth Informal Expert Meetings on the Notion of Direct Participation in Hostilities under IHL, Expert Comments and Elements of Response Concerning the Revised Draft of the Interpretive Guidance on the Notion of Direct Participation in Hostilities, Geneva, 5–6 February 2008 <www.icrc.org/eng/assets/files/other/2008-03-background-doc-icrc.pdf>.

[96] In part due to the controversy that emerged during and after the Process, discussed below.

[97] See, for example, William Boothby, 'Direct Participation in Hostilities – A Discussion of the ICRC Interpretive Guidance' (2010) 1 Journal of International Humanitarian Legal Studies 143; William Boothby, '"And for Such Time As": The Time Dimension to Direct Participation in Hostilities' (2010) 42 New York University Journal of International Law and Politics 741; Kenneth Watkin, 'Opportunity Lost: Organized Armed Groups and the ICRC "Direct Participation in Hostilities" Interpretive Guidance' (2010) 42 New York University Journal of International Law and Politics 641; Fenrick (n 94); Yoram Dinstein, 'Direct Participation in Hostilities' (2013) 18 Tilburg Law Review 3.

[98] Among those identifiable in the papers from the Expert Process as having participated in some capacity in the meetings (including, where listed, affiliations/titles at the time) are Nils Melzer (ICRC); Professor Horst Fischer (Leiden University and Ruhr Universitat); Colonel Charles Garraway (Army Legal Services, UK); Professor Michael Schmitt (George C Marshall European Centre for Security Studies); Louise Doswald Beck (International Commission of Jurists); Professor Hans-Peter Gasser (former legal advisor, ICRC); William Lietzau (US Department of Defense); Avril McDonald (TMC Asser); Jelena Pejic (ICRC); Jean-Philippe Lavoyer (ICRC); Maria Nybondas (TMC Asser); Professor Michael Bothe (Goethe University); Yves Sandoz; W Hays Parks (US Department of Defense); and Emanuela-Chiara Gillard (ICRC).

> constitutes an integral part (direct causation); and (3) the act must be specifically designed to directly cause the required threshold of harm in support of a party to the conflict and to the detriment of another (belligerent nexus).[99]

Joining this definition of direct participation were the relevant constituent elements necessary to properly understand the conceptualisation of direct participation. These included a definition of the concept of 'civilian' in international[100] and non-international armed conflict;[101] the use of private contractors and civilian employees in situations of armed conflict;[102] defining direct participation as a specific act;[103] the constitutive elements of direct participation;[104] the beginning and the end of direct participation;[105] the temporal scope of the loss of protection for direct participation;[106] precautions and presumptions in operation in situations of doubt as to the civilian status of a person;[107] restraints on the use of force when engaging in direct attack;[108] and the consequences of regaining civilian protection on the cessation of direct participation.[109] Accompanying the Recommendations was a commentary, which explained the scope of the Recommendations in more detail.

The aim of the Guidance was made clear by Nils Melzer in his comments to the American Society of International Law Annual Meeting in 2009, when he stated that the Guidance:

> [p]rovides the ICRC's recommendations as to how IHL relating to the notion of direct participation in hostilities should be interpreted in light of the circumstances prevailing in contemporary armed conflicts. In doing so, the Interpretive Guidance does not endeavour to change or amend existing rules of IHL, but to ensure their coherent interpretation in line with the fundamental principles underlying IHL as a whole. While the Interpretive Guidance is not legally binding, it may be hoped that the careful and balanced analysis underlying its recommendations will be persuasive to states, non-state actors, practitioners, and academics alike.[110]

That the final instrument adopted by the ICRC[111] was termed an 'interpretive guidance' rather than an 'expert guidance' or 'expert document' alludes to

[99] DPHIG 1016.
[100] Recommendation I.
[101] Recommendation II.
[102] Recommendation III.
[103] Recommendation IV.
[104] Recommendation V.
[105] Recommendation VI.
[106] Recommendation VII.
[107] Recommendation VIII.
[108] Recommendation IX.
[109] Recommendation X.
[110] Nils Melzer, 'The ICRC's Clarification Process' (n 90) 301.
[111] DPHIG 991–1047.

problems that arose during the Expert Process. Indeed, due to controversies that arose during the Expert Process,[112] the resulting document is the position of the ICRC alone and not a consensus document from the expert meetings.[113] The general elements of direct participation, as outlined by the ICRC, were, for the most part, acceptable to the experts. The idea that an act of direct participation required, inter alia, a belligerent nexus and a threshold of harm was relatively uncontroversial when discussed during the meetings.[114] However, a number of other elements of the Interpretive Guidance were subject to notable dissent, including the conceptualisation of membership in an organised armed group,[115] how causation was to be calculated,[116] the question of human shields,[117] and the temporal scope of loss (and reacquisition) of civilian immunity from targeting.[118] 'Perhaps most controversial was the inclusion of the section on "Restraints on the Use of Force in Direct Attack". Recommendation IX of the Guidance states that: in addition to the restraints imposed by international humanitarian law on specific means and methods of warfare, and without any prejudice to further restrictions that may arise under other applicable branches of international law, the kind and degree of force which is permissible against persons not entitled to protection against direct attack must not exceed what is actually necessary to accomplish a legitimate military purpose in the prevailing circumstances.'[119]

The inclusion of Recommendation IX (called Section IX during the drafting) in what was intended as the final draft of the Interpretive Guidance in 2007 was a cause for immediate criticism by some of the experts involved in the process.[120] According to W Hays Parks, Section IX had been inserted into the draft by the ICRC 'without consultation with participating experts or its co-sponsor, the TMC Asser Institute'.[121] The concerns regarding Section IX were that it seemed to be based on the so-called 'Pictet use of force continuum'[122]—that 'if a combatant can

[112] Discussed further later.
[113] DPHIG 992.
[114] ICRC, Fifth Informal Expert Meetings, Expert Comments and Elements of Response (n 95) 22–29.
[115] ibid 11–19.
[116] ibid 28.
[117] ibid 30–31.
[118] ibid 32–36.
[119] DPHIG 1040.
[120] ICRC, Fifth Informal Expert Meetings on the Notion of Direct Participation in Hostilities under IHL, Discussion Notes, Working Sessions I to VII, Geneva, 5–6 February 2008 <http://www.icrc.org/eng/assets/files/other/2008-04-background-doc-icrc.pdf> accessed 5 August 2021.
[121] W Hays Parks, 'Part IX of the ICRC "Direct Participation in Hostilities" Study: No Mandate, No Expertise, and Legally Incorrect' (2010) 42 New York University Journal of International Law and Politics 769, 783. This is disputed by Nils Melzer, 'Keeping the Balance between Military Necessity and Humanity: A Response to Four Critiques of the ICRC's Interpretive Guidance on the Notion of Direct Participation in Hostilities' (2010) 42 New York University Journal of International Law and Politics 831, 894.
[122] Pictet had argued that 'humanity demands capture rather than wounds, and wounds rather than death': Jean Pictet, *Humanitarian Law and the Protection of War Victims* (Henry Dunant Institute 1975) 32.

be put out of action by taking him prisoner, he should not be injured; if he can be put out of action by injury, he should not be killed; and if he can be put out of action by light injury, grave injury should be avoided'.[123] At least a dozen experts criticised the section for forwarding 'a novel argument unknown under contemporary IHL'[124]—that, in combat, one must be guided by the principle of humanity above all else, including even military necessity.[125] For the critics, this was an untenable standard for combatants to meet, requiring them to 'capture rather than kill'[126] in combat situations. According to this line of reasoning, Section IX established a legal obligation for combatants to use less than lethal force in a combat zone, contrary to State practice. As one expert put it, 'not even domestic law enforcement agencies trained their officers, let alone members of the armed forces, to shoot to wound'.[127]

The ICRC attempted to assuage concerns regarding Section IX[128] and other contentious aspects of the Guidance, including organising working groups to attempt to reach consensus[129] and proposing revisiting and revising certain formulations of rules at an additional expert meeting in 2008.[130] However, this approach did little to salve the concerns of some of the experts, with the ICRC ultimately allowing anyone who wished to remove his or her name from the final document to do so. In response, nearly a third of the experts involved in the discussions requested that their names be removed 'lest inclusion be misinterpreted as support for the Interpretive Guidance's propositions'.[131]

The Interpretive Guidance was released as an ICRC document and the names of the experts involved in the process were not published.[132] However,

[123] ICRC, Report on the Work of Experts: Weapons That May Cause Unnecessary Suffering or Have Indiscriminate Effects (ICRC 1973) 13, para 23.

[124] ICRC, Summary Report, Fourth Expert Meeting on the Notion of Direct Participation in Hostilities, 27–28 November 2006 (DPH Summary Report 2006) 75. See also ICRC, Fifth Informal Expert Meetings, Discussion Notes (n 120) 3–5.

[125] See Parks (n 121) 785.

[126] Revised Draft, Interpretive Guidance on the Notion of Direct Participation in Hostilities (2008) 63.

[127] DPH Summary Report 2006, 75.

[128] By stating that Section IX was not intended to be used in large-scale armed engagements but rather was 'primarily designed for situations where armed forces were confronted with individuals within their territorial control who did not benefit from civilian protection against direct attack although they did not pose an immediate threat at the time and could be captured without additional risk. For example, where unarmed members of armed groups were surprised while sleeping in the woods or sitting in a restaurant, it would be unacceptable for the operating forces to simply kill them without even attempting an arrest': DPH Summary Report 2006, 76.

[129] See generally ICRC, Fifth Informal Expert Meetings, Expert Comments and Elements of Response (n 95).

[130] Hays Parks comments on the process regarding Section IX: see Parks (n 121) 783–85.

[131] Michael Schmitt, 'The Interpretive Guidance on the Notion of Direct Participation in Hostilities: A Critical Analysis' (2010) 1 Harvard National Security Journal 5, 6.

[132] According to Hays Parks, the ICRC informed participants that names would not be published in an email: Parks (n 121) 785.

several participants who were involved in the process self-identified, airing their critiques in journal articles and other fora. For example, William Boothby took issue with the interpretation of the scope of DPH, specifically the way in which preparation, deployment, and return were characterised in the temporal dimension to direct participation,[133] and Kenneth Watkin was critical of the ICRC formulation of membership in armed groups.[134] Additional criticism of the Guidance came from other academics and practitioners, who argued that it was at times verging on *lex ferenda*,[135] due to its failure to adequately consult with States or to appropriately draw on State practice.[136] Others joined in criticising the inclusion of Section IX and its seeming advocacy for a *de minimus* use of lethal force against targetable persons.[137] Another criticism was that the Guidance failed to account for irregular armed groups not belonging to or attributable to a State that participate in international armed conflicts.[138] Additionally, particular concerns were raised that because the Guidance was released under the imprimatur of the ICRC, the so-called '"custodian" or "guardian"'[139] of IHL, it could have 'substantial persuasive effect'[140] beyond just serving as an ICRC interpretation, and possibly lend legitimacy to the contested sections of the Guidance. For all the criticism of the Guidance, there were those who supported the work as finally produced. Dapo Akande, while noting the limitations of the document, nonetheless praised the Guidance as providing a mechanism by which the concept of DPH could be approached,[141] while others commended the Guidance as a 'welcome and useful'[142] contribution to the debate on DPH.

[133] William Boothby, '"And for Such Time As"' (n 97) 743–50.

[134] Watkin (n 97).

[135] Jann Kleffner, 'Section IX of the ICRC Interpretive Guidance on Direct Participation in Hostilities: The End of Jus in Bello Proportionality As We Know It?' (2012) 45 Israel Law Review 35, 52.

[136] Damien van der Toorn, '"Direct Participation in Hostilities": A Legal and Practical Road Test of the International Committee of the Red Cross's Guidance through Afghanistan' (2010) 17 Australian International Law Journal 28.

[137] Kleffner (n 135) 42–43.

[138] Dapo Akande, 'Clearing the Fog of War? The ICRC's Interpretive Guidance on Direct Participation in Hostilities' (2010) 59 International and Comparative Law Quarterly 180, 185.

[139] Ka Lok Yip, 'The ICRC's Interpretive Guidance on the Notion of Direct Participation in Hostilities: Sociological and Democratic Legitimacy in Domestic Legal Orders' (2017) 8 Transnational Legal Theory 224, 235.

[140] Fenrick (n 94) 300.

[141] Akande (n 138) 192.

[142] van der Toorn (n 136). See also Fenrick (n 94) 300; Laura Hofmann, 'Strengthening the Principle of Distinction? A Critical Appraisal of the ICRC's Continuous Combat Function' (2015) 6 Journal of International Humanitarian Law Studies 377, 408; Shannon Bosch, 'The International Humanitarian Law Notion of Direct Participation in Hostilities—A Review of the ICRC Interpretive Guide and Subsequent Debate' (2014) 17 Potchefstroom Electronic Law Journal 999, 1040.

Geneva Call's Deeds of Commitment

Geneva Call is a non-governmental humanitarian organisation founded in 2000[143] with the specific aim of 'engaging armed non-State actors to adhere to a ban on landmines and to respect humanitarian and human rights norms'.[144] It was founded largely in response to work being undertaken towards the adoption of the Ottawa Treaty—itself the work of States and civil society organisations.[145] Civil society organisations were aware that a ban on land mines would only be effective if both States and armed non-State groups committed to halting their use of the weapons, particularly as non-State groups had been (and continue to be) the 'main users of the poor man's weapon'.[146] However, only States were able to sign the Ottawa Convention, with non-State actors excluded from any formalised process by which to express their commitment to such a norm. Geneva Call was established to address this gap: to encourage non-State actors to commit to a total ban on, inter alia, the use of anti-personnel mines, through signing so-called Deeds of Commitment (DoCs)—essentially quasi-treaties, whereby the non-State group agrees to stop employing a particular means or method of warfare. The first of these instruments was the Deed of Commitment for Adherence to a Total Ban on Anti-Personnel Mines and for Cooperation in Mine Action, adopted in 2000,[147] which allows non-State actors to publicly pledge their commitment to cease using anti-personnel mines. Since the adoption of the landmines DoC, additional instruments have been created by Geneva Call, including the Deed of Commitment for the Protection of Children from the Effects of Armed Conflict[148] and the Deed of Commitment for the Prohibition of Sexual Violence in Situations of Armed Conflict and towards the

[143] See <http://www.genevacall.org/who-we-are/> accessed 5 August 2021.

[144] Article 3, Statutes of Geneva Call Foundation for the Adherence of Non-State Actors to International Humanitarian Law <https://genevacall.org/wp-content/uploads/dlm_uploads/2014/01/gc-statutes-eng.pdf> accessed 5 August 2021. Indeed, members of the International Campaign to Ban Landmines were among the founders of Geneva Call. See Pascal Bongard, 'Engaging Armed Non-State Actors on Humanitarian Norms: Reflections on Geneva Call's Experience' (*Humanitarian Exchange*, No 58, July 2013) 9 <https://odihpn.org/magazine/engaging-armed-non-state-actors-on-humanitarian-norms-reflections-on-geneva-call%C2%92s-experience/> accessed 5 August 2021.

[145] For a discussion of the involvement of NGOs in the process that led to the treaty, see further John English, 'The Ottawa Process: Paths Followed, Paths Ahead' (1998) 52 Australian Journal of International Affairs 121, 121; Stefanie Herr, 'Binding Non-State Armed Groups to International Humanitarian Law: Geneva Call and the Ban of Anti-Personnel Mines—Lessons from Sudan' (2010) Peace Research Institute Frankfurt Report No 95, 3–4 <http://www.hsfk.de/fileadmin/HSFK/hsfk_downloads/prif95.pdf.pdf> accessed 5 August 2021.

[146] Anki Sjöberg 'Armed Non-State Actors: The Main Users of the "Poor Man's Weapon"' (2006) 10 Journal of Mine Action 73. See also Geneva Call, *Armed Non-State Actors and Landmines*, vol I: *A Global Report Profiling NSAs and Their Use, Acquisition, Production, Transfer, and Stockpiling of Landmines* (PSIO 2013) 14–24 <https://genevacall.org/wp-content/uploads/dlm_uploads/2013/12/5.pdf>.

[147] <http://www.genevacall.org/wp-content/uploads/dlm_uploads/2013/12/DoC-Banning-anti-personnel-mines.pdf> accessed 5 August 2021 (landmines DoC).

[148] <https://genevacall.org/wp-content/uploads/dlm_uploads/2013/12/DoC-Protecting-children-in-armed-conflict.pdf> accessed 5 August 2021 (children in armed conflict DoC).

Elimination of Gender Discrimination.[149] This was joined in 2018 with the Deed of Commitment on Health Care.[150]

The Deeds of Commitment are short instruments—normally only three to four pages in length. The landmines DoC contains 10 articles, the children in armed conflict DoC 16 articles, the prohibition on sexual violence DoC 14 articles, and the health care DoC 16 articles. As they are, essentially, publications of a single NGO, the DoCs have not gone through the kinds of processes seen in the drafting of other expert instruments—there is no intergovernmental Group of Experts contributing to a draft document that is accompanied by a commentary. Rather, the DoCs are documents that largely hew to the existing provisions in parallel instruments, often employing simplified language. For example, the landmines DoC provides that signatories commit:

> [t]o adhere to a total ban on anti-personnel mines. By anti-personnel mines, we refer to those devices which effectively explode by the presence, proximity or contact of a person, including other victim-activated explosive devices and anti-vehicle mines with the same effect whether with or without anti-handling devices. By total ban, we refer to a complete prohibition on all use, development, production, acquisition, stockpiling, retention, and transfer of such mines, under any circumstances. This includes an undertaking on the destruction of all such mines.[151]

This language largely mimics, albeit in simplified fashion, the wording of Articles 1 and 2 of the Ottawa Convention, which states that:

1. Each State Party undertakes never under any circumstances:
   a) To use anti-personnel mines;
   b) To develop, produce, otherwise acquire, stockpile, retain or transfer to anyone, directly or indirectly, anti-personnel mines;
   c) To assist, encourage or induce, in any way, anyone to engage in any activity prohibited to a State Party under this Convention.
2. Each State Party undertakes to destroy or ensure the destruction of all antipersonnel mines in accordance with the provisions of this Convention.[152]

[149] <https://genevacall.org/wp-content/uploads/dlm_uploads/2013/12/DoC-Prohibiting-sexual-violence-and-gender-discrimination.pdf> 5 August 2021 (prohibition on sexual violence DoC).

[150] <http://www.genevacall.org/wp-content/uploads/2019/07/Deed-of-Commitment-for-the-protection-of-health-care-in-armed-conflict-final-version-4.pdf> accessed 5 August 2021 (health care DoC).

[151] Landmines DoC, Art 1.

[152] 1997 Convention on the Prohibition of Anti-Personnel Mines and on their Destruction (opened for signature 3 December 1997, entered into force 1 March 1999), Art 1.

And that: 'Anti-personnel mine' means a mine designed to be exploded by the presence, proximity or contact of a person and that will incapacitate, injure or kill one or more persons. Mines designed to be detonated by the presence, proximity or contact of a vehicle as opposed to a person, that are equipped with anti-handling devices, are not considered anti-personnel mines as a result of being so equipped.'[153]

The process that follows the issuance of the DoCs is similar to that of conventional treaty-making: once an armed non-State group agrees to abide by the terms of the DoC, the leadership of the armed group signs the Deed, which is then countersigned by Geneva Call and by the Government of the Republic and Canton of Geneva, the latter of which serves as the 'depository' of the signatures, and the 'custodian of the Deeds of Commitment'.[154]

The aim of all the DoCs is the same: to ensure that all parties to an armed conflict respect existing IHL and human rights law norms as outlined in the Deed.[155] However, there is also recognition that the DoCs could have further normative effect, beyond just influencing non-State practice. As outlined in the preamble to the landmines DoC, the non-State group signing the Deed affirms its resolution to 'play our role not only as actors in armed conflicts but also as participants in the practice and development of legal and normative standards for such conflicts'.[156] This stated aim is found only in the landmines DoC and not in the later instruments, but it speaks to a notion that in influencing non-State practice, the DoCs might impact on State practice and therefore have an impact on customary international law.

Conclusion

The instruments explored in this chapter are dissimilar from the manuals and instruments examined in Chapter 4, in that they were the sole creation of civil society institutions, or they are solely addressed at non-State actors, or they were not adopted by expert consensus. However, what these instruments share with the other manuals is the stated (or implicit) aim of influencing and

[153] Ottawa Convention, Art 2.

[154] <https://genevacall.org/how-we-work/deed-of-commitment/> accessed 5 August 2021.

[155] The children in armed conflict DoC contains a commitment to 'protect the civilian population, in particular children, from the effects or dangers of military actions, and to respect their right to life, to human dignity, to education and to development, with the best interest of the child as a primary consideration'; the prohibition on sexual violence DoC affirms the signatory's commitment to determination to 'protect the civilian population and other persons no longer taking part in hostilities from the effects or dangers of military operations, and to respect their fundamental rights'.

[156] Landmines DoC, Preamble.

shaping State and non-State behaviour. That these instruments have been created at all—and continue to be created—suggests that there is some benefit to be accrued from them. This topic will be explored in the next chapter, which will look at the benefits inherent in the creation and adoption of non-binding instruments.

6

The Benefits of Soft Law in International Humanitarian Law

Why the Turn to Non-Binding Instruments and Mechanisms?

Introduction

Soft law and other non-binding instruments have increasingly been used by States and non-State entities alike as mechanisms to engage with pressing issues of international law and policy. This chapter will explore why there has been a turn to non-binding norms in international law more generally, and international humanitarian law (IHL) specifically, to see if common motivations can be found. The statements of purpose behind the adoption of the various manuals, codes of conduct, and other non-binding norms will be examined to ascertain whether they are underpinned by any common reasoning. The chapter will do this by looking to the primary documentation of the instruments themselves—that is, the officially released document containing the instrument—in order to get a better sense of what the motivations behind the instrument were. For example, in exploring the reasoning behind the *San Remo Manual on International Law Applicable to Armed Conflicts at Sea* (San Remo Naval Manual), the published text of the Manual will be examined. What does the Manual *itself* state as its *raison d'etre*? And does the *Montreux Document and the International Code of Conduct* (Montreux Document) actually state any reasons for its non-binding nature? Do the Tallinn Manuals explain why they came about by expert, rather than State-led, processes? A slightly different approach is taken with regards to the non-binding provisions in Common Article 3 and Protocol II—is those cases, the *travaux préparatoires* will be examined to see if reasons for adoption can be ascertained. While the *travaux* are not primary documents in the same way as are Common Article 3 and Protocol II, they are still official records and, as such, provide essential insight and context into how and why the relevant provisions were adopted.

The discussion of these documents will be framed by an analysis of theories of soft law compliance, looking at why other branches of international law—such as economic law and environmental law—have embraced non-binding norms. Does the theory of why soft law norms are created match the practice of creating soft law norms? This theoretical analysis of why soft law norms are adopted, coupled with

Non-Binding Norms in International Humanitarian Law. Emily Crawford, Oxford University Press. © Emily Crawford 2021.
DOI: 10.1093/oso/9780198819851.003.0007

the practical examination of why particular IHL non-binding norms have been developed, will set the parameters for the discussion and analysis that will take place in the remainder of this book.

The Benefits of Non-Binding Instruments in International Law: Theory and Practice

In the last few decades, non-binding instruments and provisions have increasingly been adopted in several fields of international law, including international economic law, international environmental law, international human rights law, and, as already noted in this book, IHL. In the realm of international environmental law,[1] soft law norms have been a mainstay, with instruments such as the Action Plan for the Human Environment, adopted by the Stockholm Conference in 1972 (the Stockholm Declaration);[2] the 1992 Rio Conference Agenda 21 (the Rio Declaration);[3] and the 1995 Food and Agriculture Organization of the United Nations (FAO) Code of Conduct for Responsible Fisheries,[4] among others. In international economic law,[5] instruments include the International Financial Reporting Standards,[6] as well as the promulgation and promotion of standards by bodies such as the International Organization of Securities Commissions (IOSCO).[7] In international human rights law,[8] there are numerous instruments, including the Guiding Principles on Internal Displacement,[9] the United Nations

[1] See generally Ulrich Beyerlin, 'Different Types of Norms in International Environmental Law: Policies, Principles, and Rules' in Daniel Bodansky, Jutta Brunnée, and Ellen Hey (eds), *The Oxford Handbook of International Environmental Law* (OUP 2007); Jürgen Friedrich, *International Environmental 'Soft Law': The Functions and Limits of Nonbinding Instruments in International Environmental Governance and Law* (Springer 2013); John Kirton and Michael Trebilcock (eds), *Hard Choices, Soft Law: Voluntary Standards in Global Trade, Environment and Social Governance* (Routledge 2016).

[2] Declaration of the United Nations Conference on the Human Environment (Stockholm, 16 June 1972), *Report of the United Nations Conference on the Human Environment, Stockholm, 5–16 June 1972*, UN Doc A/CONF.48/14/Rev.1 (1973) <http://www.un-documents.net/aconf48-14r1.pdf> accessed 6 August 2021.

[3] United Nations Conference on Environment & Development, Rio de Janeiro, Brazil, 3 to 14 June 1992, Agenda 21, UN Doc A/CONF.151/26 <http://www.unesco.org/education/pdf/RIO_E.PDF> accessed 6 August 2021.

[4] Code of Conduct for Responsible Fisheries (1995) <http://www.fao.org/3/v9878e/V9878E.pdf> accessed 6 August 2021.

[5] See generally Friedl Weiss and Armin Kammel (eds), *The Changing Landscape of Global Financial Governance and the Role of Soft Law* (Brill 2015); Emilios Avgouleas, *Governance of Global Financial Markets: The Law, the Economics, the Politics* (CUP 2012), specifically ch 5, 'The 'Softness' of Soft Law and Global Financial Governance'; Chris Brummer, 'Why Soft Law Dominates International Finance – and Not Trade' (2010) 13 Journal of International Economic Law 623.

[6] <http://www.ifrs.org/about-us/who-we-are/> accessed 6 August 2021.

[7] <http://www.iosco.org/about/pdf/IOSCO-Fact-Sheet.pdf> accessed 6 August 2021.

[8] Michèle Olivier, 'The Relevance of "Soft Law" as a Source of International Human Rights' (2002) 35 Comparative and International Law Journal of Southern Africa 289.

[9] <http://www.unhcr.org/protection/idps/43ce1cff2/guiding-principles-internal-displacement.html> accessed 6 August 2021.

Standard Minimum Rules for the Treatment of Prisoners,[10] the UN Declaration on the Rights of Indigenous Peoples,[11] and the UN Guiding Principles on Business and Human Rights.[12]

Why has soft law proliferated in international law? Various reasons have been highlighted in the literature on soft law more generally;[13] Robert Kolb provides a comprehensive and persuasive series of reasons for the development of soft law, including:

> [t]he considerable increase in the number of States after 1945 and the considerable division in ideological beliefs, which has rendered it more difficult to find compromises and agreements on hard obligations; the considerable diversification of the actors, spanning civil society, e.g. through a myriad of non-governmental organisations (NGOs), which cannot become party to hard-law instruments (treaties); the constantly increasing mobility and complexity of the questions to be regulated, which need frequent and quick revisions of the technical norms, where the conventional process is much too burdensome; an increasing fear of engaging oneself through hard-law instruments and of being caught in a net of limitations upon freedom and sovereignty; [and] the existence of an agreement on some rules and principles, but also on the choice not to render them binding in law, especially when States are not prepared to assume international legal responsibility for breaches or non-conforming behaviour.[14]

[10] Adopted by the First United Nations Congress on the Prevention of Crime and the Treatment of Offenders, held at Geneva in 1955, and approved by the Economic and Social Council by its resolutions 663 C (XXIV) of 31 July 1957 and 2076 (LXII) of 13 May 1977, now known as the Mandela Rules <http://www.unodc.org/pdf/criminal_justice/UN_Standard_Minimum_Rules_for_the_Treatment_of_Prisoners.pdf> accessed 6 August 2021.

[11] United Nations Declaration on the Rights of Indigenous Peoples, Resolution 61/295, UN Doc A/61/L.67 and Add.1 (13 September 2007) <http://www.un.org/development/desa/indigenouspeoples/wp-content/uploads/sites/19/2018/11/UNDRIP_E_web.pdf> accessed 6 August 2021.

[12] The Special Representative annexed the Guiding Principles to his Final Report to the Human Rights Council: Report of the Special Representative of the Secretary-General on the Issue of Human Rights and Transnational Corporations and Other Business Enterprises, John Ruggie, Guiding Principles on Business and Human Rights: Implementing the United Nations 'Protect, Respect and Remedy' Framework, UN Doc A/HRC/17/31 (21 March 2011) <http://www.ohchr.org/Documents/Issues/Business/A-HRC-17-31_AEV.pdf> accessed 6 August 2021.

[13] See generally John Kirkton and Michael Trebilcock, 'Hard Choices and Soft Law in Sustainable Global Governance' in John Kirkton and Michael Trebilcock (eds), *Hard Choices, Soft Law: Voluntary Standards in Global Trade, Environment and Social Governance* (Routledge 2004) 3–5; Andrew Guzman and Timothy Meyer, 'Soft Law' in Eugene Kontorovich and Francesco Parisi (eds), *Economic Analysis of International Law* (Elgar 2016) 131–34; Inger Österdahl, '(International) Law!' in Rain Liivoja and Jarna Petman (eds), *International Law-Making: Essays in Honour of Jan Klabbers* (Routledge 2015) 124; Thomas Gammeltoft-Hansen, Stéphanie Lagoutte, and John Cerone, 'Introduction: Tracing the Roles of Soft Law in Human Rights' in Stéphanie Lagoutte, Thomas Gammeltoft-Hansen, and John Cerone (eds), *Tracing the Roles of Soft Law in Human Rights* (OUP 2016) 6–8; Claire Kelly, 'The Sociological Pull of Soft Law' (2012) 106 ASIL Proceedings 327, 327; Alan Boyle and Christine Chinkin, *The Making of International Law* (OUP 2007) 214–16.

[14] Robert Kolb, *Theory of International Law* (Hart 2016) 152–53.

Turning to the instruments themselves, we can see many of the theories at work. While soft law instruments do not usually outright state the reasons for their non-binding nature, many of the instruments, in their accompanying documents or official explanations, hint at possible reasons. One common refrain behind the adoption of soft law instruments has been that rapid changes in technology and market forces in a particular field have outstripped existing legal rules, necessitating a rapid response. For example, the Preface to the FAO Code of Conduct for Responsible Fisheries states that:

> [t]he widespread introduction in the mid-seventies of exclusive economic zones (EEZs) and the adoption in 1982, after long deliberations, of the United Nations Convention on the Law of the Sea provided a new framework for the better management of marine resources ....
>
> In recent years, world fisheries have become a market-driven, dynamically developing sector of the food industry and coastal States have striven to take advantage of their new opportunities by investing in modern fishing fleets and processing factories in response to growing international demand for fish and fishery products. *By the late 1980s it became clear, however, that fisheries resources could no longer sustain such rapid and often uncontrolled exploitation and development, and that new approaches to fisheries management embracing conservation and environmental considerations were urgently needed.* The situation was aggravated by the realization that unregulated fisheries on the high seas, in some cases involving straddling and highly migratory fish species, which occur within and outside EEZs, were becoming a matter of increasing concern.[15]

Soft law, therefore, offers the opportunity to respond to new developments actively and dynamically in practice, without needing to wait for more conventional law-making processes to eventuate. As noted by Hanspeter Neubold, treaties can only be effective if they are, inter alia, speedily adopted;[16] soft law 'may be an option which permits avoidance or overcoming some of the ... difficulties of lawmaking through international treaties',[17] such as the amount of time required to draft and adopt a treaty and for the treaty to come into effect.

[15] Code of Conduct for Responsible Fisheries, Code of Conduct for Responsible Fisheries, Preface, v (emphasis added) <http://www.fao.org/3/v9878e/V9878E.pdf> accessed 6 August 2021.

[16] Hanspeter Neubold, 'The Inadequacy of Law-Making by International Treaties: "Soft Law" as an Alternative?' in Rüdiger Wolfrum and Volker Röben (eds), *Developments of International Law in Treaty Making* (Springer 2005) 40–47. Neubold argues that for treaties to be effective, they must meet four fundamental requirements: speed of adoption, clarity and uniformity of content, universality of participation in the treaty regime, and flexibility and adaptability of the regulatory regime. He further argues that treaties frequently fail to fulfil such requirements: ibid 47. Whether this is true in practice is explored in more detail in Chapter 7.

[17] ibid 47.

Likewise, soft law can be an appealing alternative to adopting a binding treaty when dealing with a controversial or difficult topic. By engaging with an instrument that has no legal sanction or consequence attached to non-compliance, soft law instruments can circumvent the improbability of being able to reach a binding consensus among States on a particular issue. This theory is borne out when looking at the background regarding the adoption of the Guiding Principles on Business and Human Rights. In his report to the Human Rights Council,[18] Special Rapporteur John Ruggie noted that the question of the intersection between transnational corporations and human rights was raising pressing concerns for the international community, but that an attempt to 'impose on companies, directly under international law, the same range of human rights duties that States have accepted for themselves under treaties'[19] was 'deeply divisive'[20] and found 'little support from Governments'.[21] In response, a non-binding framework of guiding principles was developed, which has been more warmly received by 'individual Governments, business enterprises and associations, civil society and workers' organizations, national human rights institutions, and investors'.[22]

Relatedly, soft law instruments can be useful tools that may be more adaptable than binding treaties. A set of non-binding guidelines incapable of imposing binding rules (and sanctions for non-compliance) may be more attractive to stakeholders who, for political or socio-economic reasons, might have found compliance with binding standards difficult. This very point is made in the explanation to the Standard Minimum Rules for the Treatment of Prisoners:

> In view of the great variety of legal, social, economic and geographical conditions of the world, it is evident that not all of the rules are capable of application in all places and at all times . . . .
>
> [T]he rules cover a field in which thought is constantly developing. They are not intended to preclude experiment and practices, provided these are in harmony with the principles and seek to further the purposes which derive from the text of the rules as a whole. It will always be justifiable for the central prison administration to authorize departures from the rules in this spirit.[23]

Non-binding norms can therefore be a more inclusive and adaptable response to new, changing, complex, and/or controversial topics.

[18] Report of the Special Representative of the Secretary-General (n 12).
[19] ibid 3, para 2.
[20] ibid 3, para 3.
[21] ibid.
[22] ibid 4, para 7.
[23] Standard Minimum Rules for the Treatment of Prisoners (30 August 1955), Preliminary Observations <http://www.unodc.org/pdf/criminal_justice/UN_Standard_Minimum_Rules_for_the_Treatment_of_Prisoners.pdf> accessed 6 August 2021.

The Benefits of Non-Binding Norms in International Humanitarian Law: Theory and Practice

Turning now to the law of armed conflict, we can see the various theories of soft law adoption at work in the IHL non-binding instruments. Recalling Kolb's point on the proliferation of States and the difficulties in obtaining legal and ideological consensus, the adoption of the *Copenhagen Process: Principles and Guidelines on the Handling of Detainees in International Military Operations* (Copenhagen Process) would seem to illustrate this argument, with Bruce Oswald and Thomas Winkler noting of the Process that:

> seen from a strictly legal perspective, legally binding instruments would always be the preferable way of further developing international law. The reality, however, is that it has been very difficult, bordering on the impossible, for such formal processes to reach the desired results in recent years, at least in controversial areas such as IHL and counter-terrorism. Processes like the Copenhagen Process, where states, organisations and other interested parties may in confidence exchange information, float ideas and express their common approach in non-binding documents are under these circumstances the better and often the only way ahead.[24]

Kolb's theories of the 'complexity and mobility' of technical and political issues, and the desire of States to refrain from (or at least delay) embracing binding norms, can also be seen in arguments around the adoption of the Tallinn Manuals on cyber warfare and cyber operations. Commentators have noted that the creation of the Tallinn Manuals was likely driven by the rapidly evolving technology of cyber operations,[25] and/or the reluctance of States to embrace hard law cyber norms (because of concerns either that such rules would place unacceptable limitations on sovereign powers[26] or, conversely, that new cyber norms would encroach on human rights norms[27]).

Likewise, drawing on Kolb's 'diversification of actors' theory, this is evident in the work of Geneva Call. The Deeds of Commitment (DoCs) function as parallel

[24] Bruce Oswald and Thomas Winkler, 'The Copenhagen Process: Principles and Guidelines on the Handling of Detainees in International Military Operations' (2014) 83 Nordic Journal of International Law 128, 166.

[25] Kubo Mačák, 'On the Shelf, But Close at Hand: The Contribution of Non-State Initiatives to International Cyber Law', Symposium on Dan Efrony and Yuval Shany, 'A Rule Book on the Shelf? Tallinn Manual 2.0 on Cyberoperations and Subsequent State Practice' (2019) 113 American Journal of International Law (unbound) 81, 82.

[26] See Dan Efrony and Yuval Shany, 'A Rule Book on the Shelf? Tallinn Manual 2.0 on Cyberoperations and Subsequent State Practice' (2018) 112 American Journal of International Law 583, 585.

[27] Leonhard Kreuzer, 'Disentangling the Cyber Security Debate' (*Volkerrechtsblog: International Law and International Legal Thought*, 20 June 2018) <https://voelkerrechtsblog.org/disentangling-the-cyber-security-debate/> accessed 6 August 2021.

treaties, allowing non-State actors to take on commitments and consent to enforcement mechanisms traditionally reserved for States. This is explicitly noted in the preambles to the DoCs, where signatories to a Deed affirm that they are 'resolved to play our role not only as actors in armed conflicts but also as participants in the practice and development of legal and normative standards for such conflicts, starting with a contribution to the overall humanitarian effort to solve the global landmine problem for the sake of its victims'.[28]

Connected to the 'diversification of actors' theory is an additional element that may account for the embrace of soft law norms, specifically in IHL. It has been theorised[29] that non-binding instruments formulated in conjunction with non-State actors encourage those non-State actors to comply with existing international law norms, in ways that the norms themselves do not. Put another way, there is some research to suggest that non-State armed groups are more inclined to comply with rules over which they feel 'ownership'[30]—that is, rules that they were involved in developing and codifying. There are examples of non-State armed groups denying the relevance or applicability of IHL norms, essentially on the grounds of the lack of reciprocity during the drafting and adoption stages: that because States did not include the non-States groups in the drafting or adoption of the norms, there is no obligation for them to comply with such norms.[31]

[28] Deed of Commitment for Adherence to a Total Ban on Anti-Personnel Mines and for Cooperation in Mine Action (2000) <http://www.genevacall.org/wp-content/uploads/2019/07/DoC-Banning-anti-personnel-mines.pdf> accessed 6 August 2021.

[29] See Sophie Rondeau, 'The Pragmatic Value of Reciprocity: Promoting Respect for International Humanitarian Law among Non-State Actors' in Benjamin Perrin (ed), *Modern Warfare: Armed Groups, Private Militaries, Humanitarian Organisations, and the Law* (UBC Press 2012) 45–46.

[30] Much of the literature on non-State groups and compliance with IHL employs the concept of 'ownership of norms', which is argued as being pivotal to whether non-State groups comply with IHL norms. See further, for example, Sandesh Sivakumaran, 'The Ownership of International Humanitarian Law: Non-State Armed Groups and the Formation of Enforcement of IHL Rules' in Benjamin Perrin (ed), *Modern Warfare: Armed Groups, Private Militaries, Humanitarian Organisations, and the Law* (UBC Press 2012); Pascal Bongard and Jonathan Somer, 'Monitoring Armed Non-State Actor Compliance with Humanitarian Norms: A Look at International Mechanisms and the Geneva Call Deed of Commitment' (2011) 93 International Review of the Red Cross 673, 681; Anton O Petrov, 'Non-State Actors and Law of Armed Conflict Revisited: Enforcing International Law through Domestic Engagement' (2014) 19 Journal of Conflict & Security Law 279, 287 ff; Peter Maurer, 'Establishing A Dedicated IHL Compliance System' (Opening Speech, Third Meeting of States on Strengthening Compliance with International Humanitarian Law, Geneva, 30 June–1 July 2014) < https://www.icrc.org/en/doc/resources/documents/statement/2014/06-30-compliance-ihl-maurer.htm> accessed 27 September 2021; Andrew Clapham, 'The Rights and Responsibilities of Armed Non-State Actors: The Legal Landscape & Issues Surrounding Engagement' (Geneva Academy of International Humanitarian Law and Human Rights 2010) 19 <http://ssrn.com/abstract = 1569636> accessed 6 August 2021; comments in Elisabeth Decrey Warner, 'Engaging with Non-State Armed Groups: Lessons Learned' (36th Round Table on Current Issues of International Humanitarian Law, 'Respecting IHL: Challenges and Perspectives', Institute of International Humanitarian Law, San Remo, 5–7 September 2013) <http://www.iihl.org/iihl/Documents/DECREY-WARNER.pdf> accessed 10 November 2021.

[31] In interviews conducted by Human Rights Watch, a number of Colombian non-State armed groups argued that Additional Protocol II did not apply to their conflict, as the instrument had not been 'negotiated directly with them': Human Rights Watch, *War Without Quarter: Colombia and International Humanitarian Law* (1998) <http://www.hrw.org/legacy/reports98/colombia/Colom989-03.htm#P45

The theories regarding why States and non-State actors turn to soft law instruments are varied, but all seem to draw on a central idea that soft law is (or can be) what treaty law is not. Where treaties allow participation only by States (and, in certain instances, international organisations), soft law encourages engagement with all stakeholders in a particular field. Where treaties can be time-consuming to negotiate, soft law can be dynamic and adaptive. And where treaty regimes can be limited in their efficacy through lack of universal participation (or through restricted participation, via reservations), soft law norms, due to their non-binding status, can encourage more participants.

What remains to be explored is whether these theories are borne out *in practice*. Was the San Remo Naval Manual really created because a non-binding document was quicker to produce than a treaty? Was the Copenhagen Process genuinely the only way to encourage universal participation in a regulatory regime? It is these questions that are the central focus of the next section of this chapter, which looks at the reasons *why* the non-binding instruments under examination were adopted. In doing so, the chapter will examine the instruments and provisions themselves (and any accompanying *travaux* and commentaries) to see if the theory for why soft law is embraced is borne out in practice. That is to say, do the instruments themselves expressly (or by strong implication) acknowledge that the non-binding form was necessary and desirable due to factors such as the need for a rapid response to new developments, or because consensus was elusive?

Non-Binding Norms in Binding Instruments—Why Were They Adopted?

Special Agreements in Common Article 3

As noted in Chapter 3, Common Article 3 was, in effect, the 'compromise' solution to what had been originally hoped for by the national Red Cross societies: that the laws of armed conflict, in their entirety, would apply to internal armed conflict.[32]

7_59724> accessed 6 August 2021. See also Anthea Roberts and Sandesh Sivakumaran, 'Lawmaking by Nonstate Actors: Engaging Armed Groups in the Creation of International Humanitarian Law' (2012) 37 Yale Journal of International Law 107, 127. Likewise, research undertaken by the International Council on Human Rights Policy suggests that when armed groups have been involved in the development of codes of conduct, there is an increased probability of compliance: International Council on Human Rights Policy, *Ends and Means: Human Rights Approaches to Armed Groups* (2000) 52 <https://reliefweb.int/report/world/ends-and-means-human-rights-approaches-armed-groups> accessed 6 August 2021.

[32] ICRC, *Report on the Work of the Preliminary Conference of National Red Cross Societies for the Study of the Conventions and of various Problems relative to the Red Cross, Geneva, July 26–August 3, 1946*

This proposal to extend the Conventions to all types of armed conflicts was not universally welcomed at the Diplomatic Conference in Geneva in 1949, and only after much debate in plenary and special committees was Common Article 3, as we know it today, finally adopted.[33] At Geneva in 1949, the special agreements provision in Common Article 3 was introduced during working group discussions over the scope of what was then Article 2. The original Stockholm draft of Article 2 had provided that:

> [i]n all cases of armed conflict which are not of an international character, especially cases of civil war, colonial conflicts, or wars of religion, which may occur in the territory of one or more of the High Contracting Parties, the implementing of the principles of the present Convention shall be obligatory on each of the adversaries. The application of the Convention in these circumstances shall in nowise depend on the legal status of the parties to the conflict and shall have no effect on that status.[34]

However, this provision was rejected as too broad by delegates from, inter alia, China,[35] the United States,[36] the United Kingdom,[37] France,[38] Greece,[39] Canada,[40] and Burma,[41] who considered broad extension of the law of armed conflict to civil war 'a very serious danger to sovereignty'.[42] During the working group, Article 2 went through a number of amendments and limitations in scope, with a revised Article 2(4) providing that:

> [i]n the case of armed conflicts which do not fulfil the conditions as determined above, the Parties to the conflict should endeavour to bring into force, by means

(ICRC 1947) 15. It is noteworthy that it was the ICRC that had the more sceptical (or, perhaps, realistic) appraisal of how such a recommendation would be greeted by States. As noted by the ICRC at both the 1937 expert meeting on the revision of the 1929 Conventions (Projet de revision de la Convention de Genève du 27 juillet 1929 présenté aux Sociétés nationales de la Croix-Rouge par le Comité international de la Croix-Rouge (ICRC 1937) 2) and the Sixteenth International Red Cross Conference (*Report on the Interpretation, Revision and Extension of the Geneva Convention of July 27, 1929, prepared for the Sixteenth International Red Cross Conference, London, June 1938* (ICRC 1938) 7–9), it was originally the intent of the ICRC to merely 'invite' States to apply the conventions in their entirety in civil wars, rather than compel them to do so: ibid Report on the Work of the Preliminary Conference 15.

33 See further Chapter 3 regarding the drafting history of Common Article 3.
34 Stockholm Draft, Art 2.
35 Final Record IIB, 12.
36 ibid.
37 ibid 10.
38 ibid.
39 ibid 10–11.
40 ibid 13.
41 ibid 15.
42 ibid 327.

> of special agreements, all or part of the provisions of the present Convention, or, on all circumstances, to act in accordance with the underlying humanitarian principles of the present Convention.[43]

The reason behind the adoption of the provision is straightforward: records indicate that States were concerned that full application of the Conventions to non-international armed conflicts was an unacceptable infringement on State sovereignty.[44] However, these same States still wanted the humanitarian principles of the Conventions to apply to non-international armed conflict, just in a more limited way. Therefore, by encouraging, rather than obligating, States to apply the Conventions in their entirety, the special agreements provision was a 'compromise solution permitting the reconciliation'[45] between those States that favoured the automatic application of the Conventions to non-international armed conflicts and those that preferred few, if any, of the provisions of the Convention to apply.[46] As the Swiss delegate put it: 'half a loaf is better than no bread. A comparatively modest solution is certainly better than none'.[47] This pragmatic approach is seen in the comments of other States, which noted that the automatic application to all non-international armed conflicts 'appeared complicated and of doubtful efficacy',[48] and therefore the recommendation to agree to special agreements would prevent any complications in attempting to apply provisions to non-international armed conflicts that had been clearly designed only with international armed conflicts in mind (such as the provisions on occupied territory).[49]

In this respect, we can see Kolb's theories at work—specifically, the 'increasing fear of engaging oneself through hard-law instruments and of being caught in a net of limitations upon freedom and sovereignty',[50] and the willingness of States to embrace some new rules but not to 'assume international legal responsibility for breaches or non-conforming behaviour'.[51]

[43] Annex A, First Draft drawn up by the first Working Party, Final Record IIB, 124. See Chapter 3 for a more detailed discussion of the procedural history of what became Common Article 3.
[44] See, for example, comments by French delegate Albert Lamarle, Final Record IIB, 98–99.
[45] Johan Castberg, Norwegian Delegate, Final Record IIB, 48.
[46] Though, equally, some delegates believed that the special agreements provision would produce results contrary to the intended aims, with the Romanian delegate noting that it would 'not be advisable to provide for special agreements as the only means of applying the Conventions; that might destroy all safeguards for the practical application of this Article': Final Record IIB, 331.
[47] ibid 335.
[48] ibid 76.
[49] See comments by Lamarle: ibid 94.
[50] Kolb, *Theory of International Law* (n 14) 152–53.
[51] ibid.

Article 6(5) Amnesty in Protocol II

As noted in Chapter 3, it had been hoped by the International Committee of the Red Cross (ICRC) that, in the process of updating and developing the law of non-international armed conflict, due consideration should be given to the proposal that 'members of resistance movements who participate in non-international armed conflicts and who conform to the provisions of Article 4 of the Third Geneva Convention of 12 August 1949 should when captured be protected against any inhumanity and brutality and receive treatment similar to that which that Convention lays down for prisoners of war'.[52] Eventually, the idea of prisoner-of-war treatment (if not status) was replaced with the suggestion made at the 1971 Conference of Government Experts that amnesty should be extended to persons who have taken direct part in hostilities. The ICRC proposed that:

> at the end of hostilities, it is desirable that normal life should be resumed as soon as possible. Hence, it would be fitting to generalize the proclamation of general amnesty, in the interest of both the victims and the authorities who will have to restore order and reconcile all elements of a divided people.[53]

Whether States would agree to such a broad-ranging proposal was uncertain. Indeed, both in 1971 and again in 1972 at the second session of the Conference of Government Experts,[54] the experts, while acknowledging the logic of the proposals, felt that they 'were not in a position to endorse without reservation a provision making inroads so deeply into the internal laws of States'.[55] The general consensus of the experts was that they could endorse 'nothing more than a recommendation in this regard, as they took the view that the question was within the competence of the State'.[56]

[52] Resolution XVIII, 'Status of Combatants in Non-International Armed Conflict', XXIst International Conference of the Red Cross, Istanbul 1969.

[53] ICRC, *Conference of Government Experts on the Reaffirmation and Development of International Humanitarian Law Applicable in Armed Conflicts, Geneva, 24 May – 12 June 1971, Report on the Work of the Conference* (August 1971) vol V, 59. See also the ICRC Commentary to the Draft Protocols, Draft Article 10, 143.

[54] ICRC, *Conference of Government Experts on the Reaffirmation and Development of International Humanitarian Law Applicable in Armed Conflicts, Second Session, 3 May–3 June 1972, Report on the Work of the Conference* (1972) vol I, 65–66.

[55] ICRC, *Conference of Government Experts 1971* (n 53) paras 258–59.

[56] ibid para 259; see also ICRC, *Conference of Government Experts 1972* (n 54) paras 2.220, 2.228: 'At the conclusion of the hostilities, the Parties to the conflict should endeavour to grant amnesty to as many as possible of those who have participated in the conflict or have been convicted of offences or deprived of liberty in connection with the conflict.' See also CE/COM 11/49, Proposal submitted by the experts of the United States, Draft Article 28, ICRC, *Conference of Government Experts 1972* (n 54) vol II (Annexes) 41.

When the Protocols were transmitted for debate to the diplomatic conferences in Geneva, Draft Additional Protocol II included what was then Article 10, providing that:

> [a]t the end of hostilities, the authorities in power shall endeavour to grant amnesty to as many as possible of those who have participated in the armed conflict, in particular those whose liberty has been restricted for reasons in relation to the armed conflict, whether they are interned or detained.[57]

During debate on the Protocols, the question of explicit inclusion of an amnesty provision was resisted by some delegates.[58] Among the reasons for such resistance were that amnesty provisions (or similar, such as commutation of sentence and official pardons) were generally included in the legislation of all States, and therefore it was not necessary to restate such a principle,[59] and that the non-obligatory nature of the amnesty provision rendered it irrelevant for inclusion, and thus it could be deleted without issue.[60] Other delegates felt that to recommend amnesty and to place limits on what kinds of penalties could be imposed 'was to treat some perpetrators of grave crimes leniently while the full rigour of the law would be applicable to other citizens who dared to commit similar crimes. In the case of some, conspiracy would be treated lightly or even condoned, whereas others would be liable to extreme punishment under the law'.[61]

The general tenor of State comments *against* the inclusion of the amnesty provision was that it amounted to an unacceptable infringement on State sovereignty—that, notwithstanding its non-obligatory nature, it essentially imposed a course of action on States that was impracticable. As noted by the Spanish delegate:

> [t]he adoption of measures of clemency in general and of an amnesty in particular is necessarily subject, as regards application, to considerations of expediency which can be neither appreciated nor foreseen by the drafters of a text like the one under consideration; for the same reasons, such measures fall within the exclusive competence of States, which, bearing always in mind the common good

[57] Draft Article 10, Draft Additional Protocol II, reprinted in Official Records, vol 1.

[58] Draft Article 10 was revised by a working group: Report to Committee I on the Work of Working Group B on the New Article 10 of Draft Protocol II, Geneva 21 April–11 June 1976, CDDH/I/317/Rev.2, Official Records vol X, 143–52.

[59] CDDH/SR.50, Official Records VII, 92–101, comments by delegates from Pakistan, Nigeria, Saudi Arabia, and Kenya. See also CDDH/I/SR.34, Official Records VIII, 357–65.

[60] Comments by the delegate for the Syrian Arab Republic, CDDH/SR.50, Official Records VII, 93. See also similar comments by the delegate for Canada, who supported the inclusion of the amnesty provision but also considered that because it was 'merely a recommendation, in which authorities were exhorted to grant the broadest possible amnesty to persons who had participated in the armed conflict', it could be deleted for the purpose of simplification: CDDH/SR.50, Official Records VII, 94.

[61] CDDH/SR.29, 346, para 54.

> of the community they govern, can alone decide whether or not an amnesty is conducive to the restoration of public peace.[62]

In contrast, other delegates emphasised the hortatory nature of the provisions. The delegate from Zaire noted that:

> [i]t is in no way a binding obligation; nor even a simple obligation in the technical sense, that is, a legal bond requiring any sovereign State to amnesty, no matter how and under pressure from certain forces involved, persons who have done their country serious harm by serving foreign interests. Our vote for this provision was based largely both on profound humanitarian considerations, and also and above all on national considerations. For we are convinced that in the interests of a young nation's unity, it is essential to establish a climate of understanding, and to encourage the widest degree of reconciliation in order to bring back into the fold those strayed members of the flock who unwittingly contribute to the destruction of their nation in order to please outsiders.[63]

Kolb's theories are thus visible again in the debates surrounding the amnesty provision of Protocol II. We see resistance from States to embracing binding obligations that are perceived as incursions into sovereign State prerogatives, the difficulties in achieving consensus among increased numbers of participants on the international plane, and the willingness of some States to countenance new modes of conduct—but only if such modes of conduct do not bring sanction for breach.[64]

Expert Group and Civil Society Non-Binding Instruments—Why Were They Adopted?

The San Remo Manuals

Turning now to the various manuals and other documents of instruction, several of Kolb's theories can be seen in the explanations for adoption. Starting with the San Remo Naval Manual, the drafters provide several reasons. They begin by stating that the treaty law for naval warfare is notably out of date and that:

> other instruments of importance, namely, the unratified London Declaration concerning the Laws of Naval War of 1909 and the Oxford Manual on the Laws of Naval War Governing the Relations Between Belligerents adopted by the Institute

[62] CDDH/SR.50, Official Records VII, 103.
[63] ibid 105.
[64] ibid.

of International Law in 1913 reflected the customary law of that time but could not be relied upon as a reliable guide to contemporary law.[65]

The Manual goes on to say that new technology and new means and methods of warfare have 'put into question the continuing viability of the whole of the traditional legal regime which was based on nineteenth-century traditions'[66] and that updates in the law in the form of the Additional Protocols needed to be reviewed to assess the scope of their application to naval warfare.[67] Finally, the Manuals notes that developments in the law of the sea, environmental law, and air law, as well as the adoption of the UN Charter, have changed the landscape of international law and thus the law of armed conflict.[68] Collectively, 'these factors have had the effect of introducing a great deal of uncertainty in the present state of the law';[69] therefore, it was necessary to attempt to clarify some of these uncertainties. As to the decision to adopt a non-binding document rather than a binding treaty, the Manual states that 'given the extent of uncertainty in the law, [the experts] decided that it was premature to think in terms of a draft treaty, but rather it was more appropriate to work on a document that would be a modern equivalent of the Oxford Manual of 1913 which should in itself promote a better comprehension and development of the law'.[70]

With regards to the *San Remo Manual on Non-International Armed Conflict*, it is more difficult to definitively discern Kolb's theories at work—if only because the Manual does not have the same degree of supporting documentation as the San Remo Naval Manual. While there is a commentary to the Manual, there is little in the way of a preface, introduction, or any other explanatory documentation regarding the reasons behind its adoption. What does exist is a limited background paper, published in the Israel Yearbook on Human Rights,[71] by Dieter Fleck, who originated the research project for the *Manual on the Law of Non-International Armed Conflict, with Commentary* (NIAC Manual).[72] Primary among the reasons, enunciated by Fleck, why the law of non-international armed conflicts requires additional clarification is that 'the increasing number and intensity of non-international armed conflicts in the post-World War II area have added a new dimension to the challenges of the law of armed conflict'.[73] For Fleck, the law of non-international armed conflict requires further dissemination, implementation,

65 San Remo Manual on Naval Warfare, 61.
66 ibid.
67 ibid 62.
68 ibid.
69 ibid.
70 ibid.
71 Dieter Fleck, 'Humanitarian Protection in Non-International Armed Conflicts: The New Research Project of the International Institute of Humanitarian Law' (2001) 30 Israel Yearbook on Human Rights 1.
72 See further Chapter 4 on the origins and development of the project.
73 Fleck (n 71) 1.

and development,[74] and the involvement of non-State actors in non-international armed conflicts requires more nuanced approaches to regulation if compliance with the law can ever be achieved.[75] Moreover, the involvement of other actors in the process of norm-generation and norm-compliance in non-international armed conflicts (such as the ICRC, the United Nations, and international criminal tribunals) has meant that it was considered necessary, by the Council of the International Institute of Humanitarian Law, to develop 'ambitious solutions at the forefront of legal activities to disseminate and further develop existing rules in an area of great political concern'.[76]

For both the San Remo Manuals, Kolb's argument regarding the 'mobility and complexity of the questions to be regulated … [requiring] frequent and quick revisions of the technical norms' is clearly at work.[77] Furthermore, for the San Remo Naval Manual, that the Experts agreed upon the necessity of updating the law, but that 'it was premature to think in terms of a draft treaty',[78] draws on Kolb's theory of agreement on principles and rules without further desire to see such rules adopted as a binding treaty.

The Montreux Document

The Montreux Document does not explicitly state the reasons behind its adoption. In its Preface, it simply notes the principles under which the Document proceeds, including that 'certain well-established rules of international law apply to States in their relations with private military and security companies (PMSCs) and their operation during armed conflict, in particular under international humanitarian law and human rights law',[79] and that it 'is not a legally binding instrument and does not affect existing obligations of States under customary international law or under international agreements to which they are parties'.[80] Only in the foreword to the Document is there any statement as to the reasons why it was adopted: noting that the use of private actors in armed conflict is not a new phenomenon, the authors of the foreword, Paul Seger (Head of the Directorate of International Law of the Swiss Federal Department of Foreign Affairs) and Philip Spoerri (the ICRC's Director for International Law and Cooperation within the Movement) state:

74 ibid.
75 ibid 2–3.
76 ibid 6.
77 Kolb, *Theory of International Law* (n 14) 152–53.
78 San Remo Naval Manual, 62.
79 Montreux Document, Preface, Point 1, 9.
80 ibid Point 2.

> Today, PMSCs are viewed in some quarters as an indispensable ingredient of military undertakings. Since the end of the Cold War, demand for PMSCs has increased to such an extent that there is now a lively PMSC industry offering an ever wider range of services, with some companies employing well beyond 10,000 staff. In terms of scale and scope of services involved, PMSCs today are a wholly new phenomenon. In response, several diplomatic initiatives were launched to clarify what the role of PMSCs in armed conflicts is and should be.[81]

Nowhere else in the Montreux Document is any reference made to why the Document was adopted in non-binding form. However, even with this limited information, we can see Kolb's theories at work—namely, that this new and complex practice in the realm of armed conflict (PMSCs) has meant that the absence of clarity in the law needed to be addressed in a timely manner.[82]

The Air and Missile Warfare Manual

The *HPCR Manual on International Law Applicable to Air and Missile Warfare* (AMW Manual) is clear regarding why it was adopted. After noting that the Hague Air Rules were particularly useful in determining the law relating to air warfare, the Introduction to the Manual notes that:

> much has happened in the intervening 80 years in air warfare, which was in its infancy when the Hague Rules were drawn up. Air power has become a central component of the military arsenal of States and plays a critical role in modern warfare. As for missiles, they were not even conceived in 1923. The exponential changes brought about in air and missile technology in the last few decades have transformed the face of the modern battlefield, revolutionized military strategy, and created a series of distinct challenges to the protection of civilians in time of armed conflict. Over the course of the recent decades, the challenge of applying existing law to the use of aircraft and missiles in time of hostilities has amply demonstrated that there are bones of contention regarding the scope and content of the international legal rules pertaining to air and missile warfare.[83]

The Introduction goes on to note that existing treaties have failed to adequately address the full extent of the law of air and missile warfare, and that the treaties

[81] Montreux Document, Foreword, 5.
[82] Kolb, *Theory of International Law* (n 14) 152–53.
[83] Program on Humanitarian Policy and Conflict Research at Harvard University, *HPCR Manual on International Law Applicable to Air and Missile Warfare* (AMW Manual) (CUP 2013) ix.

are not universally ratified; therefore, there is need for this kind of restatement.[84] The Manual also specifically indicates that it does not intend to be a precursor to a binding treaty; rather:

> [t]he present project uses the San Remo Manual as a model. Like the San Remo Manual, the HPCR Manual must not be confused with a draft treaty, prepared as the groundwork for a future diplomatic conference. The goal is rather to present a methodical restatement of existing international law on air and missile warfare, based on the general practice of States accepted as law (opinio juris) and treaties in force.[85]

We can therefore see the same forces in operation for the AMW Manual as we can for the San Remo Naval Manual: the increasing mobility and complexity of the practice of air and missile warfare necessitates clarity in the law, but not to the point of adopting a treaty.[86]

The Copenhagen Process

As with the Montreux Document, the Copenhagen Process does not contain any explicit elucidation of why a non-binding form was chosen. The official documents only note that State participants involved in the drafting of the Principles and Guidelines were 'not seeking to create new legal obligations or authorizations under international law',[87] but they nonetheless desired 'to develop principles to guide the implementation of the existing obligations with respect to detention in international military operations'.[88] However, the Copenhagen documents do give some indication as to why the Process and Principles were adopted in the first instance:

> Participants were motivated by the will to reinforce the principle of humane treatment of all persons who are detained or whose liberty is being restricted, to ensure respect for applicable international humanitarian law and human rights law by the detaining, transferring and receiving States and organisations as well as non-State actors and individuals .... Participants were also inspired by the good practices that States and organisations have developed in international military

84 ibid x.
85 ibid.
86 Kolb, *Theory of International Law* (n 14) 152–53. See also Neubold (n 16) 40–47.
87 Copenhagen Process and Principles, para II, at 1.
88 ibid.

> operations .... Participants [also] recognised the particular challenges that arise in handling detainees in international military operations in the context of non-international armed conflict situations and peace operations including in regard to the transfer of detainees ....[89]

The Tallinn Manuals

Turning now to the Tallinn Manuals, Tallinn 1.0 states that it was adopted because:

> [o]ne of the challenges States face in the cyber environment is that the scope and manner of international law's applicability to cyber operations, whether in offence or defence, has remained unsettled since their advent .... [T]here is a risk that cyber practice may quickly outdistance agreed understandings as to its governing legal regime ....

The community of nations is understandably concerned about this normative ambiguity.[90]

The Manual goes on to note that the motivation behind its adoption was the hope of 'bringing some degree of clarity to the complex legal issues surrounding cyber operations'.[91]

Tallinn 2.0 notes in its introduction that developments in State practice since the adoption of Tallinn 1.0—specifically, the constant cyber-attacks that States must deal with on a daily basis that do not reach the level of armed conflict (and are therefore not covered by Tallinn 1.0)—were the primary motivation behind the update of the Manual. The non-binding status of the Manual is reaffirmed,[92] but no specific statement about *why* this form was chosen (beyond the unstated, self-evident fact that, as a group of experts, rather that States, there was no possibility of adopting Tallinn 2.0 as a binding treaty). Therefore, as with other non-binding instruments, both Tallinn 1.0 and Tallinn 2.0 were seemingly a way to establish (or at least assert) the applicability of certain rules in relation to cyber space, in a timely manner, evoking Kolb's 'mobility and complexity of the questions to be regulated ... [needing] frequent and quick revisions of the technical norms'[93] theory of soft law.

[89] ibid paras V–VII.
[90] Tallinn 1.0, 3.
[91] ibid.
[92] ibid 2–3.
[93] Kolb, *Theory of International Law* (n 14) 152–53.

The *Sui Generis* Documents: The ICRC Study into Customary International Humanitarian Law, the International Code of Conduct for Private Security Service Providers, the ICRC Interpretive Guidance on the Notion of Direct Participation in Hostilities under International Humanitarian Law, and Geneva Call's Deeds of Commitment

Regarding the ICRC Study into Customary International Humanitarian Law (ICRC CIHL Study), the ICRC Direct Participation in Hostilities (DPH) Guidance, Geneva Call's Deeds of Commitment, and the International Code of Conduct (ICoC) for Private Security Service Providers, these documents were adopted in non-binding form because, in essence, there was no other option. Neither the ICRC nor Geneva Call has the international capacity to create binding international legal instruments (absent State mandate),[94] and the ICoC was intended for corporations, which, for the most part, also have limited international personality and treaty-making capacity.[95] Therefore, these documents do not generally provide any justification as to why a non-binding form (rather than a binding norm) was chosen—as there was, obviously, no real question of choice.

Nevertheless, it is possible to see Kolb's theories of soft law at work in these instruments. For the ICRC CIHL Study, the motivation to commence and produce the Study fits well with Kolb's theories about soft law norms more generally. The ICRC CIHL Study notes that it came about because of discussions undertaken at the International Conference for the Protection of War Victims in 1993.[96] Ultimately, this led to an invitation to the ICRC to 'prepare, with the assistance of experts in IHL ... a report on customary rules of international humanitarian law applicable in international and non-international armed conflicts'.[97] The aim behind the creation of such a report was to encourage better compliance with the law. As noted by in the ICRC CIHL Study itself:

> [t]he general opinion is that violations of international humanitarian law are not due to the inadequacy of its rules, but rather to a lack of willingness to respect them, to a lack of means to enforce them and to uncertainty as to their application

[94] International and NGOs can have some capacity at international law, but this generally does not include treaty-making capacity. See further Rephael Harel Ben-Ari, *The Normative Position of International Non-Governmental Organizations under International Law: An Analytical Framework* (Martinus Nijhoff 2012); Nigel White, 'Lawmaking' in Jacob Katz Cogan, Ian Hurd, and Ian Johnstone (eds), *The Oxford Handbook of International Organizations* (OUP 2016); Dan Sarooshi, 'Legal Capacity and Powers' in Jacob Katz Cogan, Ian Hurd, and Ian Johnstone (eds), *The Oxford Handbook of International Organizations* (OUP 2016).

[95] See further Merja Pentikäinen, 'Changing International "Subjectivity" and Rights and Obligations under International Law—Status of Corporations' (2012) 8 Utrecht Law Review 145.

[96] ICRC CIHL Study, xxvii

[97] ibid.

in some circumstances, but also to ignorance of the rules on the part of political leaders, commanders, combatants, and the general public.[98]

The Study makes it clear that there are several factors that contribute to a lack of compliance with the law, and that, inter alia, a lack of *awareness* of the law, as well as a lack of clarity as to its applicability—especially in situations of non-international armed conflicts—contributes to non-compliance. The Study therefore affirms the belief that 'knowledge of the rules of customary international law is therefore of use to many actors involved in the application, dissemination and enforcement of international humanitarian law . . . [and] may also be of service in a number of situations where reliance on customary international law is required' (that is, in courts and tribunals).[99] This would seem to fit with Kolb's arguments on soft law—that there exists agreement on some norms, but a lack of clarity on others.[100]

The International Code of Conduct is clear that it aims to shape non-State behaviour—and ultimately influence State behaviour.[101] The Code acknowledges the existence of the Montreux Document and notes that:

> [PMSCs] play an important role in protecting state and non-state clients engaged in relief, recovery, and reconstruction efforts, commercial business operations, diplomacy and military activity. In providing these services, the activities of PSCs can have potentially positive and negative consequences for their clients, the local population in the area of operation, the general security environment, the enjoyment of human rights and the rule of law.[102]

To that end, the Code affirms that its aim is to ensure that PMSCs:

> affirm that they have a responsibility to respect the human rights of, and fulfil humanitarian responsibilities towards, all those affected by their business activities,

[98] ibid.
[99] ibid xxix.
[100] Kolb, *Theory of International Law* (n 14) 152–53.
[101] Indeed, see the ICoC, in the Preamble, where it is stated: 'Those establishing this Code recognize that this Code acts as a founding instrument for a broader initiative to create better governance, compliance and accountability. Recognizing that further effort is necessary to implement effectively the principles of this Code, Signatory Companies accordingly commit to work with states, other Signatory Companies, Clients and other relevant stakeholders after initial endorsement of this Code to, within 18 months: a) Establish objective and measurable standards for providing Security Services based upon this Code, with the objective of realizing common and internationally-recognized operational and business practice standards; and b) Establish external independent mechanisms for effective governance and oversight, which will include Certification of Signatory Companies' compliance with the Code's principles and the standards derived from the Code, beginning with adequate policies and procedures, Auditing and Monitoring of their work in the field, including Reporting, and execution of a mechanism to address alleged violations of the Code's principles or the standards derived from the Code; and thereafter to consider the development of additional principles and standards for related services, such as training of external forces, the provision of maritime security services and the participation in operations related to detainees and other protected persons.'
[102] ICoC, Preamble, 3.

> including Personnel, Clients, suppliers, shareholders, and the population of the area in which services are provided. The Signatory Companies also recognize the importance of respecting the various cultures encountered in their work, as well as the individuals they come into contact with as a result of those activities .... The purpose of this Code is to set forth a commonly-agreed set of principles for PSCs and to establish a foundation to translate those principles into related standards as well as governance and oversight mechanisms.[103]

The Code does not go into any more detail to explain why it was adopted, but Kolb's 'diversification of actors' theory would seem to fit—that these new actors (PMSCs) on the international plane require flexibility in international law-generating processes that have traditionally not accepted non-State actors.[104]

For the ICRC DPH Guidance, the ICRC makes it clear that this was only ever to be non-binding. The ICRC nonetheless hopes that the Guidance will be influential, noting that while:

> a legally binding interpretation of IHL can only be formulated by a competent judicial organ or, collectively, by the States themselves, the ICRC hopes that the comprehensive legal analysis and the careful balance of humanitarian and military interests underlying the Interpretive Guidance will render the resulting recommendations persuasive for States, non-State actors, practitioners, and academics alike.[105]

The DPH Guidance also makes it clear that its adoption was due to the:

> [c]ontinuous shift of the conduct of hostilities into civilian population centres has led to an increased intermingling of civilians with armed actors and has facilitated their involvement in activities more closely related to military operations. Even more recently, the increased outsourcing of traditionally military functions has inserted numerous private contractors, civilian intelligence personnel, and other civilian government employees into the reality of modern armed conflict. Moreover, military operations have often attained an unprecedented level of complexity, involving the coordination of a great variety of interdependent human and technical resources in different locations. All of these aspects of contemporary warfare have given rise to confusion and uncertainty as to the distinction between legitimate military targets and persons protected against direct attacks.[106]

103 ibid 4.
104 Kolb, *Theory of International Law* (n 14) 152–53.
105 ICRC DPH Guidance, 10.
106 ibid 11–12.

Kolb's proliferation of actors and changing techniques and practices plays out here again.[107]

Finally, turning to the Geneva Call instruments, once again, as instruments designed to shape and influence the behaviour of non-State actors, there was never the possibility for them to be anything other than non-binding. However, the instruments acknowledge that they have been created because Geneva Call and the non-State actors consider themselves 'participants in the practice and development of legal and normative standards'[108] during armed conflicts. This would seem to fit with Kolb's 'diversification of actors' theory of why soft law has proliferated.[109]

Concluding Thoughts

As noted earlier, there are several reasons why soft law instruments are created—hopes of influence, adaptability, and responsiveness have driven organisations and groups of experts to create soft law instruments, with the aims of having such instruments be of use to States and non-State actors. The question now is whether these aims and objectives are realised. Do States and non-State groups engage with these instruments in practice, and abide by their rules or recommendations? The next chapter will explore these questions.

[107] Kolb, *Theory of International Law* (n 14) 152–53.

[108] Deed of Commitment for Adherence to a Total Ban on Anti-Personnel Mines and for Cooperation in Mine Action (2000), Preamble <http://www.genevacall.org/wp-content/uploads/2019/07/DoC-Banning-anti-personnel-mines.pdf> accessed 6 August 2021.

[109] Kolb, *Theory of International Law* (n 14) 152–53.

7
The Efficacy of Soft Law Norms

Introduction

Having assessed the non-binding instruments and provisions in international humanitarian law (IHL), a pertinent, if simplistic, question arises: do they actually work? Admittedly, this is a low bar to meet, but, as this chapter explores, some instruments cannot meet even that minimum standard. It is clear, from the examination undertaken in the previous chapters, that the drafters of these non-binding provisions and instruments intended for the rules and/or recommendations contained within them to influence State (and non-State) behaviour. This chapter will examine whether these aims are borne out in practice.

Preliminary Requirements: Defining and Determining Efficacy

Before determining whether the IHL non-binding instruments have been effective in practice, and how one actually measures such effectiveness, it is first necessary to define what is meant by 'effective' and/or 'efficacy'. 'Effective' is not per se a legal term; the *Oxford English Dictionary* defines 'effective' as, inter alia, 'producing a notable effect' or 'effectual'.[1] The first definition—'producing a notable effect'—is not particularly helpful, at least for the purposes of the extant analysis. Something, such as a set of rules of guidelines, can produce a notable effect, but that effect may have little to do with what was intended to be produced in the first place. More helpful is the definition of the term 'effectual', which is defined as 'produces its intended effect, or adequately answers its purpose'. 'Effectual', in this respect, is functionally the same as the term 'efficacy'—the 'power or capacity to produce effects',[2] or the 'ability to produce a desired or intended result'.[3]

However, it is necessary to distinguish 'efficacy' or 'effectiveness' as a primarily *descriptive* term, and the theory (or theories) of the effectiveness of international

[1] 'effective, adj. and n.', Oxford English Dictionary Online <http://www.oed.com/view/Entry/59674> accessed 7 August 2021.
[2] 'efficacy, n.', Oxford English Dictionary Online <http://www.oed.com/view/Entry/59736> accessed 7 August 2021.
[3] 'effectual, adj.', Oxford English Dictionary Online <http://www.oed.com/view/Entry/59682> accessed 7 August 2021.

Non-Binding Norms in International Humanitarian Law. Emily Crawford, Oxford University Press. © Emily Crawford 2021.
DOI: 10.1093/oso/9780198819851.003.0008

law as a distinct *principle* of international law. As noted by Hiroshi Taki, the term 'effectiveness' is used in the literature of public international law 'at times ambiguously, and with various meanings'.[4] At its broadest, and most simple, the term 'effectiveness' refers to 'the efficacy (actual observance) of the law as distinguished from the validity (binding force) of law'.[5] Effectiveness in this context 'corresponds to the material, factual element of the law, to its concreteness',[6] and to the 'outward impact of (primary and secondary) rules, institutions, and narratives of international law on all international actors and law-appliers'.[7] Essentially, effectiveness in this respect relates to whether a law is actually observed and respected in practice.

Within this broad overarching concept of effectiveness, there are 'sub-concepts' of effectiveness, all of which relate to the interplay between a set of facts and the legal situation connected to those facts[8]—the notion of *ex factis jus oriter*, that law arises from actions or facts.[9] Effectiveness in this sense is broadly based on the idea that 'the international legal order, given its lack of centralised structures, could have solid foundations as a legal system only insofar as its impact on reality was strong and concrete; it could not rely on legal constructs devoid of corresponding foundations in practice'.[10] This concept of effectiveness contains three distinct strands, best summarised by JHW Verzijl as:

1) That the operation of certain rules is conditional upon the existence or concurrence of certain facts or, in other words, that certain factual requirements are a precondition of their operation;
2) That there are cases in which a legal situation cannot be attributed continuing and indefinite validity in the face of long-standing factual evidence to the contrary; and
3) That the history of international law shows a frequent alteration of its rules under the impact of factual developments.[11]

[4] Hiroshi Taki, 'Effectiveness' in Anne Peters and Rüdiger Wolfrum (eds), *Max Planck Encyclopedia of Public International Law*.

[5] ibid.

[6] Enrico Milano, *Unlawful Territorial Situations in International Law: Reconciling Effectiveness, Legality and Legitimacy* (Brill 2005) 22.

[7] In this respect, effectiveness can be linked with the notion of compliance—that a rule (or institution or other regulatory entity or regime) is effective because it compels compliance with that rule (or with the edicts of the institution) or because there are consequences for non-compliance. See further Jean d'Aspremont, '"Effectivity" in International Law: Self-Empowerment against Epistemological Claustrophobia' (2014) 108 ASIL Proceedings 165.

[8] See generally J Wildeman, 'The Philosophical Background of Effectiveness' (1977) 24 Netherlands International Law Review 335.

[9] Gleider Hernández, 'Effectiveness' in Jean d'Aspremont and Sahib Singh (eds), *Concepts for International Law: Contributions to Disciplinary Thought* (Elgar 2019) 237.

[10] Salvatore Zappalà, 'Can Legality Trump Effectiveness in Today's International Law?' in Antonio Cassese (ed), *Realising Utopia: The Future of International Law* (OUP 2012) 106–07.

[11] JHW Verzijl, *International Law in Historical Perspective* (vol 1, AW Sijthoff 1968) 293.

An example of the first strand would be situations where particular facts must be present in situ before a legal result is achieved, such as the preconditions for the recognition of Statehood[12] or claims for title to territory by occupation or prescription.[13] In such scenarios, a particular factual situation must exist for corresponding legal rights to exist.[14]

An example of the second strand of effectiveness is broader and recognises that a particular state of affairs in situ (even if such a state of affairs was brought about due to an illegality) may ultimately prevail over contrary law—that the way things *are* would prevail over the way things *should be*.[15] An example would be territorial acquisition through an illegal use of force, that while 'territorial extension of State power by conquest is forbidden ... a tolerated, lasting exercise of State power over a territory which originated in conquest'[16] might result in acquisition of title. According to this approach to effectiveness, *de facto* control over the territory would, inevitably, become *de jure* control and title.

The third strand of effectiveness noted by Verzijl relates to the notion that international law can and does change according to changing facts and practice, so that a 'sudden change of social reality'[17] would produce new customary international law through changes to State practice, and/or could result in the formation of new treaty law.[18] New scientific discoveries regarding the natural environment would, for example, likely necessitate new State practice and, possibly, new treaties.

For the purposes of this chapter, the idea of efficacy or effectiveness is meant to denote whether the stated aims of the instruments are being achieved. Effectiveness in this sense is used as:

> a relational term, a measure of the relationship and congruence between a given measure or act and desired outcome or result. That relational, purposive

[12] Taki (n 4); Milano (n 6) 22; Verzijl (n 11) 293 ff.

[13] See, for example, Julius Stone, 'What Price Effectiveness?' (1956) 50 ASIL Proceedings 198, 198. This is to be distinguished from the principle of effectiveness as seen in treaty law, specifically the maxim on treaty interpretation that 'the matter may have effect rather than fail' or, in Latin, *ut res magis valiat quam pereat* (also known as the *effet utile* or *effet practique*): Richard Gardiner, *Treaty Interpretation* (2nd edn, OUP 2015) 66. For more on the principle of effectiveness in treaty law, see further Luigi Sbolci, 'Supplementary Means of Interpretation' in Enzo Cannizzaro (ed), *The Law of Treaties beyond the Vienna Convention* (OUP 2011) 159–62, 187–88; Gardiner (n 13) 179–81; Céline Braumann and August Reinisch, 'Effet Utile' in Joseph Klingler, Yuri Parkhomenko, and Constantinos Salonidis (eds), *Between the Lines of the Vienna Convention? Canons and Other Principles of Interpretation of Public International Law* (Wolters Kluwer 2019).

[14] See further Hans Kelsen, *Principles of International Law* (Rinehart 1951) 214 ff, where he analyses effectiveness in the context of acquisition of territory.

[15] As Lauterpacht notes, '[l]aw is a product of social reality. It cannot lag for long behind facts': Hersch Lauterpacht, *Recognition in International Law* (CUP 1947) 426. See also Robert Jennings, 'Nullity and Effectiveness in International Law' in Robert Jennings (ed), *Cambridge Essays in International Law: Essays in Honour of Lord McNair* (Stevens and Son 1965).

[16] Wildeman (n 8) 337–38.

[17] Charles de Visscher, *Les effectivités du droit international public* (Pedone 1967) 15–16.

[18] Wildeman (n 8) 338–39.

> quality ... [is used] as an evaluative technique to assess a legal rule or norm in relation to its impact on social reality; it concretizes a link with the material or factual element of law.[19]

In undertaking this analysis, the chapter draws on Yuval Shany's approach to the notion of effectiveness—the 'goal-based approach'[20] which holds that 'an action is effective if it accomplishes its specific objective aim'.[21] This approach does not evaluate or question the 'desirability of the goals themselves',[22] but rather whether the goals set out by the entity in question (the organisation or, as in this case of this book, the non-binding norm or instrument) are achieved.[23]

A Note on the Methodology for This Chapter

Before proceeding with the chapter, an additional preliminary comment is required, specifically regarding certain distinct methodological challenges. First, and most significant, is that, as with any attempt to determine whether a particular norm is being followed, finding appropriate and relevant State practice is particularly difficult, especially in the realm of conduct in armed conflicts. This is for several reasons; in the first instance, distinguishing between what States (and non-State actors) say they do, and what they *actually* do in their execution of armed conflicts can be notably difficult. Partially, this is an operational issue—as Sir Michael Wood has noted, during situations of armed conflict, information about '[o]perational conduct "on the ground" ... is not always easily accessible ... [and at] times it may be unclear whether it reflects official policy at all'.[24] In other instances, there can be a disjuncture between what parties to an armed conflict *say* they are doing and what they are *actually* doing in the field; as Wood also notes, 'words cannot always be taken at face value'.[25] Additionally, statements that seem to have official State imprimatur, such as military and other training manuals, can be problematic. While some training manuals *are* official State documents that restate the applicable law, other documents that emanate from the State should not be treated as declaratory of an official State position.[26]

[19] Hernández (n 9) 237.

[20] Yuval Shany, *Assessing the Effectiveness of International Courts* (OUP 2014) 13. Shany himself draws on social science literature on the definition of effectiveness (see 13 ff).

[21] Chester Barnard, *The Functions of the Executive* (Harvard University Press 1951) 20.

[22] Shany (n 20) 14.

[23] See further ibid 14 ff, for an examination of why a goal-based approach is particularly useful for a legal analysis of effectiveness, especially when examining the effectiveness of legal institutions.

[24] Michael Wood, 'The Evolution and Identification of the Customary International Law of Armed Conflict' (2018) 51 Vanderbilt Journal of Transnational Law 727, 730.

[25] ibid.

[26] See, for example, criticisms over the use of training manuals in the ICRC Study into Customary International Humanitarian Law, including non-authoritative documents such as the UK's *A Soldier's Guide to the Law of Armed Conflict*, as noted by Charles Garraway at the BIICL/RIIA

However, this chapter (and book) has a distinct methodological advantage over other endeavours to discern State practice, which have usually been undertaken for the purpose of establishing customary IHL. This book is not attempting to establish the customary status of any existing treaty provisions (such as the special agreements provision of Common Article 3 and the amnesty provision in Protocol II), nor is it attempting to discern whether individual rules in Tallinn 2.0 or the Montreux Document (or the documents in their entirety) are crystallising into, or have attained, the status of customary international law. Rather, this book has the simpler task of examining whether these various non-binding rules and instruments are having (or beginning to have) their intended impact. In this respect, this is a far lower bar to clear than that required for finding customary international law.

Nevertheless, the process of determining customary international law is still relevant—at least insofar as what *kinds* of State practice are considered relevant for the purposes of ultimately establishing the existence of customary international law. The International Law Commission issued a report in 1950[27] that listed, as evidence of customary international law, texts of international instruments,[28] the decisions of international courts,[29] the decisions of national courts,[30] national legislation,[31] diplomatic correspondence,[32] opinions of national legal advisers,[33] and the practice of international organisations.[34] When the question of

International Law Workshop on 11 October 2005, cited in Iain Scobbie, 'The Approach to Customary Law in the Study' in Elizabeth Wilmshurst and Susan Breau (eds), *Perspectives on the ICRC Study on Customary International Humanitarian Law* (CUP/Chatham House/BIICL) 39. See also the comments in George Aldrich, 'Customary International Humanitarian Law—An Interpretation on Behalf of the International Committee of the Red Cross' (2005) 76 British Yearbook of International Law 503, 507.

27 International Law Commission, Ways and Means for Making the Evidence of Customary International Law More Readily Available (Report of the International Law Commission, vol 2, 1950) <http://legal.un.org/ilc/texts/instruments/english/reports/1_4_1950.pdf> accessed 7 August 2021.

28 ibid 368.

29 ibid 369.

30 ibid 370.

31 ibid.

32 ibid 371. However, the International Law Commission notes that caution should be taken in dealing with diplomatic correspondence. Citing John Norton Moore, it advises that '[m]ere extracts from State papers or judicial decisions cannot be safely relied on as guides to the law. They may indeed be positively misleading. Especially is this true of State papers, in which arguments are often contentiously put forth which by no means represent the eventual view of the government in whose behalf they were employed': ibid 371–72.

33 ibid 372. As with diplomatic correspondence, the International Law Commission advises caution when dealing with the opinions of national legal advisers, noting that '[r]eserve may be needed in assessing the value of such opinions as evidence of customary international law, for the efforts of legal advisers are necessarily directed to the implementation of policy. Nor would a reproduction of such opinions be of much value unless it were accompanied by an adequate analysis of the history leading up to the occasions with reference to which they were given': ibid.

34 ibid.

identification of customary international law was re-examined by the International Law Commission more recently (culminating in the Draft Conclusions on Identification of Customary International Law[35]), the Commission reaffirmed and built on its 1950 position, noting that both physical and verbal acts (as well as inaction) of States are relevant as State practice and may include, inter alia:

> [d]iplomatic acts and correspondence; conduct in connection with resolutions adopted by an international organization or at an intergovernmental conference; conduct in connection with treaties; executive conduct, including operational conduct 'on the ground'; legislative and administrative acts; and decisions of national courts.[36]

The Commentaries to the Draft Conclusions on Identification of Customary International Law give additional clarification as to the scope of these forms of practice, and it is worth reprinting in full here:

> Each of the forms listed is to be interpreted broadly to reflect the multiple and diverse ways in which States act and react. The expression 'executive conduct', for example, refers comprehensively to any form of executive act, including executive orders, decrees and other measures; official statements on the international plane or before a legislature; and claims before national or international courts and tribunals. The expression 'legislative and administrative acts' similarly embraces the various forms of regulatory disposition effected by a public authority. The term 'operational conduct "on the ground"' includes law enforcement and seizure of property as well as battlefield or other military activity, such as the movement of troops or vessels, or deployment of certain weapons. The words 'conduct in connection with treaties' cover acts related to the negotiation and conclusion of treaties, as well as their implementation; by concluding a treaty a State may be engaging in practice in the domain to which the treaty relates, such as maritime delimitation agreements or host country agreements. The reference to 'conduct in connection with resolutions adopted by an international organization or at an intergovernmental conference' likewise includes acts by States related to the negotiation, adoption and implementation of resolutions, decisions and other acts adopted within international organizations or at intergovernmental conferences, whatever their designation and whether or not they are legally binding. Whether any of these examples

[35] UN Doc A/RES/73/203 (2018); see also International Law Commission, Draft Conclusions on Identification of Customary International Law, Report of the International Law Commission, 70th Session (30 April–1 June and 2 July–10 August 2018), UN Doc A/73/10 (2018) 119–56.

[36] International Law Commission, Draft Conclusions on Identification of Customary International Law, UN Doc A/RES/73/203 (2018) Conclusion 6: Forms of Practice.

> of forms of practice are in fact relevant in a particular case will depend on the specific rule under consideration and all the relevant circumstances. Decisions of national courts at all levels may count as State practice (though it is likely that greater weight will be given to the higher courts); decisions that have been overruled on the particular point are generally not considered relevant. The role of decisions of national courts as a form of State practice is to be distinguished from their potential role as a 'subsidiary means' for the determination of rules of customary international law.[37]

All these forms of practice will be looked to as evidence of the effectiveness of the non-binding norms under examination in this work.

Finally, and connected to the examples of State practice under examination, is an additional methodological issue that should be addressed: namely, how can one *prove* that a non-binding instrument has been 'effective'? What evidence will be used (and how) to support a claim for an instrument's efficacy? According to the goal-based approach to effectiveness analysis, '[w]hen a specific desired end is attained we shall say that the action is "effective" '.[38] For the non-binding norms, as seen in previous chapters, the specific stated 'desired end' has been to guide and influence State and non-State behaviour towards observance of or compliance with the outlined provisions or principles.[39] In this respect, a non-binding norm has an easier objective to reach than a binding treaty; for a non-binding norm to be effective, all it has to do is encourage a particular course of action.[40] Therefore, non-binding norms have an easier road to proving their effectiveness, as their aims are primarily to encourage or guide, rather than compel.

[37] International Law Commission, Draft Conclusions on Identification of Customary International Law, Report of the International Law Commission, 70th Session (30 April–1 June and 2 July–10 August 2018), UN Doc A/73/10 (2018) 134.

[38] Barnard (n 21) 19.

[39] For the purposes of this chapter, the related question of the *efficiency* of non-binding norms is not under examination. Efficiency analysis takes into account the unintended and unexpected results (see Shany (n 20) 27) of goal-based effectiveness analysis, as well as the costs involved in attaining such goals. Efficient analysis of rules or institutions explores how a rule or institution 'may be effective (in the sense of fulfilling all of its goals), yet inefficient by generating considerable costs and negative externalities that may offset some or all of the benefits associated with goal attainment ... [likewise] an organisation may fail to meet its designated goals and be deemed ineffective, whilst nevertheless creating unforeseen or unintended benefits that compensate for its apparent failures': ibid 28.

[40] With the correlation that non-compliance with that course of action would not be considered problematic, as there is no binding norm to breach and, therefore, no real undermining of the stated objective of the non-binding norm. This can be contrasted with the objective of a treaty or other hard law provision, whose objective is compliance with the norm, with non-compliance with the provision potentially seen as undermining the normative force of the provision.

The standard for evidence of efficacy that will be used in this chapter will be essentially quite low: to what degree have States (or the other addressees of the non-binding norm) acknowledged and adopted some or all of the recommendations or provisions in their own conduct? For the most part, the emphasis in this book will be on explicit, positive affirmation, acknowledgement, or acceptance of the non-binding norm or instrument. For example, this may be citation in a court case, incorporation in domestic legislation, or positive affirmation or acknowledgment of the norm in official State documents, such as statements by authorised representatives. In the absence of explicit evidence of acknowledgement of the instrument (in the form of direct citation), the source will be treated with caution.

With this background in mind, the chapter will look to examples of State practice to examine whether the non-binding instruments have produced, or are producing, their intended impact. Keeping in mind the stated aims of the instruments, this chapter will look to whether the non-binding norms and instruments are being referred to by States as rules (or recommendations) that they plan to implement in practice, and/or or that they have otherwise implemented in practice.

Non-Binding Norms in Binding Instruments

Common Article 3 Special Agreements

The idea of special agreements in non-international armed conflicts was rare, but not entirely unknown prior to the adoption of Common Article 3. The International Committee of the Red Cross (ICRC) notes that 'during the Spanish Civil War (1936–39) . . . the Parties signed parallel agreements with the ICRC accepting that it provide humanitarian services during that conflict',[41] and Sivakumaran points to a few instances of 'special agreement' arrangements prior to 1949, such as during the Colombian War of Independence of 1820.[42] However, given the absence of international treaty law relating to non-international armed conflicts prior to the adoption of Common Article 3, it seems uncontroversial to state that the Common Article 3 special agreements provision was an innovation to international law in 1949.

[41] 'Comité International: Guerre Civile en Espagne' (1936) 67 Revue Internationale de la Croix-Rouge 758, 758–59.

[42] Sandesh Sivakumaran, *The Law of Non-International Armed Conflict* (OUP 2012) 124, referring to the Tratado de Regularizacion de la Guerra, 26 November 1820, reproduced in (1820–21) 71 Consolidated Treaty Series 291.

Common Article 3 Special Agreements in Practice—Issues and Problems

Since the adoption of Common Article 3, there have been a number of agreements drafted between parties to non-international armed conflicts that have sought to implement additional provisions of the Geneva Conventions.[43] However, a few initial points of clarification are required. First, does the lack of specific reference to Common Article 3 and its special agreements provision in an agreement render such an agreement any less a Common Article 3 special agreement? There have been relatively few instances where an agreement has *specifically* indicated its status as a Common Article 3 special agreement—the Agreement of 22 May 1992 on the Implementation of International Humanitarian Law in the Armed Conflict in Bosnia-Herzegovina is one such example.[44] Other agreements have referenced Common Article 3 more generally. For example, Article 1 of the Agreement between the Government of the Republic of Sudan and the Sudan People's Liberation Movement to protect non-combatant civilians and civilian facilities from military attack states that '[t]he Government of the Republic of Sudan (GOS) and the Sudan People's Liberation Movement (SPLM) (hereafter referred to as the "Parties") reconfirm their obligations under international law, including common Article 3 of the 1949 Geneva Conventions'.[45] Other agreements have referred to general Geneva principles, such as protection for the Red Cross Emblem or for medical and religious personnel. For example, the Comprehensive Agreement on Respect for Human Rights and IHL in the Philippines between the Government of the Philippines and the National Democratic Front of the Philippines contains detailed provisions in Article 4 of the agreement to collect and care for the wounded and sick, and that 'the establishments, facilities, transport and equipment' of medical personnel and of the ICRC, as well as 'objects bearing the emblem of the red cross and the flag of peaceful intention; and historic monuments, cultural objects, and places of worship shall be likewise protected'.[46]

[43] It is interesting to note that, during the drafting of the Additional Protocols, the ICRC suggested the inclusion of a special agreements provision in Protocol II (in Draft Article 36: see ICRC, *Conference of Government Experts on the Reaffirmation and Development of International Humanitarian Law Applicable in Armed Conflicts, Second Session, 3 May–3 June 1972, Report on the Work of the Conference* (1972) vol I, paras 2.287–2.307). Ultimately, no Additional Protocol II (APII) special agreements provision was included in Protocol II.

[44] In Article 2 of the Agreement, entitled 'Special Agreement': 'In accordance with the Article 3 of the four Geneva Conventions of August 12, 1949, the Parties agree to bring into force the following provisions:' (Agreement of 22 May).

[45] <http://theirwords.org/media/transfer/doc/sd_splm_a_2002_09-aca3835caf6b2926ed2df65b66ae9acb.pdf> accessed 7 August 2021.

[46] Article 4, Comprehensive Agreement on Respect for Human Rights and IHL in the Philippines between the Government of the Philippines and the National Democratic Front of the Philippines,

Does a failure to specifically call an agreement a Common Article 3 special agreement as such, or even a failure to reference Common Article 3, have any bearing on whether such an agreement is a special agreement within the ambit of Common Article 3? Given the analysis in Chapter 3 on the scope and interpretation of Common Article 3 special agreements, the conclusion would have to be 'no'. Even the narrowest reading of the provision would suggest that, provided the agreement is one which seeks in bring in some or all the provisions of the Geneva Convention(s), a failure to call it a special agreement, or even to reference Common Article 3, has no bearing on whether it is a special agreement.

However, what would almost certainly be excluded from the ambit of a Common Article 3 special agreement would be any unilateral undertaking on the part of a party to a non-international armed conflict to implement some or all the provisions of the Geneva Convention. Such an undertaking would clearly be outside the plain text meaning of the term 'agreement'—an 'arrangement (typically one which is legally binding) made between two or more parties and agreed by mutual consent'.[47] This would exclude a significant number of statements and instruments, such as directives to personnel, public declarations of practice, press releases, and even internal regulations and codes of conduct that have been made by both State armed forces and non-State armed groups, in which they commit to respect or implement provisions of the Geneva Conventions in their prosecution of the conflict.[48] As they are not agreements between parties to the conflict, they would not come within the ambit of a Common Article 3 special agreement. For example, the statement made in 2011 by the Interim Transitional National Council of Libya, in which it stated that 'its policies strictly adhere to the "Geneva Convention relative to the treatment of Prisoners of War"'[49] would not be considered a Common Article 3 special agreement.

For the purposes of assessing the effectiveness of the Common Article 3 special agreements provision, only bilateral or multilateral agreements, between parties to the non-international armed conflict, are considered. This excludes any unilateral statement in which a State or non-State group proclaims itself bound by the terms of the Geneva Conventions, as well as any internal directives to troops ordering

echoing provisions in the Geneva Convention on the protection of the wounded and sick (Geneva Convention I, Art 12); and protection of medical personnel (Geneva Convention I, Art 19).

[47] 'agreement, n.' Oxford English Dictionary Online <http://www.oed.com/view/Entry/4159> 7 August 2021.

[48] See, for example, Churchill Ewumbue-Monono, 'Respect for International Humanitarian Law by Armed Non-State Actors in Africa' (2006) 88 International Review of the Red Cross 905, which lists the numerous unilateral declarations, instructions to armed forces, and other instruments and strategies employed by armed non-State opposition groups in Africa following the adoption of the Geneva Conventions.

[49] Libyan Interim Transitional National Council, Statement on the Treatment of Detainees and Prisoners, Benghazi, Libya, 25 March 2011 <http://theirwords.org/media/transfer/doc/ly_ntc_2011_05-615c0dc0f1c0ffe8dfcba03007bcead3.pdf> accessed 7 August 2021.

respect for or compliance with the Geneva Conventions. Also necessarily excluded are agreements adopted prior to the adoption of the Geneva Conventions in 1949, as well as agreements issued or adopted prior to the Conventions being ratified by the territorial State. However, agreements between non-State armed groups and an international organisation such as the United Nations or the ICRC, in which Geneva provisions are implemented, are included in the accounting. Likewise, agreements between sovereign States regarding non-international armed conflicts, which are then later acceded to by non-State armed groups, are also included.[50]

According to the Armed Conflict Dataset of the Uppsala Conflict Data Program (UCDP) at the Department of Peace and Conflict Research at Uppsala University and the Centre for the Study of Civil War at the Peace Research Institute Oslo (PRIO),[51] between the years 1949 (and the adoption of the Common Article 3 special agreements regime) and 2019, there have been over 220 armed conflicts that can be classified as State-based non-international (where a State armed force is fighting a non-State group) and over 350 incidents of organised violence[52] involving only non-State groups. Drawing on the records of peace agreements and other special agreements adopted in situations of non-international armed conflict (as recorded by Geneva Call[53] and the United Nations[54]), over 300[55] agreements were made by and between States and non-State parties in relation to armed conflicts between the years 1960 to 2019.[56] At all relevant times (that is, when the

[50] For example, the 1987 Procedure for the Establishment of a Firm and Lasting Peace in Central America, also known as the Esquipulas II Accord, was signed by five Central American States; however, the agreement was later included in agreements with non-State groups, such as Unidad Revolucionaria Nacional Guatemalteca.

[51] For the complete datasets (Uppsala Conflict Data Program/Peace Research Institute Oslo (UCDP/PRIO) Armed Conflict Dataset, UCDP Dyadic Dataset, UCDP Battle-Related Dataset, UCDP Non-State Dataset, and UCDP One-Sided Dataset) updated to 2019, see <http://ucdp.uu.se/downloads/> accessed 7 August 2021. The tables and figures in this book were created directly from the Excel sheets at the UCDP web page. For detailed descriptions of the individual cases, see the UCDP Conflict Encyclopedia at <http://www.ucdp.uu.se/> accessed 7 August 2021. For the replication data for this article, as well as the Online appendix, see <http://ucdp.uu.se/downloads/> accessed 7 August 2021 and <http://www.prio.org/jpr/datasets/Acknowledgements> accessed 7 August 2021. See also Therese Pettersson, Stina Högbladh, and Magnus Öberg, 'Organized Violence, 1989–2018 and Peace Agreements' (2019) 56 Journal of Peace Research 589; Nils Petter Gleditsch and others, 'Armed Conflict 1946–2001: A New Dataset' (2002) 39 Journal of Peace Research 615.

[52] Note that the UCDP Dataset includes situations of organised violence that would likely not be considered non-international armed conflicts under IHL, such as armed violence between organised criminal groups.

[53] <http://theirwords.org/> accessed 7 August 2021.

[54] <https://peacemaker.un.org/> accessed 7 August 2021.

[55] Christine Bell, *On the Law of Peace* (OUP 2008): in this book, Bell sets the number of agreements that could be classified as special agreements as high as 646: ibid 46. These include 'pre-negotiation, framework, and implementation agreements': ibid. Bell includes in this tally agreements for situations of civil violence that would have been contested in terms of whether they would meet the minimum threshold for classification as a non-international armed conflict according to the *Tadić* criteria, such as the conflict between Spain and the Basques.

[56] The earliest agreement in a non-international armed conflict recorded by the United Nations on the United Nations Peacemaker website, dated 1960, is the 16 Point Agreement between the Government of India and the Naga People's Convention (<https://peacemaker.un.org/sites/peacemaker.un.org/files/

agreements were adopted), the States involved in these conflicts were party to the Geneva Conventions of 1949.[57] The majority of agreements are peace agreements or ceasefire agreements between one or more non-State armed groups and their territorial government,[58] with the remainder being agreements in regards to minimum humanitarian rules to be observed by parties to the conflict.[59]

The agreements also cover a range of years, depending on the conflicts and their duration: there may be multiple agreements relating to one ongoing conflict, or a series of agreements adopted in a series of conflicts. The duration of the conflict and/or the frequency of conflicts in a particular area seem to have little impact on the frequency of the adoption of agreements. For example, despite the protracted conflicts in Sri Lanka[60] and El Salvador,[61] Geneva Call notes comparatively few agreements.[62] However, considerably shorter conflicts, such as in Bosnia and Herzegovina[63] and Tajikistan,[64] generated similar (or higher) numbers of agreements.[65] Likewise, the absence of agreements with a governmental authority is not necessarily indicative of a lack of willingness to apply and observe principles of international law. For example, only one agreement, from 1993, between

IN_600726_The%20sixteen%20point%20Agreement_0.pdf> accessed 7 August 2021). The earliest recorded post-1949 agreement recorded by Geneva Call on the *Their Words* website is dated to 1976 and the Tripoli Agreement between the Republic of the Philippines and Moro National Liberation Front (<http://theirwords.org/media/transfer/doc/ph_mnlf_1976_31-8e143f22438dc83c6199a9ce0fc94956.pdf> accessed 7 August 2021). None of these conflicts related to situations that could be classified as wars of national liberation per Additional Protocol I (API), and thus they are not considered international wars of decolonisation.

[57] For example, Sri Lanka acceded to the Geneva Conventions in February 1959 (<https://ihl-databases.icrc.org/applic/ihl/ihl.nsf/vwTreatiesByCountrySelected.xsp?xp_countrySelected = LK> accessed 7 August 2021). The Sri Lankan civil war started in 1983 (Reuters Staff, 'Timeline: Sri Lanka's 25-Year Civil War' (*Reuters*, 18 May 2009) <http://www.reuters.com/article/us-srilanka-war-timeline-sb/timeline-sri-lankas-25-year-civil-war-idUSTRE54F16620090518> accessed 7 August 2021) and agreements were signed with the Liberation Tigers of Tamil Eelam in 1995 and 2002 (<http://theirwords.org/?country = LKA> accessed 7 August 2021).

[58] For example, the Darfur Peace Agreement between the Government of the Sudan, the Sudan Liberation Movement/Army, and the Justice and Equality Movement <http://theirwords.org/media/transfer/doc/1_sd_slma_2006_19-71deb0e9f6ebf4e451ef3d997a1a5406.pdf> accessed 7 August 2021.

[59] For example, the Action Plan between MILF and the United Nations in the Philippines regarding the Issue of Recruitment and Use of Child Soldiers in the Armed Conflict in Mindanao <http://theirwords.org/media/transfer/doc/1_ph_milf_biaf_2009_13-d74703efad5c37df5ab9842bc87e67a2.pdf> accessed 7 August 2021.

[60] The 26-year conflict in Sri Lanka ended in 2009. See further Channa Wickremesekera, *The Tamil Separatist War in Sri Lanka* (Routledge 2016) ch 13.

[61] The conflict started in 1980 and did not officially end until 1992. See further Report of the UN Truth Commission on El Salvador, UN Doc S/25500 (1 April 1993) 10.

[62] Three in Sri Lanka (1995, 2002), six in El Salvador (1981, 1990, 1991, 1992).

[63] From 1992 to 1995. See ICTY, 'The Conflicts' <http://www.icty.org/en/about/what-former-yugoslavia/conflicts> accessed 7 August 2021.

[64] From 1992 to 1997. See GlobalSecurity.org, 'Tajikstan Civil War' <http://www.globalsecurity.org/military/world/war/tajikistan.htm> accessed 7 August 2021.

[65] Four for Bosnia, seven for Tajikistan.

mujahedeen groups and the Afghan government is noted by Geneva Call,[66] even though there are several examples of unilateral declarations and internal rules and regulations adopted by Afghani mujahedeen on record with Geneva Call, spanning from 1993 to 2013.[67]

On closer examination, the documents in question reveal a recognition and embrace of IHL, though perhaps not a widespread or outright adoption of an idealised Common Article 3 special agreement (whereby the Geneva Conventions in part or in their entirety are brought into effect). Over 60 instruments[68] include specific reference to IHL principles, such as ensuring the release of detainees and prisoners of war at the cessation of hostilities,[69] or noting the requirement for the clearance, removal, or destruction of explosive remnants of war.[70] However, fewer than 20 of the documents recorded by Geneva Call make specific reference to the Geneva Conventions[71] and, of those, only a handful either specifically designate themselves a Common Article 3 special agreement,[72] or otherwise clearly implement extensive Geneva Conventions provisions.[73]

[66] Afghan Peace Accord (Islamabad Accord) <http://theirwords.org/media/transfer/doc/1_af_1993_08-dc4cfedfa6c6cabc020c069efa58e596.pdf> accessed 7 August 2021.

[67] Thirteen in total. See further <http://theirwords.org/?country = AFG> accessed 7 August 2021.

[68] In agreements involving Afghanistan, Angola, Bosnia, Burundi, Colombia, Congo, Côte d'Ivoire, Croatia, the Democratic Republic of the Congo, El Salvador, Georgia, Liberia, Malaysia, Mali, Mozambique, Myanmar, Nepal, Papua New Guinea, the Philippines, Rwanda, Sierra Leone, Tajikistan, and the former Yugoslavia (regarding Kosovo).

[69] See Article IX of Peace Agreement between the Government of Liberia, the Liberians United for Reconciliation and Democracy, the Movement for Democracy in Liberia and the Political Parties, UN Doc S/2003/850 (18 August 2003).

[70] See Agreement on the Cleaning and Decontamination of the Territory of the Presence of Antipersonnel Mines (APM), Improvised Explosive Devices (IEDs) and Unexploded Ordnance (UXO), or Explosive Remnants of War (ERW) in General, between the Government of Colombia and the Revolutionary Armed Forces of Colombia—People's Army (FARC-EP), 7 March 2015 <http://theirwords.org/media/transfer/doc/farc_ep_humanitarian_demining_agreement-fd76b072d15221bf0dfac221abb3a485.pdf> accessed 7 August 2021.

[71] In agreements involving Bosnia, Croatia, the Democratic Republic of the Congo, El Salvador, and Sudan, though the Comprehensive Agreement on Respect for Human Rights and International Humanitarian Law between the Government of the Republic of the Philippines and the National Democratic Front of the Philippines does incorporate numerous IHL provisions essentially verbatim, beyond the protections of Common Article 3, while not specifically mentioning the Geneva Conventions.

[72] Agreement No 1 at the Initiative of the International Committee of the Red Cross, between the Serbian Democratic Party (SDS), the Republic of Srpska (Srpska), the Republic of Bosnia and Herzegovina, Party of Democratic Action (SDA), Croatian Democratic Community (HDZ), 22 May 1992 <http://theirwords.org/media/transfer/doc/sc_bih_sdp_pda_cdc_bih_1992_03-69c6ca85fc859359c68a5dceb777694e.pdf> accessed 7 August 2021; the Memorandum of Understanding on the Application of IHL between Croatia and the Socialist Federal Republic of Yugoslavia, 27 November 1991 <http://theirwords.org/media/transfer/doc/yu_croatia_serbia_1991_02-2a956567e705457f21f4837037ebcafc.pdf> accessed 7 August 2021.

[73] See, for example, the Comprehensive Agreement on Respect for Human Rights and International Humanitarian Law between the Government of the Republic of the Philippines and the National Democratic Front of the Philippines <https://peacemaker.un.org/sites/peacemaker.un.org/files/PH_980316_Comprehensive%20Agreement%20on%20Respect%20for%20Human%20Rights.pdf> accessed 7 August 2021. By contrast, the Comprehensive Agreement on Human Rights, between

Perhaps best known of these were the two Memoranda of Understanding (MoUs) relating to the conflict in the former Yugoslavia. The first of these was adopted in 1991 and related to the conflict in Croatia.[74] It contained 15 provisions whereby the parties to that conflict agreed to implement existing Geneva Convention provisions, including, inter alia, for the respect and care of the wounded, sick, and shipwrecked;[75] to protect and care for captured combatants[76] and civilians;[77] and for the repression of misuse of the Red Cross emblem.[78] The 1991 MoU also made specific reference to provisions in Additional Protocol I and the 1980 Conventional Weapons Convention Protocol on Mines and Booby Traps. The Agreement of 22 May 1992 on the Implementation of International Humanitarian Law in the Armed Conflict in Bosnia-Herzegovina[79] was similarly worded to the 1991 MoU, containing reference to Geneva provisions on the protection of hospitals and medical units,[80] the civilian population,[81] captured combatants,[82] and the wounded, sick, and shipwrecked.[83] However, the 1992 Agreement is also noteworthy in that, unlike the 1991 MoU, it specifically referenced the special agreements provision of Common Article 3.[84] More recently, in the 2016 agreement on cessation of hostilities in Colombia, it is specifically stated that:

> El presente Acuerdo Final para la Terminación del Conflicto y la Construcción de una Paz Estable y Duradera se suscribe por el Gobierno Nacional y las Fuerzas Armadas Revolucionarias de Colombia- Acuerdo Final 24.11.2016 Página 5 de 310 Ejército del Pueblo (FARC-EP), como Acuerdo Especial en los términos del

Guatemala and the Unidad Revolucionaria Nacional Guatemalteca, specifically notes in Section IX: 'These statements by the Parties do not constitute a special agreement, in the terms of article 3 (Common), paragraph 2, second subparagraph of the Geneva Conventions of 1949.' See further <https://peacemaker.un.org/sites/peacemaker.un.org/files/GT_940329_ComprehensiveAgreementon HumanRights.pdf> accessed 7 August 2021.

[74] Memorandum of Understanding, 27 November 1991, reproduced in Marco Sassòli, Antoine A Bouvier, and Anne Quintin (eds), *How Does Law Protect in War? Cases, Documents and Teaching Materials on Contemporary Practice in International Humanitarian Law* (3rd edn, ICRC 2011) <https://casebook.icrc.org/case-study/former-yugoslavia-special-agreements-between-parties-conflicts> accessed 7 August 2021.

[75] Articles 1, 2.

[76] Article 3.

[77] Articles 4–5, 9.

[78] Article 10.

[79] <https://casebook.icrc.org/case-study/former-yugoslavia-special-agreements-between-parties-conflicts> accessed 7 August 2021.

[80] Agreement of 22 May 1991, Art 2.2.

[81] Agreement of 22 May 1991, Art 2.3.

[82] Agreement of 22 May 1991, Art 2.4.

[83] Agreement of 22 May 1991, Art 2.1.

[84] Agreement of 22 May 1991, Art 2, entitled 'Special Agreement': 'In accordance with the Article 3 of the four Geneva Conventions of August 12, 1949, the Parties agree to bring into force the following provisions.'

artículo 3 común a los Convenios de Ginebra de 1949, para efectos de su vigencia internacional.[85]

Other agreements that can be considered as falling within the 'special agreements' category include, inter alia, the Implementing Guidelines on the Humanitarian, Rehabilitation and Development Aspects of the Government of the Philippines-Moro Islamic Liberation Front (GRP-MILF) Tripoli Agreement on Peace of 2001 between the Government of the Philippines and the Moro Islamic Liberation Front;[86] the 1998 Comprehensive Agreement on Respect for Human Rights and IHL in the Philippines[87] between the Government of the Philippines and the National Democratic Front of the Philippines; the 2006 Agreement between the Government of Uganda and the Lord's Resistance Army/Movement;[88] the Agreement between the Government of Liberia and the National Patriotic Front of Liberia;[89] the N'Djamena Protocol on the Humanitarian Ceasefire Agreement on the Conflict in Darfur;[90] the Ceasefire Code of Conduct between the Government of Nepal and Communist Party of Nepal (CPN; Maoist);[91] and the bilateral and trilateral agreements between the Government of Sudan, the Justice and Equality Movement in Sudan, and the Sudan People's Liberation Movement.[92]

[85] 'This Final Agreement for the End of Conflict and the Construction of a Stable and Lasting Peace is signed by the National Government and the Revolutionary Armed Forces of Colombia—Final Agreement 24.11.2016 Page 5 of 310 People's Army (FARC-EP), as a Special Agreement under the terms of article 3 common to the Geneva Conventions of 1949, for the purposes of its international validity' (unofficial translation). Acuerdo Final Para la Terminación del Conflicto y la Construcción de una Paz Estable y Duradera, 24 November 2016, 4–5 <https://peacemaker.un.org/sites/peacemaker.un.org/files/Colombia%20Nuevo%20Acuerdo%20Final%2024%20Nov%202016_0.pdf> accessed 7 August 2021.

[86] 7 May 2002 <https://peacemaker.un.org/sites/peacemaker.un.org/files/PH_010807_Implementing%20Guidelines%20on%20the%20Security%20Aspect%20of%20the%20Tripoli%20Agreement.pdf>.

[87] <https://peacemaker.un.org/sites/peacemaker.un.org/files/PH_980316_Comprehensive%20Agreement%20on%20Respect%20for%20Human%20Rights.pdf> accessed 10 November 2021.

[88] Cessation of Hostilities Agreement, 26 August 2006 and Addenda (for example, Addendum 6 at <https://peacemaker.un.org/sites/peacemaker.un.org/files/UG_080301_Addendum%206%20to%20the%20Cessation%20of%20Hostilities%20Agreement.pdf> accessed 7 August 2021) and Agreement on a Permanent Ceasefire, 23 February 2008 <https://peacemaker.un.org/sites/peacemaker.un.org/files/UG_080223_Agreement%20on%20a%20Permanent%20Ceasefire.pdf> accessed 7 August 2021.

[89] Cotonou Accord between Interim Government of National Unity (IGNU) of Liberia, National Patriotic Front of Liberia (NPFL) and the United Movement of Liberia for Democracy (ULIMO), 25 July 1993 <http://www.refworld.org/docid/3ae6b5796.html>.

[90] 2004 <www.un.org/zh/focus/southernsudan/pdf/dpa.pdf> accessed 7 August 2021.

[91] Available on the website of Geneva Call, which archives such agreements <http://theirwords.org/media/transfer/doc/ut_np_cpn_m_2006_07-991109f713a0d88da42e667f46e12656.pdf> accessed 7 August 2021.

[92] These include the Agreement between the Government of the Republic of Sudan and the Sudan People's Liberation Movement to Protect Non-Combatant Civilians and Civilian Facilities from Military Attack, 10 March 2002, the Protocol between the Government of Sudan, the Sudan Liberation Movement/Army, and the Justice and Equality Movement on the Improvement of the Humanitarian Situation in Darfur, and the Protocol between the Government of Sudan, the Sudan Liberation Movement/Army, and the Justice and Equality Movement on the Enhancement of the Security Situation in Darfur in Accordance with the N'Djamena Agreement, both of 9 November 2004. A complete listing

Despite the proliferation of instruments indicated above, this still leaves a considerable number of instruments adopted that do not mention IHL obligations at all. The aim of the special agreements provision was to 'encourage Parties to an armed conflict to agree to a more comprehensive set of norms',[93] to regulate conduct in a type of armed conflict for which there are scant rules, and to recognise that 'the situation of thousands of sufferers is then such that it is no longer enough for Article 3 to be respected' and so it 'becomes desirable to settle in detail the treatment they are to receive, the relief which is to be brought to them, and other matters as well'.[94] Special agreements are therefore a vital instrument whereby the most vulnerable in situations of non-international armed conflict might find themselves better protected under the law. Given the proliferation of non-international armed conflicts in the aftermath of the Second World War, and the scant international protections relating to non-international armed conflicts, the willingness of a notable number of States to negotiate and agree to special agreements to apply the Conventions is an encouraging sign.

However, when one examines the number of non-international armed conflicts that have taken place since the adoption of Common Article 3 and compares that to the number of special agreements that have been negotiated, the result is disappointing. As noted earlier, during the period 1949 to 2019, there were over 500 situations of armed violence that could potentially be classified as non-international, warranting the application of Common Article 3.[95] In that same period, the number of special agreements negotiated between the parties was notably fewer. This disjuncture between the number of conflicts and the number of agreements suggests that the adoption of the special agreements provision has been less than all-encompassing.

It should also be noted that several special agreements were adopted in armed conflicts that also saw widespread violations of the laws of armed conflict, such as in the former Yugoslavia, Rwanda, and Sierra Leone. For example, during the conflict in the former Yugoslavia, special agreements were negotiated between the parties to that conflict, but seemed to do little to prevent the participants turning that conflict into one of the most protracted and violent, marked by egregious violations of IHL.[96] Indeed, two of the signatories to the IHL agreements signed in 1991

of agreements in relation to the Sudan can be found at the Geneva Call website <http://theirwords.org/?country = SDN> accessed 7 August 2021.

[93] ICRC, *Commentary on the Second Geneva Convention: Convention (II) for the Amelioration of the Condition of the Wounded, Sick and Shipwrecked Members of Armed Forces at Sea* (CUP 2017) para 846.

[94] Jean Pictet (ed), *Commentary on the Geneva Conventions of 12 August 1949*, vol 1: *Geneva Convention for the Amelioration of the Condition of the Wounded and Sick in Armed Forces in the Field* (ICRC 1952) 59.

[95] These figures come from research undertaken by Marie Allansson, Erik Melander, and Lotta Themnér, 'Organized Violence, 1989–2016' (2017) 54 Journal of Peace Research 574. See also Gleditsch and others (n 51).

[96] For accounts of the Yugoslav War, see generally Rachel Kerr, *The International Criminal Tribunal for the Former Yugoslavia: An Exercise in Law, Politics, and Diplomacy* (OUP 2004), specifically ch 2;

were acting in their capacity as representatives of Radovan Karadžić, who would later be tried and found guilty of genocide in Srebrenica, as well as war crimes and crimes against humanity.[97]

That being said, that *any* States have been willing to engage with non-State actors in adopting more rather than less regulation is commendable. Indeed, Sivakumaran points to only a few instances of special agreements prior to 1949,[98] which suggests that the Common Article 3 special agreements provision has been in some measure beneficial. The diminution of the doctrine of recognition of belligerency[99]—itself a mechanism for triggering wider application of the international laws of armed conflict—prior to the adoption of Common Article 3 would also suggest that Common Article 3 has been a net good in encouraging more thorough application of the laws of armed conflict in all situations.

Moreover, the disparity in numbers between agreements between parties to non-international armed conflict and the implementation of IHL provisions does not necessarily mean that the Common Article 3 special agreements provision has been ineffectual. Of those more than 300 agreements, many are peace agreements directed at resolving purely political issues (such as power sharing and land distribution[100]) rather than dealing with IHL issues (such as prisoner repatriation). Therefore, that these purely political instruments fail to acknowledge IHL is not, arguably, compelling evidence of a failure of the Common Article 3 special agreements regime. Indeed, it is often the case that parties to these kinds of peace agreements also issued parallel unilateral declarations during the armed conflict announcing their intentions to respect the Geneva Conventions. For example, during the civil war in Yemen, both the Royalist and the Republican sides of the conflict made parallel commitments to the ICRC that they would respect the principles of the Geneva Conventions;[101] similar assurances were made by both parties to the Nigerian Civil War.[102]

Paul Mojzes, *Balkan Genocides: Holocaust and Ethnic Cleansing in the Twentieth Century* (Rowman Littlefield 2016), specifically chs 9–12.

[97] Marko Milanović, 'The Arrest and Impending Trial of Radovan Karadžić' (2009) 58 International and Comparative Law Quarterly 212.

[98] Sivakumaran, *The Law of Non-International Armed Conflict* (n 42) 124, referring to the Tratado de Regularizacion de la Guerra, 26 November 1820, reproduced in (1820–21) 71 Consolidated Treaty Series 291.

[99] See generally Robert McLaughlin, *Recognition of Belligerency and the Law of Armed Conflict* (OUP 2020).

[100] See further Christine Bell, *On the Law of Peace* (OUP 2008) 106–07; in which she categorises such agreements as broadly engaging in state redefinition, disaggregation of power, and dislocation of power.

[101] See, for example, the report on ICRC action in Yemen, reported in ICRC, *Annual Report 1963* (1964) 16–17 <https://international-review.icrc.org/articles/annual-report-international-committee-2> accessed 7 August 2021. See also Kathryn Boals, 'The Internal War in Yemen' in Richard Falk (ed), *The International Law of Civil War* (Johns Hopkins 1971) 314–16, and, more generally, Dana Schmidt, 'The Civil War in Yemen' in Evan Luard (ed), *The International Regulation of Civil Wars* (Thames and Hudson 1972).

[102] See the report on the work of the ICRC in Nigeria in ICRC, *Annual Report 1967* (1968) 36 <https://international-review.icrc.org/articles/annual-report-1967> accessed 7 August 2021.

This pattern is seen in other civil conflicts[103] and suggests that the special agreements provision has had *some* influence in encouraging all parties to openly state their commitment to applying the provisions of the article, and of the Conventions more generally. There is also some limited evidence to suggest that parties who publicly agree to comply with the provisions of the Geneva Conventions take steps to observe the provisions in practice. For example, in the conflict in the Congo during the 1960s, there was evidence that most persons detained in relation to the conflict were 'detained under acceptable conditions and exchanged or released in the course of hostilities'.[104] The ICRC was also able to participate actively in 'visiting prisoners, arranging prisoner releases, supplying medical relief, and educating the parties to the conflict in the law of war'.[105]

Finally, it is worth including a brief note regarding whether and how special agreements have been enforced. The Geneva Conventions obligate parties to the Convention to criminalise violations of the Convention—known as grave breaches.[106] Common Article 3 is not included in the grave breaches regime and the article has no compliance or enforcement mechanism. However, it is possible for compliance and enforcement mechanisms to be included in Common Article 3 special agreements, and there is some practice to illustrate their employment.[107] For example, the 1992 Agreement for Bosnia-Herzegovina made provision for the parties to send allegations of breaches of the agreement to the ICRC, and for the ICRC to institute enquiries into breaches.[108] Agreements between the

[103] Including in conflicts in Afghanistan (1979–89), the Dominican Republic (1965), Lebanon (1958), and Nepal (1996–2006); see further Sivakumaran, *The Law of Non-International Armed Conflict* (n 42) 114–18.

[104] Donald McNemar, 'The Postindependence War in the Congo' in Richard Falk (ed), *The International Law of Civil War* (Johns Hopkins 1971) 263.

[105] ibid 269–70.

[106] See generally Guénaël Mettraux, *International Crimes and the Ad Hoc Tribunals* (OUP 2006), specifically ch 7.

[107] See generally Ezequiel Heffes and Marcos Kotlik, 'Special Agreements as a Means of Enhancing Compliance with IHL in Non-International Armed Conflicts: An Inquiry into the Governing Legal Regime' (2014) 96 International Review of the Red Cross 1195.

[108] '**(11) Forwarding of allegations**

[1] The parties may forward to the ICRC any allegations of violations of international humanitarian law, with sufficient details to enable the party reportedly responsible to open an enquiry.

[2] The ICRC will not inform the other party of such allegations if they are expressed in abusive terms of if they are made public. Each party undertakes, when it is officially informed of such an allegation made or forwarded by the ICRC, to open an enquiry promptly and pursue it conscientiously, and to take the necessary steps to put an end to the alleged violations or prevent their recurrence and to punish those responsible in accordance with the law in force.

(12) Request for an enquiry

[1] Should the ICRC be asked to institute an enquiry, it may use its good offices to set up a commission of enquiry outside the institution and in accordance with its principles.

[2] The ICRC will take part in the establishment of such a commission only by virtue of a general agreement or an ad hoc agreement with all the parties concerned.'

government of Sudan and the Sudan People's Liberation Movement/Army also made provision for the establishment of a 'Verification Mission',[109] comprised of international experts and staff and empowered to 'investigate, evaluate and report on alleged incidents involving serious violations of the obligations or commitments'[110] contained in the agreement. A compliance mechanism was also included in the agreement between the Philippines government and the Moro Liberation Front.[111]

Regarding enforcement mechanisms, violations of Common Article 3 are part of the jurisdiction of the International Criminal Court (ICC),[112] but the ICC does not have jurisdiction to rule on special agreements—indeed, Articles 5(1) and 25(2) of the ICC Statute make it clear that the Court only has 'jurisdiction in accordance with this Statute',[113] which would seem to exclude the possibility of the Court being 'able to ground its jurisdiction on an ad hoc agreement'.[114] However, ad hoc agreements have been given consideration in the International Criminal Tribunal for the former Yugoslavia (ICTY);[115] the 1992 agreement for Bosnia and Herzegovina also explicitly provided that violations of IHL should be punished 'in accordance with the law in force'.[116]

Additional Protocol II Amnesties

Moving now to the question of the efficacy of Article 6(5), since the adoption of that article there have been numerous amnesties included in peace agreements concluded at the cessation of hostilities, as well as amnesties implemented in national legislation.

[109] Article 2, Agreement between the Government of the Republic of Sudan and the Sudan People's Liberation Movement to Protect Non-Combatant Civilians and Civilian Facilities from Military Attack.

[110] Article 2(1)(a).

[111] Comprehensive Agreement on Respect for Human Rights and International Humanitarian Law (16 March 1998), Art 6.

[112] Rome Statute of the International Criminal Court (adopted 17 July 1998, entered into force 1 July 2002) 2187 UNTS 90, Art 8(2)(c).

[113] ibid Art 5(1).

[114] Andrew Clapham, Paola Gaeta, and Marco Sassòli (eds), *The 1949 Geneva Conventions: A Commentary* (OUP 2016) 520, para 46.

[115] See *Prosecutor v Tadić (Decision on the Defence Motion for Interlocutory Appeal on Jurisdiction)* (Case No IT-94-1-AR72, 2 October 1995) para 143; *Prosecutor v Kordić (Appeals Decision)* (Case No IT-95-14/2-A, 17 December 2004) para 46. Note also *Prosecutor v Galić* (Trial Chamber I, Case No IT-98-29-T, 5 December 2003), where the Trial Chamber grounded its jurisdiction *ratione materiae* and *ratione personae* on the 22 May Agreement (paras 96–98, 124–29); however, in the Appeals Judgment of 30 November 2006, the Chamber asserted the customary nature of the offence and related international criminal responsibility, and did not consider it necessary to address the appeal on the grounds that the 22 May Agreement was not binding on the parties: *Prosecutor v Galić* (Appeals Chamber, Case No IT-98-29-A, 30 November 2006) para 86.

[116] See Luisa Vierucci, '"Special Agreements" between Conflicting Parties in the Case-Law of the ICTY' in Bert Swart, Alexander Zahar, and Göran Sluiter (eds), *The Legacy of the International Criminal Tribunal for the Former Yugoslavia* (OUP 2011) 418–21.

The ICRC Study into Customary International Humanitarian Law (ICRC CIHL) Study lists amnesties in the Central American region,[117] Georgia,[118] the former Yugoslavia,[119] the Philippines,[120] Liberia,[121] Sudan,[122] Tajikistan,[123] Sierra

[117] The Esquipulas II Accords: Procedure for the Establishment of a Firm and Lasting Peace in Central America, signed by the Presidents of Costa Rica, El Salvador, Guatemala, Honduras and Nicaragua, Guatemala City, 7 August 1987, annexed to Letter dated 27 August 1987 from the Permanent Representatives of Costa Rica, El Salvador, Guatemala and Nicaragua to the UN addressed to the UN Secretary-General, UN Doc A/42/521-S/19085 (31 August 1987)) Section 1(b).

[118] Quadripartite Agreement on Voluntary Return of Refugees and Displaced Persons in the Republic of Georgia, between the Abkhaz and Georgian Sides, the Russian Federation and UNHCR, Moscow, 4 April 1994, annexed to Letter dated 5 April 1994 from the permanent representative of Georgia to the UN addressed to the President of the Security Council, UN Doc S/1994/397 (5 April 1994) Annex II, Art 3(c).

[119] General Framework Agreement for Peace in Bosnia and Herzegovina, Annex 7, Agreement on Refugees and Displaced Persons, signed by the Republic of Bosnia and Herzegovina, the Federation of Bosnia and Herzegovina and the Republika Srpska, Dayton, 22 November 1995, Art VI. See also Agreement on the Release and Transfer of Prisoners, concluded between Representatives of Mr Alija Izetbegović (President of the Republic of Bosnia and Herzegovina and President of the Party of Democratic Action), Representative of Mr Radovan Karadžić (President of the Serbian Democratic Party), and Representative of Mr Mate Boban (President of the Croatian Democratic Community), Geneva, 1 October 1992, Art 3(1).

[120] Tripoli Agreement: Agreement between the Government of the Republic of the Philippines and the Moro National Liberation Front with the Participation of the Quadripartite Ministerial Commission Members of the Islamic Conference and the Secretary-General of the Organization of Islamic Conference, Tripoli, 23 December 1976, Section 12.

[121] Cotonou Peace Agreement on Liberia between the Interim Government of National Unity of Liberia (IGNU) of the first part and the National Patriotic Front of Liberia (NPFL) of the second part and the United Liberation Movement of Liberia for Democracy (ULIMO) of the third part, Cotonou, 25 July 1993, annexed to Letter dated 6 August 1993 from the Chargé d'affaires a.i. of the Permanent Mission of Benin to the UN addressed to the UN Secretary-General, UN Doc S/26272 (9 August 1993) Art 19.

[122] General Amnesty Proclamation Order, annexed to the Sudan Peace Agreement, Khartoum, 21 April 1997, Preamble, Arts 1–2, 6–7.

[123] Agreement between the President of the Republic of Tajikistan and the leader of the United Tajik Opposition, Moscow, 23 December 1996, annexed to Letter dated 24 December 1996 from the Permanent Representative of the Russian Federation to the UN addressed to the UN Secretary-General, UN Doc S/1996/1070 (27 December 1996) Annex I. See also General Agreement on the Establishment of Peace and National Accord in Tajikistan, Moscow, 27 June 1997, annexed to UN Doc A/52/219-S/1997/510, Letter dated 1 July 1997 from the Permanent Representative of the Russian Federation to the UN addressed to the UN Secretary-General, 2 July 1997, Annex I; Protocol on Refugees between the Government of the Republic of Tajikistan, the United Tajik Opposition and the Special Representative of the UN Secretary-General for Tajikistan, Tehran, 13 January 1997, annexed to UN Doc S/1997/56, Progress Report of the UN Secretary-General on the situation in Tajikistan, 21 January 1997, Annex III, Section 2; Statute of the Tajik Commission on National Reconciliation, Mashhad, 21 February 1997, annexed to UN Doc S/1997/169, Letter dated 24 February 1997 from the Chargé d'affaires a.i. of the Permanent Mission of the Islamic Republic of Iran to the UN addressed to the Secretary-General, 27 February 1997, Annex I, Section 7; Protocol on Political Questions between the President of the Republic of Tajikistan and the leader of the United Tajik Opposition, Bishkek, 18 May 1997, annexed to UN Doc S/1997/385, Letter dated 20 May 1997 from the Permanent Representative of Kyrgyzstan to the UN addressed to the UN Secretary-General, 20 May 1997, Annex I, Section 1; Bishkek Memorandum between the President of the Republic of Tajikistan and the leader of the United Tajik Opposition, Bishkek, 18 May 1997, annexed to UN Doc S/1997/385, Letter dated 20 May 1997 from the Permanent Representative of Kyrgyzstan to the UN addressed to the UN Secretary-General, 20 May 1997, Annex II; Protocol on the Guarantees of Implementation of the General Agreement on the Establishment of Peace and National Accord in Tajikistan, Tehran, 28 May 1997, annexed to UN Doc S/1997/410, Letter

Leone,[124] Burundi,[125] the Congo,[126] and Côte d'Ivoire.[127] These individual instances of amnesty agreements are joined by national laws on amnesty from a variety of States, including Afghanistan, Algeria, Argentina, Bosnia and Herzegovina, the Central African Republic, Chad, Chile, Colombia, Côte d'Ivoire, Croatia, the Democratic Republic of the Congo, Djibouti, El Salvador, Guatemala, Liberia, Peru, the Philippines, Poland, the Russian Federation, Rwanda, Senegal, South Africa, Tajikistan, Uganda, Uruguay, Venezuela, and Zimbabwe.[128]

All these amnesty agreements or laws came about following the adoption and entry into force of Additional Protocol II. Of the above-listed States that have entered into treaty-based amnesty agreements, or have national legislation relating to amnesty, 21 States were party to Additional Protocol II when they issued amnesty laws or adopted amnesty agreements;[129] nine were not yet party to Additional

dated 28 May 1997 from the Permanent Representative of the Islamic Republic of Iran to the UN addressed to the UN Secretary-General, 28 May 1997, Section 1.

[124] Peace Agreement Ending the Conflict between the Government of Sierra Leone and the Revolutionary United Front, Lomé, 7 July 1999, also known as the Lomé Peace Accord, Art IX.

[125] Arusha Peace and Reconciliation Agreement for Burundi, concluded between the Government of the Republic of Burundi, the National Assembly, Alliance Burundo-Africaine pour le Salut (ABASA), Alliance Nationale pour le Droit et le Développement (ANADDE), Alliance des Vaillants (AV-INTWARI), Conseil National pour la Défense de la Démocratie (CNDD), Front pour la Démocratie au Burundi (FRODEBU), Front pour la Libération Nationale (FROLINA), Parti Socialiste et Panafricaniste (INKINZO), Parti pour la Libération du Peuple Hutu (PALIPEHUTU), Parti pour le Redressement National (PARENA), Parti Indépendant des Travailleurs (PIT), Parti Libéral (PL), Parti du Peuple (PP), Parti pour la Réconciliation du Peuple (PRP), Parti Social-Démocrate (PSD), Ralliement pour la Démocratie et le Développement Economique et Social (RADDES), Rassemblement du Peuple Burundais (RPB) and Union pour le Progrès National (UPRONA), Arusha, 28 August 2000, including Protocol II on Democracy and Good Governance, Protocol II, Art 22(2)(c).

[126] Accord global et inclusif sur la transition en République Démocratique du Congo, conclu entre les composantes et entités du dialogue intercongolais, parties à l'accord: le Gouvernement de la République Démocratique du Congo, le Rassemblement Congolais pour la Démocratie (RCD), le Mouvement de Libération du Congo (MLC), l'Opposition politique, les Forces vives, le Rassemblement Congolais pour la Démocratie/Mouvement de Libération (RCD/ML), le Rassemblement Congolais pour la Démocratie/National (RCD/N), les Mai-Mai, Pretoria, 16 December 2002, Art III.8.

[127] Linas-Marcoussis Agreement between the political forces of Côte d'Ivoire, Round table of the Ivorian political forces, meeting at Linas-Marcoussis from 15 to 23 January 2003 and bringing together the following parties: FPI (Front Populaire Ivoirien), MFA (Mouvement des Forces d'Avenir), MJP (Mouvement pour la Justice et la Paix), MPCI (Mouvement Patriotique de Côte d'Ivoire), MPIGO (Mouvement Populaire Ivoirien du Grand Ouest), PDCI-RDA (Parti Démocratique de la Côte d'Ivoire-Rassemblement Démocratique Africain), PIT (Parti Ivoirien des Travailleurs), RDR (Rassemblement des Républicains), UDCY (Union Démocratique et Citoyenne), UDPCI (Union pour la Démocratie et la Paix en Côte d'Ivoire), Linas-Marcoussis, 24 January 2003, Text of the agreement, paras 1 and 3i, and Annex, para VII, 5. See also Ouagadougou Political Agreement between the Presidency of Côte d'Ivoire and the Forces Nouvelles of Côte d'Ivoire, having met at Ouagadougou from 5 February to 3 March 2007, Ouagadougou, 4 March 2007, Preamble and para VI., 6.3.

[128] See the practice relating to amnesty in the ICRC CIHL Study: ICRC, *Customary IHL Database*, Practice Relating to Rule 159 <https://ihl-databases.icrc.org/customary-ihl/eng/docs/v2_rul_rule159> accessed 7 August 2021.

[129] Algeria, Bosnia and Herzegovina, Burundi, the Central African Republic, Costa Rica, Côte d'Ivoire, Croatia, Democratic Republic of the Congo, Djibouti, El Salvador, Georgia, Liberia, Poland, Russian Federation, Rwanda, Senegal, Sierra Leone, Tajikistan, Uganda, Uruguay, and Venezuela.

Protocol II at the relevant time.[130] Of the remaining States—Chad, Guatemala, Peru, and South Africa—some amnesty agreements or laws were adopted or enacted prior to the State becoming party to Additional Protocol II.[131] The ICRC reportage of amnesty agreements differs from that of Geneva Call and the United Nations. Geneva Call[132] and the United Nations[133] note 35 amnesty agreements, with nearly all States involved party to Additional Protocol II at the relevant time.[134] This discrepancy can likely be attributed to the fact that the ICRC accounting of amnesties has not been updated to include more recent examples, such as the 2016 agreement in Colombia.

Other sources—such as the UCDP/PRIO,[135] the Transitional Justice Research Collaborative,[136] and the Transitional Justice Database Program[137]—list hundreds of amnesty agreements as having been adopted after 1977. However, many of the cited amnesties in these databases were adopted in relation to low-level riots and civil uprisings that do not reach the threshold of non-international armed conflict (as envisaged by the applicability threshold of Additional Protocol II). In some instances, the cited amnesties do not even relate to armed conflicts at all but are, rather, extended as gestures of goodwill to persons with custodial sentences to mark major national events.[138] Indeed, the UCDP/PRIO database classifies only

[130] Afghanistan, Argentina, Chile, Colombia, Honduras, Nicaragua, the Philippines, Sudan, and Zimbabwe. For a listing of when States became party to APII, see further the ICRC repository of State's parties <https://ihl-databases.icrc.org/applic/ihl/ihl.nsf/States.xsp?xp_viewStates = XPages_NORMStatesParties&xp_treatySelected = 475> accessed 7 August 2021.

[131] For example, Peru became party to APII on 14 July 1989, having signed at the Diplomatic Conference on 12 December 1977. However, Peru enacted amnesty legislation both before and after ratifying Protocol II. For example, there was a 1987 law on terrorism that included a sentence reduction and exemption provision; additional similar laws were enacted in 1989, 1991, 1992, and 1993, with the Law on Amnesty for Retired Officers of the Armed Forces and the Law on Amnesty for Military and Civil Personnel enacted in 1996.

[132] <http://theirwords.org/> accessed 27 September 2021.

[133] <https://peacemaker.un.org/> accessed 7 August 2021.

[134] Including Algeria, Angola, Bangladesh, Bosnia and Herzegovina, Burundi, the Central African Republic, Chad, Colombia, Congo, Costa Rica, Côte d'Ivoire, Croatia, Democratic Republic of the Congo, Djibouti, El Salvador, Georgia, Guatemala, Guinea, Indonesia, Liberia, Malaysia, Niger, Papua New Guinea, the Philippines, Poland, Russian Federation, Rwanda, Senegal, Sierra Leone, Sudan, Tajikistan, Uganda, Uruguay, and Venezuela. In other instances, States signed multiple amnesty agreements both prior to and after becoming party to APII—for example, Peru became party to APII on 14 July 1989, having signed at the Diplomatic Conference on 12 December 1977. However, Peru enacted amnesty legislation both before and after ratifying Protocol II.

[135] <http://www.prio.org/Data/Armed-Conflict/UCDP-PRIO/> accessed 7 August 2021.

[136] <https://transitionaljusticedata.com/> accessed 7 August 2021.

[137] As noted on its website (<http://www.tjdbproject.com/> accessed 7 August 2021): 'The Transitional Justice Data Base Project began at the University of Wisconsin in 2005 and is led by three political scientists: Leigh A. Payne, Tricia D. Olsen, and Andrew G. Reiter. The team created a global database of over 900 mechanisms (trials, truth commissions, amnesties, reparations, and lustration policies) used from 1970–2007.'

[138] For example, Vietnam has historically granted broad amnesties to prisoners on national holidays. See further AFP, 'Vietnam to Free 15,000 Prisoners to Mark Independence, Excludes "Propaganda" Detainees' (*Australia Network News* 29 August 2013) <http://www.abc.net.au/news/2013-08-29/vietnam-amnesty-to-mark-independence-day/4923726> accessed 7 August 2021.

92 amnesties as having occurred in its study of internal, non-international, and internationalised internal armed conflicts. Moreover, their data covers amnesties from 1946 to 2006, and includes both internationalised internal armed conflicts and what they call 'extra-systemic armed conflicts', which are defined as 'a conflict between a state and a non-state group outside its own territory'—essentially, wars of national liberation, according to UCDP/PRIO definitions.[139] After removing amnesties prior to the adoption of Article 6(5) in 1977, and after excluding internationalised internal armed conflicts and extra-systemic armed conflicts (as these are not classifiable as Protocol II armed conflicts), that number drops notably—to just over 30.[140]

The question then arises: did the adoption of Article 6(5) induce States to adopt amnesties following conflict? Making this determination is difficult. That there have been several amnesty agreements and decrees since the adoption of Additional Protocol II is some indication of its impact.[141] However, in none of the agreements or decrees cited by the ICRC is Article 6(5) or Additional Protocol II mentioned *at all*, nor is the language of Article 6(5) used. When one looks to the amnesties listed by Geneva Call, the United Nations, and the Stockholm International Peace Research Institute/Peace Research Institute in Oslo (SIPRI/PRIO), that number does not improve. There are relatively few instances of reference to Additional Protocol II generally, and almost no specific reference to Article 6(5). One notable exception is the 2016 Colombian peace agreement, which specifically references Article 6(5) in two articles: Article 20[142] and Article 37.[143] SIPRI/

[139] As the UCDP/PRIO definitions page notes: 'The last extra-systemic conflict ended in 1974. This category basically contains colonial conflicts' <http://www.pcr.uu.se/research/ucdp/definitions/> accessed 7 August 2021.

[140] See further Helga Malmin Binningsbø and Cyanne Loyle, 'Armed Conflict and Post-Conflict Justice Dataset: Background Narratives' (Centre for the Study of Civil War, PRIO September 2012) <http://www.justice-data.com/pcj-dataset/PCJ%20narrative%20document%20-%20Binningsbø%20et%20al%20JPR_49(5).pdf> accessed 7 August 2021.

[141] Article 6(5) has also been included in some State military manuals, including those of Canada, the United Kingdom, the Netherlands, and New Zealand.

[142] 'En aplicación del principio de favorabilidad regulado en esta ley y de lo establecido en el artículo 6.5 del Protocolo Adicional II de las Convenciones de Ginebra de 1949, la Sala aplicará la amnistía o el indulto conforme a lo establecido en esta ley y en el Acuerdo de creación de la Jurisdicción Especial para la Paz' ('In application of the principle of favorability regulated in this law and the provisions of article 6.5 of Additional Protocol II of the Geneva Conventions of 1949, the Chamber shall apply amnesty or pardon in accordance with the provisions of this law and the Agreement of creation of the Special Jurisdiction for Peace' (unofficial translation)), Acuerdo Final Para la Terminación del Conflicto y la Construcción de una Paz Estable y Duradera, 24 November 2016, 4–5.

[143] 'Se aplicará el artículo 6.5 del Protocolo II de los Convenios de Ginebra, del cual Colombia es Estado Parte, el cual dispone lo siguiente: "A la cesación de las hostilidades, las autoridades en el poder procurarán conceder la amnistía más amplia posible a las personas que hayan tomado parte en el conflicto armado o que se encuentren privadas de libertad, internadas o detenidas por motivos relacionados con el conflicto armado." ' ('Article 6.5 of Protocol II of the Geneva Conventions shall apply, of which Colombia is a State Party, which provides as follows: "Upon cessation of hostilities, the authorities in power shall endeavor to grant the widest possible amnesty to the persons who have taken part in the armed conflict or who are deprived of liberty, interned or detained for reasons related

PRIO's numbers paint an even bleaker picture; when comparing pre-Additional Protocol II and post-Additional Protocol II Non-International Armed Conflict (NIAC) amnesty agreements, there seems to be no meaningful change in the number of amnesties agreed to after the adoption of Additional Protocol II. SIPRI/PRIO notes that around 30 amnesty agreements were adopted prior to Additional Protocol II, with around 30 adopted subsequently. Given the high number of non-international armed conflicts that have taken place since 1977, it would seem that Article 6(5) has not had substantial normative force.

This assessment is further bolstered when one examines the instances of judicial notice taken with regards to Article 6(5). Some national courts *have* examined Article 6(5), but it has usually been in the context of acknowledging the article's existence as a means to address the absence of combatant status in non-international armed conflict,[144] or to facilitate post-conflict reconstruction.[145] In other instances, Article 6(5) has been cited as evidence of the validity of amnesties under international law.[146] What is absent from these cases is any examination of whether, or determination that, Article 6(5) imposes obligations on States parties to Protocol II to enact such amnesties.[147]

to the armed conflict"' (unofficial translation)), Acuerdo Final Para la Terminación del Conflicto y la Construcción de una Paz Estable y Duradera, 24 November 2016, 150–51.

[144] See the Colombian Constitutional Court, Constitutional Case No C-225/95, Re: File No LAT-040, Judgment, 18 May 1995 (original in Spanish, unofficial translation by the ICRC):

> 'In internal armed conflicts, however, those who have taken up arms do not in principle enjoy prisoner-of-war status and are consequently subject to penal sanctions imposed by the State, since they are not legally entitled to fight or to take up arms. In so doing they are guilty of an offence, such as rebellion or sedition, which is punishable under domestic legislation. […] In situations such as those of internal conflict, where those who have taken up arms do not in principle enjoy prisoner-of-war status, it is easy to understand the purpose of a provision designed to ensure that the authorities in power will grant the broadest possible amnesty for reasons related to the conflict, once hostilities are over, as this can pave the way towards national reconciliation': ibid para 42.

[145] This very point was noted by the South African Constitutional Court in *Azanian Peoples Organization (AZAPO) v President of the Republic of South Africa* [1996] 4 SA 672. The Court remarked that post-conflict amnesties in non-international armed conflicts fulfil an important social role; that for society riven by internal armed conflict: '[I]t becomes necessary after the cessation of such conflict for the society traumatized by such a conflict to reconstruct itself. The erstwhile adversaries of such a conflict inhabit the same sovereign territory. They have to live with each other and work with each other and the state concerned is best equipped to determine what measures may be most conducive for the facilitation of such reconciliation and reconstruction': ibid para 31.

[146] For example, the Criminal Chamber of the Salvadoran Supreme Court found that Article 6(5) was the relevant international law with regards to amnesties, and that amnesties were a necessary part of national reconstruction: *Guevara Portillo Case* (Sala de lo Penal de la Corte Suprema de Justicia, San Salvador, 16 August 1995) 11, cited in Naomi Roht-Arriaza and Lauren Gibson, 'The Developing Jurisprudence on Amnesty' (1998) 20 Human Rights Quarterly 843, 864. Roht-Arriaza and Gibson also point to the Chilean case of *Romo Mena* as one where Article 6(5) was cited as part of the grounds for validity for the Chilean amnesty: *Romo Mena Case* (Corte Suprema de Chile, 26 October 1995) 12: ibid.

[147] Complicating this determination is the fact that there is division in the literature as to whether grants of amnesty can be absolute or whether it is prohibited to grant them in situations of serious violations or grave breaches of IHL. The ICRC, the Inter-American Commission on Human Rights, and

Given the dispute as to the scope and permissibility of amnesties in general, let alone whether Article 6(5) of Protocol II amounts to any kind of obligation, it is unsurprising that the South African Constitutional Court remarked that it is difficult to ascertain any 'single or uniform international practice in relation to amnesty'.[148] The most that can be said is that Article 6(5) has acknowledged at international law the sovereign prerogative to grant amnesties in the context of non-international armed conflicts. However, this does not mean that Article 6(5) is entirely without merit: it stands as a rare example of acknowledgment, in treaty form, of what UN Secretary-General Kofi Annan stated in 2000: 'amnesty is an accepted legal concept and a gesture of peace and reconciliation at the end of a civil war or an internal armed conflict'[149] and '[c]arefully crafted amnesties can help in the return and reintegration of [opposing participants in armed conflict] and should be encouraged'.[150]

Non-Binding Instruments

The San Remo Manuals

Of the two San Remo Manuals—on naval warfare and non-international armed conflict—it is the manual on naval warfare that is, by far, the most successful. The *San Remo Manual on International Law Applicable to Armed Conflicts at Sea* (San Remo Naval Manual) has been hailed as having contributed 'in an invaluable manner to a clarification of the law application to naval warfare and maritime neutrality', with the 'vast majority of its provisions' being 'a contemporary

the UN Human Rights Committee are of the general opinion that amnesty can only be extended for war-like acts that are otherwise compliant with IHL obligations (that is, 'mere participation'). See ICRC CIHL Study, Rule 159 (n 128). See also the Inter-American Commission on Human Rights, *Parada Cea v El Salvador* (27 January 1999), Report No 1/99, Case 10,480, para 115; UN Human Rights Committee, 'Concluding Observations of the Human Rights Committee: Lebanon' (1 January 1997), UN Doc CCPR/C/79/Add.78, para 12; UN Human Rights Committee in its General Comment on Article 7 of the International Covenant on Civil and Political Rights. For the literature on amnesty, see generally Juan Carlos Portilla, 'Amnesty: Evolving 21st Century Constraints under International Law' (2014) 37 Fletcher Forum of World Affairs 169; Roderick O'Brien, 'Amnesty and International Law' (2005) 74 Nordic Journal of International Law 261; Andrew Reiter, 'Examining the Use of Amnesties and Pardons as a Response to Internal Armed Conflict' (2014) 47 Israel Law Review 133; Kieran McEvoy and Louise Mallinder, 'Amnesties in Transition: Punishment, Restoration, and the Governance of Mercy' (2012) 39 Journal of Law and Society 410; Mark Freeman, *Necessary Evils: Amnesties and the Search for Justice* (CUP 2009), specifically ch 4.

[148] *Azanian Peoples Organization (AZAPO) v President of the Republic of South Africa* (n 145) para 24.

[149] Report of the Secretary-General on the Establishment of a Special Court for Sierra Leone, UN Doc S/2000/915 (4 October 2000) para 22.

[150] The Rule of Law and Transitional Justice in Conflict and Post-Conflict Societies, Report of the Secretary-General, UN Doc S/2004/616 (23 August 2004) para 32.

restatement of customary international law'.[151] The San Remo Naval Manual has been referenced and cited as an 'authoritative commentary'[152] on the law of naval warfare in the case law of domestic courts, including in the United Kingdom[153] and Ireland.[154] The Manual has been given affirmative judicial attention in, or has otherwise been cited by States before, forums such as the Ethiopia-Eritrea Claims Commission,[155] the International Court of Justice (ICJ),[156] the ICC,[157] and the Permanent Court of Arbitration.[158] Additionally, the Manual has been affirmed and cited in the military manuals of a number of States[159] and has been cited in a

[151] Wolff Heintschel von Heinegg, 'The Current State of the Law of Naval Warfare: A Fresh Look at the San Remo Manual' (2006) 82 International Law Studies 269, 288. See also Steven Haines, 'War at Sea: Nineteenth-Century Laws for Twenty-First Century Wars?' (2016) 98 International Review of the Red Cross 419, 434–35.

[152] *Alseran v Ministry of Defence* [2017] EWHC 3289 (QB), [2019] QB 1251 [96].

[153] ibid.

[154] *Horgan v Ireland* [2003] IEHC 64, [2003] 2 IR 468.

[155] — *Federal Democratic Republic of Ethiopia and State of Eritrea (Ethiopia's Claim 6Ports)* [2005] ERETCC 10 (19 December 2005) 7, para 24; *State of Eritrea and Federal Democratic Republic of Ethiopia (Western Front, Aerial Bombardment and Related Claims)—Eritrea's Claims 1, 3, 5, 9–13, 14, 21, 25 & 26* [2005] ERETCC 2 (19 December 2005) 55.

[156] *Islamic Republic of Iran v United States of America (Oil Platforms)*, Rejoinder submitted by the United States of America (23 March 2001), 6.44–6.49; Counter-Memorial and Counter-Claim submitted by the United States of America (23 June 1997) 136; Reply and Defence to Counter-Claim submitted by the Islamic Republic of Iran (10 March 1999)—vol I, 151–53, 204–05; Further Response to the United States' Counter-Claim submitted by the Islamic Republic of Iran (24 September 2001)—vol I, 92, 95, 98, 102; *Islamic Republic of Iran v United States of America (Oil Platforms)*, Public sitting held on 26 February 2003, President Shi presiding—Verbatim record, 39.

[157] *Situation on the Registered Vessels of the Union of the Comoros, the Hellenic Republic and the Kingdom of Cambodia* (Pre-Trial Chamber I, No ICC-01/13, 23 June 2015) 41, 42, 45; Corrigendum of Annex, Partly Dissenting Opinion of Judge Péter Kovács, Pre-Trial Chamber [2015] IntCrimC 827, No ICC-01/13-34-Anx-Corr, 15–16; Public Redacted Version of Prosecution's Consolidated Response to the Observations of the Victims [2015] IntCrimC 781, No ICC-01/13-29-Red, 47; Referral of the 'Union of the Comoros' with respect to the 31 May 2010 Israeli raid on the Humanitarian Aid Flotilla bound for Gaza Strip, requesting the Prosecutor of the International Criminal Court pursuant to Articles 12, 13 and 14 of the Rome Statute to initiate an investigation into the crimes committed within the Court's jurisdiction, arising from this raid; Article 53(1) Report—Situation on Registered Vessels of Comoros, Greece and Cambodia (6 November 2014); Appendix B—Letter dated 30 September 2014 from Der Generalbundesanwalt Beim Bundesgerichtschof to Frau Inge Höger, MdB (unofficial translation of Letter into English), No ICC-01/13-45-AnxB (13-08-2015).

[158] *Federal Democratic Republic of Ethiopia v State of Eritrea (Ports)* [2005] PC Arb 2 (Eritrea Ethiopia Claims Commission, 19 December 2005).

[159] See, for example, Office of the Chief of Naval Operations, US Department of the Navy, *The Commander's Handbook on the Law of Naval Operations* (2007, Naval Warfare Publication No NWP 1-14M); UK Ministry of Defence, *The Manual of the Law of Armed Conflict* (OUP 2004) ch 13; *German Navy, Commander's Handbook—Kommandanten-Handbuch* (Bonn 2002), 19, 140; the Norwegian armed forces manual—*Manual i krigens folkerett* (2013), 99, 168, 198. The French military manual is slightly more circumspect, noting that 'Bien qu'elles soient incluses dans le recueil de "droit international régissant la conduite des hostilités" publié par le Comité International de la Croix-Rouge (CICR) en 1996, les dispositions du manuel de San Remo ne constituent pas encore à proprement parler des règles de droit positif: la note liminaire rédigée par le CICR précise d'ailleurs que si la plupart des dispositions figurant dans le manuel sont considérées comme énonçant le droit actuellement en vigueur, certaines peuvent apparaître comme de simples développements du droit. Il convient donc de rester prudent dans l'appréciation de la valeur de ce texte, et de comparer ses dispositions avec le droit antérieur.' ('Although included in the collection of "international law governing the conduct of hostilities" published by the International Committee of the Red Cross (ICRC) in 1996, the provisions of the

number of other international forums[160]—most recently, in relation to the *Mavi Marmara* incident. The Turkel Commission,[161] the Turkish National Commission of Inquiry,[162] and various UN bodies[163] all cite the significance of the San Remo Manual. For example, in the September 2011 Palmer Report, a key recommendation was that: '[a]ll States should act with prudence and caution in relation to the imposition and enforcement of a naval blockade. The established norms of customary international law must be respected and complied with by all relevant parties. The San Remo Manual provides a useful reference in identifying those rules.'[164]

The San Remo Naval Manual has also impacted on ICRC practice: the Manual is repeatedly referenced and cited in the updated Commentary to the Second Geneva Convention for the Amelioration of the Condition of Wounded, Sick and Shipwrecked Members of Armed Forces at Sea,[165] with the ICRC singling it out for 'special mention … [as] a valid restatement of customary and treaty international law applicable to armed conflicts at sea.'[166]

Moving now to the *San Remo Manual on Non-International Armed Conflicts*, the Manual has been praised as the work of 'three highly respected LOAC [law of armed conflict] scholars and practitioners and built on the *Tadic* foundation … [providing] a much more comprehensive analysis of the content of the

San Remo Handbook are not yet properly speaking positive rule of law: the ICRC's introductory note states that while most of the provisions contained in the manual are regarded as stating the law currently in force, some may appear as mere developments in law. It is therefore necessary to remain cautious in assessing the value of this text, and compare its provisions with the law prior'): Ministère de la Défense, *Manuel De Droit Des Conflits Armés* (2012) 42.

[160] United Nations Office for the Coordination of Humanitarian Affairs, 'Oxford Guidance on the Law Relating to Humanitarian Relief Operations in Situations of Armed Conflict' 36–37 <http://www.unocha.org/sites/dms/Documents/Oxford%20Guidance%20pdf.pdf> accessed 7 August 2021; Report of the Commission to the General Assembly on the work of its sixty-third session, Yearbook of the International Law Commission (2011) vol 2, part 2, UN Doc A/CN.4/SER.A/2011/Add.1 (Part 2), 213; International Law Commission, Sixty-seventh session at Geneva (4 May–5 June and 6 July–7 August 2015), 'Second Report on the Protection of the Environment in Relation to Armed Conflicts', submitted by Marie G Jacobsson, Special Rapporteur, UN Doc A/CN.4/685 (28 May 2015) 55–56.

[161] Turkel Commission, 'Public Commission to Examine the Maritime Incident of 31 May 2010' (January 2010), Report: Part 1, 42–45, 49, 59–60, 82–86, 90–91, 93–94, 103, 109, 110, 115 <http://www.gov.il/BlobFolder/generalpage/alternatefiles/he/turkel_eng_a_0.pdf> accessed 7 August 2021.

[162] Turkish National Commission of Inquiry, Report on the Israeli Attack on the Humanitarian Aid Convoy to Gaza on 31 May 2010 (February 2011) 7, 60–64, 68–69, 83–84, 87–88, 93, 95, 98, 100, 103 <http://www.mfa.gov.tr/data/Turkish%20Report%20Final%20-%20UN%20Copy.pdf> accessed 7 August 2021.

[163] Human Rights Council, Report of the international fact-finding mission to investigate violations of international law, including international humanitarian and human rights law, resulting from the Israeli attacks on the flotilla of ships carrying humanitarian assistance, UN Doc A/HRC/15/21 (27 September 2010) 9, 12–14; Geoffrey Palmer, Alvaro Uribe, Joseph Ciechanover Itzhar, and Süleyman Özdem Sanberk, Report of the Secretary-General's Panel of Inquiry on the 31 May 2010 Flotilla Incident (September 2011) 5, 15, 18, 22–23, 29–29, 34, 70–71, 73, 79–80, 81, 84–96 <https://unispal.un.org/pdfs/GazaFlotillaPanelReport.pdf> accessed 7 August 2021.

[164] Report of the Secretary-General's Panel of Inquiry on the 31 May 2010 Flotilla Incident (n 164) 5.

[165] ICRC, *Commentary on the Second Geneva Convention* (n 93).

[166] ibid 31–32.

law that regulates non-international armed conflicts'.[167] However, the impact of the NIAC Manual in practice has been notably subdued. The Manual was cited by lawyers in the UK case *R v Gul*,[168] and referred to in reports of the International Law Commission regarding the protection of the environment in relation to armed conflicts.[169] However, it is not mentioned in the publicly available military manuals, such as those of the United States, the United Kingdom, Canada, New Zealand, Germany, and Norway,[170] nor is it cited in the updated Commentary to Geneva Convention I.[171]

Montreux Document

In the 10 years since its adoption, the *Montreux Document on Pertinent International Legal Obligations and Good Practices for States related to Operations of Private Military and Security Companies during Armed Conflict* (Montreux Document) has been widely cited and referenced by States, intergovernmental organisations, and non-governmental organisations (NGOs), as well as by private entities. For example, the Document is cited in the German law of armed conflict manual,[172] as well as the New Zealand and Danish manuals.[173] It has been cited in State practice in and before UN bodies,[174] as well as by UN

[167] Geoffrey Corn and Eric Talbot Jensen, 'Transnational Armed Conflict: A "Principled" Approach to the Regulation of Counter-Terror Combat Operations' (2009) 42 Israel Law Review 46, 56.

[168] *R v Gul* [2012] 3 All ER 83 [30].

[169] International Law Commission, Sixty-seventh session at Geneva (4 May–5 June and 6 July–7 August 2015), 'Second report on the protection of the environment in relation to armed conflicts', submitted by Marie G Jacobsson, Special Rapporteur, UN Doc A/CN.4/685 (28 May 2015) 55, para 180; International Law Commission, Seventy-first session at Geneva (29 April–7 June 2019 and 8 July–9 August 2019), 'Second report on protection of the environment in relation to armed conflicts' prepared by Marja Lehto, Special Rapporteur, UN Doc A/CN.4/728 (27 March 2019) 75, para 167.

[170] See, for example, UK's *Manual of the Law of Armed Conflict* (n 159) ch 15 on Internal Armed Conflict; Canada's *Law of Armed Conflict at the Operational and Tactical Levels* (B-GJ-005-104/FP-021, 2003) ch 17; US Department of Defense's *Law of War Manual* (2015) ch XVII.

[171] ICRC, *Commentary on the First Geneva Convention: Convention (I) for the Amelioration of the Condition of the Wounded and Sick in Armed Forces in the Field* (CUP 2017).

[172] German Federal Ministry of Defence, *Law of Armed Conflict Manual* (Joint Service Regulation (ZDv) 15/2, DSK AV230100262, 2013) 19, paras 131, 46, and 334.

[173] New Zealand Defence Force/Te Ope Kaatua O Aotearoa, *Manual of Armed Forces Law*, vol 4: *Law of Armed Conflict* (DM 69, 2nd edn, 2017) 1–30, 6–25, 6–26; Danish Ministry of Defence, Defence Command Denmark, *Military Manual on International Law Relevant to Danish Armed Forces in International Operations* (2016) 120.

[174] See Note Verbale dated 7 June 2012 from the Permanent Mission of Switzerland to the United Nations addressed to the Secretary-General of the United Nations, 202/12 SXN/ULN; Letter dated 2 October 2009 from the Permanent Representative of Switzerland to the United Nations addressed to the Secretary-General—United Nations General Assembly Sixty-third session, Agenda item 76, Status of the Protocols Additional to the Geneva Conventions of 1949 and relating to the protection of victims of armed conflicts, A/63/467-S/2008/636 (6 October 2008); UN Committee on the Rights of the Child, Consideration of reports submitted by States parties under article 8 of the Optional Protocol to the Convention on the Rights of Child on involvement of children in armed conflict, Initial reports of States parties due in 2008—Slovakia—30 October 2009, UN Doc CRC/C/OPAC/SVK/1 (14 June 2011) para

bodies themselves,[175] the European Parliament,[176] the European Commission for Democracy through Law,[177] and the Permanent Council of the Organisation

105; UN Security Council, Meetings Coverage, 8456th Meeting, 'Better Control of Borders, Private Security Firms Key to Stopping "Guns for Hire", Speakers Say at Security Council Debate on Mercenary Activities in Africa', SC/13688 (4 February 2019); UNSC, Meetings Coverage, 6427th Meeting, 'In Presidential Statement, Security Council Reaffirms Commitment to Protection of Civilians in Armed Conflict, Adopts Updated Aide Memoire on Issue', SC/10089 (22 November 2010); Meetings Coverage, 6151st Meeting, 'Despite Progress, Civilians Continue to Bear Brunt of Conflict, Says Under-Secretary-General in Briefing to Security Council', SC/9692 (26 June 2009); Note Verbale from the Permanent Mission of Croatia to the United Nations, UN Doc A/71/225 (26 July 2016); Committee against Torture, List of issues in connection with the consideration of the fifth periodic report of the United Kingdom of Great Britain and Northern Ireland, adopted by the Committee at its Forty-ninth session (29 October–23 November 2012), UN Doc CAT/C/GBR/Q/5/Add.1 (2 May 2013); US, Summary record of the 15th meeting, UN GAOR, 6th Comm, UN Doc A/C.6/69/SR.15 (2 December 2014); Committee on the Rights of the Child, Slovakia—Consideration of reports submitted by States parties under Article 8(1) of the Optional Protocol to the Convention on the Rights of the Child on the Involvement of Children in Armed Conflict: Initial reports of States parties due in 2008, UN Doc CRC/C/OPAC/SVK/1 (14 June 2011); Mexico—UN Doc S/PV.6151 (26 June 2009); Comments by Poland, France, Germany, UK, South Africa—Security Council, UN Doc S/PV.8456 (4 February 2019).

[175] See, inter alia, Human Rights Council, Report of the Open-Ended Intergovernmental Working Group to Consider the Possibility of Elaborating an International Regulatory Framework on the Regulation, Monitoring and Oversight of the Activities of Private Military and Security Companies on its Second Session, Twenty-second session, Agenda item 3, UN Doc A/HRC/22/41 (24 December 2012); Human Rights Council, Report of Open-Ended Intergovernmental Working Group to Consider the Possibility of Elaborating an International Regulatory Framework on the Regulation, Monitoring and Oversight of the Activities of Private Military and Security Companies on its Fourth Session, Thirtieth session, Agenda item 3, UN Doc A/HRC/30/47 (9 July 2015); Human Rights Council, 'Promotion and Protection of all Human Rights, Civil, Political, Economic, Social and Cultural Rights, including the Right to Development—Report of the Working Group on the Use of Mercenaries as a Means of Violating Human Rights and Impeding the Exercise of the Right of peoples to Self-Determination, Tenth session, Agenda item 3, UN Doc A/HRC/10/14 (21 January 2009); Human Rights Council, Report of the Working Group on the Use of Mercenaries as a Means of Violating Human Rights and Impeding the Exercise of the Right of Peoples to Self-determination', Fifteenth session, Agenda item 3, UN Doc A/HRC/15/25 (5 July 2010); International Law Commission, Seventy-first session at Geneva (29 April–7 June 2019 and 8 July–9 August 2019), 'Second Report on Protection of the Environment in Relation to Armed Conflicts' prepared by Marja Lehto, Special Rapporteur, UN Doc A/CN.4/728 (27 March 2019); United Nations Office on Drugs and Crime (UNODC), State Regulation concerning Civilian Private Security Services and their Contribution to Crime Prevention and Security Safety (2014), 83–84. There have also been numerous discussions of the Montreux Document in the Third and Sixth Committees. See, for example, Meetings Coverage, Sixty-sixth General Assembly, 37th and 38th Meetings, 'Flouting International Law, Racism Pervades All Countries, Third Committee Hears at Start of Debate', GA/SHC/4115 (3 November 2014); Meetings Coverage, Sixty-fifth session, thirteenth and fourteenth meetings, 'Responsibility of States to Ensure Protection of Diplomatic Personnel, Premises Is Reviewed by Assembly's Legal Committee', GA/L/3394 (18 October 2010).

[176] European Parliament, European Parliament Resolution of 21 January 2016 on Estonian and UK Seamen under Detention in India (2016/2522(RSP)), P8_TA(2016)0022, para 6; European Parliament, European Parliament Resolution of 8 October 2013 on Corruption in the Public and Private Sectors: The Impact on Human Rights in Third Countries (2013/2074(INI)), P7_TA(2013)0394, Preamble, para 44; European Parliament, Joint Answer given by High Representative/Vice-President Ashton on behalf of the Commission, 2 August 2012, Official Journal of the European Union, C 262 E/131, 11.9.2013; Committee of Foreign Affairs, Draft Report on Human Rights Concerns in Private Military and Security Companies' Operations Affecting Third Countries (Draft Report, European Parliament, 17 July 2018).

[177] Report on Private Military and Security Firms and Erosion of the State Monopoly on the Use of Force, adopted by the Venice Commission at its 79th Plenary Session (Venice, 12–13 March 2009) on

of American States,[178] as well as in official US,[179] UK,[180] Canadian,[181] and Australian[182] governmental and parliamentary documentation.

However, actual implementation of the Montreux Document in State practice has been slow. The 'Montreux Five Years On' report,[183] undertaken in 2013, was the first study to examine, in detail, whether the provisions of the Document had been taken up in practice by States involved with private military and security companies (PMSCs), as either Contracting States, Home States, or Territorial States.[184] The report looked at the practice of the United States, the United Kingdom, Iraq, and Afghanistan. Among its findings was that while the United States was taking numerous positive steps in implementing many of Montreux's 'Good Practices for Contracting States',[185] the United Kingdom was falling behind on licensing,

the basis of comments by Mr Iain Cameron (Member, Sweden), Study No 531/2009 (29 June 2009), 3, 5–8, 12–14, 19; Venice Commission, *Annual Activity Report 2009* (2010) 40–41.

[178] Committee on Juridical and Political Affairs, Special Meeting on International Humanitarian Law (Final Report, Permanent Council of the Organization of American States, 25 March 2009).

[179] Including that the Afghan Public Protection Force 'adhere to the Afghan Public Protection Force Code of Conduct and applicable international standards, such as the Montreux Document, and the International Code of Conduct for private security service providers', outlined in Section 1535, Subtitle C (c)(3)(iii), National Defense Authorization Act for Fiscal Year 2013, 112 HR 4310, 2012 HR 4310, 112 HR 4310. See also Moshe Schwartz, 'The Department of Defense's Use of Private Security Contractors in Iraq and Afghanistan: Background, Analysis, and Options for Congress' (Congressional Research Service Report No R40835, 21 February 2011); Jennifer K Elsea, Private Security Contractors in Iraq and Afghanistan: Legal Issues (Congressional Research Service Report No R40991, 7 January 2010).

[180] See Letter from Secretary of State, Ministry of Defence to Rt Hon James Arbuthnot MP, on the MoD's Approach towards Private Security Companies (12 May 2014) <http://www.parliament.uk/documents/commons-committees/defence/140512-SoS-to-Chair-re-Private-Security-Companies.pdf> accessed 7 August 2021; UK Parliament, House of Lords, HL Deb 30 October 2012, vol 740, col 495 <https://publications.parliament.uk/pa/ld201213/ldhansrd/text/121030-0001.htm> accessed 7 August 2021.

[181] Oral Questions (6 May 2009): response of Peter MacKay, Minister of National Defence and Minister of the Atlantic Gateway, 40th Parliament, 2nd Session, Hansard, vol 144, no 052; Oral Questions (7 February 2011): response of Lawrence Cannon, Minister for Foreign Affairs, Hansard, vol 145, no 125, 3rd Session, 40th Parliament; Oral Questions (9 February 2011): responses of Lawrence Cannon, Minister for Foreign Affairs, Hansard, vol 145, no 127, 3rd Session, 40th Parliament.

[182] Australian Parliamentary Debates, Senate, Foreign Affairs, Defence and Trade Legislation Committee, 'Estimates', (Supplementary Budget Estimates) (18 October 2010) <https://parlinfo.aph.gov.au/parlInfo/download/committees/estimate/13304/toc_pdf/7774-4.pdf;fileType = application%2Fpdf#search=%22committees/estimate/13304/0001%22> accessed 7 August 2021.

[183] Rebecca DeWinter-Schmitt (ed), *Montreux Five Years On: An Analysis of State Efforts to Implement Montreux Document Legal Obligations and Good Practices* (International Institute of Non-violent Action (NOVACT)/The Center for Human Rights and Humanitarian Law/International Coalition Control PMSC 2013) <https://novact.org/wp-content/uploads/2013/12/MontreuxFinal.pdf> accessed 7 August 2021.

[184] As noted in the Preface to the Montreux Document, in paras 9(c)–(e), '"Contracting States" are States that directly contract for the services of PMSCs, including, as appropriate, where such a PMSC subcontracts with another PMSC ... "Territorial States" are States on whose territory PMSCs operate ... "Home States" are States of nationality of a PMSC, i.e. where a PMSC is registered or incorporated; if the State where the PMSC is incorporated is not the one where it has its principal place of management, then the State where the PMSC has its principal place of management is the "Home State"'.

[185] DeWinter-Schmitt (n 183) 8–9.

monitoring, accountability, and remedies regarding PMSCs.[186] Likewise, the practices of Iraq and Afghanistan were falling well short of Montreux best practice.[187] These conclusions were confirmed during the Montreux + 5 Conference, held in 2013 as a review of the first five years of the Document.[188]

As a result of reviews of the Document, the Montreux Document Forum (MDF) was established in 2014. The Forum is designed to: 'support national implementation of the Montreux Document, as well as to bring more states and international organisations to actively support it. The MDF further aims to strengthen dialogue on lessons learned, good practices and challenges related to the regulation of PMSCs.'[189]

The MDF produced a study in 2017 which suggested that the Montreux Document is indeed having a positive impact on the regulation of PMSCs.[190] For example, the study notes:

> most MD participants have passed relatively recent laws to address the industry. About 60% of MD states have passed one or more new bills to regulate PMSCs since the year 2000. Other states have added amendments to preexisting military or defence law. Only 27% of MD states have national legislation for PMSCs that pre-dates 2000, which indicates that these states have adapted older laws to fit new contexts, or perhaps that these states have fit the regulation of PMSCs under the umbrella of a pre-existing framework.[191]

The study also found that 32 of the 54 (at that time) Montreux States had implemented distinction and identification requirements for PMSC personnel and transport;[192] 29 Montreux States had established firearms and weapons licensing and registration systems;[193] 32 Montreux States required a use of force policy and weapons training for PMSCs and personnel, and placed restrictions on the weapons that may be carried on duty;[194] 19 Montreux States had implemented specific provisions for the monitoring of PMSC compliance with legislation, licences,

[186] ibid 9.

[187] ibid 10–11.

[188] <https://www.eda.admin.ch/dam/eda/en/documents/aussenpolitik/voelkerrecht/Chairs-Conclusions-montreux-final_en.pdf> accessed 10 November 2021.

[189] <https://www.montreuxdocument.org/about/the-forum.html > accessed 10 November 2021.

[190] Geneva Centre for the Democratic Control of Armed Forces, *The Montreux Document: A Mapping Study on Outreach and Implementation* (DCAF/Swiss Confederation 2017) <http://www.mdforum.ch/pdf/mapping-study.pdf> accessed 7 August 2021. See also Benjamin S Buckland and Anna Marie Burdz, *Progress and Opportunities: Challenges and Recommendations for Montreux Document Participants* (2nd edn, Geneva Centre for the Democratic Control of Armed Forces 2015) <http://www.mdforum.ch/pdf/Progress-and-Opportunities-Challenges-and-Recommendations-for-Montreux-Document-Participants-2nd-edition.pdf>.

[191] ibid The Montreux Document 12.

[192] ibid.

[193] ibid 13.

[194] ibid.

or regulations by a regulatory national regulatory body; and 32 Montreux States had implemented 'legislation containing clear provisions for cancelling contract or removing a [PMSC's] licence/registration to operate under specific terms of misconduct'.[195] The study also noted that many of Montreux's good practice recommendations had been integrated into the practice of non-Montreux States and organisations, such as the United Nations and the Economic Community of West African States.[196] Considerable parts of the Montreux Document have also been incorporated into the practice of private entities: ASIS International, one of the world's largest peak bodies for security professionals, has incorporated the Montreux Document into its management system standards.[197]

The Montreux Document, though initially hampered by slow uptake, now seems to be having a tangible impact on the practice of States in their dealings with PMSCs. This conclusion is further affirmed when one looks at the practice of PMSCs themselves, and the engagement with the International Code of Conduct for Private Security Providers. The text of the ICoC was officially adopted on 9 November 2010, with 58 private security companies[198] signing up to the Code.[199] By 2013, over 700 companies had signed up.[200] However, as noted in Chapter 5, shortcomings in oversight and monitoring mechanisms in the Code meant that a signature did not always equal compliance. The creation of the International Code of Conduct Association (ICoCA)—the monitoring body for the ICoC—seems to have gone some way to addressing the problems of monitoring and compliance. As of this writing, seven States,[201] 97 PMSCs, and 40 civil society organisations[202] are members of ICoCA, with the PMSCs operating in more than 90 States and headquartered in 34 States.[203] Membership of the ICoCA means that the organisation is certified by the ICoCA and submits to ongoing independent monitoring, auditing, and verification, including regular self-reporting.[204] Members of the ICoCA must re-certify every three years to maintain membership.[205]

195 ibid.

196 ibid 22.

197 PSC.1-2012 and PSC.4-2013; Private Security Monitor, 'ANSI/ASIS International Standards' (University of Denver, Sié Chéou-Kang Center for International Security & Diplomacy) <http://psm.du.edu/international_regulation/global_standards_codes_of_conduct/asis_standard.html> accessed 7 August 2021.

198 The companies are listed in David Wallace, 'International Code of Conduct for Private Security Service Providers' (2011) 50 International Legal Materials 89, 103–04.

199 See further 'The International Code of Conduct for Private Security Service Providers' (Geneva Academy of International Humanitarian Law and Human Rights Academy Briefing No 4, August 2013) <http://www.geneva-academy.ch/joomlatools-files/docman-files/Publications/Academy%20Briefings/Icoc_web_final.pdf> accessed 10 November 2021.

200 <www.icoca.ch/en> accessed 7 August 2021. See also <http://www.admin.ch/gov/en/start/dokumentation/medienmitteilungen.msg-id-47889.html> accessed 7 August 2021.

201 Australia, Canada, Norway, Sweden, Switzerland, the United Kingdom, and the United States.

202 See <https://icoca.ch/en/membership> accessed 7 August 2021.

203 ICoCA, *Annual Report 2017–2018*, 2 < https://icoca.ch/wp-content/uploads/2018/12/Annual-Report-2017-2018_0.pdf> accessed 7 August 2021.

204 < https://icoca.ch/what-we-do/> accessed 27 September 2021.

205 ibid.

Member numbers would seem to suggest that the ICoC is having an impact on promoting compliance and monitoring. The ICoCA had 88 industry members in 2014,[206] rising to 98 in 2016[207] and 101 in 2017.[208] Numbers dropped to 92 in 2018,[209] but rose again in 2019, to 97, reaching 100 in 2020.[210] In addition, the ICoC has been cited in UN bodies,[211] in UN practice,[212] and in the practice of States.[213] For example, in an appearance before the International Maritime Organization, Singapore and the Philippines cited the Code as part of their call for the need for guidance regarding the use of PMSCs in anti-piracy operations.[214]

The Air and Missile Warfare Manual

The *HPCR Manual on International Law Applicable to Air and Missile Warfare* (AMW Manual) has achieved some impact on State practice. The Manual

[206] ICoCA, *Annual Report 2013–2014* (2014) 4 (can be requested from the ICoCA Secretariat).

[207] ICoCA, *Annual Report 2015–2016* (2016) 5 (can be requested from the ICoCA Secretariat).

[208] ICoCA, *Annual Report 2016–2017* (2017) 6, (can be requested from the ICoCA Secretariat).

[209] ICoCA, *Annual Report 2017–2018* (2018) 5 <https://icoca.ch/?s = annual+report> accessed 27 September 2021.

[210] See <https://icoca.ch/en/membership> accessed 7 August 2021.

[211] Human Rights Council, 'Summary of the third session of the Open-ended Intergovernmental Working Group to Consider the Possibility of Elaborating an International Regulatory Framework on the Regulation, Monitoring and Oversight of the Activities of Private Military and Security', Third session, Geneva, 21–25 July 2014, UN Doc A/HRC/WG.10/3/2 (2 September 2014); Human Rights Council, Report of the Open-ended Intergovernmental Working Group to Consider the Possibility of Elaborating an International Regulatory Framework on the Regulation, Monitoring and Oversight of the Activities of Private Military and Security, Twenty-second session, Agenda item 3, UN Doc A/HRC/22/41 (24 December 2014); Human Rights Council, 'Summary of the first session of the Open-Ended Intergovernmental Working Group to Consider the Possibility of Elaborating an International Regulatory Framework on the Regulation, Monitoring and Oversight of the Activities of Private Military and Security Companies', First session, Geneva, 23–27 May 2011, UN Doc A/HRC/WG.10/1/4 (22 November 2011); Human Rights Council, Report of the Open-Ended Intergovernmental Working Group to Consider the Possibility of Elaborating an International Regulatory Framework on the Regulation, Monitoring and Oversight of the Activities of Private Military and Security Companies, Thirtieth session, Agenda item 3, UN Doc A/HRC/30/47 (9 July 2015); International Law Commission, Sixty-seventh session (second part), Provision summary record of the 3275th meeting, UN Doc A/CN.4/SR.3275 (22 September 2015); UN Security Council, 'Better Control of Borders, Private Security Firms Key to Stopping "Guns for Hire", Speakers Say at Security Council Debate on Mercenary Activities in Africa', Meetings Coverage, 8456th meeting, SC/13688 (4 February 2019) (comments by France).

[212] United Nations Department of Safety and Security, *United Nations Security Management System—Security Policy Manual* (2011) 95; Human Rights Council, Report of the Working Group on the Use of Mercenaries as a Means of Violating Human Rights and Impeding the Exercise of The right of Peoples to Self-determination: Mission to Ghana (8 to 15 December 2017), 39th session, Agenda item 3, UN Doc A/HRC/39/49/Add.1 (7 December 2018).

[213] Note Verbale dated 26 October 2016 from the Permanent Mission of the United States of America to the United Nations addressed to the President of the General Assembly, 71st session, UN Doc A/71/585 (31 October 2016); Consideration of reports submitted by States parties under article 40 of the International Covenant on Civil and Political Rights, UN Doc CCPR/C/USA/4 (30 December 2011).

[214] International Maritime Organization, Maritime Safety Committee 89th Session, Agenda item 18, 'Piracy and Armed Robbery against Ships: Development of guidance for the Industry on the Employment of Private Armed Security Service Providers to deter and Counter Piracy Against Ships',

is mentioned in several State military manuals, including the US *Law of War Manual*.[215] New Zealand,[216] Denmark,[217] and Switzerland[218] all cite the Manual in their own manuals of military instruction, as does the French military manual, which references the Air and Missile Warfare (AMW) Manual as a 'documentary source'[219] for the law of armed conflict (but affirms its non-binding nature). The German manual on the law of armed conflict also cites the AMW Manual,[220] but makes it clear that, when examining such manuals, 'it should not be assumed that their contents automatically coincide with the positions of the German Government and/or the Federal Ministry of Defence'.[221] The Manual has also been cited in UN bodies, such as the Human Rights Council[222] and the International Law Commission.[223] The Manual was also cited in the US

submitted by the Philippines, Singapore, Baltic and International Maritime Council (BIMCO) and International Chamber of Shipping (ICS), MSC/89/18/5 (8 March 2011).

215 US *Law of War Manual* (n 170) 933, n 103; 1021, n 52.

216 New Zealand *Manual of Armed Forces Law*, vol 4 (n 173) 8-4, 8-7, 8-8, 8-9, 8-16, 8-17, 8-22, 10-4, 10-5, 10-7, 10-8, 10-11, 10-14, 10-17, 10-19, 10-24, 10-25, 10-28, 10-29, 10-30, 10-32.

217 Danish Ministry of Defence, Defence Command Denmark, *Military Manual on International Law Relevant to Danish Armed Forces in International Operations* (2016) 486, 545 (where it is stated: 'To a great extent, reference is made to the HPCR Manual on International Law Applicable to Air and Missile Warfare (AMW Manual) for inspiration even though the document as such is not legally binding and has not been adopted by States').

218 Confédération Suisse, Swiss Armed Forces, *Law of Air and Missile Warfare: Instructor's Manual*. As noted on page 6, the instructor's manual 'is a follow-on product [to the AMW], which aims to provide military instructors with practical guidance as to the translation of the HPCR's AMW Manual and the accompanying Commentary into a course curriculum with case studies and exercises tailored to the specific needs of the armed forces, units or individuals in question'.

219 'Un groupe d'expert dirigés par l'université d'Harvard a tenté de codifier le droit des operations aériennes, suivant l'exemple du manuel de San Remo codifiant le droit des opérations maritimes. Cet effort a abouti à la publication d'un manuel, appelé Manuel HPCR (Humanitarian Policy and Conflict Research) du droit applicable à la guerre aérienne et à l'utilisation des missiles, qui regroupe l'ensemble des règles coutumières applicables à ce domaine. Bien que ce document n'ait pas de valeur juridique contraignante, il offre un panorama du droit applicable et constitue une source documentaire' ('A group of experts led by Harvard University tried to codify the law of operations following the example of the San Remo manual codifying the law of maritime operations. This effort resulted in the publication of a manual, called HPCR Manual (Humanitarian Policy and Conflict Research) of the law applicable to air warfare and the use of missiles, which includes all customary rules applicable to this area. Although this document has no legal value it offers a panorama of the applicable law and constitutes a documentary source': French military manual 41–42, unofficial translation).

220 German Federal Ministry of Defence (n 172) 20, para 131; 159, n 1.

221 ibid 20, para 131.

222 Human Rights Council, Promotion and Protection of all Human Rights, Civil, Political, Economic, Social and Cultural Rights, including the Right to Development—Report of the Special Rapporteur on Extrajudicial, Summary, or Arbitrary Executions, Philip Alston, Agenda item 3, Addendum, UN Doc A/HRC/14/24/Add.6 (28 May 2010) 10; Human Rights Council, Human Rights Situation in Palestine and Other Occupied Arab Territories—Report of the Detailed Findings of the Independent Commission of Inquiry Established Pursuant to Human Rights Council Resolution, Twenty-ninth session, Agenda items 7, S-21/1, UN Doc A/HRC/29/CRP.4 (24 June 2015) 103.

223 International Law Commission, Report of the Commission to the General Assembly on the Work of its Sixty-third Session, Yearbook of the International Law Commission (2011) vol 2, part 2, UN Doc A/CN.4/SER.A/2011/Add.1 (Part 2) 213; International Law Commission, Report of the International Law Commission, Sixty-third session (26 April–3 June and 4 July–12 August 2011), Supplement No 10

case *Flores*, in which the court employed the Manual to help define the word 'missile'.[224]

The Copenhagen Process and Principles

There is some indication that the *Copenhagen Process Principles and Guidelines on the Handling of Detainees in International Military Operations* (Copenhagen Principles) are gaining traction in State practice. The Principles have been cited a number of times in UN bodies,[225] and by States before UN bodies,[226] and were referred to repeatedly by States during regional discussions with the ICRC on its 2013 report on 'Strengthening International Humanitarian Law Protecting Persons Deprived of their Liberty'.[227] The Principles have also been cited in cases including *Al-Jedda*,[228] *Mohammed*,[229] and *Al-Waheed*[230] (though the non-binding nature of

(A/66/10) 360; International Law Commission, 'Second Report on the Protection of the Environment in Relation to Armed Conflicts', submitted by Marie G Jacobsson, Special Rapporteur, Sixty-seventh session at Geneva (4 May–5 June and 6 July–7 August 2015), UN Doc A/CN.4/685 (28 May 2015) 55, 58–60.

[224] 'International law definitions of the term "missile" are similar to those discussed above. The United Nations 2002 Report on "The Issue of Missiles in All Its Aspects" defines a missile as "an unmanned, self-propelled, self-contained, unrecallable, guided or unguided vehicle designed to deliver a weapon or other payload." U.N. Secretary-General, The issue of missiles in all its aspects, ¶ 19, U.N. Doc. A/57/229 (July 23, 2002). Harvard University's Humanitarian Policy and Conflict Research Program's "Manual on International Law Applicable to Air and Missile Warfare" defines a missile as a "self-propelled unmanned weapon—launched from aircraft, warships or land-based launchers—that [is] either guided or ballistic." Program on Humanitarian Policy and Conflict Research at Harvard University, Manual on International Law Applicable to Air and Missile Warfare, 5–6 (2009), <http://ihlresearch.org/amw/HPCRManual.pdf>. In sum, every modern military definition of missile we have encountered includes a self-propulsion requirement. Many definitions also suggest that missiles have guidance systems. We therefore hold that the definition of a missile, under U.S.S.G. § 2K2.1(b)(3)(A) and 26 U.S.C. § 5845(f), is a self-propelled device designed to deliver an explosive. We leave the question of whether the definition of a missile under U.S.S.G. § 2K2.1(b)(3)(A) and 26 U.S.C. § 5845(f) should also include a guidance requirement for another day.' *US v Flores* 729 F 3d 910 (9th Cir 2013).

[225] Secretary-General, Torture and other Cruel, Inhuman or Degrading Treatment or Punishment, 70th session, UN Doc A/70/303 (7 August 2015).

[226] Australian Permanent Mission to the UN Geneva, Views of the Australian Government on Preliminary Draft Principles and Guidelines on Remedies and Procedures of Anyone Deprived of His Liberty to Bring Proceedings Before a Court, in Order that the Court May Decide the Lawfulness of Detention (Note No 658/2014, 1 October 2014); Permanent Mission of the United States of America to Geneva (Diplomatic Notes No 041-15, 21 April 2015); United Kingdom and Australia, Summary record of the 14th meeting, UN GAOR, 6th Comm, 69th session, UN Doc A/C.6/69/SR.14 (10 December 2014).

[227] ICRC, Strengthening International Humanitarian Law Protecting Persons Deprived of Their Liberty: Synthesis Report from Regional Consultations of Government Experts (ICRC 2013) 17, 19–20, 24, 26 <http://www.icrc.org/en/doc/assets/files/2013/strengthening-protection-detention-consultations-synthesis-2013-icrc.pdf> accessed 8 August 2021.

[228] *Al-Jedda v UK* (2011) 53 EHRR 23 [58].

[229] *Mohammed v Ministry of Defence* [2014] EWHC 1369 (QB) [262].

[230] 'For reasons already given, I consider that this guidance is equally relevant in relation to the NIAC in which United Kingdom forces were engaged and in the context of which SM was captured and detained. In October 2012, a wide range of 24 states together with international organisations including

the Principles was noted), as well as in State practice. For instance, in 2015, the Australian government specifically acknowledged the Copenhagen Principles in its comments on the UN Working Group on Arbitrary Detention's Draft Principles and Guidelines on Remedies and Procedures of Anyone Deprived of His or Her Liberty to Bring Proceedings Before a Court.[231] The Copenhagen Principles were also affirmed by New Zealand during the Operation Burnham Inquiry.[232] The Principles are referred to repeatedly in the US Law of War Manual,[233] as well as the US Digest of United States Practice in International Law[234] and the Rule of Law Handbook for Judge Advocates.[235]

The Tallinn Manuals

Since the adoption of Tallinn 1.0 and 2.0, the Manuals have been acknowledged to some degree in State practice. The Australian government noted that the Tallinn Manuals are 'an important academic contribution to international legal dialogue in this area'.[236] The Manuals have been referenced in State practice, such as in statements by US government officials,[237] as well as in the New

the UN, NATO, the African Union, the European Union, and the ICRC agreed on the Copenhagen Principles. These were specifically intended to reflect "generally accepted standards" (Commentary, para 16.2) applicable "to international military operations in the context of non-international armed conflicts and peace operations" (Introductory para IX). Principle and Guideline 12 reads: "A detainee whose liberty has been deprived for security reasons is to, in addition to a prompt initial review, have the decision to detain reconsidered periodically by an impartial and objective authority that is authorised to determine the lawfulness and appropriateness of continued detention." This is both consistent with and supports the application to detention in the course of a NIAC of principles similar to those recognised in *Hassan* as appropriate in relation to an IAC.' *Al-Waheed v Ministry of Defence; Mohammed v Ministry of Defence* [2017] UKSC 2 [206].

[231] Note 23/2015 <http://www.ohchr.org/Documents/Issues/Detention/DraftBasicPrinciples/March2015/Australia.pdf> accessed 8 August 2021.

[232] Operation Burnham Inquiry, Overview of engagement with partners in Afghanistan on detention issues—Heath Fisher, Ministry of Foreign Affairs and Trade Divisional Manager, International Security and Disarmament Division, Operation Burnham Inquiry, Module Two: Detention, 4–5 <https://operationburnham.inquiry.govt.nz/assets/IOB-Files/23-May-2019-Module-2-Presentation-MFAT-Detention.pdf?SubsiteID = 1> accessed 8 August 2021.

[233] US *Law of War Manual* (n 170), in the section on the treatment of detainees, at 510, 513–14, 516–18, 521–22, 524–28.

[234] US Department of State, *Digest of United States Practice in International Law* (2009–17) ch 18, 605–06.

[235] Judge Advocate General's Legal Center & School, US Army Center for Law and Military Operations, *Rule of Law Handbook: A Practitioner's Guide for Judge Advocates* (2015) 20–21.

[236] Commonwealth of Australia, Department of Foreign Affairs and Trade, Australia's International Cyber Engagement Strategy, October 2017 <https://www.internationalcybertech.gov.au/sites/default/files/2021-04/21045%20DFAT%20Cyber%20Affairs%20Strategy%20Internals_Acc_update_1_0.pdf>accessed 27 September 2021.

[237] See comments by Homeland Security adviser Tom Bossert during an official press briefing at the White House on 11 May 2017, in which he stated that, in making a determination about the character of a cyber-attack: 'There's a whole lot that we'll talk about in terms of what constitutes a cyberattack, what's

Zealand,[238] German,[239] and Danish military manuals.[240] They have also been cited in the United Nations, the International Law Commission,[241] and the United Nations Office for Disarmament Affairs.[242] They have also been cited before the courts in a number of US jurisdictions, primarily in relation to domestic criminal cyber offences.[243] However, one case relating to international law—*Blumstein v Biden*[244]—drew on the Tallinn Manual's formulation of the rule of sovereignty over cyberspace as part of the argument that the US had failed to protect itself from cyber-incursion during the 2016 election.[245] In that instance, the Supreme Court, in hearing an emergency writ for a plea of mandamus, noted that:

> [w]hile Petitioners were not able to identify precedent in support of its 'novel constitutional claim', Petitioners did provide fact-based evidence from cyber experts confirming a State's right to control its cyber infrastructure and the cyber activities within its cyber territory.... The Tallinn manual sets forth non-binding standards governing a nation-state's sovereignty and right to exercise jurisdiction and control over its cyberspace. It states: Although no state may claim sovereignty over cyberspace per se, states may exercise sovereign prerogatives over any cyber infrastructure located on their territory, as well as activities associated with that cyber infrastructure.[246]

war and what's not war. The Tallinn Manual and other things are important.' < https://trumpwhitehouse.archives.gov/briefings-statements/press-briefing-principal-deputy-press-secretary-sarah-sanders-homeland-security-advisor-tom-bossert-051117/>.

[238] New Zealand *Manual of Armed Forces Law*, vol 4 (n 173) 5-8, 5-10, 6-22, 6-23, 8-4, 8-32, 8-38, 8-39, 8-40.

[239] German Federal Ministry of Defence (n 172) 20, 74.

[240] Danish *Military Manual* (n 217) 97, 120, 287, 363, 424, 703.

[241] International Law Commission, Sixty-seventh session at Geneva (4 May–5 June and 6 July–7 August 2015), 'Second Report on the Protection of the Environment in relation to Armed Conflicts', submitted by Marie G Jacobsson, Special Rapporteur, UN Doc A/CN.4/685 (28 May 2015) 61; International Law Commission, Sixty-seventh session (second part), Provisional summary record of the 3266th meeting, Held at the Palais des Nations, Geneva, on Wednesday, 8 July 2015, at 10 a.m. (30 May 2016), UN Doc A/CN.4/SR.3266, 55; International Law Commission, Sixty-seventh session (second part), Provisional summary record of the 3268th meeting, Held at the Palais des Nations, Geneva, on Friday, 10 July 2015, at 10 a.m. (11 May 2016), UN Doc A/CN.4/SR.3268, 9.

[242] United Nations Office for Disarmament Affairs, Civil Society and Disarmament 2017, Voluntary, Non-Binding Norms for Responsible State Behaviour in the Use of Information and Communications Technology: A Commentary (2017) <http://www.un.org/disarmament/publications/civilsociety/civil-society-and-disarmament-2017/> accessed 8 August 2021.

[243] In appellate briefs in *US v Darby* No 17-4212 (4th Cir 2018); *US v Eure* No 17-4167 (4th Cir 2017); *US v Tippens* No 17-30117 (9th Cir 2019); *US v Werdene* No 16-3588 (3rd Cir 2018); *US v McLamb* No 17-4299 (4th Cir 2018).

[244] US Supreme Court, No 16-907, Emergency Petition for Writ of Mandamus, filed 18 January 2017.

[245] ibid 6.

[246] ibid, mandamus denied, 20 March 2017.

Geneva Call's Deeds of Commitment

The four Deeds of Commitment (DoCs) have had varying degrees of success in implementation. Most successful has been the DoC with regards to anti-personnel mines. A report by Geneva Call on the first seven years of operation of the DoC for landmines[247] noted that after signing the DoC on landmines, non-State armed groups almost universally began to engage with demining and mine disposal activities. For example, in Western Sahara, following the signing of the DoC by the Polisario Front, 'the British NGO Landmine Action, with the support of UNMAS [United Nations Mine Action Service], started a technical survey and Explosive Ordnance Disposal (EOD) project in the areas controlled by this signatory group'.[248] By 2007, Geneva Call noted that of the then-34 signatories to the Mine DoC:

> 16 signatories have established mine action coordination structures or appointed focal persons to follow up on the implementation of the *Deed of Commitment*. 14 signatories have reportedly carried out mine clearance and related operations (mapping, marking and surveying) and/or cooperated with international and local specialized organizations in that respect. In many cases, the action was limited and consisted of *ad hoc* marking, EOD and removal of mines.
>
> ... nearly all signatories (29) have complied with their obligation to cooperate in the monitoring of their pledge.
>
> 29 signatory NSAs have provided information and reports to Geneva Call on measures they have taken to implement the *Deed of Commitment*.[249]

Non-State engagement with DoCs has influenced not only non-State behaviour, but also State behaviour. There is evidence to suggest that the signing of the landmines DoC by the Sudan People's Liberation Movement/Army (SPLM/A) in October 2001[250] was pivotal in prompting Sudan to sign and ratify the Ottawa Convention in 2003.[251] The timing of the acts by the SPLM/A and the Sudanese government is

[247] Geneva Call, *Engaging Armed Non-State Actors in a Landmine Ban: The Geneva Call Progress Report 2000–2007* <http://www.genevacall.org/wp-content/uploads/2019/02/gc-progress-report-07.pdf> accessed 8 August 2021.

[248] ibid 9.

[249] ibid 16, 18.

[250] See <http://www.genevacall.org/country-page/sudan/> accessed 8 August 2021.

[251] For a full listing of signatories and dates of signing/ratification, see <http://www.icrc.org/applic/ihl/ihl.nsf/States.xsp?xp_viewStates = XPages_NORMStatesParties&xp_treatySelected = 580> accessed 8 August 2021. Indeed, within a year of the SPLM/A signing the DoC, the government of Sudan was negotiating and adopting a memorandum of understanding with the SPML/A and the United Nations, with the aim of reducing mine and unexploded ordnance injuries in Sudan, and working towards the development of a jointly agreed upon Mine Action Plan. See further the Memorandum of Understanding between the Government of Sudan, the Sudan People's Liberation Movement and the United Nations Regarding United Nations Mine Action Support to Sudan, 19 September 2002 <http://

noteworthy; despite the SPLM/A in 1996 declaring its intention to demine areas within its control,[252] the Sudanese government had not signed the Ottawa Treaty prior to Geneva Call engaging with the SPLM/A and the SPLM/A signing the DoC. As noted in 2005 by Martin Barber, the Director of the UN Mine Action Service, 'it is clear from conversations with senior officials of the Government [in Sudan], that they would not have felt able to ratify the [Ottawa] Treaty, if the SPLM/A had not already made a formal commitment to observe its provisions in the territory under its control'.[253]

In terms of the reception of the Deeds, the level of engagement with them has been extensive. Armed non-State actors in Africa, Asia, South America, Europe, and the Middle East have agreed to commit to the terms of the DoCs. The landmines DoC currently has 53 signatories, with the children in armed conflict DoC and the prohibition on sexual violence DoC having 27 and 25 signatories, respectively.[254] The DoC on health care currently has one signatory. Research also indicates that non-State armed groups have been largely receptive to the work of Geneva Call, with 'nearly all signatories to the Deeds ... [abiding] by their monitoring obligation, providing information and report to Geneva Call on their implementation and allowing field follow-up missions'.[255] Evidence from Geneva Call and other sources, such as Landmine Monitor, has indicated an overall decline in the use of anti-personnel landmines, with the work of Geneva Call in-country directly linked to the reduction or elimination of stockpiles of anti-personnel weapons in the hands of armed non-State groups.[256]

reliefweb.int/report/sudan/memorandum-understanding-between-govt-sudan-splm-and-un-regarding-un-mine-action> accessed 8 August 2021.

[252] Resolution on Problem Posed by Proliferation of Anti-Personnel Mines in Liberated Parts of New Sudan, 1 November 1996, available on the affiliated website of Geneva Call, *Their Words: Directory of Armed Non-State Actor Humanitarian Commitments* <http://theirwords.org/media/transfer/doc/sc_sd_splm_a_1996_07-f22cfb3dee8032a783d5df4c3d1f2bae.pdf> accessed 8 August 2021.

[253] Martin Barber, 'Preface', *Armed Non-State Actors and Landmines: Volume I—A Global Report Profiling NSAs and Their Use, Acquisition, Production, Transfer and Stockpiling of Landmines* (Geneva Call and the Program for the Study of International Organisations 2005) 1 <http://www.genevacall.org/wp-content/uploads/dlm_uploads/2013/12/5.pdf> accessed 8 August 2021.

[254] <https://genevacall.org/how-we-work/deed-of-commitment/> accessed 8 August 2021. For a complete list of non-State actors approached by Geneva Call, and for a record of who has signed which DoC, see <https://genevacall.org/how-we-work/armed-non-state-actors/> accessed 8 August 2021.

[255] See Pascal Bongard, 'Engaging Armed Non-State Actors on Humanitarian Norms: Reflections on Geneva Call's Experience' *Humanitarian Exchange* (No 58, July 2013) 9 <https://odihpn.org/magazine/engaging-armed-non-state-actors-on-humanitarian-norms-reflections-on-geneva-call%C2%92s-experience/> accessed 8 August 2021.

[256] ibid.

This pattern of respect and implementation of all the DoCs continues: the 2018 Annual Report noted that Geneva Call now engages with 86 armed non-State groups, 18 of which have not previously engaged with Geneva Call.[257] During 2018, 81 armed non-State groups received training on child protection and access to education for children;[258] 86 armed non-State groups received visits from Geneva Call field teams for training or other forms of engagement;[259] 16 armed groups participated in training sessions on gender issues and adopted new internal rules and regulations on gender equality and the prohibition of sexual violence, among them groups in Myanmar, Colombia, the Democratic Republic of the Congo, Iran, Lebanon, the Philippines, Sudan, Syria, and Turkey;[260] and Geneva Call monitored the destruction of 2,500 stockpiled anti-personnel mines by the Sahrawi Mine Action Coordination Office in accordance with the DoC signed by the Polisario Front in 2005.[261]

The reception by States of the work undertaken by Geneva Call has been more muted, but still receptive. In the first instance, Geneva Call can only engage with a non-State armed group 'in country' with the permission of the State.[262] That States have allowed Geneva Call to engage with these non-State groups, for the purposes of site visits for monitoring compliance with the DoCs, indicates a degree of success and receptivity. Indeed, there is evidence that many States:

> have supported engagement efforts and have allowed Geneva Call to engage with ANSAs [armed non-state actors] on their territory. At the initiative of Geneva Call, a few – such as the governments of the Philippines, Senegal and Sudan—have even agreed to meeting opposing ANSAs to discuss humanitarian issues. Colombia has allowed Geneva Call to meet imprisoned leaders .... Other States have prohibited direct interaction on the part of Geneva Call, but have allowed its local partners to meet ANSAs. Still others have funded Geneva Call to engage with ANSAs proscribed on their terrorist lists.[263]

[257] Geneva Call, Annual Report 2018 (2019) 5 <http://www.genevacall.org/wp-content/uploads/2019/07/GEC-RA2018A4_web-compressed-1.pdf> accessed 8 August 2021.
[258] ibid 10.
[259] ibid 9.
[260] ibid 11.
[261] ibid 12.
[262] See Bongard (n 255).
[263] See ibid. However, there have also been examples of States refusing to allow Geneva Call to undertake in-country compliance visits. See ibid regarding the refusal to allow an in-country compliance visit for the Kurdistan Workers Party.

The work of Geneva Call has been noted and affirmed by the United Nations,[264] the European Union,[265] and the African Union,[266] and has been cited in the ICC.[267]

The ICRC CIHL and Direct Participation in Hostilities Instruments

The ICRC's two soft law documents—the CIHL Study and the Direct Participation in Hostilities (DPH) Guidance—have had significant impact. The DPH Guidance has been cited numerous times by and before international courts,[268] including the ICC[269]

[264] See, for example, UN Security Council, Protection of Civilians in Armed Conflict, Report of the Secretary-General, S/2018/462 (14 May 2018) 11 <http://www.securitycouncilreport.org/atf/cf/%7B65BFCF9B-6D27-4E9C-8CD3-CF6E4FF96FF9%7D/s_2018_462.pdf> accessed 8 August 2021.

[265] '[T]he European Union has regularly expressed its political support, notably during the meetings of State Parties of the Mine ban Treaty. This endorsement has recently been reiterated in November 2007 at the 8th MSP to the MBT in Amman: "The EU recognizes the importance of engaging non-state Actors with the objectives of this Convention, and therefore supports the work of the organisation Geneva Call and its efforts to bring non-state actors in compliance with the provisions of the Convention. The European Union stresses the importance of continuing the support, as appropriate, to mine action in order to assist affected populations in areas under the control of armed non-state actors" [Statement by Portugal on behalf of the European Union at the 8th meeting of States Parties to the Anti-Personnel Mine Ban Convention, Amman, 18 November 2007]': Geneva Call, 'Geneva Call Position Paper: The EU-Africa Strategy and the Humanitarian Engagement of Armed Non-State Actors (ANSAs)' (1 December 2007) < https://www.genevacall.org/geneva-call-position-paper-eu-africa-strategy-humanitarian-engagement-armed-non-state-actors-nsas/> accessed 8 August 2021. See also Final Report of the Eighth Meeting of the States Parties to the Convention on the Prohibition of the Use, Stockpiling, Production and Transfer of Anti-Personnel Mines and on Their Destruction, APLC/MSP.8/2007/6 (30 January 2008) 12, 14 <http://www.apminebanconvention.org/fileadmin/APMBC/MSP/8MSP/8MSP-FinalReport-30Nov2007-en.pdf> accessed 8 August 2021; Meeting of the States Parties to the Convention on the Prohibition of the Use, Stockpiling, Production and Transfer of Anti-Personnel Mines and on Their Destruction, Final Report, APLC/MSP.11/2011/8, (16 February 2012) 16, 42–43 <http://www.apminebanconvention.org/fileadmin/APMBC/MSP/11MSP/11MSP-FinalReport-16Fev2012-en.pdf> accessed 8 August 2021.

[266] <https://genevacall.org/african-states-commend-work-geneva-call-acknowledge-importance-engaging-armed-non-state-actors-landmine-ban/> accessed 8 August 2021. See also African Union, Common African Position on Anti-Personnel Landmines, adopted at the 2nd Continental Conference of African Experts on Landmines, 17 September 2004, reprinted in Project Document: The African Union Mine Action and Explosive Remnants of War Strategic Framework, April 2014–December 2017, Annex 3 <http://www.peaceau.org/uploads/au-mine-action-project-document.pdf> accessed 8 August 2021 (though the Common Position does not mention Geneva Call by name).

[267] Prosecution Appeal Brief, *Prosecutor v Ntaganda* (Appeals Chamber, No ICC-01/04-02/06-2432, 7 October 2019) para 51. See also *R v Lelikan (No 5)* [2019] NSWSC 494.

[268] See generally Ka Lok Yip, 'The ICRC's Interpretive Guidance on the Notion of Direct Participation in Hostilities: Sociological and Democratic Legitimacy in Domestic Legal Orders' (2017) 8 Transnational Legal Theory 224.

[269] Prosecution Appeal Brief, *Situation in the Islamic Republic of Afghanistan* (Appeals Chamber, No ICC-02/17-7430 September 2019) paras 48–49; *Prosecutor v Mbarushimana (Decision on the Confirmation of Charges)* (Pre-Trial Chamber I, No ICC-01/04-01/10-465-Red, 16 December 2011) paras 66–67; Closing Submissions of the Defence, *Prosecutor v Lubanga* (Trial Chamber I, No ICC-01/04-01/06-2773, 15 July 2011) para 12; Confirmation of Changes Hearing, Prosecution Closing Statement, *Prosecutor v Ntaganda* (No ICC-01/04-02/06-258-AnxA10, 14 February 2014) para 17; Document in Support of the Appeal on Behalf of Mr Ntaganda against Trial Chamber VI's Decision on the Defence's Challenge to the Jurisdiction of the Court in Respect of Counts 6 and

and the ICTY;[270] in domestic courts in Israel,[271] the United States,[272] Germany,[273] and the United Kingdom;[274] in the Australian parliament;[275] and in the United Nations.[276] In the UK case *Mohammad*, the Court noted:

9', No ICC-01/04-02/06-892, *Prosecutor v Ntaganda* (Appeals Chamber, No ICC-01/04-02/06-972, 2 November 2015) para 10; Mr Thomas Lubanga's Appellate Brief against the 14 March 2012 Judgment Pursuant to Article 74 of the Statute, *Prosecutor v Lubanga* (Appeals Chamber, No ICC-01/04-01/06-2948, 3 December 2012) paras 68–70; Prosecution's Response to Thomas Lubanga's Appeal against Trial Chamber I's Judgment Pursuant to Article 74, *Prosecutor v Lubanga* (Appeals Chamber, No ICC-01/04-01/06-2969s, 18 February 2013) paras 89–90; Public Redacted Version of 'Request for Authorisation of an Investigation Pursuant to Article 15', 6 September 2017, No ICC-01/17-5-US-Exp, *Situation in Burundi* (Pre-Trial Chamber III, No ICC-01/17-5-Red, 15 November 2017) para 28; Office of the Prosecutor, International Criminal Court, Situation on Registered Vessels of Comoros, Greece and Cambodia: Article 53(1) Report (6 November 2014), Annex A, No ICC-01/13-6-AnxA, 26–27; Defence Request for a Disclosure Order Regarding Material Related to the Circumstances of Hostilities between the LRA and Ugandan Government Pursuant to Article 67(2) and Rule 77, Defence for Dominic Ongwen, *Prosecutor v Ongwen* (Trial Chamber IX, No ICC-02/04-01/15-759, 15 March 2017) 11.

[270] Final Brief on Behalf of Milan Gvero, *Prosecutor v Popovic* (Trial Chamber, Case No IT-05-88-T, 30 July 2010) 57–58; Redacted Public Version, Vlastimir Dordevic's Appeal Brief, *Prosecutor v Dordević* (Case No IT-05-87/1-A, 15 August 2011) 109–10; *Prosecutor v Tolimir (Separate and Partly Dissenting Opinion of Judge Antonetti)* (Case No IT-05-88/2-A, 14 July 2015) para 67; *Prosecutor v Boskoski* (Case No IT-04-82-A, Open Session, 29 October 2009) para 82.

[271] *Yesh Din—Volunteers for Human Rights v Chief of General Staff* (IDF, HCJ 3003/18, 30 April 2018) 14–15.

[272] *Al-Bihani v Obama* 389 US App DC 26, 590 F 3d 866, 884–85 (2010); *NY Times Co v US Department of Justice* 756 F 3d 100 (2d Cir 2014); *Al-Aulaqi v Panetta* 2013 WL 440710 (DDC) (Trial Motion, Memorandum and Affidavit) US District Court, District of Columbia, 5 February 2013, Plaintiffs' Opposition to Defendants' Motion to Dismiss; *US v Elhuzayel* 2016 WL 3459287 (CDCal) (Trial Motion, Memorandum and Affidavit) US District Court, CD California, Santa Ana Division, Defendant's Motion to Dismiss Indictment Counts 1 and 2 Rule 12; *US v Hamidullin* 2015 WL 4722285 (EDVa) (Trial Motion, Memorandum and Affidavit) US District Court, ED Virginia, Richmond Division, Defendant's Motion to Dismiss the Indictment; *Atchley v Astrazeneca UK Ltd* 2018 WL 3859918 (DDC) (Trial Motion, Memorandum and Affidavit) US District Court, District of Columbia, Defendants' Reply in Support of Their Rule 12(b)(1) and 12(b)(6) Motions to Dismiss; *Jaber v US* 2016 WL 4440276 (CADC) (Appellate Brief) US Court of Appeals, District of Columbia Circuit, Brief of Appellants, 28; *Al Bahlul v US* 2017 WL 2417309 (US) (Appellate Petition, Motion and Filing) Supreme Court, Brief of Amicus Curiae Center for Constitutional Rights in Support of Petitioner, 12; *Hamdan v US* 2011 WL 5942215 (CADC) (Appellate Brief) US Court of Appeals, DC Circuit, Corrected Brief of Amicus Curiae Center for Constitutional Rights in Support of Petitioner, 17–18; *Obaydullah v Obama* 2011 WL 5859053 (CADC) (Appellate Brief) US Court of Appeals, DC Circuit, (Corrected) Brief of Appellant, 67–68; *Doe v Drummond Company Inc* 2014 WL 1870569 (CA11) (Appellate Brief) US Court of Appeals, 11th Circuit, Brief of Amici Curiae Colombian Human Rights Advocates and Legal Scholars in Support of Plaintiffs–Appellants, 2.

[273] Der Generalbundesanwalt beim Bundesgerichtshof, Ermittlungsverfahren gegen Oberst Klein und Hauptfeldwebel W. wegen des Verdachts einer Strafbarkeit nach dem VStGB und anderer Delikte hier: Einstellung des Verfahrens gemäß § 170 Abs. 2 Satz 1 StPO, 16.04.2010, 48 et seq <http://www.generalbundesanwalt.de/docs/einstellungsvermerk20100416offen.pdf> accessed 8 August 2021; Der Generalbundesanwalt beim Bundesgerichtshof, Betr: Drohneneinsatz vom 4. Oktober 2010 in Mir Ali/Pakistan—Verfügung des Generalbundesanwalts vom 20. Juni 2013–3 BJs 7/12-4, 23 July 2013 23 et seq https://dserver.bundestag.de/btd/18/CD12850/D_IV_Ausgewaehlte_Dokumente_zum_Ersten_und_Zweiten_Teil_des_Berichts/D_IV_7_Zum_Zweiten_Teil_Kapitel_H/H07.pdf accessed 27 September 2021.

[274] *Mohammed v Secretary of State for Defence* [2015] EWCA Civ 843; *Al-Saadoon v Secretary of State for Defence* [2016] EWHC 773 (Admin).

[275] Criminal Code Amendment (War Crimes) Bill 2016, Bills Digest No 43, 2016–17, 23 November 2016, 43.

[276] Yearbook of the International Law Commission (2013) vol 2, part 2, Report of the Commission to the General Assembly on the work of its sixty-fifth session, UN Doc A/CN.4/SER.A/2013/Add.1

For the first stage of this submission (namely that there was power to attack and use lethal force on insurgents who participate in the conflict) the Secretary of State relied on the ICRC's *Interpretative Guidance on the Notion of Direct Participation in Hostilities under International Humanitarian Law* (2009). This states:

'Most notably, for the duration of their direct participation in hostilities, civilians *may* be directly attacked as if they were combatants. Derived from Article 3 common to the Geneva Conventions, the notion of taking a direct or active part in hostilities is found in many provisions of international humanitarian law...' (at 12)[277]

The ICRC CIHL Study has likewise been taken up in State practice, being cited in parliamentary debates prior to legislative reform in Australia;[278] in courts in Canada,[279] Israel,[280] the Philippines,[281] the United Kingdom,[282] and the United States,[283] as well as in the European Court of Human Rights,[284] the ICJ,[285] the

(Part 2), 36; International Commission, Sixty-fifth session, First report on subsequent agreements and subsequent practice in relation to treaty interpretation, by George Nolte, Special Rapporteur (19 March 2013), UN Doc A/CN.4/660, 53–54.

277 *Mohammed v Secretary of State for Defence* [2015] EWCA Civ 843, 205.

278 Crimes Legislation Amendment (Powers, Offences and Other Measures) Bill 2015, Bills Digest No 1, 2015–16, 5 August 2015, 14 <https://parlinfo.aph.gov.au/parlInfo/download/legislation/billsdgs/3994284/upload_binary/3994284.pdf;fileType = application/pdf> accessed 8 August 2021; Counter-Terrorism Legislation Amendment Bill (No 1) 2014—Concluded Matter [2015] AUPJCHR 75 (13 May 2015), 141; Criminal Code Amendment (War Crimes) Bill 2016, Bills Digest No 43, 2016–17, 23 November 2016, 6–7.

279 *R v Y (N)* 2008 CarswellOnt 3032 (Ont SCJ) 77 WCB (2d) 686, 8–10.

280 *Public Committee Against Torture v Government* HCJ 769/02 (14 December 2016) 491–92; *Al-Bassiouni v Prime Minister and Minister of Defence* HCJ 9132/07 (27 January 2008) para 14.

281 Representatives *Lagman v Medialdea* [2017] PHSC 351.

282 *Mohammed v Secretary of State for Defence* [2015] EWCA Civ 843 [761]–[767], [778]–[780], [794]–[796]; *Al-Waheed v Ministry of Defence; Mohammed v Ministry of Defence* [2017] UKSC 2, [2017] HRLR 1 [98]–[99]; *Mohammed v Ministry of Defence* [2014] EWHC 1369 (QB) [56]; *R v Mohammed Gul* [2012] EWCA Crim 280 [12]; *KS v Secretary of State for the Home Department* [2014] UKUT 00552 (IAC).

283 *Hamdan v Rumsfeld* 48 US 557 (2006).

284 *Sargsyan v Azerbaijan* (2017) 64 EHRR 4 [225], [260]; *Korbeley v Hungary* (2010) 50 EHRR 48 [1221]–[1222]; *Muršić v Croatia* (2017) 65 EHRR 1 [77]; *Marguš v Croatia* (2016) 62 EHRR 17 [575]; *Chiragov v Armenia* (2016) 63 EHRR 9 [427]; *Mocanu v Romania* (2015) 60 EHRR 19 [900].

285 Public sitting held 7 March 2017, at 10 am, at the Peace Palace, President Abraham presiding, in *Application of the International Convention for the Suppression of the Financing of Terrorism and of the International Convention on the Elimination of All Forms of Racial Discrimination (Ukraine v Russian Federation)*, Verbatim Record (2017), CR 2017/2, 25–26; *Jurisdictional immunities of the State (Germany v Italy: Greece intervening)*, Dissenting opinion of Judge Cançado Trindade, 223–24 (128–29), 267 (172); *Questions relating to the Obligation to Prosecute or Extradite (Belgium v Senegal)*, Separate Opinion of Judge Cançado Trindade, 541 (123); Public sitting held 25 April 2005, at 3 pm, at the Peace Palace, President Shi presiding, in *Armed Activities on the Territory of the Congo (Democratic Republic of the Congo v Uganda)*, Verbatim Record, CR 2005/13, 31–32.

ICC,[286] the ICTY,[287] the Special Court for Sierra Leone,[288] the Ethiopia-Eritrea Claims Commission;[289] and in UN bodies.[290]

Assessing the Impact of Soft Law Instruments

Looking at the practice of States and non-State groups in relation to the various soft law instruments, what can be said about their efficacy? Nearly all the instruments meet the admittedly low bar of having an impact on State practice. Through either citations in court cases, recognition in military manuals, or employment of the instruments before UN bodies, States and non-State groups are engaging with the soft law instruments. Moreover, as noted in this chapter, there is clear evidence that the rules contained in these instruments are being implemented in practice. However, as is also evident above, implementation and engagement with the instruments is inconsistent, and the degrees of engagement vary significantly between the types

[286] Public Redacted Version of Prosecution's Submissions on Issues That Were Raised during the Confirmation of Charges Hearing, 7 March 2014, No ICC-01/04-02/06-276-Conf, *Prosecutor v Ntaganda* (No ICC-01/04-02/06-276-Red, 24 March 2014) 75; *Prosecutor v Abu Garda (Decision on the Confirmation of Charges)* (Pre-Trial Chamber I, No ICC-02/05-02/09, 8 February 2010) 40; Public redacted version of 'Prosecution's Response to the Defence Closing Brief', 15 September 2014, No ICC-01/05-01/08-3141-Conf, *Prosecutor v Bemba Gombo* (Trial Chamber III, No ICC-01/05-01/08, 22 April 2016) 35–36; United Nations Joint Submission on Reparations, *Prosecutor v in Katanga* (Trial Chamber II, No ICC-01/04-01/07, 14 May 2015).

[287] *Prosecutor v Hadžihasanović (Decision on Joint Defence Interlocutory Appeal of Trial Chamber Decision on Rule 98BIS Motions for Acquittal)* (Appeals Chamber, Case No IT-01-47-AR73.3, 11 March 2005); *Prosecutor v Stakic (Judgment)* (Appeals Chamber, Case No IT-97-24-A, 22 March 2006); *Prosecutor v Boškoski (Judgment)* (Trial Chamber II, Case No IT-04-82-T, 10 July 2008) 93; *Prosecutor v Orić (Judgment)* (Appeals Chamber, IT-03-68-A, 83–84, 3 July 2008); *Prosecutor v Rašević (Decision on Referral of Case Under Rule 11 BIS)* (Referral Bench, Case No IT-97-25/1-PT, 8 July 2005) 23; *Prosecutor v Hadžihasanović (Judgment)* (Trial Chamber, Case No IT-01-47-T, 15 March 2006) 69–70.

[288] *Prosecutor v Norman (Decision on Preliminary Motion Based on Lack of Jurisdiction (Child Recruitment))* (Appeals Chamber, Case No SCSL-2004-14-AR72(E), 31 May 2004).

[289] Eritrea-Ethiopia Claims Commission, Partial Award, Prisoners of War, Eritrea's Claim 17, 1 July 2003, para 41 and Partial Award, Prisoners of War, Ethiopia's Claim 4, para. 32 (concerning the Geneva Conventions); Eritrea-Ethiopia Claims Commission, Partial Award, Central Front, Eritrea's Claims 2, 4, 6, 7, 8 and 22, 28 April 2004, para. 23 and Partial Award, Central Front, Ethiopia's Claim 2, para. 17; Eritrea-Ethiopia Claims Commission, Partial Award, Western Front, Aerial Bombardment and Related Claims, 19 December 2005, para 95; Eritrea-Ethiopia Claims Commission, Partial Award, Western Front, Aerial Bombardment and Related Claims, 19 December 2005, paras 104–05.

[290] International Law Commission, Seventy-first session at Geneva (29 April–7 June 2019 and 8 July–9 August 2019), 'Second report on protection of the environment in relation to armed conflicts' prepared by Marja Lehto, Special Rapporteur, UN Doc A/CN.4/728 (27 March 2019) 12, 24, 26–28, 74–76; Human Rights Council, Third session, Item 2 of the provisional agenda, Implementation of General Assembly Resolution 60/251 of 15 March 2006 Entitled 'Human Rights Council', Report of the Commission of Inquiry on Lebanon pursuant to Human Rights Council resolution S-2/1 (23 November 2006), UN Doc A/HRC/3/2, 24; Report of the International Law Commission, Seventy-first session (29 April–7 June and 8 July–9 August 2019), Supplement No 10 (A/74/10), 73–74; Report of the International Law Commission, Sixty-eighth session (2 May–10 June and 4 July–12 August 2016), Supplement No 10 (A/71/10), 87, 90, 161–62, 323–24; International Commission of Inquiry on Darfur, Report to the UN Secretary-General pursuant to Security Council Resolution 1564 of 18 September 2004, 25 January 2005.

of instruments. Of the instruments aimed at modifying or influencing *State* behaviour, those that have significant State engagement in their formation (such as the Montreux Document and, to a lesser extent, the Copenhagen Principles) seem overall to have been more enthusiastically received by States than those that are the product of expert groups (with the notable exception of the San Remo Naval Manual). This seems especially so if those expert groups are small and/or have had limited State involvement in their formation (such as with the NIAC Manual or the AMW Manual). Instruments that have involved the ICRC also seem to have been more warmly received, likely due to perceptions of the neutrality and gravitas of the ICRC (discussed in further detail in Chapter 8).

However, that 'enthusiastic reception' is somewhat measured in situations where the instruments have been perceived as attempting to introduce innovations into the law. Therefore, instruments that encourage States to embrace what might be considered new obligations, such as amnesty for non-State armed fighters, or expansive definitions of sovereignty in cyberspace, seem to have been less successful in changing State behaviour on a broad or wide-reaching scale. In those instances, it does not appear to matter that the instrument involved States in its formation, or consulted with States, or that the ICRC was the architect of the rule. Where the instrument is perceived as pushing the limits of State obligation beyond pre-existing hard law, the efficacy of the instrument seems limited.

Given the varied reception to the non-binding instruments, Chapter 8 will look at whether the processes surrounding the creation and adoption of these instruments influence how they are received in practice. In doing so, the chapter will draw on legal theory regarding the concepts of legality and legitimacy.

8

Legitimacy and Legality and Non-Binding Instruments in International Humanitarian Law

Introduction

The various non-binding instruments have had different levels of success in their uptake by States and non-State actors. Some instruments have had immediate impact on State behaviour while others have been received with circumspection. How can we account for why some instruments are more successful than others, and how can we account for whether and why these instruments are used and received as legal (or quasi-legal) instruments, given their non-binding nature? One promising approach that might help account for the differing reception of these instruments is to examine the instruments through the lens of theories of legitimacy and legality, and their relationship to international law.

In undertaking this analysis, this chapter will explore whether theories regarding the legitimacy of law (and international law more generally) can account for whether a non-binding instrument is more readily welcomed in State practice. That is to say, do perceptions about an instrument's legitimacy impact on whether it is more readily received by States and non-State groups? Utilising the academic debate on the notion of legitimacy, this chapter will examine what factors might contribute to whether an instrument is perceived as having some measure of legitimacy. These factors may include the provenance of the instrument, the process by which the instrument is created, the participants involved in its drafting, and whether the outcomes are considered a reasonable restatement of applicable law or an unacceptable progressive development. In undertaking this analysis, the chapter will explore and analyse some of the issues that are unique to international humanitarian law (IHL) soft law instruments, looking at who initiated the process that led to the adoption of the instrument, the objectives behind the adoption, who was involved in the adoption, and how the instrument has been received and perceived by its intended audience. The chapter will also assess whether questions of legitimacy are relevant for non-binding norms, or whether their non-binding status frees them, in some respect, from the debates surrounding the legitimacy of international law.

Non-Binding Norms in International Humanitarian Law. Emily Crawford, Oxford University Press. © Emily Crawford 2021.
DOI: 10.1093/oso/9780198819851.003.0009

This chapter will also look at the connected question of the legality of non-binding instruments: what is their legal status, if any, and does that impact on their reception and impact? Non-binding norms are, clearly, not law, in that they have no binding effect, and there is no consequence that follows from non-compliance with the instrument: it is not possible, for example, to make a legal case for a State having 'breached' the *Tallinn Manual on the International Law Applicable to Cyber Warfare* (Tallinn Manual), or for having failed to conclude a Common Article 3 special agreement. However, the non-binding instruments are not totally devoid of legality or legal-ness. They make claims to some form of authority and compliance; moreover, they are employed in legal forums and in legal ways, to support and bolster legal argumentation. It is therefore instructive to look at theories of legality and international law to explore what we can say about the legal quality or legal nature of non-binding instruments. This brings us to the central issue for non-binding instruments, and specifically their legitimacy and legality: namely, how should such instruments be treated? Do they have any authority to claim themselves as being instructive, or to hope to influence behaviour? Do they deserve any deference or respect as (semi-)authoritative statements despite their non-binding status? Essentially, simplistically, the question becomes: what right do non-binding norms have to make any claims on behaviour?

Legitimacy, Legality, and Non-Binding Norms

What is the relevance of theories of legitimacy and legality for non-binding instruments in IHL? Theories of legitimacy and legality are more often seen in jurisprudential analyses attempting to ascertain the source of law as a force of authority and compliance, or in the fields of political science and international relations.[1] What then is the relevance of these theories to non-binding norms? If legitimacy and legality are primarily of concern for understanding the nature of law as a binding force, what then is the relevance of these theories to instruments and provisions that do not profess to be law (or, at least, profess to be legally binding)? Why analyse an instrument for its legal authority, and for the legitimacy of its calls for particular kinds of behaviour, if the instrument makes no such claims to authority, and/or holds no position that requires legitimation?

[1] The concepts of legitimacy and legality are a focus of legal literature, as well as the disciplines of international relations and political science. While law and international relations/political science have distinct disciplinary objectives and approaches regarding their study of legitimacy and legality, both fields share a common interest—namely, theorising why rules are or are not followed, and what makes rules 'rules'. See, for example, Filipe dos Reis and Oliver Kessler, 'The Power of Legality, Legitimacy and the (Im)possibility of Interdisciplinary Research' in Nikolas Rajkovic, Tanja Aalberts, and Thomas Gammeltoft-Hansen (eds), *The Power of Legality: Practices of International Law and Their Politics* (CUP 2016).

The relevance of theories of legitimacy and legality to non-binding instruments is, firstly, related to connected theories of compliance, and the relationship between the legitimacy and legality of norms and compliance with those norms. As will be explored in this chapter, the legitimacy and legality of a norm often influences its ability to compel behaviour. Therefore, for instruments seeking to influence behaviour—like the non-binding norms under examination in this book—understanding what contributes to and fosters compliance is important.

Secondly, it is true that the extant non-binding instruments under examination make it clear that they are *not* law. For example, the Montreux Document states in its Preface that 'this document is not a legally binding instrument', as does the *HPCR Manual on International Law Applicable to Air and Missile Warfare* (AMW Manual),[2] which states in its introduction that it 'does not [itself] have binding force'.[3] However, regardless of their non-binding status, the non-binding instruments *are* assertions of authority on their particular subject areas and *do* make claims for compliance. It is therefore instructive to look at theories of legitimacy and legality, and whether the debates surrounding the legitimacy and legality of 'binding' international law (such as treaties and custom) are equally relevant for non-binding instruments in international law. As noted in the introduction, instruments that demonstrate high levels of legitimacy seem to have higher levels of normative and rhetorical power; therefore, non-binding instruments that engage with and embody the principles of legitimacy and legality may be more likely to compel and encourage compliance. If this is true, then it may prove instructive for the drafters of future non-binding norms to pay attention to legitimacy and legality issues when creating new instruments.

Defining Legitimacy: Theories of Legitimacy in International Law

Legitimacy, as a concept and theory, is complex, and the literature on the topic is vast and varied.[4] At its simplest, legitimacy is generally considered to refer to

[2] Montreux Document, Preface, 9. See also Program on Humanitarian Policy and Conflict Research at Harvard University, *HPCR Manual on International Law Applicable to Air and Missile Warfare* (AMW Manual) (CUP 2013) xiii.

[3] AMW Manual, xiii.

[4] See, for example, Max Weber, who distinguished between traditional, charismatic, and legal legitimacy: Max Weber, *Economy and Society* (Guenther Roth and Claus Wittich eds, University of California Press 1978) 31–38, 212–97; Thomas Franck, *The Power of Legitimacy among Nations* (OUP 1990); Jean-Marc Coicaud and Veijo Heiskanen (eds), *The Legitimacy of International Organizations* (United Nations University Press 2001); Allen Buchanan, *Justice, Legitimacy, and Self-Determination: Moral Foundations for International Law* (OUP 2003); Mattias Kumm, 'The Legitimacy of International Law: A Constitutionalist Framework of Analysis' (2004) 15 European Journal of International Law 907; Thomas Franck, 'The Power of Legitimacy and the Legitimacy of Power: Law in an Age of Power Disequilibrium' (2006) 100 American Journal of International Law 88; Rüdiger Wolfrum and Volker Röben (eds), *Legitimacy in International Law* (Springer 2008) 109–30, 169–88.

the 'justification of the exercise of public authority, the latter being understood as equivalent to having the power to take binding decisions'.[5] Or, as Thomas Franck puts it, '[l]egitimacy is a property of a rule or rule-making institution which itself exerts a pull toward compliance on those addressed normatively because those addressed believe that the rule or institution has come into being and operates in accordance with generally accepted principles of right process'.[6] Legitimacy, therefore, is connected to a justification to assert authority, as well as an expectation of compliance with such assertions.[7] A set of rules issued by an institution or organisation will have more normative impact or exert a stronger 'compliance pull'[8] if those rules are considered legitimate, and if the organisation that promulgates the rules is likewise considered legitimate. As Franck argues:

> *Why do nations obey rules? ... Because they perceive the rule and its institutional penumbra to have a high degree of legitimacy* ... legitimacy is [therefore] ... an independent variable, one which controls the extent to which a rule is perceived to exert a powerful pull towards compliance on those to whom it is addressed.[9]

If, as Franck seems to suggest, a rule is perceived as legitimate if it demonstrates particular qualities,[10] then there is more likelihood that the rule will be followed or more likelihood that the rule will exert a compliance pull. In international law, this is particularly relevant: lacking the vertical normative hierarchy and compulsory adjudicative framework of domestic law, international law relies heavily on rules being followed because there is a perception that the rules *should* be followed, even (or perhaps especially) in the absence of a compulsory adjudicator. The place of legitimacy in non-binding norms would therefore seem particularly pertinent. For, if legitimacy is a significant factor accounting for why rules are followed, theories of legitimacy could help explain why certain non-binding rules are more impactful than others. Perceptions of legitimacy relating to non-binding norms in IHL could

[5] Rüdiger Wolfrum, 'Legitimacy in International Law' in Anne Peters and Rüdiger Wolfrum (eds), *Max Planck Encyclopedia of Public International Law*. See also Daniel Bodansky, who argues that legitimacy is the 'justification and acceptance of political authority': Daniel Bodansky, 'The Concept of Legitimacy in International Law' in Rüdiger Wolfrum and Volker Röben (eds), *Legitimacy in International Law* (Springer 2008) 310.

[6] Franck, *The Power of Legitimacy among Nations* (n 4) 24.

[7] Bodansky, 'The Concept of Legitimacy in International Law' (n 5) 312. See also Joseph Raz, *The Authority of Law* (2nd edn, OUP 2009) 8–11, where he connects authority to legitimacy, based on the notion that law claims authority.

[8] Franck, *The Power of Legitimacy among Nations* (n 4) 50.

[9] ibid 25 (emphasis in original).

[10] For Franck, these qualities are determinacy, symbolic validation, coherence, and adherence: 'determinacy is related to the semantic clarity of a rule; the symbolic validation of a rule relates to a rule's authenticity (e.g., through pedigrees or rituals in courts); coherence describes the consistency with other rules; and, finally, adherence relates to H.L.A. Hart's idea of primary and secondary rules and shows how a rule is connected to a hierarchy of rules.' Dos Reis and Kessler (n 1), paraphrasing Franck, *The Power of Legitimacy among Nations* (n 4) 233.

account for why some instruments have been readily embraced by States, while others have been received more guardedly.

This chapter now turns to examine theories of legitimacy and apply them to the existing non-binding norms under examination to see if there is correlation between the theory and the practice. The chapter will use the typology of theories of legitimacy of international law as outlined by, inter alia, Daniel Bodansky[11] and Rüdiger Wolfrum,[12] who divide theories of legitimacy into the categories of source-based theories of legitimacy, process-based theories of legitimacy, and outcome-based theories of legitimacy.[13]

Source Legitimacy (Including Organisational and Structural Legitimacy)

Source-based theories of the legitimacy of international law posit that authority is legitimated by its origin—that a law will be legitimate (and, it is argued, will more likely be observed and respected[14]) if it emanates from a legitimate source. According to the 'traditional'[15] view, States are the legitimate bearers of authority in the domestic plane and, by consenting to international law on the international plane, they legitimate international law by that act of consent.[16] Accordingly, international laws, when based on State consent, are legitimate exercises of authority and exert a normative force and compliance pull. As Keller notes: '[s]tate sovereignty ... serves as the defining organisational principle of the international system. In keeping with this principle, states may accordingly incur international obligations only to the extent that they submit to them by virtue of consent. From the finding that the international legal order is premised on state consent, which in

[11] Daniel Bodansky, 'Legitimacy' in Daniel Bodansky, Jutta Brunnée, and Ellen Hey (eds), *The Oxford Handbook of International Environmental Law* (OUP 2008) 710–11.

[12] Rüdiger Wolfrum, 'Legitimacy of International Law from a Legal Perspective: Some Introductory Considerations' in Rüdiger Wolfrum and Volker Röben (eds), *Legitimacy in International Law* (Springer 2008) 6–7.

[13] Other theorists divide legitimacy into two broad categories: input legitimacy and output legitimacy. Input legitimacy correlates to source legitimacy (including organisational and participant legitimacy), while output legitimacy correlates to outcome legitimacy, incorporating process legitimacy. See, for example, Matthias Hartwig, 'ICANN—Governance by Technical Necessity' in Armin von Bogdandy and others (eds), *The Exercise of Public Authority by International Institutions: Advancing International Institutional Law* (Springer 2010) 598–99); David Easton, *A Systems Analysis of Political Life* (Wiley 1965); David Easton, 'A Reassessment of the Concept of Political Support' (1975) 5 British Journal of Political Science 435; Fritz Scharpf, *Demokratietheorie zwischen Utopie und Anpassung* (Universitätsverlag 1970).

[14] See Ian Hurd, 'Legitimacy and Authority in International Politics' (1999) 53 International Organisation 379, 387, where he cites legitimacy as one of the reasons behind compliance with rules.

[15] Wolfrum, 'Legitimacy of International Law from a Legal Perspective' (n 12) 6.

[16] Bodansky, 'Legitimacy' (n 11) 710–11.

turn is a sovereign act, it follows that state sovereignty constitutes the traditional basis of legitimacy.'[17]

Also broadly captured under the umbrella of source legitimacy is the theory that laws and law-making by certain international organisations can be imbued with the same legitimacy as States and State-made law. Legitimacy for international organisations exists either because States consent to the law-making by the international organisation (through their membership of or participation in the organisation), or because the organisation is considered to have particular subject-matter interest and expertise in the area, which marks it as having a right to engage in law-making.[18] An international institution or organisation is therefore considered legitimate if it possesses what Robert Keohane and Allen Buchanan have identified as the twofold elements of legitimacy: normative and sociological, both the right to rule and the widely held belief in the right to rule:[19]

> To say that an institution is legitimate in the normative sense is to assert that it has the right to rule—where ruling is promulgating rules and attempting to secure compliance with them by attaching costs to noncompliance and/or benefits to compliance. Ruling in this broad sense does not require that the rules be backed by coercion, much less that the rulemaker claims a rightful monopoly on coercion within a jurisdiction, so it does not presuppose the state ... an institution is legitimate in the sociological sense when it is widely believed to have the right to rule.[20]

How an international organisation attains such legitimate authority is itself based on several possible theories. The primary theory is that an institutional organisation is given legitimacy through the participation or sanction of the State. Therefore, a system created by, or consented to by, the State is imbued with that State's legitimacy, at least in some measure[21]—as noted by Buchanan and Keohane:

[17] Helen Keller, 'Codes of Conduct and Their Implementation: The Question of Legitimacy' in Rüdiger Wolfrum and Volker Röben (eds), *Legitimacy in International Law* (Springer 2008) 256.

[18] See, for example, Katharina Coleman's *International Organisations and Peace Enforcement: The Politics of International Legitimacy* (CUP, 2007). Coleman argues that the UN can be seen as a 'gatekeeper' for international legitimacy, especially in relation to military interventions, in part because of the role of the UN as a State-based organisation, and in part because of its subject-matter purview with regards to the use of force: 70–72. See also Steven Wheatley, 'Democratic Governance beyond the State: The Legitimacy of Non-State Actors as Standard Setters' in Anne Peters and others (eds), *Non-State Actors as Standard Setters* (CUP 2009), in which he argues that the authority that accrues to international institutions is 'provided by a recognition of their institutional competence and epistemic authority': 215–16.

[19] Allen Buchanan and Robert Keohane, 'The Legitimacy of Global Governance Institutions' (2006) 20 Ethics and International Affairs 405.

[20] Allen Buchanan and Robert Keohane, 'The Legitimacy of Global Governance Institutions' in Rüdiger Wolfrum and Volker Röben (eds), *Legitimacy in International Law* (Springer 2008) 25.

[21] As Matthias Hartwig defines it, 'the classical form of legitimacy of an international institution ... is the principle of consent which is achieved by the accession of the member states to the treaty establishing the international organisation, as well as their participation in the bodies of the international organisation': Hartwig (n 13) 597.

> [I]nstitutions are sometimes said to be legitimate if they were created by the right sort of process, and, more specifically, if they were created by legitimate institutions, the idea being that legitimacy can be transferred, as it were. In international legal scholarship it is often assumed that global governance institutions are legitimate if they are created through state consent.[22]

However, State participation is not the sole means by which an institution can generate legitimacy. One theory—output legitimacy—posits that an organisation is legitimate if it is based on 'shared beliefs about normatively desirable outcomes, and the ability of institutions to achieve them'.[23] As Buchanan and Keohane note:

> [t]he justification for having global governance institutions is primarily if not exclusively instrumental: we value them because of the benefits they bring, rather than regarding them as intrinsically valuable. The basic reason for states or other addressees of institutional rules to take them as binding and for individuals generally to support or at least not interfere with the operation of these institutions is that they provide benefits that cannot otherwise be obtained.[24]

Another theory—process legitimacy—posits that an international organisation is legitimate if it follows open, democratic, transparent rules, with clear procedures for accountability and participation.[25] This theory is largely based on the notion that:

> [b]ecause democracy is now widely thought to be the gold standard for legitimacy in the case of the state, it may seem obvious that global governance institutions are legitimate if and only if they are democratic. And since these institutions increasingly affect the welfare of people everywhere, surely this must mean that they ought to be democratic in the sense of giving everyone an equal say in how they operate.[26]

Finally, structural legitimacy[27] emanates from the 'beliefs about the identity and particular qualities of an institution',[28] such as its 'epistemic capacities, its perceived ability to muster particular resources and expertise, or from certain qualities of

22 Buchanan and Keohane, 'The Legitimacy of Global Governance Institutions' (n 20) 35.

23 Dominik Zaum, 'Legitimacy' in Jacob Katz Cogan, Ian Hurd, and Ian Johnstone (eds), *The Oxford Handbook of International Organizations* (OUP 2016) 1109; see also Fritz Scharpf, *Governing in Europe: Effective and Democratic?* (OUP 1999).

24 Buchanan and Keohane, 'The Legitimacy of Global Governance Institutions' (n 20) 46–47.

25 Zaum (n 23) 1110; see also Thomas Franck, *Fairness in International Law and Institutions* (Clarendon 1995).

26 Buchanan and Keohane, 'The Legitimacy of Global Governance Institutions' (n 20) 38–39.

27 Mark Sutchman, 'Managing Legitimacy: Strategic and Institutional Approaches' (1995) 20 Academy of Management Review 571.

28 Zaum (n 23) 1110.

its membership, such as the involvement of regional powers, or the democratic character of member states'.[29] In this respect, structural legitimacy can encompass participant legitimacy—that the people and/or entities involved in the law-making endeavour are considered as having a legitimate right to participate—due to subject-matter expertise, or because they participate with the sanction or authority of a legitimate actor such as the State. In this respect, theories of legitimacy with relation to international organisations overlap with process and outcome legitimacy, in addition to source legitimacy.

Process Legitimacy

Connected to theories of structural legitimacy, a law may be considered legitimate because the *process* that brought it into being is considered legitimate. According to this approach, a rule is legitimate because it emanates from a legitimate process: the procedures that resulted in the rule-creation or rule-adoption are considered procedurally fair, transparent, predictable, and accountable.[30] As noted by David Wirth, '[p]rocedure matters … The structure of international procedures can affect the substantive content of international law … [and] procedural integrity is itself an important source of authority and legitimacy for international law'.[31] Process legitimacy exists when an institution or organisation makes law according to a fair process—that is, 'the process met our pre-exi[s]ting expectations from institutional conduct that conform to specific standards'[32] of procedural fairness, such as consistency of procedure and lack of bias.[33] Process legitimacy can be evidenced in relation to broader, general procedural aspects—such as the structure of the institution and who participates in it—as well as adhering to a pre-agreed procedure that is fair and open.

In this respect, process legitimacy is deeply enmeshed with source legitimacy—particularly for international institutions. Legitimacy for international organisations, and for the norms they promulgate, therefore:

> depends on the extent to which the norm (1) emanates from a fair and accepted procedure, (2) is applied equally and without invidious discrimination,

[29] ibid 1110.

[30] As Renate Mayntz notes, 'legitimacy is a given if the formal procedure used to generate decisions or policies meets specific criteria': Renate Mayntz, 'Legitimacy and Compliance in Transnational Governance' (2010) Max Planck Institute for the Study of Societies Working Paper 10/5, 7. See also Franck, *The Power of Legitimacy among Nations* (n 4) 91–134, on the importance of procedure to legitimacy.

[31] David Wirth, 'Reexamining Decision-Making Processes in International Environmental Law' (1994) 79 Iowa Law Review 797, 797–98.

[32] Yuval Shany, *Assessing the Effectiveness of International Courts* (OUP 2014) 142.

[33] ibid.

and (3) does not offend minimum substantive standards of fairness and equity. These are admittedly nebulous criteria, and they are admittedly aspirational. No existing legal system fully meets them. As Thomas Franck says, 'legitimacy is a matter of degree'.[34]

Outcome Legitimacy

Legitimacy for a law or law-making institution or process can also be dependent on, or result from, its outcomes. According to this theory, if a law (or the institution that promulgates the law) produces outputs that are accepted as beneficial[35] and effective[36] to purpose, then the law/institution will be considered legitimate.[37] This outcome or output legitimacy will, in turn, be more likely to encourage compliance.[38] Output legitimacy is therefore concerned with 'the problem-solving quality of the law and rules'[39] created by particular institutions, and is demonstrated through the ability of the institution in question 'to solve collective problems and to meet the expectations of the governed citizens'.[40]

Output legitimacy is also closely connected to notions of expertise—specifically, that an organisation's output legitimacy will be enhanced if the output is the result of expert involvement of the process. As Mayntz notes:

> a lay population lacks the expertise and information needed to formulate effective policies—this is a well-recognised drawback of democratic procedure ... [if] policy is concerned mainly with effective problem-solving ... expertise should play a particularly important role in transnational governance ... expert authority is often judged to be yet another form of rational legitimacy.[41]

An organisation that produces effective rules, as created by experts, would therefore seem to demonstrate a high level of outcome legitimacy.[42]

[34] Abram Chayes and Antonia Handler Chayes, *The New Sovereignty: Compliance with International Regulatory Agreements* (Harvard University Press 1988) 127, citing Franck, *The Power of Legitimacy among Nations* (n 4) 26.

[35] Easton, *A Systems Analysis of Political Life* (n 13) 382.

[36] Thomas Risse, 'Transnational Governance and Legitimacy' in Arthur Benz and Yannis Papadopoulos (eds), *Governance and Democracy: Comparing National, European and International Experiences* (Routledge 2006) 183.

[37] See further Simona Piattoni, *The Theory of Multi-Level Governance: Conceptual, Empirical, and Normative Challenges* (OUP 2010), specifically ch 11, 'Output Legitimacy'.

[38] As Thomas Risse argues, 'actors will comply voluntarily with norms and rules, the more they are convinced of the legitimacy of the rule': Risse (n 36) 183.

[39] Vivien Schmidt, 'Democracy and Legitimacy in the European Union Revisited: Input, Output *and* "Throughput"' (2013) 61 Political Studies 2, 4.

[40] Mayntz (n 30) 10.

[41] ibid 12.

[42] See further Jens Steffek, 'The Output Legitimacy of International Organisations and the Global Public Interest' (2015) 7 International Theory 263.

These broad characterisations of legitimacy theory do not exist in distinct silos, separate from one another—an institution may be considered legitimate because of the outcomes it produces, which are connected to the processes it follows. The legitimacy of a regulatory regime is in many instances based on a number of distinct sources of legitimacy—'input as well as output, participation and expertise as well as effectiveness'.[43]

The Relevance of Legitimacy to Non-Binding Norms

From the brief review of the literature mentioned earlier, it seems that legitimacy is a central (but not the sole) reason as to whether a rule is or is not followed: the legitimacy of the rule creator, the rule creation process, or the outcome of the rule's application will impact on whether the rule is observed or rejected. As noted by Franck, it is not that 'a rule's legitimacy is the sole or, in some instances, even the primary reason a state chooses to obey the law. It does not maintain that lack of legitimacy is necessarily the sole or primary reason for any state's decision not to comply'.[44] However, Franck does argue that States obey rules 'because they perceive the rule and its institutional penumbra to have a high degree of legitimacy'.[45]

If legitimacy is important in law-making, should theories of legitimacy apply equally to 'non-law-making'—that is, to non-binding rules? Do non-binding norms need to be legitimate? They are instruments that do not have, nor claim to have, the same normative force as treaties or custom and no penalties result from non-compliance, so it is arguable that the non-binding instruments are not subject to the same legitimacy concerns as are binding rules. However, as noted in previous chapters, all the instruments under present examination seek to influence the behaviour of their addressees and present themselves as statements of (soft) authority. These instruments do not exert *de jure* authority over their addressees,[46] but there is still a hope—perhaps even an expectation—of compliance. Therefore, these instruments 'exercise de facto authority in a variety of ways and hence also raise issues of legitimacy'.[47] Moreover, practice would suggest that legitimacy perceptions *are* of significant relevance to non-binding instruments generally. In analyses of compliance with rules that do not have binding force or that lack 'coercive order',[48] perceptions of the legitimacy of the rules or of the rule-making institution

[43] Mayntz (n 30) 12. See also Robert Baldwin, Martin Cave, and Martin Lodge, *Understanding Regulation: Theory, Strategy, and Practice* (2nd edn, OUP 2012) 26–31; Ingo Take, 'Legitimacy in Global Governance: International, Transnational and Private Institutions Compared' (2012) 18 Swiss Political Science Review 220, 222–28.

[44] Franck, 'The Power of Legitimacy and the Legitimacy of Power' (n 4) 93.

[45] ibid.

[46] Excluding those non-binding provisions in Common Article 3 and Additional Protocol II.

[47] Bodansky, 'The Concept of Legitimacy in International Law' (n 5) 312.

[48] To use the phrase coined by Hans Kelsen to define law, as distinct from religion and morality: Hans Kelsen, *Principles of International Law* (Holt, Rinehart, Winston 1966) 5.

are a fundamental consideration and a significant contributor to compliance with those rules.[49]

If legitimacy theories apply to non-binding instruments, the next question to ask is this: do the existing non-binding norms meet supposed minimum legitimacy requirements (that is, demonstrate the qualities typically evidenced by legitimate exercises of authority) or do they suffer from a legitimacy gap (that is, lack commonly required factors that demonstrate legitimacy)? Do perceptions of legitimacy or illegitimacy (of origin, of process, of outcome) explain why a particular non-binding instrument has or has not been successful in influencing State behaviour in situations of armed conflict? If legitimacy is central to compliance, then it would follow that an *absence* of legitimacy would make it less likely for a rule or instrument to exert a compliance pull. Additionally, if we accept the premise that State consent is central to claims for legitimacy, a 'decoupling of State consent from international legal processes'[50] could likewise undermine the legitimacy of the non-binding norms (and therefore their compliance pull), specifically those developed by non-State groups.

At first glance, most of the non-binding norms (except for those contained in Common Article 3 and Protocol II, which are part of a treaty regime and therefore accrue legitimacy by virtue of State consent) fail to demonstrate the conventional requirements deemed necessary for designation as 'legitimate' under international law. For legitimacy theorists, international law is legitimate because it 'is established through the consent of States supposedly representing the will of their nationals'.[51] In the alternative, legitimacy can be found 'in public deliberation conducted with communicative rationality under Jürgen Habermas's model of deliberative democracy',[52] whereby public deliberation 'lends legitimacy to its outcomes by being sensitive to the quality of reasons and the force of the better argument and fostering participants' openness to change their initial preferences'.[53] Many of the non-binding norms lack these features entirely: for example, the International Committee of the Red Cross' Direct Participation in Hostilities (ICRC DPH) Guidance was the creation of 'an organisation established under Swiss law, with no specific mandate from the State parties to the Geneva Conventions to interpret

[49] See generally Michael Zürn and Christian Joerges (eds), *Law and Governance in Postnational Europe: Compliance beyond the Nation-State* (CUP 2005) for a series of case studies on compliance with supranational and/or non-binding international rules and regulations.

[50] Helen Keller, 'Codes of Conduct and Their Implementation: The Question of Legitimacy' in Rüdiger Wolfrum and Volker Röben (eds), *Legitimacy in International Law* (Springer 2008) 257.

[51] Known as 'consent-based democratic theory'. See further Wolfrum and Röben (n 4) 6; Steven Wheatley, 'A Democratic Rule of International Law' (2011) 22 European Journal of International Law 525, 527.

[52] Ka Lok Yip, 'The ICRC's Interpretive Guidance on the Notion of Direct Participation in Hostilities: Sociological and Democratic Legitimacy in Domestic Legal Orders' (2017) 8 Transnational Legal Theory 224, 240.

[53] ibid. See also Jürgen Habermas, *Between Facts and Norms: Contributions to a Discourse Theory of Law and Democracy* (MIT Press 1998) 3–10.

IHL, following consultation with independent experts with no better mandate'.[54] Instruments such as the AMW Manual, the *San Remo Manual on International Law Applicable to Armed Conflicts at Sea* (San Remo Naval Manual), the Tallinn Manuals, and the Deeds of Commitment (DoCs) have likewise emanated from institutions or groups of experts who cannot claim any specific mandate from States to engage in the interpretation and development of IHL, or to have engaged in any process that would seem to satisfy Habermas's requirements of deliberative democratic process. With drafting meetings often held 'behind closed doors'[55] and with 'unelected and unaccountable "experts"'[56] in charge of the drafting, how could such instruments be considered legitimate?

That being said, most of the non-binding instruments do engage, intentionally or not, with legitimacy theory. Embracing some form of source, process, and/or outcome legitimacy, the non-binding instruments, consciously or otherwise, recognise that their credibility and success are, in some measure, dependent on legitimation through their source, their process, or their outcomes. The classic basis for source legitimacy—the involvement or imprimatur of the State[57]—is obviously present in non-binding norms such as the *Copenhagen Process Principles and Guidelines on the Handling of Detainees in International Military Operations* (Copenhagen Principles) and the Montreux Document. In both instruments, States have been the initiators of the projects and, as States are the legitimate bearers of authority domestically and internationally, these instruments are legitimated by State involvement.[58]

However, some of the non-binding instruments have not involved States in their creation. Where this has happened, the creators of the non-binding instruments have engaged in acts of process legitimacy. This process legitimacy has taken the form of consultations with States in the later stages of the document's creation (as with the AMW Manual and Tallinn 2.0), or else the adoption of some limited deliberative processes—for example, the inclusion of relevant stakeholders,[59] such as civil society organisations and intergovernmental organisations (as seen during the Copenhagen Process). These consultations with relevant stakeholders would seem to fulfil Buchanan and Keohane's theory of process legitimacy as being demonstrated by institutions that are democratic 'in the sense of giving everyone an equal say in how they operate'.[60] By providing opportunities for States and other

[54] Ka Lok Yip, 'The ICRC's Interpretive Guidance on the Notion of Direct Participation in Hostilities: Sociological and Democratic Legitimacy in Domestic Legal Orders' (2017) 8 Transnational Legal Theory 224, 239.

[55] Amnesty International, 'Copenhagen "Principles" on Military Detainees Undermine Human Rights' (22 October 2012) <http://www.amnesty.org/en/latest/news/2012/10/copenhagen-principles-military-detainees-undermine-human-rights/> accessed 9 August 2021.

[56] Yip (n 54) 239.

[57] Wolfrum, 'Legitimacy of International Law from a Legal Perspective' (n 12) 6.

[58] Bodansky, 'Legitimacy' (n 11) 710–11.

[59] Mayntz (n 30) 9. See also Scharpf, *Governing in Europe* (n 23) 10.

[60] Buchanan and Keohane, 'The Legitimacy of Global Governance Institutions' (n 20) 38–39.

interested stakeholders to provide input into the non-binding instrument, the creators of these instruments ensure that the process (if not the source) is legitimated.

Finally, for those non-binding instruments that have not involved States in any substantive manner, such as the DoCs and the International Code of Conduct, output legitimacy comes into play. The effectiveness of these documents, as drawn up by experts in the field (in relation to armed non-State actors and private military and security companies (PMSCs) respectively), draws on the central tenet of output legitimacy: that outputs that are accepted as beneficial[61] and effective[62] to solve particular problems will be considered legitimate, especially if those outputs are the result of the work of experts.[63] As noted in the previous chapter, the DoCs have clearly proven effective in achieving their stated aims; therefore, the Deeds are legitimated by their outcomes.

This engagement with legitimacy discourse is often seen in the positive feedback the instruments in question have received. The documents are frequently commented on in ways that implicitly acknowledge notions of source legitimacy, process legitimacy, and/or outcome legitimacy. For example, the AMW Manual highlighted the involvement of international law experts such as Yoram Dinstein and Claude Bruderlein, whose expertise was considered 'crucial for the authority'[64] of the Manual; the ICRC is noted as the 'acknowledged custodians of the Geneva Conventions';[65] and the San Remo Naval Manual is 'broadly regarded as authoritative'.[66] Even criticisms of the non-binding instruments have frequently been framed in terms that, intentionally or not, evoke legitimacy discourse, which would seem to reaffirm the significance of legitimacy discourse to the non-binding norms. Criticisms of some of the non-binding norms have often been framed to suggest that there is something problematic in either the source, the process, or the outcomes of the non-binding instruments, which, in turn, undermines any authority on the part of the instruments to make claims for particular modes of behaviour.[67] For example, many of the non-binding norms have been critiqued

[61] Easton, A *Systems Analysis of Political Life* (n 13) 382.

[62] Risse (n 36) 183.

[63] See further Steffek (n 42).

[64] AMW Manual, iii.

[65] William Boothby, 'Direct Participation in Hostilities—A Discussion of the ICRC Interpretive Guidance' (2010) 1 International Humanitarian Legal Studies 143, 145.

[66] Wolff Heintschel von Heinegg, 'The Current State of the Law of Naval Warfare: A Fresh Look at the San Remo Manual' (2006) 82 International Law Studies 269, 269.

[67] The centrality of the State to notions of legitimacy underscores debates regarding the legitimacy gap inherent in transnational governance. Transnational and supranational institutions are 'widely considered to be impaired by the absence or weakness of democratic procedures of decision-making … supranational institutions are not held accountable to voters; they lack sanctioning power; there is no … global demos; and there are few institutionalised forms for the direct expression of popular preferences': Mayntz (n 30) 9. See also Scharpf, *Governing in Europe* (n 23). Similar characteristics can be seen regarding those groups and institutions involved in the creation of many of the non-binding norms under present examination. There is an absence of popular input from the citizenry, a lack of power to sanction, and, in some cases, an absence of accountability mechanisms for the decision-makers involved in their creation.

for an absence of process legitimacy—that the methods employed to create the instrument fail to meet a fundamental requirement of process legitimacy, such as a lack of bias.[68] Criticism of Tallinn 1.0 focused on the participants having 'distinctly American and Old European backgrounds',[69] which, it was argued, gave the Manual 'a certain neo-imperialist aftertaste'.[70] Likewise, the decision during the Tallinn drafting process to consult the military manuals of only four States (Canada, Germany, the United Kingdom, and the United States) led to a 'clear problem of representativeness'.[71]

Even instruments emanating from sources with high levels of legitimacy have been critiqued for failures in process. For example, the ICRC was criticised for the methodology employed for the Customary IHL Study, and for being too eager to assert the customary status of a rule, when there seemed insufficient facts or evidence to support such a conclusion.[72] In critiques of the Study, the strong implication is that the entire Study was motivated not by a desire to genuinely ascertain the customary (or non-customary) status of the Additional Protocols, but rather 'from an unrealistic desire to show that controversial provisions of API are declaratory of customary international law'.[73]

Other non-binding instruments have been criticised for failures in outcome, suggesting that the instruments would be unable 'to solve collective problems and to meet the expectations of the governed citizens'.[74] For example, the ICRC DPH Guidance was famously excoriated for perceived procedural failures during the drafting,[75] which risked producing rules 'that will be regarded by states' armed forces as impractical or worse, and which may therefore be ignored'.[76] The AMW Manual was criticised for its outcomes, with one commentator arguing that the Manual's inclusion of 'restrictive, regressive, and reprehensible rules'[77] in the

[68] Shany (n 32) 142.

[69] Lauri Mälksoo, 'The Tallinn Manual as an International Event' (*Diplomaatia*, 8 August 2013) <https://icds.ee/en/the-tallinn-manual-as-an-international-event/> accessed 9 August 2021.

[70] ibid.

[71] ibid.

[72] John B Bellinger III and William J Haynes II, 'A US Government Response to the International Committee of the Red Cross Study Customary International Humanitarian Law' (2007) 89 International Review of the Red Cross 443, 444.

[73] Yoram Dinstein, 'The ICRC Customary International Humanitarian Law Study' (2006) 82 International Law Studies 99, 110.

[74] Mayntz (n 30) 10.

[75] W Hays Parks, 'Part IX of the ICRC "Direct Participation in Hostilities" Study: No Mandate, No Expertise, and Legally Incorrect' (2010) 42 New York University Journal of International Law and Politics 769; William Boothby, '"And for Such Time As": The Time Dimension to Direct Participation in Hostilities' (2010) 42 New York University Journal of International Law and Politics 741; Kenneth Watkin, 'Opportunity Lost: Organised Armed Groups and the ICRC "Direct Participation in Hostilities" Interpretive Guidance' (2010) 42 New York University Journal of International Law and Politics 641; Jann Kleffner, 'Section IX of the ICRC Interpretive Guidance on Direct Participation in Hostilities: The End of Jus in Bello Proportionality As We Know It?' (2012) 45 Israel Law Review 35.

[76] William Boothby, '"And for Such Time As"' (n 75) 768.

[77] Jordan J Paust, 'A Critical Appraisal of the Air and Missile Warfare Manual' (2012) 47 Texas International Law Journal 277, 282.

final document could 'lead to war crime responsibility if they are followed'.[78] The Copenhagen Principles were also disparaged as adding 'little to fulfil the stated objective of 'develop[ing] principles to guide the implementation of the existing obligations with respect to detention in international military operations'.[79]

Do Legitimacy Theories Explain the Success or Failure of Non-Binding Instruments?

Responses to and reception of the non-binding norms in practice leads to the next question, which is whether legitimacy (or its absence) plays any role in the effectiveness of the non-binding norm. Are State-led non-binding instruments more likely to be taken up in practice? Are institutions that seem to fulfil the criteria for legitimacy (such as process legitimacy and structural legitimacy) more likely to create a 'successful' instrument, one that is used in practice? From the examination undertaken in the previous chapter, we can broadly see that, of the 16 distinct non-binding instruments and provisions, those instruments that had a high level of State involvement at all stages of their formulation or adoption seem to have had more impact in practice than those that did not involve States: the Montreux Document, the Copenhagen Principles, and the special agreements provision in Common Article 3 have all had notable impact on State behaviour. This impact in practice is marked when one compares equivalent non-binding instruments that were the outcome of expert groups—in particular, the AMW Manual, the Tallinn Manuals, and the *San Remo Non-International Armed Conflict Manual* (NIAC Manual). The expert group instruments, with the exception of the San Remo Naval Manual, have been less likely to be cited by States before UN bodies, or in domestic practice such as court cases, or in governmental deliberations. However, the absence of State involvement is not itself a predictor of lack of impact; instruments that emanated from the ICRC have had significant impact on State practice, and the Geneva Call Deeds of Commitment, addressed solely at non-State actors, have also been notably successful.

What, then, can we make of this trend? One must of course be careful not to draw absolute conclusions based on limited evidence, but it is possible to make some tentative assessments. The relative impact of the instruments seems very broadly to map to theories of source legitimacy—specifically, that State (or specific institutional) involvement brings legitimacy, which itself compels compliance. In the realm of non-binding instruments, those instruments that have had States or

[78] ibid.

[79] Jacques Hartmann, 'The Copenhagen Process: Principles and Guidelines' (*EJIL:Talk!*, 3 November 2012) <http://www.ejiltalk.org/the-copenhagen-process-principles-and-guidelines/> accessed 9 August 2021.

international institutions[80] involved in their creation have been more likely to be embraced than those that came from expert groups where there was little or no State involvement.

Criticisms of the legitimacy of non-binding instruments raise a larger issue: namely, if the instruments in question are not intended to have legal effect, and are non-binding, why critique their legitimacy when they are not exercises of authority in the first place? A possible answer is that, while these instruments are non-binding, they nonetheless have an impact (and are intended to have an impact) on State behaviour. This conclusion leads to the next question: is this impact legal in nature? Do the instruments have a legal character and, if so, what are the consequences and issues as a result of that (quasi) legality? The non-binding instruments are, prima facie, not law, because of their non-binding nature, but it would be simplistic to assert that they have no legal character at all. As Joost Pauwelyn notes, 'the mere fact that something falls on the non-law side does not mean that it has no legal effect'.[81] As noted in Chapter 7, the non-binding norms have been cited before by domestic and international courts and by States before international bodies such as the United Nations. They have been included in military manuals and other manuals of instruction. Though not law, they are nonetheless law-like.[82] Therefore, this chapter now turns to examine the concept of legality, and how that applies to the non-binding norms under examination.

Defining Legality

Legality, like legitimacy, is a complicated concept, and the focus of considerable literature.[83] It also has several meanings: in international criminal law and international human rights law, the principle of legality—also known as *nullum crimen, nulla poena sine lege*—requires that an act can be punished only if, at the time of its commission, the act was the object of a valid, sufficiently precise, written criminal

[80] Only specific institutions, however—ones that themselves have high levels of institutional legitimacy due to, for example, subject matter expertise.

[81] Joost Pauwelyn, 'Is It International Law or Not, and Does It Even Matter?' in Joost Pauwelyn, Ramses Wessel, and Jan Wouters (eds), *Informal International Lawmaking* (OUP 2012) 130.

[82] Moreover, to consider that law is only law if a sanction applies to non-compliance is a particularly narrow view—indeed, as Joost Pauwelyn notes, if one were to take only this approach, 'little, if anything of today's traditional international law . . . would be law': ibid 131.

[83] See, for example, Carl Schmitt, *Legality and Legitimacy* (Jeffrey Seitzer tr and ed, Duke University Press 2004); Scott Shapiro, *Legality* (Harvard University Press 2011); Fleur Johns, *Non-Legality in International Law: Unruly Law* (CUP 2013); Hans Lindahl, *Fault Lines of Globalization: Legal Order and the Politics of A-Legality* (OUP 2013); Nikolas Rajkovic, Tanja Aalberts, and Thomas Gammeltoft-Hansen (eds), *The Power of Legality: Practices of International Law and Their Politics* (CUP 2016); Jutta Brunnée and Stephen J Toope, *Legitimacy and Legality in International Law* (CUP 2010); David Dyzenhaus, *Legality and Legitimacy: Carl Schmitt, Hans Kelsen and Hermann Heller in Weimar* (OUP 1997).

law to which a sufficiently certain sanction was attached.[84] Legality also has a distinct definition in domestic common law. In English and Australian jurisdictions, the principle of legality relates to the 'interpretive presumption against legislative abrogation of fundamental common law rights'.[85] It is a ' "clear statement principle" according to which courts will not, in the absence of clear statutory words, impute to legislatures an intention to abrogate fundamental common law rights'.[86]

However, in the context of international law literature, legality is most often theorised as a 'generic descriptor attached to certain conduct, phenomena, institutions, systems, people and forms of knowledge deemed to fall within the province, or to possess properties distinctive, of lawfulness'.[87] According to this approach, legality relates to and defines behaviour (or instruments or systems/instructions) as being compliant with existing law. In this respect, legality can be understood in opposition to the idea of illegality—that of acting contrary to existing law. Legality is understood as 'conformity or non-conformity of a body politic, or a national or international mechanism, with the legal rules that regulate its establishment'.[88] An example of legality in this context would be the argument put forward by the defence in the *Tadić* case: that the creation of the Tribunal was illegal because the Security Council lacked the power to establish it.[89] Legality is assessed 'by reference to legal texts, case law, and precedents. Challenges and appeals may be raised as part of the adjudicative process, but there is a clear and final view either in favour or against. An action is always legal or illegal; it cannot be partly legal'.[90]

[84] In its broadest sense, the principle of legality can be considered as including a number of elements. These include the principle of non-retroactivity (*nullum crimen, nulla poena sine lege praevia*); the prohibition against analogy (*nullum crimen, nulla poena sine lege stricta*); the principle of certainty (*nullum crimen, nulla poena sine lege certa*); and the prohibition against uncodified or judge-made criminal provisions (*nullum crimen, nulla poena sine lege scripta*). See generally Susan Lamb, 'Nullum Crimen, Nulla Poena Sine Lege in International Criminal Law' in Antonio Cassese, Paola Gaeta, and John Jones (eds), *The Rome Statute of the International Criminal Court* (OUP 2002).

[85] Brendan Lim, 'The Normativity of the Principle of Legality' (2013) 37 Melbourne University Law Review 372, 373.

[86] ibid.

[87] Fleur Johns, 'Legality' in Jean d'Aspremont and Sahib Singh (eds), *Concepts for International Law: Contributions to Disciplinary Thought* (Elgar 2019) 637.

[88] Antonio Cassese, 'The Legitimacy of International Criminal Tribunals and the Current Prospects of International Criminal Justice' (2012) 25 Leiden Journal of International Law 491, 493.

[89] *Prosecutor v Tadić (Decision on the Defence Motion for Interlocutory Appeal on Jurisdiction)* (Appeals Chamber, Case No IT-94-l-A, 2 October 1995) para 5.

[90] Vesselin Popovski and Nicholas Turner, 'Legality and Legitimacy in International Order' (2008) United Nations University Policy Brief 5, 3. There is also an approach to legality that conceives of the term 'not as a positivist legal study of whether someone or something is in conformity with doctrinal international law but rather as an evolving conceptual nexus between law and politics': Nikolas Rajkovic, Tanja Aalberts, and Thomas Gammeltoft-Hansen, 'Introduction: Legality, Interdisciplinarity and the Study of Practices' in Nikolas Rajkovic, Tanja Aalberts, and Thomas Gammeltoft-Hansen (eds), *The Power of Legality: Practices of International Law and Their Politics* (CUP 2016) 3). For these theorists, legality is a 'product of overlapping practices that order our social world through creating symbols, mobilising concepts and giving legal meanings to entities and actions': ibid 'Introduction: Legality, Interdisciplinarity and the Study of Practices' 11. Legality, in this respect, is collection of 'social performances by various kinds of actors that confirm, reproduce and contest the nexus between/of politics and law': ibid 'Introduction: Legality, Interdisciplinarity and the Study of Practices' 12.

Legality can also be conceived of as defining a behaviour (or instruments or systems/instructions) as having a legal quality—that there are certain consequences due to the 'legal-ness' of the conduct (or system or institution) in question. This can be contrasted with the idea of non-legality[91] and non-law—that 'which stands opposed to or outside the reach of legal norms'.[92] Therefore, legality refers to the legal quality of an object, entity, or mode of behaviour—that is, it has a legal characteristic (rather than an exclusively political, social, or moral quality,[93] notwithstanding that legal-ness can also intersect with these other qualities). Legality, in this respect, is a way of distinguishing between 'social rules formed on the basis of shared understandings'[94] and rules that cross a 'threshold of legal normativity'.[95] If that normative threshold is crossed—by, for example, fulfilling criteria for legality[96]—then 'legal rules are formed and will guide decision-making'.[97] As Nicole Roughan notes, this definition of legality is conceptualised as 'the property of being legal, in the sense of being *of the law* rather than being in accordance with the law. In other words, the relevant distinction is between being legal or non-legal and not between being legal or illegal'.[98]

It is this last approach to legality—that of the property of being legal—that will inform the analysis in the remainder of this chapter, which will look to the legal-ness and legal quality of non-binding instruments. With this definition in mind, the next question to ask is, what makes something international law (such that non-binding instruments would be either law or non-law)?

An (arguably simplistic) approach would posit that international law can be found in Article 38(1) of the Statute of the International Court of Justice (ICJ), which lists the traditional sources of law—treaties, custom, general principles of law, and, as a subsidiary means of determining the content of the law, judicial decisions, and the teachings of eminent publicists. Therefore, to be law, the soft law instruments would need to be characterised as one of the Article 38 sources of law. Indeed, the soft law instruments frequently demonstrate many of the characteristics of the conventional sources of international law—they mimic treaty form or,

91 Johns, *Non-Legality in International Law* (n 83) 1.

92 ibid.

93 Johns, 'Legality' (n 87) 637.

94 Andrea Bianchi, *International Law Theories: An Inquiry into Different Ways of Thinking* (OUP 2016) 120.

95 ibid.

96 Which, for Lon Fuller, would be that 'justice must take the shape of general rules, not of decisions in individual cases; people must be able to acquaint themselves with the content of the rules; laws must apply to future cases; legal rules must be intelligible; legal rules may not contradict one another; legal rules must not make requirements that people are unable to meet; legal rules must not change too often; [and] the rules must be imposed by the government': Paul Cliteur and Afshin Ellian, *A New Introduction to Jurisprudence: Legality, Legitimacy and the Foundations of the Law* (Routledge 2019) 17–18, drawing on Fuller's *The Morality of Law* (Yale University Press 1969) 46–90.

97 Andrea Bianchi (n 94) 120.

98 Nicole Roughan, 'Mind the Gaps: Authority and Legality in International Law' (2016) 27 European Journal of International Law 329, 332.

as in the case of Common Article 3 special agreements and Protocol II amnesties, they are included in binding treaties. Likewise, they have sometimes involved States in their formation and application. Soft law instruments can also stand as examples of State practice, and they are frequently the work of eminent publicists. However, the soft law instruments also fail to sit easily within the Article 38 framework in several ways. While the notion of what makes law 'law' was discussed to some degree in Chapter 1 of this book, it is useful to recollect the arguments here to inform the rest of this chapter. Drawing on the framework outlined by Pauwelyn,[99] the remainder of the chapter will examine the literature on distinguishing law from non-law, which Pauwelyn argues can be divided into five general categories, focusing on sanction, form, intent, effect, and substance.[100]

Law as Sanction

The first of these categories—'law as sanction'—posits that an instrument can be considered law only if it is accompanied by effective and centralised sanctions.[101] If no sanction applies for failure to observe the provisions of the instrument, then the instrument cannot be law. This theory would seem to exclude nearly all the IHL non-binding instruments from being considered law. For example, no sanction follows from failing to observe the terms of the Copenhagen Principles; therefore, they are not law. Even those non-binding principles in binding instruments—the Common Article 3 special agreements provision and the Article 6(5) amnesty provision—do not carry sanction for non-observance.[102]

[99] Pauwelyn, 'Is It International Law or Not' (n 81).

[100] ibid 131.

[101] For example, as espoused by Thomas Hobbes in *Leviathan* (Clarendon Press 1965, reprinted from the edition of 1651) ch XXVI, para 137. See also Mark C Murphy, 'Hobbes (and Austin, and Aquinas) on Law as Command of the Sovereign' in Al P Martinich and Kinch Hoekstra (eds), *The Oxford Handbook of Hobbes* (OUP 2016).

[102] There is debate, however, as to how and whether the question of legality arises in relation to any special agreements adopted under Common Article 3. There is significant literature that looks at the legal effect of special agreements. See further Luisa Vierucci, '"Special Agreements" between Conflicting Parties in the Case-law of the ICTY' in Bert Swart, Alexander Zahar, and Göran Sluiter (eds), *The Legacy of the International Criminal Tribunal for the Former Yugoslavia* (OUP 2011); Georg Schwarzenberger, *International Law as Applied by International Courts and Tribunals* (Stevens and Son 1968) 729. International case law has also explored whether special agreements can be considered treaties, and therefore binding. See further the Special Court for Sierra Leone in *Prosecutor v Kallon (Decision on Challenge to Jurisdiction: Lomé Accord Amnesty)* (Appeals Chamber, Case No SCSL-2004-15-AR72(E) and Case No SCSL-2004-16-AR72(E), 13 March 2004); *Prosecutor v Fofana (Decision on Preliminary Motion on Lack of Jurisdiction: Illegal Delegation of Jurisdiction by Sierra Leone)* (Case No SCSL-2004-14-AR72(E)) para 4; and *Prosecutor v Kondewa (Decision on Lack of Jurisdiction/Abuse of Process: Amnesty Provided by the Lomé Accord)* (Case No SCSL-2004-14-AR72(E), 25 May 2004), as well as the Colombian Constitutional Court, where it was stated that Common Article 3 special agreements are not treaties, as 'they are not established between entities subject to public international law but between the parties to an internal conflict, which are subject to international humanitarian law': Corte Constitucional de la República de Colombia, sentencia C-225/95, Re: File No LAT-040; 18 May 2005, Constitutional review of the Protocol Additional to the Geneva Conventions of 12 August 1949, and

According to the law-as-sanction approach, most, if not all, of the non-binding instruments would have no legal quality or character. The non-binding norms have not been issued by a single sovereign authority that expects compliance or claims unilateral authority, nor is there a possibility of imposing sanctions for purported 'breaches' of the instrument. Non-binding instruments in IHL would be what Austin would consider 'laws of the third class'[103]—rules of positive morality, which embrace:

> human laws of the two following species: 1. The laws (properly so called) which are set by men to men, but not by men as political superiors, nor by men, as private persons, in pursuance of legal rights: 2. The laws which are closely analogous to laws proper, but are merely opinions or sentiments held or felt by men in regard to human conduct.[104]

However, the absence of sanction is not, for some theorists, sufficient to deprive an instrument of legality or legal-ness. For Jutta Brunnée and Stephen Toope, 'fidelity to law . . . is generated because adherence to the criteria of legality in the creation and application of norms produce law that is legitimate in the eyes of those to whom it is addressed'.[105] According to this approach, legal obligation is generated not by the presence of externally imposed sanctions but because the practice of legality is carried out by a community of practice—a community of persons who 'share collective understandings of what they are doing and why'.[106] The interaction of shared understandings with the criteria and practice of legality can create a sense of obligation, even in the absence of an externally imposed sanction.[107] In relation to non-binding instruments, both Brunnée and Toope,[108] as well as Christine Chinkin,[109] note that non-binding norms 'may sometimes possess more obligatory force than norms derived from formal sources of law'[110] due to the interaction

relating to the Protection of Victims of Non-International Armed Conflicts (Protocol II), drawn up in Geneva on 8 June 1977, and of Law 171 of 16 December 1994, whereby said Protocol is approved, para 17 (original in Spanish, unofficial translation, in Marco Sassòli, Antoine A Bouvier, and Anne Quintin, *How Does Law Protect in War: Cases, Documents and Teaching Materials on Contemporary Practice in International Humanitarian Law,* vol 3 (3rd edn, ICRC 2011) 2240). cf Antonio Cassese, 'The Special Court and International Law' (2004) 2 Journal of International Criminal Justice 1130, who contends that non-State armed groups can have international personality.

[103] John Austin, *The Province of Jurisprudence Determined: Being the First Part of a Series of Lectures on Jurisprudence, or, the Philosophy of Positive Law* (2nd edn, 3 vols, London, 1861–63) vol 1, 111.

[104] ibid.

[105] Jutta Brunnée and Stephen J Toope, 'Interactional International Law: An Introduction' (2011) 3 International Theory 307, 308.

[106] Andrea Bianchi, *International Law Theories: An Inquiry into Different Ways of Thinking* (OUP 2016) 120.

[107] Brunnée and Toope, *Legitimacy and Legality* (n 83) 51.

[108] ibid.

[109] Christine Chinkin, 'The Challenge of Soft Law: Development and Change in International Law' (1989) 38 International and Comparative Law Quarterly 850, 850–51.

[110] Brunnée and Toope, *Legitimacy and Legality* (n 83) 51.

between the norm in question, and the sense of legitimacy and engagement with the practice of legality that accompanies it.

Law as Form

A second school of thought considers an instrument to be law if 'certain formalities or procedural steps'[111] are followed—steps which 'elevate an instrument from non-law to law'.[112] These steps vary according to the type of law; for domestic law, the requisite formalities might include enactment as legislation, while in international law, registration as a treaty with the UN Secretary-General under Article 102 of the UN Charter would be a relevant indicium of legality. Applying the 'form' theory of legality to the non-binding norms under extant examination, most of non-binding norms would not be considered law (apart from Common Article 3 and Article 6(5) of Protocol II). All the non-binding instruments under examination meet some basic formal requirements—for example, they are all in written form. However, they do not usually evidence common international legal formalities, such as signature by a representative endowed with full powers (such as a Foreign Minister)[113] or lodgement with the United Nations under Article 102 of the UN Charter.

That being said, lack of strict legal formality does not prima facie exclude the non-binding instruments from the realm of law. As noted by Pauwelyn,[114] and Jan Klabbers,[115] both the European Court of Justice and the ICJ have been prepared to consider a wide variety of instruments as having legal status, including codes of conduct, guidelines, and resolutions.[116] It would seem that strict compliance with legal formalities is not necessarily a requirement for legality; that while the 'form or instrument chosen (*instrumentum*) may not be a formal treaty, the underlying, substantive agreement it embodies (*negotium*) can still be part of international law'.[117] By this reasoning, the non-binding norms in IHL might have a measure of legality—while they are not meant to be binding, they are intended to be treated with a degree of seriousness and consideration. As noted in previous chapters of this book, nearly all the non-binding norms include statements to the effect that they hope to shape State behaviour. Moreover, the rules embodied in the

[111] Pauwelyn, 'Is It International Law or Not' (n 81) 131.
[112] ibid.
[113] Vienna Convention on the Law of Treaties, Arts 2(1)(c), 7.
[114] Pauwelyn, 'Is It International Law or Not' (n 81) 132.
[115] Jan Klabbers, 'The Undesirability of Soft Law' (1998) 67 Nordic Journal of International Law 381, 388–89.
[116] For example, in *Pulp Mills on the River Uruguay (Argentina v Uruguay) (Judgment)* ICJ Rep (20 April 2010) paras 132–50. It should also be noted that the Article 38 list of sources is not considered exhaustive in any event. See further Ole Spiermann, *International Legal Argument in the Permanent Court of International Justice: The Rise of the International Judiciary* (CUP 2005) 207.
[117] Pauwelyn, 'Is It International Law or Not' (n 81) 132.

non-binding instruments can be reflective of existing customary law (as with the San Remo Naval Manual). Therefore, while the instrument itself may not be law, it may embody legal rules, and therefore retain a measure of legality.

Law as Intent to Be Law

The intent of the instrument can also distinguish it as international law: if the drafters of the instrument intended for it to have legally binding effect, then it can be considered law.[118] This approach emphasises the intentions of the drafters, rather than any adherence to questions of form: as noted by Pauwelyn, 'it is fair to say that the criterion of intent of the parties is the criterion generally accepted under international law for purposes of distinguishing what is international law and what is not'.[119] According to this reasoning, non-binding instruments could be binding law if the parties intended for them to be so; as noted above and in previous chapters of this book, the drafters of all of the non-binding instruments have intended for the instruments and provisions to influence and shape the behaviour of the addressees. In this respect, there is some measure of legality due to intent. However, intending to influence and guide behaviour is not equivalent to intending for the instruments to have binding force. It is clear that, apart from Common Article 3's special agreements and Additional Protocol II's amnesty provision, none of the non-binding norms under examination have intended to have binding force—indeed, as noted in chapters 4 and 5, most of the non-binding norms expressly state that the instrument is not intended to be binding. Therefore, the non-binding instruments would lack legality due to a lack of legally binding intent.

Law as Having Legal Effect

A fourth approach to legality states that an instrument could be considered international law if it has, as José Alvarez has termed it, 'normative ripples'[120]—that is, if it has changed State behaviour. It is this type of legality that seems most relevant for the non-binding norms in IHL. According to this approach, international law 'is comprised of those instruments or norms which change State behaviour'.[121] As demonstrated in Chapter 7, several of the non-binding instruments have impacted on and influenced State behaviour; therefore, if we follow an effects-based approach to legality, many of the non-binding instruments would qualify. Indeed,

[118] ibid 134.
[119] ibid.
[120] José Alvarez, *The Impact of International Organizations on International Law* (Brill 2017) 329.
[121] Pauwelyn, 'Is It International Law or Not' (n 81) 136.

the instruments are used in quasi-legal ways by governments and adjudicative bodies—as noted in Chapter 7, the non-binding instruments have been cited alongside binding treaties by States before judicial bodies.

However, one would need to be careful in adopting this approach too thoroughly; as noted in Chapter 7, measuring the impact and influence of the non-binding norms is difficult. It is sometimes unclear whether a particular non-binding instrument has created new practice or is simply reflecting existing practice (for example, the practice of granting amnesties). If we accept that an instrument is legal because of its *effects*, this could lead to a counterintuitive result: that an instrument has legal qualities *only* if it changes behaviour. An effects-based approach to legality might have the contrary outcome with formal sources of law—that is, Common Article 3 special agreements and Protocol II amnesties—being considered as *less* than law, because they have failed to produce the intended effects.

Law as Substance

Finally, an instrument can be considered law if it meets certain substantive criteria, such as legitimacy[122] or what Benedict Kingsbury has termed 'publicness'.[123] Legitimacy and publicness would include adherence to certain principles, including the principles of legality, rationality, proportionality, the rule of law, and human rights.[124] According to this approach, many non-binding instruments might be considered as having legal character in the sense that they reflect 'agreements aimed at influencing the behaviour of states' and/or meet 'basic requirements of legitimacy'.[125] Again, as noted in previous chapters, many of the non-binding norms under examination would seem to meet these standards. They are clearly intended to influence the behaviour of States and they engage with and demonstrate many of the hallmarks of legitimacy. The non-binding instruments would also meet (or at least come close to meeting) proposed standards of publicness. 'Publicness', for Benedict Kingsbury, 'is the claim made for law that it has been wrought by the whole society, by the public, and the connected claim that law addresses matters of concern to the society as such'.[126] On a very simplistic level, many of the non-binding norms address matters of concern to society as a whole, and have involved many aspects of society in their creation—including civil society organisations, governments, industry, and academia.

[122] As proposed by Franck, *The Power of Legitimacy among Nations* (n 4).
[123] Benedict Kingsbury, 'The Concept of "Law" in Global Administrative Law' (2009) 20 European Journal of International Law 23, 29, 31.
[124] ibid 23.
[125] Pauwelyn, 'Is It International Law or Not' (n 81) 136.
[126] Kingsbury (n 123) 31.

However, when we look more closely at Kingsbury's criteria for publicness, the non-binding norms would *not* seem to meet such criteria (or, at least, would not seem appropriate objects of a publicness analysis). Kingsbury draws attention to fundamental requirements of public law, such as having avenues of review of decisions, a practice of reason-giving by decision-makers, and a commitment to publicity and transparency by rule-makers and decision-makers.[127] The non-binding norms do not easily fit within this framework; for example, they are not exercises in decision-making power. Therefore, while the non-binding instruments might meet requirements of legitimacy, they are less likely to fit with notions of publicness.

The Legality of Non-Binding Norms

Can non-binding norms ever be law? Differing approaches to legality would seem to cover the entirety of the spectrum: one approach would see non-binding norms as having legal or law-like qualities, while other approaches would take a far more binary view—that something is either law or not law, and that, unlike with legitimacy, there cannot be a spectrum of legality. However, there is an additional element in relation to legality and international law—as Pauwelyn has noted, whether something can be considered law also depends on the question of capacity, rather than effect.[128] Namely, are those actors involved in the creation of the non-binding instrument endowed with the capacity to make law in the first instance, regardless of how the instrument is ultimately received and perceived? How one answers this question depends on how one views the capacity of the participants in the first instance. If one takes the position that *only* States can make international law (and even then, *only* through designated persons endowed with full powers[129]), then the non-binding instruments cannot ever be law, because, even though States have been involved in the creation of some instruments, the instruments were not intended to be binding, and they have not resulted in a document signed by an authorised representative of the State (with the signature the designated method of indicating an intention to be bound under international law).

A broader view would argue that any official State involvement, even at lower levels of government, would be sufficient to contribute to the legal status of the instrument: that any representative of the State, serving in that capacity and engaging in the negotiation and adoption of a non-binding instrument, would be sufficient to contribute to an instrument's international legality.[130] A broader view still argues that *any* actor with *any* quantum of international legal personality—including

[127] ibid 32.
[128] Pauwelyn, 'Is It International Law or Not' (n 81) 141.
[129] As provided in Articles 6 and 7 of the Vienna Convention on the Law of Treaties.
[130] Pauwelyn, 'Is It International Law or Not' (n 81) 143.

international organisations, non-governmental organisations, and even armed non-State groups—can make international law. This line of reasoning is premised on the fact that, by virtue of these actors' position as bearers of rights and responsibilities under international law, they 'enjoy a fledgling position as international law-makers'[131] and are therefore capable of making law both through their practice (as contributing to customary international law) and through positive acts such as participation in instrument negotiation and adoption.[132] The consequences of taking a broad view of the legal capacity of participants in the creation of non-binding norms would be significant (and will be explored in more detail in the final chapter (Chapter 9) of this book).

The non-binding norms under examination are not law, but they are clearly not without legal impact. Additionally, the instruments engage with discourses and practices of legitimacy, which evidences an intent that the instruments are meant to be treated with a degree of seriousness by addressees. What are the consequences of treating the non-binding norms as quasi-legal, quasi-legitimate exercises of authority in IHL? It is this question that will be explored in the final chapter of this book.

[131] ibid. See also Gunther Teubner, 'Global Bukowina: Legal Pluralism in the World Society' in Gunther Teubner (ed), *Global Law without a State* (Dartmouth 1997); Anthony Clark Arend, *Legal Rules and International Society* (OUP 1999) 176–85.

[132] Arend (n 131) 177. However, see further Jean d'Aspremont, who argues that 'whatever the influence of these non-state actors may be, states and international organisations remain the exclusive international law-makers': Jean d'Aspremont, 'Non-State Actors from the Perspective of Legal Positivism' in Jean d'Aspremont (ed), *Participants in the International Legal System: Multiple Perspectives on Non-State Actors in International Law* (Routledge 2011) 25.

9

The Impact of the Turn towards the Non-Binding in International Humanitarian Law and the Way Forward for Non-Binding Norms in International Humanitarian Law

Introduction

International law now increasingly involves 'new actors, processes and instruments that escape the narrow confines of traditional international law [leading] to increasing engagement with informal international law'.[1] As noted in Chapter 6, there are notable benefits that come from engaging with non-binding instruments. Such instruments bring with them a degree of 'speed, flexibility',[2] and dynamism that formal treaty-making processes can lack. Likewise, non-binding instruments can engage with a broader range of stakeholders, potentially exerting a greater compliance pull. The impact of these non-binding and informal instruments is notable; as explored in previous chapters of this book, the instruments have influenced State practice, are treated as quasi-legal documents by stakeholders, and 'are more and more discussed side-by-side with treaties, State and judicial practice'.[3] However, while there has been attention paid to these immediate impacts of non-binding instruments, it is also important to note potential long-term impacts connected to non-binding instruments. Primary among these is whether the turn to non-binding instruments presents a problem for traditional law-making processes: that is to say, are non-binding instruments being embraced *instead* of binding norms? Moreover, if the non-binding form is gaining precedence as a normative format, does the involvement of other actors in the creation of non-binding instruments itself create problems of accountability, bias, or representativeness (which may ultimately have implications for legitimacy and efficacy)? This final chapter will return to some of the debates examined in Chapter 1 regarding the 'problems' of soft law and non-binding instruments and will explore whether the

[1] Eve Kassoti, 'Beyond State Consent? International Legal Scholarship and the Challenge of Informal International Law-Making' (2016) 63 Netherlands International Law Review 99, 99–100.
[2] Anthony Aust, 'The Theory and Practice of Informal International Instruments' (1986) 35 International and Comparative Law Quarterly 787, 807.
[3] Kassoti (n 1) 100.

Non-Binding Norms in International Humanitarian Law. Emily Crawford, Oxford University Press. © Emily Crawford 2021.
DOI: 10.1093/oso/9780198819851.003.0010

proliferation of non-binding instruments (and the proliferation of stakeholders involved in their creation) is problematic or an opportunity for international humanitarian law (IHL)—or, perhaps, both.

Exploring the Effect of the Turn to Non-Binding Instruments in International Humanitarian Law: The Impact on Formal Law-Making

A recent common theme in the literature on the sources of international law, and the process of international law-making, is that States are taking something of a step back from traditional or formal international law-making processes—specifically, treaty-making.[4] Articles and books speak of a 'widespread deadlock in multi-lateral treaty making',[5] and note that 'formal international law is stagnating in both terms of quantity and quality ... increasingly superseded by "informal international lawmaking" involving new actors, new processes, and new outputs'.[6] This seems to be the case in IHL particularly, an arena where, as Michael Schmitt and Sean Watts have commented, 'the guns of State IHL *opinio juris* have fallen silent'.[7] Into this purported gap, 'norm entrepreneurs'[8]—people interested in effecting social change—have emerged. In addition to State-made law, we now have various international actors all engaging in processes that look very much like treaty-making or law-making,[9] including international organisations,[10] non-State

[4] Joost Pauwelyn, Ramses Wessel, and Jan Wouters, 'When Structures Become Shackles: Stagnation and Dynamics in International Lawmaking' (2014) 25 European Journal of International Law 733, 734–38.

[5] Anton Orlinov Petrov, *Expert Laws of War: Restating and Making Law in Expert Processes* (Elgar 2020) 11. See also Joost Pauwelyn, Ramses Wessel, and Jan Wouters, 'Informal International Law as Presumptive Law: Exploring New Modes of Law-Making' in Rain Liivoja and Jarna Petman (eds), *International Law-Making: Essays in Honour of Jan Klabbers* (Routledge 2014) 76–78.

[6] Pauwelyn, Wessel, and Wouters, 'When Structures Become Shackles' (n 4).

[7] Michael Schmitt and Sean Watts, 'The Decline of International Humanitarian Law *Opinio Juris* and the Law of Cyber Warfare' (2015) 50 Texas International Law Journal 189, 191.

[8] Cass R Sunstein, 'Social Norms and Social Roles' (1996) 96 Columbia Law Review 903, 909.

[9] This topic has been comprehensively examined by numerous scholars, not least including Pauwelyn, Wessel, and Wouters, who have undertaken immensely valuable research into the examination of law-making by non-States and law-making in informal contexts: Joost Pauwelyn, Ramses Wessel, and Jan Wouters, *Informal International Lawmaking* (OUP 2012). See also Jean d'Aspremont (ed), *Participants in the International Legal System: Multiple Perspectives on Non-State Actors in International Law* (Routledge 2011); Patrick Capps and Henrik Palmer Olsen (eds), *Legal Authority beyond the State* (CUP 2018); Math Noortmann and Cedric Ryngaert (eds), *Non-State Actor Dynamics in International Law: From Law-Takers to Law-Makers* (Ashgate 2010).

[10] See generally Nigel White, 'Lawmaking' in Jacob Katz Cogen, Ian Hurd, and Ian Johnstone (eds), *The Oxford Handbook of International Organisation* (OUP 2016); José Alvarez, *International Organizations as Lawmakers* (OUP 2005); Inger-Johanne Sand, 'Varieties of Authority in International Law: State Consent, International Organisations, Courts, Experts and Citizens' in Patrick Capps and Henrik Palmer Olsen (eds), *Legal Authority Beyond the State* (CUP 2018); Krzysztof Skubiszewski, 'Forms of Participation of International Organizations in the Lawmaking Processes' (1964) 18 International Organization 790; Ramses Wessel, 'Institutional Lawmaking: The Emergence of a Global

civil society organisations,[11] international and transnational corporations,[12] and groups of individuals.[13] These 'new actors'[14] are engaging in 'new processes'[15] of norm and rule generation, and producing 'new outputs'[16]—outputs that forward 'more flexible norms or guidelines, grounded in practical experience and expertise and continuously corrected to take account of new developments and learning'.[17]

This turn to the informal and the non-binding has led observers to comment that States are, voluntarily or not, abdicating their traditionally central role as law-makers on the international plane, with the related development that treaties are no longer the singular mechanism for international governance—as Anne Peters, Lucy Koechlin, and Gretta Fenner Zinkernagel note, 'on all levels of governance, standard setting (norm formation or regulation) is no longer the exclusive domain of states',[18] a sentiment echoed by Laurence Boisson de Chazournes, who notes that, given the manifold changes wrought by the process of globalisation, the quintessential form of law-making—the treaty—'might not be of great help for regulating behaviours'.[19] The proliferation of non-binding norms in IHL—as examined in this book—might indicate that, as Yahli Shereshevsky has argued, States are 'reluctant to directly engage in the making of IHL'.[20] Anton Petrov notes something similar:

Normative Web' in Catherine Brölmann and Yannick Radi (eds), *Research Handbook on the Theory and Practice of International Lawmaking* (Elgar 2016).

[11] See generally Barbara K Woodward, 'International Lawmaking and Civil Society' in Catherine Brölmann and Yannick Radi (eds), *Research Handbook on the Theory and Practice of International Lawmaking* (Elgar 2016); Steve Charnovitz, 'Two Centuries of Participation: NGOs and International Governance' (1997) 18 Michigan Journal of International Law 183; Laura Pedraza-Farina, 'Conceptions of Civil Society in International Lawmaking and Implementation: A Theoretical Framework' (2013) 34 Michigan Journal of International Law 605.

[12] Peter Muchlinski, 'Multinational Enterprises as Actors in International Law: Creating "Soft Law" Obligations and "Hard Law" Rights' in Math Noortman and Cedric Ryngaert (eds), *Non-State Actors Dynamics in International Law: From Law-Takers to Law Makers* (Ashgate 2010); Stephen Tully, *Corporations and International Lawmaking* (Martinus Nijhoff 2007); Daniel Thürer, 'The Emergence of NGOs and Transnational Enterprises in International Law and the Changing Role of the State' in Rainer von Hofmann and Nils Geissler (eds), *Non-State Actors as New Subjects of International Law: International Law—From the Traditional State Order towards the Law of the Global Community. Proceedings of an International Symposium of the Kiel Walther-Schücking-Institute of International Law, March 25 to 28, 1998* (Duncker and Humblot 1999); David Snyder, 'Private Lawmaking' (2003) 64 Ohio State Law Journal 371.

[13] Petrov, *Expert Laws of War* (n 5); Jörg Kammerhofer, 'Lawmaking by Scholars' in Catherine Brölmann and Yannick Radi (eds), *Research Handbook on the Theory and Practice of International Lawmaking* (Elgar 2016).

[14] Pauwelyn, Wessel, and Wouters, 'When Structures Become Shackles' (n 4) 741.

[15] ibid 734.

[16] ibid.

[17] ibid 742–43.

[18] Anne Peters, Lucy Koechlin, and Gretta Fenner Zinkernagel, 'Non-State Actors as Standard Setters: Framing the Issue in an Interdisciplinary Fashion' in Anne Peters and others (eds), *Non-State Actors as Standard Setters* (CUP 2009) 1.

[19] Laurence Boisson de Chazournes, 'Treaty Law-Making and Non-Treaty Law-Making: The Evolving Structure of the International Legal Order' in Rüdiger Wolfrum and Volker Röben (eds), *Developments of International Law in Treaty Making* (Springer 2005) 463.

[20] Yahli Shereshevsky, 'Back in the Game: International Humanitarian Lawmaking by States' (2019) 37 Berkeley Journal of International Law 1, 4.

> Interpretations [of the law] by states have legal effect according to the doctrine of sources and could effectively steer the [expert process] discourse and add elements of formal law to it. However, states do not actively participate in these processes. This opens up space for expert processes to leave their mark. Does this invite another instance of *expert rule*, an often-used commonplace to designate today's technocratic regulation of global affairs?
>
> If that were the case, one would wonder when states will wake up and intervene.[21]

However, while there *has* been a diminution of treaties more generally,[22] this does not necessarily mean that *no* meaningful or significant IHL treaties have been adopted. Over the last 25 years, a considerable number of IHL treaties have been adopted on topics including, inter alia, blinding laser weapons,[23] cultural property,[24] landmines,[25] cluster munitions,[26] the trade in small arms,[27] the creation of a third protected emblem,[28] nuclear weapons,[29] and the creation of the International Criminal Court (ICC).[30] These treaties—all of them in force—do not seem to suggest that States are not engaging with treaty-making or treaty-adoption in IHL. What is undoubtedly true is that States are no longer the sole or primary drivers of IHL—for example, several of the abovementioned treaties came to fruition, in large part, only because of advocacy undertaken by civil society organisations.[31] Furthermore, as noted in previous chapters, civil society organisations and

[21] Petrov, *Expert Laws of War* (n 5) 233.

[22] Pauwelyn, Wessel, and Wouters, 'When Structures Become Shackles' (n 4) 734–38.

[23] Convention on Prohibitions or Restrictions on the Use of Certain Conventional Weapons which may be deemed to Be Excessively Injurious or to Have Indiscriminate Effects (Protocol on Blinding Laser Weapons) (Protocol IV to the 1980 Convention) (adopted 13 October 1995, entered into force 30 July 1998) 1380 UNTS 370.

[24] Second Protocol to the Hague Convention of 1954 for the Protection of Cultural Property in the Event of Armed Conflict (adopted 26 March 1999, entered into force 9 March 2004) 2253 UNTS 172.

[25] Convention on the Prohibition of the Use, Stockpiling, Production and Transfer of Anti-Personnel Mines and on their Destruction (adopted 18 September 1997, entered into force 1 March 1999) 2056 UNTS 211.

[26] Convention on Cluster Munitions (adopted 30 May 2008, entered into force 1 August 2010) 2688 UNTS 30.

[27] Arms Trade Treaty (adopted 2 April 2013, entered into force 24 December 2014) 3013 UNTS 1.

[28] Protocol additional to the Geneva Conventions of 12 August 1949, and relating to the Adoption of an Additional Distinctive Emblem (Protocol III) (adopted 8 December 2005, entered into force 14 January 2007) 2404 UNTS 261.

[29] Treaty on the Prohibition of Nuclear Weapons (adopted 7 July 2017, entered into force 22 January 2021).

[30] Rome Statute of the International Criminal Court (adopted 17 July 1998, entered into force 1 July 2002) 2187 UNTS 90.

[31] For example, the Treaty on the Prohibition of Nuclear Weapons was influenced greatly by the work of the International Campaign to Abolish Nuclear Weapons (ICAN); likewise, the International Campaign to Ban Landmines was instrumental in the adoption of the 1997 mine ban treaty. See further Motoko Mekata, 'How Transnational Civil Society Realized the Ban Treaty: An Interview with Beatrice Fihn' (2018) 1 Journal for Peace and Nuclear Disarmament 79; Kenneth Anderson, 'The Ottawa Convention Banning Landmines, the Role of International Non-Governmental Organisations and the Idea of International Civil Society' (2000) 11 European Journal of International Law 91.

non-State groups have been pivotal in the development and production of the non-binding norms that have proliferated in IHL. States are now clearly sharing the norm-generation stage with 'a wide array of entities ... [that] have entered into the scene and challenged the norm-making monopoly of traditional subjects'.[32] The question becomes whether this development in IHL is problematic. In this respect, it is useful to return to the debate on soft law, and on informal international law-making more specifically.[33]

In their examination of informal international law-making,[34] Joost Pauwelyn, Ramses Wessel, and Jan Wouters note that there are three elements that can mark law-making as informal—output informality, actor informality, and process informality.[35] Output informality relates to the production of a document that cannot be categorised as a traditional source of law, as outlined in Article 38 of the International Court of Justice Statute;[36] process informality relates to situations where 'international cooperation occurs in a loosely organised network or forum rather than a traditional international organisation';[37] and actor informality relates to the participation of non-traditional actors in international processes, including private actors, non-governmental and civil society organisations, and other actors not traditionally capable of making international law.[38] Does 'author informality' or informality in process or output cause (or have the potential to cause) problems for how or whether IHL is observed and implemented? As noted in Chapter 8 on legitimacy and legality, informality at any or all stages of law-making can have the effect of impacting on the perceived legitimacy of the instrument, which in turn may impact its legality and effectiveness. However, as also noted in Chapter 8, these informal instruments *do* engage in measures to bolster their legitimacy, which, arguably, serve to offset any issues that may arise regarding their informality. As Jean d'Aspremont has noted, non-State actors have been 'involved in international law-making for more than 200 years',[39] though the extent of their contribution has 'undergone a noteworthy increase'[40] in recent years. Arguably, the involvement

[32] Kassoti (n 1) 102. See also Nico Krisch and Benedict Kingsbury, 'Introduction: Global Governance and Global Administrative Law in the International Legal Order' (2006) 17 European Journal of International Law 1, 1.

[33] Though it should be noted that the concepts of soft law and informal international law-making are not necessarily coextensive. See further Joost Pauwelyn, 'Informal International Lawmaking: Framing the Concept and Research Questions' in Joost Pauwelyn, Ramses Wessel, and Jan Wouters (eds), *Informal International Lawmaking* (OUP 2012).

[34] Pauwelyn, 'Informal International Lawmaking' (n 33).

[35] ibid 15.

[36] ibid.

[37] ibid 17.

[38] ibid 19.

[39] Jean d'Aspremont, 'International Law-Making by Non-State Actors: Changing the Model or Putting the Phenomenon into Perspective' in Math Noortmann and Cedric Ryngaert (eds), *Non-State Actor Dynamics in International Law: From Law-Takers to Law-Makers* (Ashgate 2010) 175.

[40] ibid 176.

of non-State actors at *any* stage of norm-generating processes does not 'suggest a major upheaval of the entire international law-making system'.[41]

In any event, as evidenced in Chapter 6 of this book, States *are* engaging with non-binding norms—either during or after their creation. By choosing to engage (or not engage) with non-binding norms or informal law-making processes and outputs, States are themselves contributing to the generation of formal law, in the form of customary international law. It therefore cannot be said that States are not involved, in some way, in the norm-creating process. Moreover, the parallel proliferation of treaties in IHL (alongside the non-binding instruments) would not seem to suggest a repudiation of formal law-making in IHL, nor the outright rejection of the State as lawmaker in international law.

If the incorporation of informal means of norm generation exists, quite comfortably, alongside more formal means in IHL, what then is the problem? As was explored in Chapter 6 of this book, there are manifold benefits that come with these new actors, processes, and outputs—they overcome the strict and often rigid structures of formal international law-making processes and outputs, allowing for *all* interested stakeholders to provide input to the system that governs their behaviour. However, as identified by Pauwelyn, Wessel, and Wouters, informal instruments in international law do have distinct drawbacks, namely in the areas of accountability and transparency.[42] These distinct structural problems may indeed cause later problems for IHL and are discussed in the next section.

Non-Binding Norms and Accountability, Transparency, and Bias

The first, and most obvious, drawback of non-binding norms is the absence of formal accountability or transparency mechanisms. As Pauwelyn, Wessel, and Wouters have noted, 'whether an instrument is "legally binding" under international law is simply no longer the right criterion or proxy. To the extent that new forms of cooperation matter or have an impact, they must be justified'.[43] Many of the non-binding documents have no mechanism for review—if a State decides to adopt the provisions of a non-binding instrument in practice, there may be 'limited opportunities for judicial review because informality weakens the ability of individuals to invoke the policy in court or to challenge its validity'.[44]

[41] ibid.

[42] Pauwelyn, 'Informal International Lawmaking' (n 33) 19.

[43] Joost Pauwelyn, Ramses Wessel, and Jan Wouters, 'Informal International Lawmaking: An Assessment and Template to Keep It Both Effective and Accountable' in Joost Pauwelyn, Ramses Wessel, and Jan Wouters (eds), *Informal International Lawmaking* (OUP 2012) 510.

[44] Eyal Benvenisti, 'Towards a Typology of Informal International Lawmaking Mechanisms and Their Distinct Accountability Gaps' in Joost Pauwelyn, Ramses Wessel, and Jan Wouters (eds), *Informal International Lawmaking* (OUP 2012) 306.

Many non-binding norms lack a degree of domestic accountability and might be considered as 'unreflective of democratic choices'.[45] Additionally, as was seen in Chapters 4 and 5, publicly available information regarding how these instruments have originated, and what processes were involved in their creation, can often be scant or even entirely absent. This lack of accountability and transparency means that the creation of non-binding instruments may be a process susceptible to manipulation or influence by interest groups with a particular perspective to promote. As Benvenisti has argued:

> the informality of international cooperation, with their lack of accountability and transparency, lends itself to capture by narrow interest groups ... the more informal the policy-making, the more capture is possible and the less the process and outcome are open to public scrutiny. Such concerns intensify when governments take the back seat and allow private actors to set their own standards without public scrutiny.[46]

An example of this would be the controversy that arose surrounding procedural and substantive accountability and transparency issues during the creation of the International Committee of the Red Cross Direct Participation in Hostilities (ICRC DPH) Guidance, specifically, the inclusion of Section IX (as it was then termed) in the final draft of the interpretive guidance in 2007. Section IX had been purportedly inserted into the draft DPH document by the ICRC, allegedly 'without consultation with participating experts or its co-sponsor, the TMC Asser Institute'.[47] This allegation would seem to suggest that the DPH Expert Process was subject to processes that were not entirely accountable or transparent to their participants, let alone to those who would ultimately be the addressees of the instrument. Additional to these procedural concerns was the substantive issue of the underlying approach that Section IX seemed to espouse: that 'if a combatant can be put out of action by taking him prisoner, he should not be injured; if he can be put out of action by injury, he should not be killed; and if he can be put out of action by light injury, grave injury should be avoided'.[48] At least 15 of the experts involved in the DPH expert process believed that the Section was making 'a novel argument unknown under contemporary IHL'[49]—that in combat, one must be guided by the

[45] ibid.

[46] ibid 306.

[47] W Hays Parks, 'Part IX of the ICRC "Direct Participation in Hostilities" Study: No Mandate, No Expertise, and Legally Incorrect' (2010) 42 New York University Journal of International Law and Politics 769, 783. This is disputed in Nils Melzer, 'Keeping the Balance between Military Necessity and Humanity: A Response to Four Critiques of the ICRC's Interpretive Guidance on the Notion of Direct Participation in Hostilities' (2010) 42 New York University Journal of International Law and Politics 831, 894.

[48] ICRC, *Report on the Work of Experts: Weapons That May Cause Unnecessary Suffering or Have Indiscriminate Effects* (ICRC 1973) 13, para 23.

[49] ICRC, Summary Report, Fourth Expert Meeting on the Notion of Direct Participation in Hostilities, 27–28 November 2006, 75.

principle of humanity above all else, including even military necessity.[50] Critics of Section IX felt that it essentially implied that there was a legal obligation for combatants to use less than lethal force in a combat zone, contrary to State practice.[51] The ICRC DPH Guidance would seem be an example of what Eyal Benvenisti has noted regarding soft law and informal international law-making: that the process of '"legislating from below" may benefit some disadvantaged groups ... at the expense of others. While NGOs [non-governmental organisations] may be effective in enhancing the accountability of others to the interests the NGOs represent, it is less clear whether NGOs are equally committed to accountability to those whom they do not represent'.[52]

Another accountability issue for informal and non-binding instruments is that such instruments circumvent traditional domestic mechanisms of accountability and transparency.[53] Non-binding and informal instruments do not require the same kinds of domestic affirmation as do treaties—they do not need to be transformed into legislation,[54] or to be otherwise approved by the primary legislative body.[55] For Pauwelyn, Wessel, and Wouters, '[t]he circumvention of domestic formalities linked to lawmaking must be taken more seriously. Domestic accountability mechanisms are at the core of keeping new models of international cooperation in check ... [c]ertain new forms of cooperation ... avoid this legitimising step'.[56] For them, accountability in informal instruments is vital for, if there is no oversight over the instruments, they would 'turn ineffective as neutrality, quality, and trust in the norms created is likely to wane and with it their legitimacy and effectiveness ... [U]ltimately, effectiveness and accountability go hand in hand'.[57] In order to overcome this legitimacy gap, Pauwelyn, Wessel, and Wouters recommend that a 'minimum degree of congressional or parliamentary oversight of all international cooperation that limits individual freedom—treaty or not—must be available'.[58]

[50] Parks (n 47) 785. This theory of humanity over military necessity has been called 'Pictet's use-of-force continuum', as Pictet had argued that 'humanity demands capture rather than wounds, and wounds rather than death': Jean Pictet, *Humanitarian Law and the Protection of War Victims* (Henry Dunant Institute 1975) 32.

[51] ICRC, Summary Report (n 49) 75.

[52] Benvenisti (n 44) 308.

[53] Pauwelyn, Wessel, and Wouters, 'Informal International Lawmaking' (n 43) 513.

[54] For example, in Australia, while the executive has essentially unfettered power to enter into treaties (under section 51(xxix) of the Australian Constitution), only Parliament can give the treaty binding force by way of legislative act. See further Annemarie Devereux and Sarah McCosker, 'International Law and Australian Law' in Donald Rothwell and Emily Crawford (eds), *International Law in Australia* (3rd edn, Thomson Reuters 2017).

[55] For example, in the United States, any treaty action taken by the Executive requires approval by Congress. See generally Johan van der Vyver, *Implementation of International Law in the United States* (Peter Lang 2010).

[56] Pauwelyn, Wessel, and Wouters, 'Informal International Lawmaking' (n 43) 513.

[57] ibid 518.

[58] ibid 514.

That being said, non-binding norms in IHL may not be subject to concerns about oversight, at least not in the same ways as informal international instruments (such as those examined by Pauwelyn, Wessel, and Wouters). As noted in Chapter 2 of this book, States have long engaged with non-binding norms in IHL and, as with other forms of State and non-State practice, it is for States to decide whether they choose to engage with such instruments. If States have concerns about the validity, legitimacy, or legality of a particular non-binding instrument, they can, much like with customary international law, choose to openly reject some or all of the rules put forward in that particular instrument—which, arguably, is the ultimate form of democratic oversight.

An additional concern regarding non-binding norms is that they may be susceptible to bias. As noted in Chapters 4 and 5, many of the IHL non-binding instruments are the work of small groups of experts. Those experts are often drawn from predominantly Western European and Others Group (WEOG) States, with little to no representation from Central or Eastern Asian States, African States, or South American States. This raises the spectre that the instruments are subject to what Anthea Roberts has called 'westernizing influences'[59] that 'reinforce particular approaches to international law'.[60] A predominance of Western and Western-educated experts in the expert processes makes the selection of experts a critical factor and, with it, 'representativeness, or a lack thereof'.[61] As Roberts has pointed out, there is an overrepresentation of WEOG experts working in international law practice, primarily coming from 'Anglophone and Francophone core Western States'.[62] This overrepresentation in practice is largely mirrored in the expert processes[63] and could potentially play a role in entrenching what might be considered a Western idea of international law.[64] This is particularly evident in many of the IHL expert processes, where there is a clear 'geographical imbalance in favour of Australia, Canada, Germany, the United Kingdom and the United States, whereby many individuals have participated in multiple expert processes'.[65]

Institutional bias may also be present; while the experts in many of these expert processes serve in their personal capacity, even so it is difficult to escape the conclusion that experts representing, say, the ICRC or a State military would likely not depart too radically from their institutional training when advocating for a particular position or interpretation of the law. As Ka Lok Yip notes of the participants in the ICRC DPH Guidance, 'those working for their government's armed forces clearly had a direct vested interest at stake in the interpretation of the notion of

[59] Anthea Roberts, *Is International Law International?* (OUP 2017) 44.
[60] ibid 48.
[61] Petrov, *Expert Laws of War* (n 5) 59.
[62] Roberts (n 59) 256.
[63] For a full detailing of participants in the instruments and States of origin, see further Chapter 4.
[64] See further Roberts (n 59) ch 5.
[65] Petrov, *Expert Laws of War* (n 5) 79.

direct participation in hostilities as it could affect the scope of their freedom in planning combat operations'.[66] Likewise, the ICRC's controversial introduction of Section IX in its DPH Guidance could be considered an example of a particular institutional bias coming out during the drafting of a non-binding instrument.

Transparency of process and outcome is also a key consideration for the non-binding norms. As evidenced in Chapters 4 and 5, there is considerable variation regarding the publicly available information relating to the non-binding instruments. While many of the instruments have the entirety of the drafting documents published (either in print or online, such as the ICRC DPH Process), some (like the Non-International Armed Conflict (NIAC) Manual) have little or no publicly available information regarding their procedure or how they arrived at their substantive outcomes. While some documents have been open regarding drafting participants and drafting procedures, others have been less so. Openness and transparency are vital for ensuring that an instrument is not biased and is engaging in practices of legitimacy.

Non-binding norms can therefore potentially raise several issues regarding accountability, transparency, and bias. They are frequently created by unappointed and unelected experts without a mandate from States, engaging in closed-door procedures whose processes and participants are only made evident after the process is completed, if at all,[67] and with no mechanism by which those being governed by such new rules can challenge their validity. As Anton Petrov has noted: 'expert processes deny the possibility of accountability ... they circumvent the requirements of formalised settings, such as geographical representation. In this regard, they are even worse than most other actors who often show similar deficiencies with a view to methodology, but at least, follow procedural safeguards'.[68]

In professing to be merely restating the law, rather than making new law, many non-binding instruments 'seek to avoid responsibility for their claims by presenting their restatements as findings that are not binding'.[69] But many non-binding norms *do* essentially engage in something that looks very similar to law creation: for example, while the drafters of the *Tallinn Manual on the International Law Applicable to Cyber Warfare* (Tallinn Manual) did not create the law on individual criminal liability for war crimes, they did say that it applies in cyber warfare,[70] even while commentators acknowledge that there have been few, if any, instances of cyber operations that could be considered as reaching the level of armed conflict.[71] Issues

[66] Ka Lok Yip, 'The ICRC's Interpretive Guidance on the Notion of Direct Participation in Hostilities: Sociological and Democratic Legitimacy in Domestic Legal Orders' (2017) 8 Transnational Legal Theory 224, 241.

[67] Petrov, *Expert Laws of War* (n 5) 79.

[68] ibid 233.

[69] ibid 232.

[70] Tallinn 2.0, Rule 84, 391.

[71] Stilgherrian, 'Suppose They Started a Cyber War and No-One Knew' (*SBS*, 14 November 2016) <http://www.sbs.com.au/guide/article/2016/11/11/suppose-they-started-cyber-war-and-no-one-knew> accessed 9 August 2021; Thomas Rid, *Cyber War Will Not Take Place* (C Hurst & Co 2013); Lior

of accountability and transparency of process and outcome, as well as possible procedural and substantive bias, are therefore 'live' issues.

Despite these potential pitfalls, it seems likely that non-binding instruments will continue to proliferate in IHL. They offer a mechanism for prompt, dynamic, and adaptive responses to new and pressing challenges in IHL, and international law more generally. As demonstrated in this book, non-binding norms are having an impact on State practice and are being treated in legal ways by States and other international law institutions. Therefore, despite their non-binding nature, these instruments are, in effect, making claims to authority and, as such, need to possess a degree of legitimacy in order to assert a compliance pull. In this respect, ensuring that there is some accountability, transparency, and a lack of bias in the non-binding norms seems crucial to their legitimacy and legality—and, therefore, their effectiveness. What this accountability, transparency, and lack of bias would look like is something of which all drafters of future non-binding instruments should be mindful. This may mean more transparency during the drafting process (such as more systematic engagement with civil society and States); more assiduous attempts to ensure broad geographical representation among participants; more extensive State consultations before and during the drafting process; more open communication regarding participants and drafting procedures; and perhaps even ongoing efforts to revise and update documents in light of State and non-State practice. Indeed, some of the new non-binding norms being written are engaging in precisely these practices, with information readily available about the participants and processes involved in both the *Woomera Manual*[72] and the *Manual on International Law Applicable to Military Uses of Outer Space*.[73]

In the future, a more comprehensive study on the legality, legitimacy, and efficacy of non-binding norms in other regions of the globe would be beneficial. The present study was limited in a number of ways—having access only to publicly available records, and in only a limited array of languages, from a limited array of legal systems. More comprehensive analysis of the impact of these norms in practice in regions such as Asia, Africa, the Middle East, and South America would be enormously instructive to explore whether these non-binding instruments are influencing State practice globally and whether the hopes to guide and

Tabansky, 'The Current State of Cyber Warfare' (May 2015) *Cyber Security Review* <https://www.cybersecurity-review.com/articles/the-current-state-of-cyber-warfare/> accessed 9 August 2021: 'Centrally, war is a violent act, where the threat of force and violence is instrumental to achieving a political goal. Neither denial-of-service, web hacking, nor espionage are even potentially violent, even when Stuxnet is considered—no cyber incident has yet been violent nor caused loss of human life. Since none of the cyber events have yet met the requirements to constitute a war, the "cyberwar" metaphor should be relinquished, at least for the time being.'

[72] University of Adelaide, *Woomera Manual* https://law.adelaide.edu.au/woomera/ accessed 9 August 2021.

[73] McGill University, *Manual on International Law Applicable to Military Uses of Outer Space* https://www.mcgill.ca/milamos/ accessed 9 August 2021.

instruct State and non-State behaviour during armed conflict are being borne out. But what the present study has shown is that, contrary to practitioners' critiques of non-binding and soft instruments and possible concerns regarding their legitimacy, both the creators of the instruments and the addressees and recipients of the instruments treat these instruments with care and consideration. For the most part, the creators of most of these non-binding instruments—particularly those that are the results of expert processes or that emanate from civil society—take steps to ensure that their work is a careful consideration of the law, frequently engaging with the central tenets of legitimacy discourse to ensure that it is well-received and effective. Likewise, the addressees and recipients of the non-binding instruments also seem to treat the instruments with careful attention, with clear evidence that those instruments that may not have scrupulously hewn to the *lex lata* are being less welcomed in practice. Where all the non-binding instruments can clearly improve is in the realm of transparency of process—better, and more publicly available, information regarding the processes involved in their creation will likely contribute to enhanced legitimacy, which will potentially impact on the legitimacy and legality of such instruments and assuage concerns regarding accountability and bias.

Bibliography

Abbott K and Snidal D, 'Hard and Soft Law in International Governance' (2000) 54 International Organisation 421

Abbott K and others, 'The Concept of Legalisation' (2000) 54 International Organisation 401

Abi-Saab G, 'Wars of National Liberation and the Development of Humanitarian Law' in Akkerman R, van Krieken P, and Pannenborg C (eds), *Declarations on Principles: A Quest for Universal Peace* (Sijthoff 1977) 143–73

Abi-Saab G, 'Cours général de droit international public' (1987) 207 Recueil des Cours 1

Abi-Saab G, 'Human Rights and Humanitarian Law in Internal Conflicts' in Warner D (ed), *Human Rights and Humanitarian Law: The Quest for Universality* (Martinus Nijhoff 1997) 107–24

Akande D, 'Clearing the Fog of War? The ICRC's Interpretive Guidance on Direct Participation in Hostilities' (2010) 59 International and Comparative Law Quarterly 180

Aldrich G, 'Customary International Humanitarian Law—An Interpretation on Behalf of the International Committee of the Red Cross' (2005) 76 British Yearbook of International Law 503

Alkan Olsson I, 'Four Competing Approaches to International Soft Law' (2013) 58 Scandinavian Studies in Law 177

Allansson M, Melander E, and Themnér L, 'Organized Violence, 1989–2016' (2017) 54 Journal of Peace Research 574

Alvarez J, *International Organizations as Lawmakers* (OUP 2005)

Alvarez J, *The Impact of International Organizations on International Law* (Brill 2017)

Anderson K, 'The Ottawa Convention Banning Landmines, the Role of International Non-Governmental Organisations and the Idea of International Civil Society' (2000) 11 European Journal of International Law 91

Arai-Takahashi Y, *The Law of Occupation: Continuity and Change of International Humanitarian Law, and Its Interaction with International Human Rights Law* (Brill 2009)

Arend AC, *Legal Rules and International Society* (OUP 1999)

Aust A, 'The Theory and Practice of Informal International Instruments' (1986) 35 International and Comparative Law Quarterly 787

Austin J, *The Province of Jurisprudence Determined: Being the First Part of a Series of Lectures on Jurisprudence, or, the Philosophy of Positive Law* (2nd edn, 3 vols, London 1861–63)

Avgouleas E, *Governance of Global Financial Markets: The Law, the Economics, the Politics* (CUP 2012)

Bacon JM, 'The Balloon in Warfare', *Macmillan's Magazine* (1 May 1904)

Baldwin R, Cave M, and Lodge M, *Understanding Regulation: Theory, Strategy, and Practice* (2nd edn, OUP 2012)

Barnard C, *The Functions of the Executive* (Harvard University Press 1951)

Barnsby R and Reeves S, 'Give Them an Inch, They'll Take a Terabyte: How States May Interpret Tallinn Manual 2.0's International Human Rights Law Chapter' (2017) 95 Texas Law Review 1515

Baxter RR, 'International Law in "Her Infinite Variety"' (1980) 29 International and Comparative Law Quarterly 549 (1980)

Bell C, *On the Law of Peace* (OUP 2008)

Bellinger JB, III and Haynes WJ, II, 'A US Government Response to the International Committee of the Red Cross Study Customary International Humanitarian Law' (2007) 89 International Review of the Red Cross 443

Ben-Ari RH, *The Normative Position of International Non-Governmental Organizations under International Law: An Analytical Framework* (Martinus Nijhoff 2012)

Benvenisti E, 'Towards a Typology of Informal International Lawmaking Mechanisms and Their Distinct Accountability Gaps' in Pauwelyn J, Wessel R, and Wouters J (eds), *Informal International Lawmaking* (OUP 2012) 297–309

Besson S, 'Theorising the Sources of International Law' in Besson S and Tasioulas J (eds), *The Philosophy of International Law* (OUP 2010) 163–85

Best G, *Humanity in Warfare: The Modern History of the International Law of Armed Conflicts* (Weidenfeld and Nicolson 1980)

Bethlehem D, 'The Methodological Framework of the Study' in Wilmshurst E and Breau S (eds), *Perspectives on the ICRC Study on Customary International Humanitarian Law* (CUP/Chatham House/BIICL 2007) 3–14

Betti A, '"Slay This Monster": The United States and Opposition to the Rome Statute on the International Criminal Court' (2016) 17 Human Rights Review 417

Beyerlin U, 'Different Types of Norms in International Environmental Law: Policies, Principles, and Rules' in Bodansky D, Brunnée J, and Hey E (eds), *The Oxford Handbook of International Environmental Law* (OUP 2007) 425–48

Bianchi A, *International Law Theories: An Inquiry into Different Ways of Thinking* (OUP 2016)

Blutman L, 'In the Trap of a Legal Metaphor: International Soft Law' (2010) 59 International and Comparative Law Quarterly 605

Boals K, 'The Internal War in Yemen' in Falk R (ed), *The International Law of Civil War* (Johns Hopkins 1971) 303–47

Bodansky D, 'The Concept of Legitimacy in International Law' in Wolfrum R and Röben V (eds), *Legitimacy in International Law* (Springer 2008) 309–17

Bodansky D, 'Legitimacy' in Bodansky D, Brunnée J, and Hey E (eds), *The Oxford Handbook of International Environmental Law* (OUP 2008) 704–26

Boisson de Chazournes L, 'Treaty Law-Making and Non-Treaty Law-Making: The Evolving Structure of the International Legal Order' in Wolfrum R and Röben V (eds), *Developments of International Law in Treaty Making* (Springer 2005) 463–79

Bongard P and Somer J, 'Monitoring Armed Non-State Actor Compliance with Humanitarian Norms: A Look at International Mechanisms and the Geneva Call Deed of Commitment' (2011) 93 International Review of the Red Cross 673

Boon K, 'Charter of Economic Rights and Duties of States (1974)' in Peters A and Wolfrum R (eds), *Max Planck Encyclopedia of Public International Law* (OUP 2013)

Boothby W, '"And for Such Time As": The Time Dimension to Direct Participation in Hostilities' (2010) 42 New York University Journal of International Law and Politics 741

Boothby W, 'Direct Participation in Hostilities—A Discussion of the ICRC Interpretive Guidance' (2010) 1 Journal of International Humanitarian Law Studies 143

Boothby W, *Conflict Law* (Springer 2014)

Bosch S, 'The International Humanitarian Law Notion of Direct Participation in Hostilities—A Review of the ICRC Interpretive Guide and Subsequent Debate' (2014) 17 Potchefstroom Electronic Law Journal 999

Bothe M, 'Legal and Non-Legal Norms—A Meaningful Distinction in International Relations?' (1980) 11 Netherlands Yearbook of International Law 65

Bothe M, 'Customary International Humanitarian Law: Some Reflections on the ICRC Study' (2005) 8 Yearbook of International Humanitarian Law 143
Bothe M and others (eds), *New Rules for Victims of Armed Conflicts: Commentary on the Two 1977 Protocols Additional to the Geneva Conventions of 1949* (2nd edn, Martinus Nijhoff 2013)
Boyle A and Chinkin C, *The Making of International Law* (OUP 2007)
Braumann C and Reinisch A, 'Effet Utile' in Klingler J, Parkhomenko Y, and Salonidis C (eds), *Between the Lines of the Vienna Convention? Canons and Other Principles of Interpretation of Public International Law* (Wolters Kluwer 2019) 47–72
Brummer C, 'Why Soft Law Dominates International Finance—and Not Trade' (2010) 13 Journal of International Economic Law 623
Brunnée J and Toope SJ, *Legitimacy and Legality in International Law* (CUP 2010)
Brunnée J and Toope SJ, 'Interactional International Law: An Introduction' (2011) 3 International Theory 307
Buchanan A, *Justice, Legitimacy, and Self-Determination: Moral Foundations for International Law* (OUP 2003)
Buchanan A and Keohane R, 'The Legitimacy of Global Governance Institutions' (2006) 20 Ethics and International Affairs 405
Buchanan A and Keohane R, 'The Legitimacy of Global Governance Institutions' in Wolfrum R and Röben V (eds), *Legitimacy in International Law* (Springer 2008) 25–62
Burke R, 'From Individual Rights to National Development: The First UN International Conference on Human Rights, Tehran, 1968' (2008) 19 Journal of World History 275
Buzatu A-M, 'Towards an International Code of Conduct for Private Security Providers: A View from Inside a Multi-Stakeholder Process' (Geneva Centre for the Democratic Control of Armed Forces, SSR Paper 12, 2015)
Capps P and Olsen HP (eds), *Legal Authority beyond the State* (CUP 2018)
Carlson J, 'Hunger, Agricultural Trade Liberalisation, and Soft International Law: Addressing the Legal Dimensions of a Political Problem' (1984–85) 70 Iowa Law Review 1187
Cassese A, 'The Special Court and International Law' (2004) 2 Journal of International Criminal Justice 1130
Cassese A, *International Law* (2nd edn, OUP 2005)
Cassese A, 'The Legitimacy of International Criminal Tribunals and the Current Prospects of International Criminal Justice' (2012) 25 Leiden Journal of International Law 491
Castañeda J, *Legal Effects of United Nations Resolutions* (Amoia A tr, Columbia University Press 1969)
Chadwick E, 'Merchant Ship Conversion in Warfare, the Falklands (Malvinas) Conflict and the Requisition of the QE2' (2010) 12 Journal of the History of International Law 71
Chaisse J, 'Demystifying Public Security Exception and Limitations on Capital Movement: Hard Law, Soft Law and Sovereign Investments in the EU Internal Market' (2015–16) 37 University of Pennsylvania Journal of International Law 583
Charlesworth H, 'Law-Making and Sources' in Crawford J and Koskenniemi M (eds), *The Cambridge Companion to International Law* (CUP 2012) 187–202
Charnovitz S, 'Two Centuries of Participation: NGOs and International Governance' (1997) 18 Michigan Journal of International Law 183
Chatterjee SK, 'The Charter of Economic Rights and Duties of States: An Evaluation after 15 Years' (1991) 40 International and Comparative Law Quarterly 669
Chayes A and Chayes AH, *The New Sovereignty: Compliance with International Regulatory Agreements* (Harvard University Press 1988)

Chinkin C, 'The Challenge of Soft Law: Development and Change in International Law' (1989) 38 International and Comparative Law Quarterly 850

Chinkin C, 'Normative Development in the International Legal System' in Shelton D (ed), *Commitment and Compliance: The Role of Non-Binding Norms in the International Legal System* (OUP 2000) 21–42

Clapham A, 'The Rights and Responsibilities of Armed Non-State Actors: The Legal Landscape & Issues Surrounding Engagement' (Geneva Academy of International Humanitarian Law and Human Rights 2010) <ssrn.com/abstract=1569636> accessed 10 August 2021

Clapham A, Gaeta P, and Sassòli M (eds), *The 1949 Geneva Conventions: A Commentary* (OUP 2016)

Cliteur P and Ellian A, *A New Introduction to Jurisprudence: Legality, Legitimacy and the Foundations of the Law* (Routledge 2019)

Cockayne J, 'Regulating Private Military and Security Companies: The Context, Negotiation, Weaknesses and Promise of the Montreux Document' (2008) 13 Journal of Conflict & Security Law 401

Coicaud J-M and Heiskanen V (eds), *The Legitimacy of International Organizations* (United Nations University Press 2001)

Cole A and others (eds), *San Remo Handbook on Rules of Engagement* (Institute of International Humanitarian Law 2009)

Coleman K, *International Organisations and Peace Enforcement: The Politics of International Legitimacy* (CUP 2007)

Corn G and Jensen ET, 'Transnational Armed Conflict: A "Principled" Approach to the Regulation of Counter-Terror Combat Operations' (2009) 42 Israel Law Review 46

Corn G and Taylor R, 'Sovereignty in the Age of Cyber' (2017) 111 American Journal of International Law (unbound) 207

Crawford E, *Identifying the Enemy: Civilian Participation in Armed Conflict* (OUP 2015)

Crawford E, 'Accounting for the ENMOD Convention: Cold War Influences on the Origins and Development of the 1976 Convention on Environmental Modification Techniques' in Craven M, Pahuja S, and Simpson G (eds), *International Law and the Cold War* (CUP 2020) 81–97

Crosland M, 'Science and the Franco-Prussian War' (1976) 6 Social Studies of Science 185

Crowe D, *War Crimes, Genocide, and Justice* (Springer 2014)

Cryer R, 'Of Custom, Treaties, Scholars and the Gavel: The Influence of the International Criminal Tribunals on the ICRC Customary Law Study' (2006) 11 Journal of Conflict & Security Law 239

Cullen A, 'Key Developments Affecting the Scope of Internal Armed Conflict in International Humanitarian Law' (2005) 183 Military Law Review 66

Cullen A, *The Concept of Non-International Armed Conflict in International Humanitarian Law* (CUP 2012)

D'Amato A, 'Softness in International Law: A Self-Serving Quest for New Legal Materials: A Reply to Jean d'Aspremont' (2009) 20 European Journal of International Law 897

d'Aspremont J, 'Softness in International Law: A Self-Serving Quest for New Legal Materials' (2008) 19 European Journal of International Law 1075

d'Aspremont J, 'International Law-Making by Non-State Actors: Changing the Model or Putting the Phenomenon into Perspective' in Noortmann M and Ryngaert C (eds), *Non-State Actor Dynamics in International Law: From Law-Takers to Law-Makers* (Ashgate 2010) 171–94

d'Aspremont J, *Formalism and the Sources of International Law: A Theory of the Ascertainment of Legal Rules* (OUP 2011)
d'Aspremont J, 'Non-State Actors from the Perspective of Legal Positivism' in d'Aspremont J (ed), *Participants in the International Legal System: Multiple Perspectives on Non-State Actors in International Law* (Routledge 2011) 23–40
d'Aspremont J, (ed), *Participants in the International Legal System: Multiple Perspectives on Non-State Actors in International Law* (Routledge 2011)
d'Aspremont J, '"Effectivity" in International Law: Self-Empowerment against Epistemological Claustrophobia' (2014) 108 ASIL Proceedings 165
DB, 'The Brussels International Declaration of 1874 concerning the Laws and Customs of War' (1974) 14 International Review of the Red Cross 616
De Koker C, 'The Copenhagen Process on the Handling of Detainees in International Military Operations: Principles and Guidelines—A Critical Appraisal' in Shapland J and others (eds), *Desistance, Social Order and Responses to Crime* (Maklu 2014) 167–84
de Visscher C, *Les Effectivités du Droit International Public* (Pedone 1967)
Demeyere B and others, 'The Updated ICRC Commentary on the Second Geneva Convention: Demystifying the Law of Armed Conflict at Sea' (2016) 98 International Review of the Red Cross 401
Despagnet F, *Cours de Droit International Public* (de Boeck C ed, 4th edn, Librairie de la Société du Recueil Sirey; L Larose et L Tenin 1910)
Devereux A and McCosker S, 'International Law and Australian Law' in Rothwell D and Crawford E (eds), *International Law in Australia* (3rd edn, Thomson Reuters 2017) 23–47
Dinstein Y, 'The ICRC Customary International Humanitarian Law Study' (2006) 82 International Law Studies 99
Dinstein Y, 'Direct Participation in Hostilities' (2013) 18 Tilburg Law Review 3
Dinstein Y, *Non-International Armed Conflicts in International Law* (2nd edn, CUP 2021)
dos Reis Fe and Kessler O, 'The Power of Legality, Legitimacy and the (Im)possibility of Interdisciplinary Research' in Rajkovic N, Aalberts T, and Gammeltoft-Hansen T (eds), *The Power of Legality: Practices of International Law and Their Politics* (CUP 2016) 99–124
Doswald-Beck L, 'San Remo Manual on International Law Applicable to Armed Conflicts at Sea' (1995) 35 International Review of the Red Cross 583
Doswald-Beck L, (ed), *San Remo Manual on International Law Applicable to Armed Conflicts at Sea* (CUP 1995)
Doswald-Beck L and Vité S, 'Origin and Nature of Human Rights Law and Humanitarian Law' (1993) 293 International Review of the Red Cross 94
Dowdeswell TL, 'The Brussels Peace Conference of 1874 and the Modern Laws of Belligerent Qualification' (2017) 54 Osgoode Hall Law Journal 805
Dunlap C, 'Law of War Manuals and Warfighting: A Perspective' (2012) 47 Texas International Law Journal 265
Dupuy P-M, 'Soft Law and the International Law of the Environment' (1991) 12 Michigan Journal of International Law 420
Dupuy R-J, 'Declaratory Law and Programmatory Law: From Revolutionary Custom to "Soft Law"' in Akkerman R, van Krieken P, and Pannenborg C (eds), *Declarations on Principles: A Quest for Universal Peace* (Leiden 1977) 247–58
Dyzenhaus D, *Legality and Legitimacy: Carl Schmitt, Hans Kelsen and Hermann Heller in Weimar* (OUP 1997)
Easton D, *A Systems Analysis of Political Life* (Wiley 1965)
Easton D, 'A Reassessment of the Concept of Political Support (1975) 5 British Journal of Political Science 435

Efrony D and Shany Y, 'A Rule Book on the Shelf? Tallinn Manual 2.0 on Cyberoperations and Subsequent State Practice' (2018) 112 American Journal of International Law 583

Eichensehr K, 'Review: The Tallinn Manual on the International Law Applicable to Cyber Warfare' (2014) 108 American Journal of International Law 585

Eide A, Rosas A, and Meron T, 'Combating Lawlessness in Gray Zone Conflicts through Minimum Humanitarian Standards' (1995) 89 American Journal of International Law 215

Elder D, 'The Historical Background of Common Article 3 of the Geneva Convention of 1949' (1979) 11 Case Western Reserve Journal of International Law 37

Ellis J, 'Shades of Grey: Soft Law and the Validity of Public International Law' (2012) 25 Leiden Journal of International Law 313

Emanuelli C, 'Comments on the ICRC Study on Customary International Humanitarian Law' (2006) 44 Canadian Yearbook of International Law 437

Emerson J, 'Great Weapon or "Fanciful Contraption"? The Rise and Fall of the Union Balloon Corps' (2012) 51 Civil War Times 33

English J, 'The Ottawa Process: Paths Followed, Paths Ahead' (1998) 52 Australian Journal of International Affairs 121

Ewumbue-Monono C, 'Respect for International Humanitarian Law by Armed Non-State Actors in Africa' (2006) 88 International Review of the Red Cross 905

Fastenrath U, 'Relative Normativity in International Law' (1993) 4 European Journal of International Law 305

Fenrick W, 'ICRC Guidance on Direct Participation in Hostilities' (2009) 12 Yearbook of International Humanitarian Law 287

Fitzmaurice G, 'Report on the Law of Treaties' (1956) 2 Yearbook of the International Law Commission 104

Fitzmaurice M and Elias O, *Contemporary Issues in the Law of Treaties* (Eleven 2005)

Fleck D, 'Humanitarian Protection in Non-International Armed Conflicts: The New Research Project of the International Institute of Humanitarian Law' (2000) 30 Israel Yearbook on Human Rights 1

Francioni F, 'International "Soft Law": A Contemporary Assessment' in Lowe V and Fitzmaurice M (eds), *Fifty Years of the International Court of Justice: Essays in Honour of Sir Robert Jennings* (CUP 1996) 167–78

Franck T, *The Power of Legitimacy among Nations* (OUP 1990)

Franck T, *Fairness in International Law and Institutions* (Clarendon 1995)

Franck T, 'The Power of Legitimacy and the Legitimacy of Power: Law in an Age of Power Disequilibrium' (2006) 100 American Journal of International Law 88

Freeman M, *Necessary Evils: Amnesties and the Search for Justice* (CUP 2009)

Freidel F, *Francis Lieber: Nineteenth Century Liberal* (Peter Smith 1968)

Friedrich J, *International Environmental 'Soft Law': The Functions and Limits of Nonbinding Instruments in International Environmental Governance and Law* (Springer 2013)

Fuller L, *The Morality of Law* (Yale University Press 1969)

Gammeltoft-Hansen T, Lagoutte S, and Cerone J, 'Introduction: Tracing the Roles of Soft Law in Human Rights' in Lagoutte S, Gammeltoft-Hansen T, and Cerone J (eds), *Tracing the Roles of Soft Law in Human Rights* (OUP 2016) 1–13

Garcia-Peña Jaramillo D, 'Humanitarian Protection in Non-International Armed Conflicts: A Case Study of Colombia' (2000) 30 Israel Yearbook on Human Rights 179

Gardiner R, *Treaty Interpretation* (2nd edn, OUP 2015)

Garner JW, *The German War Code: A Comparison of the German Manual of the Laws of War with Those of the United States, Great Britain, and France and with the Hague Convention Respecting the Laws and Customs of War on Land* (University of Illinois 1918)

Garner JW, *International Law and the World War* (Longmans Green 1920)

Garner JW, 'International Regulation of Air Warfare' (1932) 3 Air Law Review 309

Gill T and others (eds), *Leuven Manual on the International Law Applicable to Peace Operations* (CUP 2017)

Gleditsch NP and others, 'Armed Conflict 1946–2001: A New Dataset' (2002) 39 Journal of Peace Research 615

Göcke K, 'The Brussels Declaration' in Peters A and Wolfrum R (eds), *Max Planck Encyclopedia of Public International Law* (OUP 2013)

Gold J, 'Strengthening the Soft International Law of Exchange Arrangements' (1983) 77 American Journal of International Law 443

Graber D, *The Development of the Law of Belligerent Occupation, 1863–1914: A Historical Survey* (Columbia University Press 1949)

Green L, *The Contemporary Law of Armed Conflict* (3rd edn, Manchester University Press 2008)

Grespin W, 'An Act of Faith: Building the International Code of Conduct for Private Security Providers' (*Diplomatic Courier* July/August 2012)

Gruchalla-Wesierski T, 'A Framework for Understanding "Soft Law"' (1984) 30 McGill Law Journal 38

Guzman A and Meyer T, 'International Soft Law' (2010) 2 Journal of Legal Analysis 171

Guzman A and Meyer T, 'Soft Law' in Kontorovich E and Parisi F (eds), *Economic Analysis of International Law* (Elgar 2016) 123–54

Habermas J, *Between Facts and Norms: Contributions to a Discourse Theory of Law and Democracy* (MIT Press 1998)

Haines S, 'War at Sea: Nineteenth-Century Laws for Twenty-First Century Wars?' (2016) 98 International Review of the Red Cross 419

Hanke HM, 'The 1923 Hague Rules of Air Warfare: A Contribution to the Development of International Law Protecting Civilians from Air Attack' (1993) 292 International Review of the Red Cross 12

Hannam H, 'The Status of the Universal Declaration of Human Rights in National and International Law' (1995–96) 25 Georgia Journal of International and Comparative Law 287

Hart HLA, *The Concept of Law* (2nd edn, Clarendon 1994)

Hartigan R, *Lieber's Code and the Law of War* (Gryphon 1983)

Hartwig M, 'ICANN—Governance by Technical Necessity' in von Bogdandy A and others (eds), *The Exercise of Public Authority by International Institutions: Advancing International Institutional Law* (Springer 2010) 575–605

Hayashi N, *The Role and Importance of the Hague Conferences: A Historical Perspective* (UNIDIR 2017)

Heffes E and Kotlik M, 'Special Agreements as a Means of Enhancing Compliance with IHL in Non-International Armed Conflicts: An Inquiry into the Governing Legal Regime' (2014) 96 International Review of the Red Cross 1195

Heintschel von Heinegg W, 'The Current State of the Law of Naval Warfare: A Fresh Look at the San Remo Manual' (2006) 82 International Law Studies 269

Heintschel von Heinegg W, 'The Law of Armed Conflict at Sea' in Fleck D (ed), *The Handbook of International Humanitarian Law* (OUP 2013) 475–568

Heintschel von Heinegg W, 'Maritime Warfare' in Clapham A and Gaeta P (eds), *The Oxford Handbook of International Law in Armed Conflict* (OUP 2014) 145–81

Heintschel von Heinegg W, 'The San Remo Manual—History, Methodology and Future Application' in Stephens D and Stubbs M (eds), *The Law of Naval Warfare* (LexisNexis Butterworths 2019) 11–25

Henckaerts J-M, 'Customary International Humanitarian Law: Taking Stock of the ICRC Study' (2010) 78 Nordic Journal of International Law 435

Henckaerts J-M and Doswald-Beck L (eds), *Customary International Humanitarian Law* (ICRC 2005)

Hernández G, 'Effectiveness' in d'Aspremont J and Singh S (eds), *Concepts for International Law: Contributions to Disciplinary Thought* (Elgar 2019) 237–50

Herst H, 'The Civil War's Attempt at Aerial Warfare' (1995) 253 Stamps 8

Higgins R, *Problems and Process: International Law and How We Use It* (Clarendon 1994)

Hill-Cawthorne L, 'The Copenhagen Principles of the Handling of Detainees: Implications for the Procedural Regulation of Internment' (2013) 18 Journal of Conflict & Security Law 481

Hillgenberg H, 'A Fresh Look at Soft Law' (1999) 10 European Journal of International Law 499

Hobbes T, *Leviathan* (Clarendon Press 1965, original published 1651)

Hoffman M, 'The Application of International Humanitarian Law in Sri Lanka: A Compliance Based Case Study on the Rules of War' (2000) 30 Israel Yearbook on Human Rights 209

Hofmann L, 'Strengthening the Principle of Distinction? A Critical Appraisal of the ICRC's Continuous Combat Function' (2015) 6 Journal of International Humanitarian Law Studies 377

Holland TE, *The Laws of War on Land: Written and Unwritten* (Clarendon 1908)

Horowitz J, 'Introductory Note to the Copenhagen Process Principles and Guidelines on the Handling of Detainees in International Military Operations' (2012) 51 International Legal Materials 1364

Hume D, *A Treatise of Human Nature* (Clarendon Press 1896)

Hurd I, 'Legitimacy and Authority in International Politics' (1999) 53 International Organisation 379

International Committee of the Red Cross, 'Interpretive Guidance on the Notion of Direct Participation in Hostilities under International Humanitarian Law, Adopted by the Assembly of the International Committee of the Red Cross on 26 February 2009' (2008) 90 International Review of the Red Cross 991

International Committee of the Red Cross, *Commentary on the Second Geneva Convention: Convention (II) for the Amelioration of the Condition of the Wounded, Sick and Shipwrecked Members of Armed Forces at Sea* (2nd edn, ICRC 2017)

International Committee of the Red Cross, *Customary IHL Database* <https://ihl-databases.icrc.org/customary-ihl/eng/docs/home> accessed 10 August 2021

Jakovljević B and Patrnogić J, 'The Urgent Need to Apply the Rules of Humanitarian Law to So-Called Internal Armed Conflicts' (1961) 1 International Review of the Red Cross 250

Jennings R, 'Nullity and Effectiveness in International Law' in Jennings R (ed), *Cambridge Essays in International Law: Essays in Honour of Lord McNair* (Stevens and Son 1965) 64–87

Jennings R, 'An International Lawyer Takes Stock' (1990) 39 International and Comparative Law Quarterly 513

Jensen ET, 'The Future of the Law of Armed Conflict: Ostriches, Butterflies, and Nanobots' (2014) 35 Michigan Journal of International Law 253

Jensen ET and Watts S, 'A Cyber Duty of Due Diligence: Gentle Civilizer or Crude Destabiliser?' (2017) 95 Texas Law Review 1555

Johns F, *Non-Legality in International Law: Unruly Law* (CUP 2013)

Johns F, 'Legality' in d'Aspremont J and Singh S (eds), *Concepts for International Law: Contributions to Disciplinary Thought* (Elgar 2019) 636–49

Kalshoven F, 'The Conference of Government Experts on the Reaffirmation and Development of International Humanitarian Law Applicable in Armed Conflicts, 24 May–12 June, 1971' (1971) 2 Netherlands Yearbook of International Law 68

Kalshoven F, 'The Conference of Government Experts on the Reaffirmation and Development of International Humanitarian Law Applicable in Armed Conflicts (Second Session), 3 May–2 June, 1972' (1972) 3 Netherlands Yearbook of International Law 18

Kammerhofer J, 'Lawmaking by Scholars' in Brölmann C and Radi Y (eds), *Research Handbook on the Theory and Practice of International Lawmaking* (Elgar 2016) 305–26

Kassoti E, 'Beyond State Consent? International Legal Scholarship and the Challenge of Informal International Law-Making' (2016) 63 Netherlands International Law Review 99

Keller H, 'Codes of Conduct and Their Implementation: The Question of Legitimacy' in Wolfrum R and Röben V (eds), *Legitimacy in International Law* (Springer 2008) 219–98

Kelly C, 'The Sociological Pull of Soft Law' (2012) 106 ASIL Proceedings 327

Kelsen H, *Principles of International Law* (Holt, Rinehart, Winston 1966)

Kelsey JTG, 'Hacking into International Law: The Principles of Distinction and Neutrality in the Age of Cyber Warfare' (2008) 106 Michigan Law Review 1427

Kerr R, *The International Criminal Tribunal for the Former Yugoslavia: An Exercise in Law, Politics, and Diplomacy* (OUP 2004)

Kingsbury B, 'The Concept of "Law" in Global Administrative Law' (2009) 20 European Journal of International Law 23

Kirton J and Trebilcock M, 'Hard Choices and Soft Law in Sustainable Global Governance' in Kirkton J and Trebilcock M (eds), *Hard Choices, Soft Law: Voluntary Standards in Global Trade, Environment and Social Governance* (Routledge 2004) 3–29

Kirton J and Trebilcock M (eds), *Hard Choices, Soft Law: Voluntary Standards in Global Trade, Environment and Social Governance* (Routledge 2016)

Klabbers J, *The Concept of Treaty in International Law* (Kluwer 1996)

Klabbers J, 'The Redundancy of Soft Law' (1996) 65 Nordic Journal of International Law 167

Klabbers J, 'The Undesirability of Soft Law' (1998) 67 Nordic Journal of International Law 381

Kleffner J, 'Section IX of the ICRC Interpretive Guidance on Direct Participation in Hostilities: The End of Jus in Bello Proportionality As We Know It?' (2012) 45 Israel Law Review 35

Kolb R, 'The Relationship between International Humanitarian Law and Human Rights Law: A Brief History of the 1948 Universal Declaration of Human Rights and the 1949 Geneva Conventions' (1998) 324 International Review of the Red Cross 400

Kolb R, 'Human Rights Law and International Humanitarian Law between 1945 and the Aftermath of the Teheran Conference of 1968' in Kolb R and Gaggioli G (eds), *Research Handbook on Human Rights and Humanitarian Law* (Elgar 2013) 35–52

Kolb R, *Theory of International Law* (Hart 2016)

Korns S and Kastenberg J, 'Georgia's Cyber Left Hook' (2008–09) 38 Parameters 60

Kreß C, 'War Crimes Committed in Non-International Armed Conflict and the Emerging System of International Criminal Justice' (2000) 30 Israel Yearbook on Human Rights 103

Krisch N and Kingsbury B, 'Introduction: Global Governance and Global Administrative Law in the International Legal Order' (2006) 17 European Journal of International Law 1

Kritsiotis D, 'International Humanitarian Law and the Disintegration of States' (2000) 30 Israel Yearbook on Human Rights 17

Kumm M, 'The Legitimacy of International Law: A Constitutionalist Framework of Analysis' (2004) 15 European Journal of International Law 907

Labuda P, 'The Lieber Code' in Peters A and Wolfrum R (eds), *Max Planck Encyclopedia of Public International Law* (OUP 2013)

Lamb S, 'Nullum Crimen, Nulla Poena Sine Lege in International Criminal Law' in Cassese A, Gaeta P, and Jones J (eds), *The Rome Statute of the International Criminal Court* (OUP 2002) 733–66

Lauterpacht H, *Recognition in International Law* (CUP 1947)

Lim B, 'The Normativity of the Principle of Legality' (2013) 37 Melbourne University Law Review 372

Lindahl H, *Fault Lines of Globalization: Legal Order and the Politics of A-Legality* (OUP 2013)

Liu IY, 'The Due Diligence Doctrine under Tallinn Manual 2.0' (2017) 33 Computer Law and Security Review 390

Lorimer J, *The Institutes of the Law of Nations: A Treatise on the Jural Relations of Separate Political Communities* (vol 2, Blackwood 1884)

Lowe V, 'The Impact of the Law of the Sea on Naval Warfare' (1987) 14 Syracuse Journal of International Law and Commerce 657

Lowe V, *International Law* (OUP 2007)

Mačák K, 'Military Objectives 2.0: The Case for Interpreting Computer Data as Objects under International Humanitarian Law' (2015) 48 Israel Law Review 55

Mačák K, 'On the Shelf, But Close at Hand: The Contribution of Non-State Initiatives to International Cyber Law', Symposium on Efrony D and Shany Y, 'A Rule Book on the Shelf? Tallinn Manual 2.0 on Cyberoperations and Subsequent State Practice' (2019) 113 American Journal of International Law (unbound) 81

MacLaren M and Schwendimann F, 'An Exercise in the Development of International Law: The New ICRC Study on Customary International Humanitarian Law' (2005) 6 German Law Journal 1217

MacLeod S, 'Private Security Companies and Shared Responsibility: The Turn to Multistakeholder Standard-Setting and Monitoring through Self-Regulation-"Plus"' (2015) 62 Netherlands International Law Review 119

Mälksoo L, 'The Tallinn Manual as an International Event' (*Diplomaatia*, 8 August 2013) <https://icds.ee/en/the-tallinn-manual-as-an-international-event/> accessed 10 August 2021

Marr S, 'The Southern Blue Fin Tuna Cases: The Precautionary Approach and Conservation and Management of Fish Resources' (2000) 11 European Journal of International Law 815

Martens FF, *La paix et la guerre: la conférence de Bruxelles 1874. Droits et devoirs des belligérants (leur application pendant la guerre d'Orient 1874–1878) la conférence de La Haye 1899* (Arthur Rousseau 1901)

Mayntz R, 'Legitimacy and Compliance in Transnational Governance' (2010) Max Planck Institute for the Study of Societies Working Paper 10/5

McCormack T and Liivoja R, 'Law in the Virtual Battlespace: The Tallinn Manual and the Jus in Bello' (2012) 15 Yearbook of International Humanitarian Law 45

McEvoy K and Mallinder L, 'Amnesties in Transition: Punishment, Restoration, and the Governance of Mercy' (2012) 39 Journal of Law and Society 410

McLaughlin R, *Recognition of Belligerency and the Law of Armed Conflict* (OUP 2020)

McNair A, *The Law of Treaties: British Practice and Opinions* (OUP 1938)
McNair A, *International Law Opinions, Selected and Annotated*, vol 1: *Peace* (CUP 1956)
McNair A, *The Law of Treaties* (OUP 1961)
McNemar D, 'The Postindependence War in the Congo' in Falk R (ed), *The International Law of Civil War* (Johns Hopkins 1971) 244–302
Mekata M, 'How Transnational Civil Society Realized the Ban Treaty: An Interview with Beatrice Fihn' (2018) 1 Journal for Peace and Nuclear Disarmament 79
Melzer N, 'The ICRC's Clarification Process on the Notion of Direct Participation in Hostilities under International Humanitarian Law' (2009) 103 ASIL Proceedings 299
Melzer N (ed), *Interpretive Guidance on the Notion of Direct Participation in Hostilities under International Humanitarian Law* (ICRC 2009)
Melzer N, 'Keeping the Balance between Military Necessity and Humanity: A Response to Four Critiques of the ICRC's Interpretive Guidance on the Notion of Direct Participation in Hostilities' (2010) 42 New York University Journal of International Law and Politics 831
Meron T, 'On the Inadequate Reach of Humanitarian and Human Rights Law and the Need for a New Instrument' (1983) 77 American Journal of International Law 589
Meron T, 'Towards a Humanitarian Declaration on Internal Strife' (1984) 78 American Journal of International Law 859
Meron T, *Human Rights in Internal Strife: Their International Protection* (CUP 1987)
Meron T, 'Draft Model Declaration on Internal Strife' (1988) 262 International Review of the Red Cross 59
Meron T and Vagts D, 'The Geneva Conventions of 1949 and Wars of National Liberation' in Baxter R and others (eds), *Humanizing the Laws of War: Selected Writings of Richard Baxter* (OUP 2013) 277–85
Mettraux G, *International Crimes and the Ad Hoc Tribunals* (OUP 2006)
Milano E, *Unlawful Territorial Situations in International Law: Reconciling Effectiveness, Legality and Legitimacy* (Brill 2005)
Milanović M, 'The Arrest and Impending Trial of Radovan Karadžić' (2009) 58 International and Comparative Law Quarterly 212
Ministry of Foreign Affairs of Denmark, 'Copenhagen Process on the Handling of Detainees in International Military Operations: Introductory Comments by the Chair, Principles and Guidelines with Chairman's Commentary, and Minutes of the Third Copenhagen Conference' (2012) 51 Military Law and the Law of War Review 187
Ministry of Foreign Affairs of Denmark, Legal Department, 'The Copenhagen Process on the Handling of Detainees in International Military Operations' (2007) 46 Military Law and the Law of War Review 363
Moir L, *The Law of Internal Armed Conflicts* (CUP 2002)
Mojzes P, *Balkan Genocides: Holocaust and Ethnic Cleansing in the Twentieth Century* (Rowman Littlefield 2016)
Monroe L, 'The United States and the Statute of Rome' (2001) 95 American Journal of International Law 124
Mörth U, 'Introduction' in Mörth U (ed), *Soft Law in Governance and Regulation: An Interdisciplinary Analysis* (Elgar 2004) 1–10
Muchlinski P, 'Multinational Enterprises as Actors in International Law: Creating "Soft Law" Obligations and "Hard Law" Rights' in Noortman M and Ryngaert C (eds), *Non-State Actor Dynamics in International Law: From Law-Takers to Law Makers* (Ashgate 2010) 9–39
Murphy MC, 'Hobbes (and Austin, and Aquinas) on Law as Command of the Sovereign' in Martinich AP and Hoekstra K (eds), *The Oxford Handbook of Hobbes* (OUP 2016) 41–62

Nabulsi K, *Traditions of War: Occupation, Resistance and the Law* (OUP 1999)
Neubold H, 'The Inadequacy of Law-Making by International Treaties: "Soft Law" as an Alternative?' in Wolfrum R and Röben V (eds), *Developments of International Law in Treaty Making* (Springer 2005) 627–53
Noortmann M and Ryngaert C (eds), *Non-State Actor Dynamics in International Law: From Law-Takers to Law-Makers* (Ashgate 2010)
Nünlist C, 'Helsinki+40 in the Historical Context' (2014) 25 Security and Human Rights 198
O'Brien R, 'Amnesty and International Law' (2005) 74 Nordic Journal of International Law 261
O'Connell D, *International Law* (2nd edn, Stevens 1970)
Olivier M, 'The Relevance of "Soft Law" as a Source of International Human Rights' (2002) 35 Comparative and International Law Journal of Southern Africa 289
Oppenheim L, *International Law: A Treatise*, vol 2: *War and Neutrality* (Lauterpacht H ed, 7th edn, Longmans 1952)
Österdahl I, '(International) Law!' in Liivoja R and Petman J (eds), *International Law-Making: Essays in Honour of Jan Klabbers* (Routledge 2015) 121–35
Oswald B, 'The Copenhagen Process: Some Reflecting Concerning Soft Law' in Lagoutte S, Gammeltoft-Hansen T, and Cerone J (eds), *Tracing the Roles of Soft Law in Human Rights* (OUP 2016) 109–28
Oswald B and Winkler T, 'The Copenhagen Process: Principles and Guidelines on the Handling of Detainees in International Military Operations' (2014) 83 Nordic Journal of International Law 128
Parks WH, 'Part IX of the ICRC "Direct Participation in Hostilities" Study: No Mandate, No Expertise, and Legally Incorrect' (2010) 42 New York University Journal of International Law and Politics 769
Paust JJ, 'A Critical Appraisal of the Air and Missile Warfare Manual' (2012) 47 Texas International Law Journal 277
Pauwelyn J, 'Informal International Lawmaking: Framing the Concept and Research Questions' in Pauwelyn J, Wessel R, and Wouters J (eds), *Informal International Lawmaking* (OUP 2012) 13–34
Pauwelyn J, 'Is It International Law or Not, and Does It Even Matter?' in Pauwelyn J, Wessel R, and Wouters J (eds), *Informal International Lawmaking* (OUP 2012) 125–61
Pauwelyn J, Wessel R, and Wouters J (eds), *Informal International Lawmaking* (OUP 2012)
Pauwelyn J, Wessel R, and Wouters J, 'Informal International Lawmaking: An Assessment and Template to Keep It Both Effective and Accountable' in Pauwelyn J, Wessel R, and Wouters J (eds), *Informal International Lawmaking* (OUP 2012) 500–37
Pauwelyn J, Wessel R, and Wouters J, 'Informal International Law as Presumptive Law: Exploring New Modes of Law-Making' in Liivoja R and Petman J (eds), *International Law-Making: Essays in Honour of Jan Klabbers* (Routledge 2014) 75–102
Pauwelyn J, Wessel R, and Wouters J, 'When Structures Become Shackles: Stagnation and Dynamics in International Lawmaking' (2014) 25 European Journal of International Law 733
Pedersen O, 'From Abundance to Indeterminacy: The Precautionary Principle and Its Two Camps of Custom' (2014) 3 Transnational Environmental Law 323
Pedraza-Farina L, 'Conceptions of Civil Society in International Lawmaking and Implementation: A Theoretical Framework' (2013) 34 Michigan Journal of International Law 605
Pentikäinen M, 'Changing International "Subjectivity" and Rights and Obligations under International Law—Status of Corporations' (2012) 8 Utrecht Law Review 145

Perna L, *The Formation of the Treaty Law of Non-International Armed Conflicts* (Martinus Nijhoff 2006)

Perry TS (ed), *The Life and Letters of Francis Lieber* (Osgood and Company 1882)

Peters A, Koechlin L, and Zinkernagel GF, 'Non-State Actors as Standard Setters: Framing the Issue in an Interdisciplinary Fashion' in Peters A and others (eds), *Non-State Actors as Standard Setters* (CUP 2009) 1–32

Petrasek D, 'Moving Forward on the Development of Minimum Humanitarian Standards' (1998) 92 American Journal of International Law 557

Petrov AO, 'Non-State Actors and Law of Armed Conflict Revisited: Enforcing International Law through Domestic Engagement' (2014) 19 Journal of Conflict & Security Law 279

Petrov AO, *Expert Laws of War: Restating and Making Law in Expert Processes* (Elgar 2020)

Pettersson T, Högbladh S, and Öberg M, 'Organized Violence, 1989–2018 and Peace Agreements' (2019) 56 Journal of Peace Research 589

Piattoni S, *The Theory of Multi-Level Governance: Conceptual, Empirical, and Normative Challenges* (OUP 2010)

Pictet J (ed), *Commentary on the Geneva Conventions of 12 August 1949, vol 1: Geneva Convention for the Amelioration of the Condition of the Wounded and Sick in Armed Forces in the Field* (ICRC 1952)

Pictet J (ed), *Humanitarian Law and the Protection of War Victims* (Henry Dunant Institute 1975)

Pilloud C and others (eds), *Commentary on the Additional Protocols of 8 June 1977 to the Geneva Conventions of 12 August 1949* (ICRC 1987)

PoKempner D, 'Squinting through the Pinhole: A Dim View of Human Rights from Tallinn 2.0' (2017) 95 Texas Law Review 1599

Popovski V and Turner N, 'Legality and Legitimacy in International Order' (United Nations University Policy Brief 5, 2008)

Portilla JC, 'Amnesty: Evolving 21st Century Constraints under International Law' (2014) 37 Fletcher Forum of World Affairs 169

Program on Humanitarian Policy and Conflict Research at Harvard University, *Manual on International Law Applicable to Air and Missile Warfare* (CUP 2013)

Pustogarov VV, *Our Martens: F.F. Martens, International Lawyer and Architect of Peace* (intro Butler WE, Simmonds 2000)

Quénivet N, 'The History of the Relationship between International Humanitarian Law and Human Rights Law' in Arnold R and Quénivet N (eds), *International Humanitarian Law and Human Rights Law: Towards a New Merger in International Law* (Martinus Nijhoff 2008) 1–14

Radziwill Y, *Cyber Attacks and the Exploitable Imperfections of International* Law (Brill 2015)

Rajkovic N, Aalberts T, and Gammeltoft-Hansen Y, 'Introduction: Legality, Interdisciplinarity and the Study of Practices' in Rajkovic N, Aalberts T, and Gammeltoft-Hansen T (eds), *The Power of Legality: Practices of International Law and Their Politics* (CUP 2016) 1–26

Rajkovic N, Aalberts T, and Gammeltoft-Hansen T (eds), *The Power of Legality: Practices of International Law and Their Politics* (CUP 2016)

Ramlogan R, *Sustainable Development: Towards a Judicial Interpretation* (Martinus Nijhoff 2011)

Raz J, *The Authority of Law* (2nd edn, OUP 2009)

Reisman WM, 'The Concept and Functions of Soft Law in International Politics' in Bello E and Ajibola BA (eds), *Essays in Honour of Judge Taslim Olawale Elias* (Martinus Nijhoff 1992) 135–44

Reiter A, 'Examining the Use of Amnesties and Pardons as a Response to Internal Armed Conflict' (2014) 47 Israel Law Review 133

Rid T, *Cyber War Will Not Take Place* (C Hurst & Co 2013)

Risse T, 'Transnational Governance and Legitimacy' in Benz A and Papadopoulos Y (eds), *Governance and Democracy: Comparing National, European and International Experiences* (Routledge 2006) 179–99

Roach JA, 'The Law of Naval Warfare at the Turn of Two Centuries' (2000) 94 American Journal of International Law 64

Roberts A, *Is International Law International?* (OUP 2017)

Roberts A and Sivakumaran S, 'Lawmaking by Nonstate Actors: Engaging Armed Groups in the Creation of International Humanitarian Law' (2012) 37 Yale Journal of International Law 107

Roht-Arriaza N and Gibson L, 'The Developing Jurisprudence on Amnesty' (1998) 20 Human Rights Quarterly 843

Rolin-Jaequemyns G, 'Chronique du Droit International—1871–1874' (1875) 7 Revue de droit international et de législation comparée (1st ser)

Rondeau S, 'The Pragmatic Value of Reciprocity: Promoting Respect for International Humanitarian Law among Non-State Actors' in Perrin B (ed), *Modern Warfare: Armed Groups, Private Militaries, Humanitarian Organisations, and the Law* (UBC Press 2012) 43–72

Ronzitti N (ed), *Commentary to 1913 Manual on Naval Warfare: A Collection of Agreements and Documents with Commentaries* (Martinus Nijhoff 1988)

Root E, 'Francis Lieber' (1913) 7 American Journal of International Law 453

Roughan N, 'Mind the Gaps: Authority and Legality in International Law' (2016) 27 European Journal of International Law 329

Sand I-J, 'Varieties of Authority in International Law: State Consent, International Organisations, Courts, Experts and Citizens' in Capps P and Olsen HP (eds), *Legal Authority Beyond the State* (CUP 2018) 161–87

Sarooshi D, 'Legal Capacity and Powers' in Cogan JK, Hurd I, and Johnstone I (eds), *The Oxford Handbook of International Organisations* (OUP 2016) 985–1005

Sassòli M, Bouvier AA, and Quintin A (eds), *How Does Law Protect in War? Cases, Documents and Teaching Materials on Contemporary Practice in International Humanitarian Law* (3rd edn, ICRC 2011)

Sbolci L, 'Supplementary Means of Interpretation' in Cannizzaro E (ed), *The Law of Treaties beyond the Vienna Convention* (OUP 2011) 144–63

Schabas W, *Genocide in International Law: The Crime of Crimes* (CUP 2000)

Schachter O, 'The Twilight Existence of Nonbinding International Agreements' (1977) 71 American Journal of International Law 296

Schaller C, 'Beyond Self-Defence and Countermeasures: A Critical Assessment of the Tallinn Manual's Conception of Necessity' (2017) 95 Texas Law Review 1619

Scharpf F, *Demokratietheorie zwischen Utopie und Anpassung* (Universitätsverlag 1970)

Scharpf F, *Governing in Europe: Effective and Democratic?* (OUP 1999)

Schindler D, 'The Different Types of Armed Conflicts According to the Geneva Conventions and Protocols' (1979) 163 Recueil des Cours 117

Schindler D and Toman J (eds), The Laws of Armed Conflicts: A Collection of Conventions, Resolutions, and Other Documents (4th edn, Martinus Nijhoff 2004)

Schmidt D, 'The Civil War in Yemen' in Luard E (ed), *The International Regulation of Civil Wars* (Thames and Hudson 1972) 169–86

Schmidt V, 'Democracy and Legitimacy in the European Union Revisited: Input, Output *and* "Throughput"' (2013) 61 Political Studies 2

Schmitt C, *Legality and Legitimacy* (Seitzer J tr and ed, Duke University Press 2004)
Schmitt M, 'Computer Network Attack and the Use of Force in International Law: Thoughts on a Normative Framework' (1999) 37 Columbia Journal of Transnational Law 885
Schmitt M, 'The Interpretive Guidance on the Notion of Direct Participation in Hostilities: A Critical Analysis' (2010) 1 Harvard National Security Journal 5
Schmitt M (ed), *Tallinn Manual on the International Law Applicable to Cyber Warfare* (CUP 2013)
Schmitt M (ed), *Tallinn Manual 2.0 on the International Law Applicable to Cyber Operations* (CUP 2017)
Schmitt M, Garraway C, and Dinstein Y (eds), *The Manual on the Law of Non-International Armed Conflict* (International Institute of Humanitarian Law 2006)
Schmitt M and Vihul L, 'Sovereignty in Cyberspace: Lex Lata Vel Non?' (2017) 111 American Journal of International Law (unbound) 213
Schmitt M and Watts S, 'The Decline of International Humanitarian Law *Opinio Juris* and the Law of Cyber Warfare' (2015) 50 Texas International Law Journal 189
Schröder M, 'Precautionary Approach/Principle' in Peters A and Wolfrum R (eds), *Max Planck Encyclopedia of Public International Law* (OUP 2013)
Schwarzenberger G, *International Law as Applied by International Courts and Tribunals* (Stevens and Son 1968)
Schwebel S, 'Wars of Liberation—as Fought in UN Organs' in Moore JN (ed), *Law and Civil War in the Modern World* (Johns Hopkins Press 1974) 446–57
Schwebel S, 'The Effect of Resolutions of the UN General Assembly on Customary International Law' (1979) 73 ASIL Proceedings 301
Schwelb E, 'The Influence of the Universal Declaration of Human Rights on International and National Law' (1959) 53 ASIL Proceedings 217
Scobbie I, 'The Approach to Customary International Law in the Study' in Wilmshurst E and Breau S (eds), *Perspectives on the ICRC Study on Customary International Humanitarian Law* (CUP/Chatham House/BIICL 2007) 15–49
Seiberth C, *Private Military and Security Companies in International Law* (Intersentia 2014)
Shah R, 'Beating Blackwater: Using Domestic Legislation to Enforce the International Code of Conduct for Private Military Companies' (2014) 123 Yale Law Journal 2559
Shany Y, *Assessing the Effectiveness of International Courts* (OUP 2014)
Shapiro S, *Legality* (Harvard University Press 2011)
Shelton D, 'Soft Law' in Armstrong D (ed), *Routledge Handbook of International Law* (Abingdon 2009) 68–80
Shelton D, 'International Law and Relative Normativity' in Evans M (ed), *International Law* (OUP 2010) 141–71
Shelton D, 'Stockholm Declaration (1972) and Rio Declaration (1992)' in Peters A and Wolfrum R (eds), *Max Planck Encyclopedia of Public International Law* (OUP 2013)
Shereshevsky Y, 'Back in the Game: International Humanitarian Lawmaking by States' (2019) 37 Berkeley Journal of International Law 1
Simma B and others (eds), *The Charter of the United Nations: A Commentary* (vol 1, 3rd edn, OUP 2012)
Singer P, 'War, Profits, and the Vacuum of Law: Privatized Military Firms and International Law' (2003) 42 Columbia Journal of Transnational Law 521
Singer P, *Corporate Warriors: The Rise of the Private Military Industry* (Cornell University Press 2008)
Sirinskiene A, 'The Status of Precautionary Principle: Moving towards a Rule of Customary Law' (2009) 4 Jurisprudence 349

Sivakumaran S, *The Law of Non-International Armed Conflict* (OUP 2012)
Sivakumaran S, 'The Ownership of International Humanitarian Law: Non-State Armed Groups and the Formation of Enforcement of IHL Rules' in Perrin B (ed), *Modern Warfare: Armed Groups, Private Militaries, Humanitarian Organisations, and the Law* (UBC Press 2012) 86–101
Sjöberg A, 'Armed Non-State Actors: The Main Users of the "Poor Man's Weapon"' (2006) 10 Journal of Mine Action 73
Skjærseth JB, Stokke OS, and Wettestad J, 'Soft Law, Hard Law, and Effective Implementation of International Environmental Norms' (2006) 6 Global Environmental Politics 104
Skubiszewski K, 'Forms of Participation of International Organizations in the Lawmaking Processes' (1964) 18 International Organization 790
Snyder D, 'Private Lawmaking' (2003) 64 Ohio State Law Journal 371
Snyder F, 'The Effectiveness of European Community Law: Institutions, Processes, Tools and Techniques' (1993) 56 Modern Law Review 19
Snyder F, 'Soft Law and Institutional Practice in the European Community' in Martin S (ed), *The Construction of Europe: Essays in Honour of Emile Noël* (Kluwer 1994) 197–225
Sohn L, 'The Universal Declaration of Human Rights: A Common Standard of Achievement? The Status of the Universal Declaration in International Law' (1967) 8 International Commission of Jurists Review 17
Solis G, *The Law of Armed Conflict: International Humanitarian Law in War* (2nd edn, CUP 2016)
Spaight JM, *Aircraft in War* (MacMillan 1914)
Spaight JM, *Air Power and War Rights* (Longmans 1925)
Spiermann O, *International Legal Argument in the Permanent Court of International Justice: The Rise of the International Judiciary* (CUP 2005)
Steffek J, 'The Output Legitimacy of International Organisations and the Global Public Interest' (2015) 7 International Theory 263
Stone J, 'What Price Effectiveness?' (1956) 50 ASIL Proceedings 198
Sulmasy GM, 'The Law of Armed Conflict in the Global War on Terror: International Lawyers Fighting the Last War' (2014) 19 Notre Dame Journal of Law, Ethics & Public Policy 309
Sunstein CR, 'Social Norms and Social Roles' (1996) 96 Columbia Law Review 903
Sutchman M, 'Managing Legitimacy: Strategic and Institutional Approaches' (1995) 20 Academy of Management Review 571
Sutherland D, *A Savage Conflict: The Decisive Role of Guerrillas in the American Civil War* (University of North Carolina Press 2009)
Suy E, 'Innovations in International Law-Making Processes' in McDonald RSJ, Johnston D, and Morris G (eds), *The International Law and Policy of Human Welfare* (Sijthoff and Noordhoof 1978) 187–207
Sweet C, 'Review: The Tallinn Manual on the International Law Applicable to Cyber Warfare' (2014) 66 Europe-Asia Studies 669
Take I, 'Legitimacy in Global Governance: International, Transnational and Private Institutions Compared' (2012) 18 Swiss Political Science Review 220
Taki H, 'Effectiveness' in Peters A and Wolfrum R (eds), *Max Planck Encyclopedia of Public International Law* (OUP 2013)
Tammes AJP, 'Soft Law' in TMC Asser Institute and Board of the Netherlands International Law Review (eds), *Essays on International and Comparative Law in Honour of Judge Erades* (TMC Asser 1983) 187–95

Terry J, 'The Lawfulness of Attacking Computer Networks in Armed Conflict and in Self-Defence in Periods Short of Armed Conflict: What Are the Targeting Constraints?' (2001) 169 Military Law Review 70

Teubner G, 'Global Bukowina: Legal Pluralism in the World Society' in Teubner G (ed), *Global Law without a State* (Dartmouth 1997) 3–28

Thirlway H, *The Sources of International Law* (OUP 2012)

Thomas D, *The Helsinki Effect: International Norms, Human Rights, and the Demise of Communism* (Princeton University Press 2001)

Thürer D, 'The Emergence of NGOs and Transnational Enterprises in International Law and the Changing Role of the State' in von Hofmann R and Geissler N (eds), *Non-State Actors as New Subjects of International Law: International Law—From the Traditional State Order towards the Law of the Global Community. Proceedings of an International Symposium of the Kiel Walther-Schücking-Institute of International Law, March 25 to 28, 1998* (Duncker and Humblot 1999) 37–58

Thürer D, 'Comment—The Democratization of Contemporary International Law-Making Processes and the Differentiation of Their Application' in Wolfrum R and Röben V (eds), *Developments of International Law in Treaty Making* (Springer 2005) 53–63

Thürer D, 'Soft Law' in Peters A and Wolfrum R (eds), *Max Planck Encyclopedia of Public International Law* (OUP 2013)

Tougas M-L, 'Some Comments and Observations on the Montreux Document' (2009) 12 Yearbook of International Humanitarian Law 312

Tully S, *Corporations and International Lawmaking* (Martinus Nijhoff 2007)

van der Toorn D, '"Direct Participation in Hostilities": A Legal and Practical Road Test of the International Committee of the Red Cross's Guidance through Afghanistan' (2010) 17 Australian International Law Journal 28

van der Vyver J, *Implementation of International Law in the United States* (Peter Lang 2010)

van Dijk P, 'The Implementation of the Final Act of Helsinki: The Creation of New Structures or the Involvement of Existing Ones?' (1989) 10 Michigan Journal of International Law 110

Verzijl JHW, *International Law in Historical Perspective* (vol 1, AW Sijthoff 1968)

Veuthey M, 'Remedies to Promote the Respect of Fundamental Human Values in Non-International Armed Conflict' (2000) 30 Israel Yearbook on Human Rights 37

Vierucci L, '"Special Agreements" between Conflicting Parties in the Case-Law of the ICTY' in Swart B, Zahar A, and Sluiter G (eds), *The Legacy of the International Criminal Tribunal for the Former Yugoslavia* (OUP 2011) 401–33

Vigny J-D and Thompson C, 'Fundamental Standards of Humanity: What Future?' (2002) 20 Netherlands Quarterly of Human Rights 185

Viñuales JE (ed), *The Rio Declaration on Environment and Development: A Commentary* (OUP 2015)

Virally M, 'La distinction entre textes internationaux ayant une portee juridique dans les relations mutuelles entres leurs auteurs et texts qui en sont depourvus' (1983) 60 IDI Annuaire 166

Walker G, 'Responses to Humanitarian Law Violations in Non-International Armed Conflicts: Historical Perspectives and Considerations on Conflicts of Jurisdiction' (2000) 30 Israel Yearbook on Human Rights 79

Wallace D, 'International Code of Conduct for Private Security Service Providers' (2011) 50 International Legal Materials 89

Watkin K, 'Opportunity Lost: Organized Armed Groups and the ICRC "Direct Participation in Hostilities" Interpretive Guidance' (2010) 42 New York University Journal of International Law and Politics 641

Weber M, *Economy and Society* (Roth G and Wittich C ed, University of California Press 1978)

Wedgwood R, 'Proportionality, Cyberwar and the Law of War' (2000) 76 International Law Studies 219

Wehberg H, 'Pacta Sunt Servanda' (1959) 53 American Journal of International Law 775

Weil P, 'Towards Relative Normativity in International Law' (1983) 77 American Journal of International Law 413

Weiss F and Kammel A (eds), *The Changing Landscape of Global Financial Governance and the Role of Soft Law* (Brill 2015)

Wellens KC and Borchardt GM, 'Soft Law in European Community Law' (1989) 14 European Law Review 267

Wessel R, 'Institutional Lawmaking: The Emergence of a Global Normative Web' in Brölmann C and Radi Y (eds), *Research Handbook on the Theory and Practice of International Lawmaking* (Elgar 2016) 179–99

Wheatley S, 'Democratic Governance beyond the State: The Legitimacy of Non-State Actors as Standard Setters' in Peters A and others (eds), *Non-State Actors as Standard Setters* (CUP 2009) 215–40

Wheatley S, 'A Democratic Rule of International Law' (2011) 22 European Journal of International Law 525

Wherry W, 'Aerial Warfare in International Law' (Contemporary Law Pamphlets 1939)

White A, 'The Third Peace Conference at the Hague' (1914) 76 The Advocate of Peace 183

White N, 'Regulatory Initiatives at the International Level' in Bakker C and Sossai M (eds), *Multilevel Regulation of Military and Security Contractors: The Interplay between International, European and Domestic Norms* (Hart 2011) 11–30

White N, 'Lawmaking' in Cogan JK, Hurd I, and Johnstone I (eds), *The Oxford Handbook of International Organisations* (OUP 2016) 559–80

Whyte J, 'The "Dangerous Concept of the Just War": Decolonization, Wars of National Liberation, and the Additional Protocols to the Geneva Conventions' (2018) 9 Humanity 313

Wickremesekera C, *The Tamil Separatist War in Sri Lanka* (Routledge 2016)

Wildeman J, 'The Philosophical Background of Effectiveness' (1977) 24 Netherlands International Law Review 335

Wilson H, *International Law and the Use of Force by National Liberation Movements* (Clarendon 1988)

Winkler T, 'The Copenhagen Process on Detainees: A Necessity' (2010) 78 Nordic Journal of International Law 489

Winkler T and Oswald B, 'The Copenhagen Process Principles and Guidelines on the Handling of Detainees in International Military Operations' (2012) 16(39) ASIL Insights. https://www.asil.org/insights/volume/16/issue/39/copenhagen-process-principles-and-guidelines-handling-detainees accessed 10 August 2021

Wirth D, 'Reexamining Decision-Making Processes in International Environmental Law' (1994) 79 Iowa Law Review 797

Witt JF, *Lincoln's Code: The Laws of War in American History* (Free Press 2012)

Wolfrum R, 'Legitimacy of International Law from a Legal Perspective: Some Introductory Considerations' in Wolfrum R and Röben V (eds), *Legitimacy in International Law* (Springer 2008) 1–24

Wolfrum R, 'Legitimacy in International Law' in Peters A and Wolfrum R (eds), *Max Planck Encyclopedia of Public International Law* (OUP 2013)

Wolfrum R, and Röben V (eds), *Legitimacy in International Law* (Springer 2008)

Wood M, 'The Evolution and Identification of the Customary International Law of Armed Conflict' (2018) 51 Vanderbilt Journal of Transnational Law 727
Wood M and Purisch D, 'Helsinki Final Act (1975)' in Peters A and Wolfrum R (eds), *Max Planck Encyclopedia of Public International Law* (OUP 2013)
Woodward BK, 'International Lawmaking and Civil Society' in Brölmann C and Radi Y (eds), *Research Handbook on the Theory and Practice of International Lawmaking* (Elgar 2016) 105–49
Wyman R, 'The First Rules of Air Warfare' (1984) 35 Air University Review 94
Yasuaki O, *A Transcivilizational Perspective on International Law* (Martinus Nijhoff 2010)
Yip KL, 'The ICRC's Interpretive Guidance on the Notion of Direct Participation in Hostilities: Sociological and Democratic Legitimacy in Domestic Legal Orders' (2017) 8 Transnational Legal Theory 224
Zander J, *The Application of the Precautionary Principle in Practice* (CUP 2010)
Zappalà S, 'Can Legality Trump Effectiveness in Today's International Law?' in Cassese A (ed), *Realising Utopia: The Future of International Law* (OUP 2012) 105–17
Zaum D, 'Legitimacy' in Cogan JK, Hurd I, and Johnstone I (eds), *The Oxford Handbook of International Organizations* (OUP 2016) 1107–25
Zegveld L, *The Accountability of Armed Opposition Groups in International Law* (CUP 2002)
Zürn M and Joerges C (eds), *Law and Governance in Postnational Europe: Compliance beyond the Nation-State* (CUP 2005)

Index

For the benefit of digital users, indexed terms that span two pages (e.g., 52–53) may, on occasion, appear on only one of those pages.